Poetry Markets
for
Canadians

**The most comprehensive guide to publishing opportunities for
Canadian poets ever assembled.**

Poetry Markets
for
Canadians

SIXTH EDITION

Edited by James Deahl

THE MERCURY PRESS
&
THE LEAGUE OF CANADIAN POETS

Stratford / Toronto

The publishers gratefully acknowledge the financial assistance of the Canada Council and the Ontario Arts Council in their ongoing operations.

Edited by James Deahl
Cover design by Orange Griffin
Cover photograph by Anna Rumley
Composition and page design by TASK

Printed and bound in Canada by Metropole Litho

Canadian Cataloguing in Publication Data
The National Library of Canada has catalogued this publication as follows:
Main entry under title:
Poetry markets for Canadians
Biennial.
Continues: Poetry markets in Canada.
Publisher varies.
ISSN 0843-2287
ISBN 1-55128-030-2 (6th ed.)
1. Poetry - Authorship - Periodicals. 2. Publishers and publishing - Canada - Directories. 3. Canadian Periodicals (English) - Directories. I. League of Canadian Poets.
PN155.P6 070.5'2'0971 C89-032442-5

THE MERCURY PRESS
Represented in Canada by the Literary Press Group
Distributed in Canada by General Distribution Services

ACKNOWLEDGEMENTS

Several people assisted with this guide. I am indebted to Michael Wurster for serving as consultant for the American periodical listings. Welsh poet Peter Finch provided a large portion of the address list for the British periodicals. He helped make the British section better than ever before.

I also wish to acknowledge the support of Edita Petrauskaite, LCP Executive Director and Betsy Struthers, LCP President. A final thank you is extended to Gilda Mekler for copyediting the manuscript.

CONTENTS

INTRODUCTION TO THE SIXTH EDITION *James Deahl*

A NOTE ON THE LISTINGS

THE LEAGUE OF CANADIAN POETS

INTRODUCTION TO THE SIXTH EDITION

This edition of *Poetry Markets for Canadians* covers all English-language poetry markets in the world. With the exception of the American market, letters were sent to every periodical we could locate that publishes poetry in English. In the case of the huge market in the United States, only the finest journals were surveyed.

Letters also went to every Canadian publisher of poetry books or chapbooks in English. The result is the most comprehensive guide to publishing opportunities for Canadians ever assembled. But this is not simply a list of magazines and publishers who accept poetry. Such a list was the starting point. The data in the present volume cover ONLY those magazines and publishers that welcome unsolicited manuscripts of Canadian poetry or unsolicited letters of inquiry from Canadian poets. Thus, you can avoid writing to, or making submissions to, editors who are not interested in reading Canadian material.

Because the goal was to be as inclusive as possible, with the exception of the American list, no claims can be made as to the quality or appropriateness of the book publishers and magazines included here. Some meet the highest professional standards, while others are thoroughly amateur. It is for you, the poet, to ensure that you deal only with those publishers and editors who conduct their affairs in a manner acceptable to you. For example, you may decide not to publish in a magazine that wants to buy all rights to your poems. Likewise, you may not favour journals that fail to provide contributors' copies. The word is: know your market.

Because there are over two thousand periodicals in the United States that publish poetry, and our goal was to be exclusive, the noted American poet Michael Wurster, of Pittsburgh, PA, was asked for advice. (Readers who wish to study the entire American market are referred to: *The International Directory of Little Magazines and Small Presses*, Len Fulton, editor, Dustbooks, PO Box 100, Paradise, CA, 95969.) Basically, only those journals with a circulation of 1,000 or more that were typeset, perfect-bound, and published at least twice per year were sent forms. Exceptions were made when a magazine was of outstanding quality, was a journal of haiku, or was recommended by Michael Wurster (who also suggested dropping certain titles from our list). A very few periodicals that failed to meet the criteria were included if they displayed a strong interest in Canadian work.

Thus, *Seneca Review* is included despite a circulation of less than 1,000 because a good editor keeps the quality up. *The American Poetry Review*, one of the very best poetry journals anywhere, is included despite being a tabloid. *Pig Iron*, an annual, is listed here because of the hearty welcome it extends to Canadian poetry.

In the end, even the best market guide is no more than a guide. It is up to you to study your markets as best you can.

Because the French and English literary scenes in Canada function quite separately, no attempt has been made to cover French-language markets.

James Deahl
Editor

A NOTE ON THE LISTINGS

In this volume a complete periodical listing will provide the following data: 1, full name of magazine; 2, complete editorial address; 3, editor(s); 4, poetry editor(s); 5, year founded; 6, total circulation; 7, average number of pages per issue; 8, number of issues per year; 9, page size (width and height); 10, type of binding (perfect-bound or saddle-stitched); 11, cost of a sample copy; 12, cost of a subscription; 13, whether the copyright rests with the author or the magazine; 14, whether book reviews are used; 15, if book reviews are used, number per year; 16, whether translations are used; 17, whether interviews are used; 18, whether fiction is used; 19, whether essays or other non-fiction articles are used; 20, whether contributor's copies are provided; 21, terms of money payment, if any; 22, time required to reply to a submission; 23, the name of any publisher of poetry books or chapbooks associated with the magazine; 24, the names of up to four poets whose work has been published; and 25, a short editorial statement.

A complete publisher listing will provide the following data: 1, full name of press; 2, complete editorial address; 3, telephone, fax number, and E-mail address; 4, poetry editor(s); 5, year founded; 6, average press run; 7, average number of pages per book or chapbook; 8, number of poetry titles published during 1994; 9, whether the press publishes full-size books, chapbooks, or both; 10, whether fiction is published; 11, whether drama is published; 12, whether art books are published; 13, whether children's books are published; 14, whether textbooks are published; 15, whether non-fiction trade books are published; 16, whether the Writers' Union contract is used or a standard contract that is similar to the Union's contract in its provisions; 17, whether royalties are paid and, if so, the rate of payment; 18, if full-length unsolicited poetry manuscripts are accepted or if the press wishes to examine a few sample poems first; 19, whether written guidelines are provided on request; 20, the names of up to four authors published by the press; and 21, a short editorial statement.

Finally, I appeal to you for help in making the next edition even better. After all, this guide is for you and should serve your needs. I would like to know about any errors of fact and/or omission. As well, I would like to hear how the information and its presentation may be improved. Suggestions can be sent to me c/o The League of Canadian Poets. They will be gratefully received.

THE LEAGUE OF CANADIAN POETS

The League of Canadian Poets was founded in 1966 by Raymond Souster, Ralph Gustafson, Ronald G. Everson, Louis Dudek, and Michael Gnarowski. The League's purpose has always been to actively promote the works of Canadian poets to the general public and in the education system and to encourage talented poets in their creative endeavours. In the years since 1966, the LCP has grown into a national organization of some four hundred poets.

The LCP offers two types of membership. Full membership (at a fee of $175 + GST per year in 1995) is offered to poets who have published at least one full-sized volume of poetry, and/or two chapbooks, and/or have substantial magazine publications, and/or have produced an audiotape or CD of their poetry in performance. Associate membership (at a fee of $60 + GST per year in 1995) is open to poets with some journal publications who are not yet eligible for full membership.

LCP services and benefits include:

PUBLIC READINGS PROGRAM
In cooperation with the Canada Council, the Ontario Arts Council, and municipal arts councils, the LCP organizes hundreds of poetry readings in urban centres, remote outposts, native settlements, company towns, public libraries, universities, and colleges. These public events do much to advance the appreciation of poetry in Canada.

EDUCATIONAL WORKSHOPS AND SEMINARS
Members of the LCP spend considerable time working with teachers and educational administrators to promote the study of Canadian literature and to offer their professional advice on the teaching of poetry in the classroom.

POETS IN THE SCHOOLS PROGRAM
In cooperation with the Ontario Arts Council, the LCP has developed an exciting program of readings and workshops in schools across Ontario at both

the elementary and secondary levels. The lives of children, teachers, and poets are greatly enriched by these encounters. Teachers say that the program inspires students to read more and to express themselves by showing that poetry is a living, accessible art form.

ADMINISTRATION OF LITERARY PRIZES
Each year the LCP sponsors the following two literary prizes: 1. The Pat Lowther Memorial Award, for the best book of poems by a woman. Value: $1,000. 2. The Gerald Lampert Memorial Award, for the best first book of poems. Value: $1,000.

POETS ABROAD
With assistance from External Affairs, the Canada Council, the Saskatchewan Arts Board, the Ontario Ministry of Culture, Citizenship and Recreation, and other provincial bodies, the LCP has sent its members to the U.K., China, France, Finland, Mexico, Italy, Chile, Germany, and many other countries to bear witness for Canada and to promote cultural exchange.

PUBLISHING OF EDUCATIONAL MATERIALS
The LCP publishes materials of use to the literary and educational communities, including *Who's Who in the League of Canadian Poets*, which contains biographical and bibliographical material for easy reference, and a guide to the teaching of poetry called *Poets in the Classroom* (Pembroke Press, 1995).

LITERARY ARCHIVES OF BOOKS AND TAPE RECORDINGS
In order to preserve our cultural heritage, the LCP has produced a sound archive of readings by senior members. It also maintains a comprehensive library of books by LCP members. The National Archives holds League papers from the period before 1985.

NATIONAL POETRY CONTEST
The LCP runs an annual poetry contest with cash prizes of $1,000, $750, and $500. The LCP and a literary press also publish an anthology of the best fifty poems entered in the contest. This national competition serves to increase the awareness of, and interest in, poetry at all levels of society.

NEWSLETTER / MUSELETTER

The LCP publishes a regular newsletter, available to members as well as by subscription to non-members. This publication offers information about current LCP and members' activities, poetry events and markets, and serves as a liaison between poets and the larger community. It also publishes the *Museletter*, which appears twice a year and features poetry, poetics, and articles on other topics of interest to working poets.

MARKETING PROJECT

In 1995, the League instituted a direct mail marketing project. Four times a year, over 10,000 flyers listing new and award-winning books of poetry by members are sent to libraries, universities, booksellers, interested individuals, embassies, and other arts organizations in Canada and abroad.

As part of this campaign to increase awareness of the vitality of the Canadian poetry scene, the League also publishes *Poetry Spoken Here*, a bi-monthly calendar of public readings by members across the country.

ADVOCACY

The LCP also represents the interests of Canadian poets to government and other bodies. The LCP is an active member of the Canadian Conference of the Arts, the Canadian Copyright Institute, and the Book and Periodical Council (which serves all parties involved in Canadian publishing and deals with issues affecting literature such as copyright, censorship, public lending right, reprography, taxation, and literacy).

For more information on the services and resources of The League of Canadian Poets, write to 54 Wolseley Street, Suite 204, Toronto, Ontario, M5T 1A5. Phone (416) 504-1657; Fax. (416) 703-0059; E-mail league@io.org; Web site http://www.swifty.com/lc

ONE: GETTING PUBLISHED: PERIODICALS

Almost everyone who writes poetry wants to place it before the public. This is because poetry is communication and becomes a completed act when it "speaks" to another person. There are two ways to achieve this end: oral presentation and print.

In Canada there are no less than two hundred magazines that publish poetry. Some, like *Canadian Author*, use very little poetry, while others, like *Arc*, focus entirely on poetry. Some look for free verse; others prefer more traditional work. It does not matter if you write haiku or epics — there is something for everyone.

Most poets, at some stage in their lives, will begin to submit manuscripts to journals. And most will receive a fair quota of rejection slips along with a few acceptances. Some poets enjoy sending their stuff out to magazines. Others hate the whole process. This is the business side of writing, as opposed to the more interesting creative side.

1.1 HOW TO SUBMIT POETRY TO MAGAZINES

To improve your chances, here are eight suggestions.

1. Always send a professional-looking submission. This will consist of about six to eight poems, neatly typed. Your name and address should appear on each sheet. Never single-space your poems.

2. Along with the poems should be a short covering letter offering the poems for publication and thanking the editors for their time and consideration.

3. A self-addressed stamped envelope (SASE) is also essential. Indeed, many editors will not return your poems without one. If you are making a foreign submission and cannot acquire proper stamps for your SASE, you should send International Reply Coupons (IRCs). These can be purchased at any Canadian post office.

4. If you wish to create a good impression you should ensure that you have enclosed sufficient postage (or IRCs). I have done my share of editing and from what I've seen it would seem that at least half of all submissions come with insufficient return postage. But you don't have to take my word for it. Here is what Mary Hollingsworth, editor of *Cotton Boll*, has to say: "Please make note that it is my observation that Canadians rarely, if ever, enclose adequate postage for return of manuscripts."

5. You may elect to include a short bio note and a short bibliography. The key word here is "short." You do not need to send a list of the fifty periodicals that have already published your work.

6. Avoid making simultaneous submissions unless you have made sure that the magazines you are dealing with will accept them.

7. Even with a proper SASE, some poems go astray. Always keep copies of the work that you send out.

8. Do not become too depressed when you receive a rejection slip. Send your poems off again straightaway. Every poet gets rejection slips; they do not mean that you are not a good writer. Rest assured that even "ten-book poets" can, and do, have work rejected.

The most important part of the business of publishing poems (and yes, publishing is a business as well as an art) is market research. In the pages that follow you will find information on almost four hundred periodicals that are interested in receiving submissions from Canadian poets. It is up to you to study these publications to ensure that you make wise choices. For example, there is little point in sending formal, rhymed poems to *Unmuzzled OX*, where the order of the day is "pre-anti-post-modern" poetry and prose poetry. You would have more luck submitting them to *Orbis*, where traditional verse is welcomed.

Thus, it always pays to read before you submit your poems.

You can do this by purchasing a specimen copy, or you can study many of the journals listed here at a public or university library. Remember, you will waste a lot of time and money if you proceed to submit your work blindly (to say nothing of wasting some already overworked editor's time).

Once you have identified a dozen or so literary magazines that accept the sort of poem you write, it is time to start. If your work wins easy acceptance, fine. If not, try to see the editor's point of view. Some editors say they do not reject, they merely select. Editors are limited by the space available, and may reject poetry they actually like because it does not seem to them to have that extra spark; because it is too different from, or too similar to, other work; or because it does not fit their image of the journal. (If you are like most poets, however, rejection slips will continue to irk, despite your best attempts at philosophy.)

If an editor comments on your work, it is an expression of interest: take it in good part. Seriously consider the editor's comments; they may be valid. Remember how difficult it is to be objective about your own work, but also keep in mind how personal such judgments may be: the very points that bother one editor may constitute your poem's appeal to another. Which, of course, is why you can save a lot of frustration by conducting proper research in the first place. With almost four hundred magazines from which to choose, it is best to submit only to those who may view your work favourably.

Keep your rejection slips, and note who rejected what. They indicate your success/failure rate, and give you information for future submissions. You can submit rejected poems to another magazine, or you can submit new poems to a magazine that has rejected earlier submissions, especially if you have received encouraging comments. As long as you continue to believe in a poem you should keep sending it out. Many quite fine poems are published after ten or more rejections.

Most poets realize early on that publishing poetry does not pay. Still, you should receive something for your hard work. The minimum ethical payment for periodical publication is a copy of the issue containing the work. Many magazines, including some very highly regarded ones, such as *The Literary Review* and *Prairie Schooner*, offer no monetary payment. Others will pay modest honoraria, ranging from $5 up. Publishing poetry, whether in magazines, books, or anthologies, is a business arrangement. You should be satisfied with the terms. If you have any concerns about the form or method of payment, do not hesitate to query the editor.

Unsolicited submission of work usually constitutes an offer of permission to publish. Notification of acceptance constitutes the closing of the business deal.

If you change your mind, you must withdraw your work in writing; remaining silent will imply your acceptance of the deal and its terms.

1.2   TOP TO BOTTOM OR BOTTOM TO TOP?

We now come to the question of where to start. Some periodicals are thoroughly professional. They are nicely designed, perfect-bound, typeset, and mostly tend to publish professional writers. Others are clearly amateur. They may be photocopied and stapled, look awful, and publish people that, for good reason, you've never heard of. Each fills its niche. Most fall between these extremes.

If you have publishable poetry and elect to work from the bottom up, you will likely, after a few rejection slips, get into print. If, on the other hand, you start from the top and work down, you could also get into print. You can expect more rejections along the way, but you will be publishing your poetry at a higher level. Working from the top down takes longer and is more trying, to be sure. Just keep in mind that, when your work is accepted, it will appear in journals that are more highly respected and enjoy larger readerships.

Most poets want to write the best poems that they are capable of writing. Quite understandably, they want to publish them in the best possible journals. There is no easy way to achieve these goals. It is hard work, it takes time, and the way is lined with rejection slips.

1.3   RIGHTS AND PERMISSIONS

"Rights" are what publishers purchase when accepting your poetry. There are several types of rights that pertain to publishing in periodicals. You must make sure that you understand what rights are being given up and what rights you, as the author, retain.

First Serial Rights. This is what most magazines will purchase. It is the right to publish your work for the first time. This implies an assurance from you that the work has not already been published. You cannot sell first serial rights twice. First rights are sometimes called first Canadian rights or first North American rights. It is reasonable for a journal to receive North American rights if it is distributed in both the United States and Canada. It should be noted that North American rights include Canadian rights; you cannot sell Canadian rights if you have already agreed to give North American rights to another magazine.

First Anthology Rights. A few periodicals want the right to use your poem in a future anthology as well as in the periodical itself. If you agree to this you are relinquishing one of the subsequent rights. It is probably to your benefit to agree; having a poem in a *The Best of XXXXX Review* anthology will help your poetry become better known.

All Rights. Although it is no longer common, some periodicals still attempt to purchase all rights. If you give up all rights, the periodical will own your work and you will have no further legal rights to it. (All rights are what you, as the author, own to begin with.) Should you sell all rights to a poem, you will be forced to obtain the publisher's permission to use that poem in any future book or anthology. This is considered unreasonable and unethical. Think carefully before you sell all rights. (This practice, it is interesting to note, is forbidden by law in Britain.)

Some periodicals will buy all rights and give the subsequent rights back to you at your written request. There are several possible variations.

Do not necessarily go by what you read in this market guide. Most magazines have formal contributors' guidelines in which the issue of rights will normally be covered. If you are in doubt, or if you want to be completely certain, write for the guidelines. (You should always send an SASE when you request this type of information.)

Permissions. This usually refers to the granting of permission to a publishing house to reprint a poem in a book or anthology. The permission applies only to the book for which it is granted. Any further use of the work must be negotiated separately.

While many literary compilations pay only in contributors' copies, it is reasonable to expect a permission fee for appearances in major anthologies. You should always charge a fee for the inclusion of your poetry in textbooks.

Fees per poem range from $25 to $500 or more, depending on the publisher, the nature of the collection, the length of the poem, and the reputation of its author. Permission fees are negotiable.

A publisher seeking a permission will contact either the author or the original publisher. If the original publishing contract assigned reprint rights to the publisher rather than the author, the publisher will negotiate the fee. If the author retained these rights, the author will handle the negotiations. Most book contracts call for the fee to be split between the author and the original publisher.

Permission forms should clearly identify the title of the work requested and the title, intended market, size, and estimated press run of the proposed anthology or textbook. A projected publication date should also be part of this little contract. In addition to your fee you should request a copy of the book. You may also wish to add a line to the permission form stipulating that the poem must not be altered in any way without written approval.

Additional fees are not automatically payable for second and subsequent printings of the proposed book. These are usually negotiated separately. (Textbooks commonly run to several editions.)

1.4 COPYRIGHT

Copyright is the property right that arises initially from authorship alone. You own what you make, and this is a right that can be sold. You should, however, NEVER SELL THE COPYRIGHT. When publishing your poems, always make sure that the copyright remains in your name and is not transferred to the periodical or book publisher. (Never take anything for granted. When publishing in periodicals, chapbooks, books, anthologies, or textbooks, make sure that the copyright remains with you.) In the normal course of events, the copyright will be your property until you die. It will then become the property of your heirs or estate for a further fifty years, unless it has been assigned (by sale or gift) to someone else.

For complete information and appropriate forms, write to: The Commissioner of Patents, Copyright Office, Hull, Quebec, K1A 0E1.

For American information and registration, you can write to the Copyright Office, Library of Congress, Washington, DC, 20540-4320.

Information on copyright is also obtainable from the League of Canadian Poets, The Writers' Union of Canada, and from the various provincial writers' groups listed elsewhere in this guide.

For information about the Canadian reprography collective, please contact CanCopy, Suite 900, 6 Adelaide Street East, Toronto, Ontario, M5C 1H6; (800) 893-5777.

And be sure to remember— never sell your copyright. It is your responsibility to thoroughly understand the terms of publication when you deal with book publishers or magazines.

1.5 CANADIAN PERIODICAL LISTINGS

The following 148 Canadian periodicals welcome submissions of poetry. Some publish only poetry; others publish very little poetry. Some have national distribution; others only circulate locally.

You should always study a journal before you submit your work. Many of these magazines can be found in public or university libraries. It may also be wise to send for sample copies. It is important to look before you leap.

Always send a self-addressed stamped envelope (SASE) with your material.

Note: Not all of these periodicals meet the professional standards advocated by the League of Canadian Poets. The goal here has been to cover ALL journals in Canada that publish poetry. Thus, it may happen that a few of the publishers on this list conduct their business in a way that is unfair to poets.

absinthe
Box 61113, Kensington Postal Outlet, Calgary, Alberta T2N 4S6
Ed: by Collective   Poetry Ed: n/a

Since: 1988	Circ: 750	Pages: 80	Per Year: 2
Size: 8 X 11	Binding: ?	Sample: $6	Sub: $10
Copyright: author	Book reviews: no	Reviews/year: n/a	Translations: yes
Interviews: ?	Fiction: yes	Essays: yes	Copies: yes
Money: yes	Time: 1-6 months		

Authors published: David Daniel Moses

As our editorial collective is concerned with publishing writing from disenfranchised communities, please read our most recent issue to determine what sort of work we are looking for.

ACTA VICTORIANA
150 Charles Street West, Toronto, Ontario M5S 1K9
Telephone: (416) 944-1055
Ed and Poetry Ed: Abbie Levin

Since: 1878	Circ: 1,000	Pages: 45	Per Year: 2
Size: 8 1/2 X 11	Saddle stitched	Sample: $1.60	Sub: $5
Copyright: author	Book reviews: no	Reviews/year: n/a	Translations: no
Interviews: yes	Fiction: yes	Essays: yes	Copies: 2
Money: no	Time: 2 months		

Authors published: Margaret Atwood, Clive Thompson, Nicole Nolan, & Heidi Tredemann

We especially welcome essays about media/cultural issues as well as other topics.

THE AFFILIATE
777 Barb Road, Vankleek Hill, Ontario K0B 1R0
Ed and Poetry Ed: Peter Riden

Since: 1987	Circ: 2,000	Pages: 44	Per Year: 12
Size: 8 1/2 X 11	Saddle stitched	Sample: $7 (U.S.)	Sub: $75 (U.S.)
Copyright: ?	Book reviews: yes	Reviews/year: ?	Translations: no
Interviews: yes	Fiction: no	Essays: yes	Copies: yes
Money: no	Time: 2-5 months		

Authors published: Patricia Sutton. Joseph Farley, Kendra Usack, & Woody Raymer

We suggest that you ask for a trial copy upon contacting us so that you'll know what we're about. Cost of sample copy ourside North America: $10 (U.S.); cost of subscription outside North America: $100 (U.S.).

AFTERTHOUGHTS
Pacific Centre North, 701 Granville St., PO Box 54039, Vancouver, BC V7Y 1K6
Ed and Poetry Ed: J.K. Andromeda

Since: 1994	Circ: 400	Pages: 68	Per Year: 4
Size: 13.5cm X 21.2 cm	Prefect bound	Sample: $4	Sub: $10
Copyright: author	Book reviews: no	Reviews/year: n/a	Translations: no
Interviews: no	Fiction: no	Essays: no	Copies: 1
Money: no	Time: 2-4 weeks		

Authors published: Gregory William Gunn, Beryl Baigent, Monika Lee, & Vic Elias

Will consider all types of poetry, but prefer free verse that is imaginative, clear, and smooth-flowing; it should actually say something of significance as well. Uncensored, open forum for both new and established writers. Features poets from anywhere in the world. Submissions accepted all year. We have taken a vegan stance. Magazine is associated with Lakewood Press.

AMBER
40 Rose Street, Apt. 404, Dartmouth, Nova Scotia B3A 2T6
Telephone: (902) 461-4934
Ed and Poetry Ed: Hazel Firth Goddard

Since: 1967	Circ: 100	Pages: 28	Per Year: 4
Size: 9 X 5	Saddle stitched	Sample: $2	Sub: $10
Copyright: author	Book reviews: no	Reviews/year: n/a	Translations: no
Interviews: yes	Fiction: no	Essays: no	Copies: 1
Money: no	Time: ?		

Authors published: Elizabeth St Jacques, Tony Cosier, Herb Barrett, & Jack Brooks

Definitely no religious poems, nor pornographic poems. Modern and traditional, nature, life, etc. Will accept only half page length poems. Also interested in short shorts, haiku, etc. for "Marsh & Maple" insert. One free copy with published poem only. Writers must subscribe to be published.

THE AMETHYST REVIEW
23 Riverside Avenue, Truro, Nova Scotia B2N 4G2
Telephone: (902) 895-1345
Ed: Penny L. Ferguson

Since: ?	Circ: ?	Pages: ?	Per Year: 2
Size: ?	Binding: ?	Sample: $6	Sub: $12
Copyright: author	Book reviews: ?	Reviews/year: ?	Translations: ?
Interviews: ?	Fiction: yes	Essays: ?	Copies: 1
Money: no	Time: ?		

Poetry can be up to 200 lines. Fiction can be up to 5,000 words. Also interested in black & white artwork (Max. size: 5 X 6). Runs an annual writing contest. Please send SASE for details.

THE ANTIGONISH REVIEW
PO Box 5000, St. Francis Xavier University, Antigonish, Nova Scotia B2G 2W5
Telephone: (902) 867-3962   Fax: (902) 867-5153
Ed: George Sanderson   Poetry Ed: Peter Sanger

Since: 1970	Circ: 800	Pages: 150	Per Year: 4
Size: 6 X 9	Perfect bound	Sample: $3	Sub: $20
Copyright: author	Book reviews: yes	Reviews/year: 12-15	Translations: yes
Interviews: rarely	Fiction: yes	Essays: yes	Copies: 2
Money: no	Time: 2-3 months		

Authors published: Michael Hulse, Sue Nevill, Barry Butson, & Amy Barrutt

ARC
PO Box 7368, Ottawa, Ontario K1L 8E4
Eds and Poetry Eds: John Barton & Rita Donovan

Since: 1978	Circ: 680	Pages: 80-88	Per Year: 2
Size: ?	Perfect bound	Sample: $6.50	Sub: $25
Copyright: author	Book reviews: yes	Reviews/year: ?	Translations: yes
Interviews: yes	Fiction: no	Essays: yes	Copies: 2
Money: $25/page	Time: 3-6 months		

Authors published: Erin Mouré, Robin Skelton, & Anne Szumigalski

Please query first when submitting reviews, interviews, essays, translations and artwork because these items are usually solicited. One issue per year tends to be a special theme issue; send SASE for information.

ARIEL: A Review of International English Literature
The University of Calgary, Department of English, 2500 University Drive N.W., Calgary, Alberta T2N 1N4
Telephone: (403) 220-4657   Fax: (403) 289-1123
Ed: Victor J. Ramraj   Poetry Ed: by Committee

Since: 1970	Circ: 1,000	Pages: 160	Per Year: 4
Size: 8 1/2 X 5 1/2	Perfect bound	Sample: $10	Sub: $18
Copyright: ?	Book reviews: yes	Reviews/year: 20-25	Translations: yes
Interviews: yes	Fiction: no	Essays: yes	Copies: 2
Money: ?	Time: 2-3 months		

Authors published: Claire Harris, David Dabydeen, Emma LèRocque, & Robert Hillies

Primarily a journal of essays. About 10 to 12 poems are published in each issue. Fiction is only used in special issues. Work published in *Ariel* can only be reprinted with the approval of the journal. Subscriptions are $18 regular, $15 student, $27 institutional. E-mail address: ariel@acs.ucalgary.ca

ARTSbeat
Hamilton & Region Arts Council, 116 King Street West, Hamilton, Ontario L8P 4V3
Telephone: (905) 529-9485   Fax: (905) 529-0238
Ed: Ivan Jurakic

Since: 1969	Circ: 3,500	Pages: 12	Per Year: 6
Size: tabloid	Newspaper	Sample: free	Sub: $25
Copyright: author	Book reviews: yes	Reviews/year: ?	Translations: yes
Interviews: yes	Fiction: yes	Essays: yes	Copies: no
Money: no	Time: 2 weeks		

Authors published: Jim Strecker & Soraya Erian

Preference is for material, essays, reviews, etc. that pertains to the Hamilton-Wentworth/Burlington region. E-mail address: harac@freenet.hamilton.on.ca

AT THE CROSSROADS
PO Box 317, Station P, Toronto, Ontario M5S 2S8
Telephone: (416) 538-4296   Fax: (416) 538-3206
Ed: karenmiranda augustine   Poetry Ed: amuna baraka

Since: 1992	Circ: 2,000	Pages: 64	Per Year: 3
Size: 10 1/2 X 15	Saddle stitched	Sample: $5	Sub: $13.65
Copyright: author	Book reviews: yes	Reviews/year: 1	Translations: yes
Interviews: yes	Fiction: yes	Essays: yes	Copies: yes
Money: yes	Time: 1 month		

Authors published: Terri Saunders, e.jaw.sé, Sapphire, & T.S. Pratt

An interdisciplinary journal of Black art and culture, promoting Black women's work. We encourage submissions which are creative in approach, thought-provoking, and critical. E-mail address: atc@nugraphix.com

BARDIC RUNES
424 Cambridge Street South, Ottawa, Ontario K1S 4H5
Ed: Michael McKenny

Since: 1990	Circ: ?	Pages: 60	Per Year: ?
Size: digest	Binding: ?	Sample: $4	Sub: $10/3 issues
Copyright: author	Book reviews: no	Reviews/year: n/a	Translations: yes
Interviews: no	Fiction: yes	Essays: no	Copies: ?
Money: $5	Time: 2 weeks		

Authors published: Janet Reedman, Owen Neill, Mildred Keating, & Denyse Bridger

Essentially a fiction magazine. I stopped advertising the fact we publish poetry as we were inundated with modern garbage. Send us what every century but this one considered poetry as to form. Content must be traditional high fantasy. E-mail address: bn872@freenet.carleton.ca

BENEATH THE SURFACE
McMaster University, Department of English, Chester New Hall, Hamilton, Ontario L8S 4S8
Ed and Poetry Ed: changes annually

Since: 1983	Circ: 150-250	Pages: 40-50	Per Year: 2
Size: varies	Saddle stitched	Sample: $4	Sub: $8
Copyright: author	Book reviews: no	Reviews/year: n/a	Translations: no
Interviews: yes	Fiction: yes	Essays: yes	Copies: 1
Money: no	Time: 4-8 months		

Authors published: R.J. Nesbitt, Rose Mary Hunold, Robert Cook, & Susan Benjamin

Open to all types of poetry. Reads manuscripts between September and April.

BETWEEN THE LINES
McMaster University, Wentworth House B118, Hamilton, Ontario L8S 4K1
Telephone: (905) 525-9140, Ex. 27543
Ed: by Committee

Since: 1988	Circ: ?	Pages: 20	Per Year: monthly
Size: 11 1/2 X 13	Newspaper	Sample: free	Sub: n/a

Copyright: ?	Book reviews: yes	Reviews/year: ?	Translations: ?
Interviews: ?	Fiction: yes	Essays: yes	Copies: ?
Money: no	Time: ?		

Authors published: Tim Madden, Jeff Andersen, Lisa Hannan, & Debi Raposo

blue buffalo

922 9th Avenue S.E., Calgary, Alberta T2G 0S4

Telephone: (403) 265-0524

Ed: Tony King   Poetry Eds: Rick Miles, Sarah Murphy, Chris Hogan, & Leila Sujrr

Since: 1982	Circ: 250	Pages: 25-30	Per Year: 2
Size: 6 X 9	Saddle stitched	Sample: $2	Sub: $4
Copyright: author	Book reviews: no	Reviews/year: n/a	Translations: no
Interviews: no	Fiction: yes	Essays: no	Copies: 1
Money: yes	Time: 4 months		

Authors published: Rob Branden, Vanna Tesslar, Erin Michie, & M.G. Meneghetti

Pays $40 for fiction and $15 per poem. Deadline for spring issue: December 31; deadline for Fall issue: June 30. Publishes new and emerging writers and artists from Alberta only.

THE BRITISH COLUMBIA MONTHLY

PO Box 48884, Station Bentall, Vancouver, British Columbia V7X 1A8

Ed and Poetry Ed: Gerry Gilbert

Since: 1972	Circ: 600	Pages: 16	Per Year: 1
Size: 7 X 8 1/2	Saddle stitched	Sample: $1	Sub: n/a
Copyright: author	Book reviews: yes	Reviews/year: seldom	Translations: yes
Interviews: no	Fiction: yes	Essays: yes	Copies: yes
Money: no	Time: n/a		

Authors published: Marie Annharte Baker, Peter Culley, Yvonne Parent, & Goh Pohseng

B.C. Monthly is both an annual monograph and a radio program on CFRO (102.7 FM), RADIOFREERAINFOREST (RFRF). Backlog is 1,000 months long, but we welcome poetry submissions on CD and audiotape. RFRF is a one-hour weekly broadcast. The spoken word hits home. Please send SASE for details.

BYWORDS

University of Ottawa, English Department, 175 Waller Street, Ottawa, Ontario K1N 6N5

Telephone: (613) 562-5764   Fax: (613) 562-5990

Eds and Poetry Eds: Gwendolyn Guth & Maria Scala

Since: 1990	Circ: 500	Pages: 8	Per Year: 11 or 12
Size: 5 1/2 X 8 1/2	Saddle stitched	Sample: free	Sub: $12
Copyright: author	Book reviews: no	Reviews/year: n/a	Translations: no
Interviews: no	Fiction: no	Essays: no	Copies: 4
Money: no	Time: 2-3 months		

Authors published: Seymour Mayne, Enid Delgatty Rutland, Joseph Dandurand, & Leslie Smith Dow

Bywords will publish three chapbooks featuring Canada'a diverse poetic community; the first one, Remembered Earth, is available for $2. The monthly magazine features eclectic, well-crafted poems, usually 1 to 2 pages in length.

We also publish the winners of Ottawa's annual Jane Jordan Competition. Subscriptions for institutions are $20/year.

CABARET VERT MAGAZINE
PO Box 157, Station P, Toronto, Ontario M5S 2S7
Eds and Poetry Eds: Beth & Joy Learn

Since: ?	Circ: ?	Pages: 36	Per Year: varies
Size: 8 1/2 X 11	Saddle stitched	Sample: $7	Sub: $20/3 issues
Copyright: author	Book reviews: yes	Reviews/year: ?	Translations: ?
Interviews: ?	Fiction: yes	Essays: yes	Copies: yes
Money: no	Time: ?		

Authors published: Yves Troendle, Sheila Murphy, bpNichol, & Adeena Karasick
An occasional magazine of experimental poetic text, language arts, cross-over art/science, language technology, fusion-esque, photography, etc.

CANADIAN AUTHOR
27 Doxsee Avenue North, Campbellford, Ontario K0L 1L0
Telephone: (705) 653-0323 Fax: (705) 653-0593
Ed: Welwyn Wilton Katz   Poetry Ed: Sheila Martindale

Since: 1921	Circ: 5,000	Pages: 32	Per Year: 4
Size: 8 1/2 X 11	Saddle stitched	Sample: $4.50	Sub: $15
Copyright: author	Book reviews: yes	Reviews/year: 24	Translations: no
Interviews: yes	Fiction: yes	Essays: yes	Copies: yes
Money: yes	Time: ?		

Authors published: Liliane Welch, George Whipple, Sylvia Adams, & John Wilson
Publishes book reviews, but not of poetry books. No epic poems. No profanity or vulgarity. Submit poetry any time.

CANADIAN DIMENSION
228 Notre Dame Avenue, Suite 401, Winnipeg, Manitoba R3B 1N7
Telephone: (204) 957-1519 Fax: (204) 943-4617
Ed: by Collective

Since: 1963	Circ: 3,500	Pages: 48	Per Year: 6
Size: ?	Binding: ?	Sample: $3	Sub: $24.50
Copyright: magazine	Book reviews: yes	Reviews/year: varies	Translations: no
Interviews: yes	Fiction: no	Essays: yes	Copies: yes
Money: ?	Time: 6 months		

Broadly political— that is, not narrowly sloganeering but profoundly sensitive to the connections between words and the state of the world. This can be personal as well as "political" in the usual sense of being about social issues.

CANADIAN FORUM
251 Laurier Avenue West, Suite 804, Ottawa, Ontario K1P 5J6
Telephone: (613) 230-3078 Fax: (613) 233-1458
Ed: Duncan Cameron   Poetry Ed: Pat Smart

Since: 1920	Circ: 10,000	Pages: 48	Per Year: 10
Size: 8 1/2 X 11	Binding: ?	Sample: $3	Sub: $23.54
Copyright: author	Book reviews: yes	Reviews/year: 80	Translations: yes
Interviews: yes	Fiction: yes	Essays: yes	Copies: 2
Money: $75	Time: 6 weeks		

Authors published: Margaret Atwood, Irving Layton, Gwendolyn MacEwen, & Leonard Cohen

Prefers submissions of 8 to 10 shorter poems per author. Two pages for a single poet per issue.

CANADIAN JEWISH OUTLOOK
6184 Ash Street, #3, Vancouver, British Columbia V5Z 3G9
Telephone: (604) 324-5101   Fax: (604) 325-2470
Eds: Henry Rosenthal, Sylvia Friedman, & Carl Rosenberg

Since: 1962	Circ: 2,000	Pages: 32	Per Year: 8
Size: 8 X 10 1/2	Perfect bound	Sample: free	Sub: $30
Copyright: author	Book reviews: yes	Reviews/year: 30	Translations: yes
Interviews: yes	Fiction: yes	Essays: yes	Copies: yes
Money: no	Time: 3 months		

Authors published: Miriam Waddington, Aaron Kramer, Philip Resnick, & Ray Shankman
Imagery— Judaic, secular heritage, humanism.

CANADIAN LITERATURE
The University of British Columbia, 2029 West Mall, Room 225, Vancouver, British Columbia V6T 1Z2
Telephone: (604) 822-2780   Fax: (604) 822-9452
Ed: Eva-Marie Kröller   Poetry Ed: Iain Higgins

Since: 1957	Circ: 1,400	Pages: 200	Per Year: 4
Size: 6 X 9	Perfect bound	Sample: $20	Sub: $42.80
Copyright: author	Book reviews: yes	Reviews/year: 80-100	Translations: no
Interviews: no	Fiction: no	Essays: yes	Copies: ?
Money: ?	Time: 6-8 week		

Authors published: Teruko Anderson-Jones, Jorge Etcheverry, Cheryl Faggo, & Steve Luxton
Primarily a journal of criticism. Canadian poets and/or Canadian content only.

CANADIAN WOMAN STUDIES/LES CAHIERS DE LA FEMME
York University, 212 Founders College, 4700 Keele Street, North York, Ontario M3J 1P3
Ed: Shelagh Wilkinson   Poetry Ed: Maria Jacobs

CANADIAN WRITER'S JOURNAL
Box 6618, Station LCD 1, Victoria, British Columbia V8P 5N7
Telephone: (604) 477-8807
Ed: Gordon M. Smart   Poetry Ed: Elizabeth St Jacques

Since: 1984	Circ: 300	Pages: 64	Per Year: 4
Size: 5 1/5 X 8 1/2	Saddle stitched	Sample: $4	Sub: $15
Copyright: author	Book reviews: yes	Reviews/year: 6-10	Translations: no
Interviews: few	Fiction: yes	Essays: yes	Copies: 1
Money: $5/page	Time: 4-6 weeks		

Authors published: Sharron R. McMillan, Ruth Latta, Hazel Firth Goddard, & Linda Holeman
We use limited poetry except in the Wind Songs column; looks for haiku, senryu, tanka, sijo, and renga. A few other poems related to writing, or used in an article on poetry writing, are published. Runs an annual poetry competition.

CAPERS AWEIGH MAGAZINE
PO Box 96, Sydney, Nova Scotia B1P 6G9
Telephone: (902) 567-1449
Eds: John MacNeil & C. Fairn Kennedy   Poetry Ed: John MacNeil

Since: 1992	Circ: 500	Pages: 92	Per Year: 2
Size: 5 1/5 X 8 1/2	Saddle stitched	Sample: $5	Sub: $10
Copyright: author	Book reviews: yes	Reviews/year: ?	Translations: no
Interviews: no	Fiction: yes	Essays: no	Copies: no
Money: no	Time: 6 months		

Authors published: Shirley Kiju Kawi, James Seminal. J.M. Neil, & Joe Gale

Regional publication of, for, and by Cape Bretoners. Will publish non-Cape Bretoners only if they write about Cape Breton. Associated with Capers Aweigh Small Press, a publisher of books and chapbooks by Cape Bretoners.

THE CAPILANO REVIEW
Capilano College, 2055 Purcell Way, North Vancouver, British Columbia V7J 3H5
Telephone: (604) 984-1712 Fax: (604) 983-7520
Ed: Robert Sherrin

Since: 1972	Circ: 850	Pages: 120	Per Year: 3
Size: 6 X 9	Perfect bound	Sample: $9	Sub: $25
Copyright: author	Book reviews: no	Reviews/year: n/a	Translations: ?
Interviews: yes	Fiction: yes	Essays: yes	Copies: 2
Money: $50-$200	Time: 4 months		

Authors published: Patrick Friesen, Evelyn Lau, Robin Blaser, & Hilary Clark

CARLETON ARTS REVIEW
Cartleton University, Box 78, 18th Floor, Davidson Dunton Tower, Ottawa, Ontario K1S 5B6

Since: 1985	Circ: 300-500	Pages: 50	Per Year: 2
Size: 8 1/2 X 7	Perfect bound	Sample: $3.50	Sub: $7
Copyright: author	Book reviews: yes	Reviews/year: 4-6	Translations: no
Interviews: yes	Fiction: yes	Essays: yes	Copies: yes
Money: no	Time: 2-4 months		

Authors published: Ken Norris, Patricia Young, Brian Burke, & Joanne Epp

We take poetry from all over the world, although we like to see Canadian work show up on our front porch. Poetry that tells an interesting and evocative story is always welcome. Poetry by minorities and women is also welcome. We consider manuscripts all year.

CAROUSEL MAGAZINE
University of Guelph, Room 217, University Centre, Guelph, Ontario N1G 2W1
Eds and Poetry Eds: Michael Carbert & Ross Bolton

CHASTITY AND HOLINESS
71 Thorncliffe Park Drive, Apt. 215, Toronto, Ontario M4H 1L3
Telephone: (416) 696-2350 Fax: same
Ed: Cecil Justin Lam   Poetry Ed: Janet King

Since: 1988	Circ: 1,000	Pages: 32	Per Year: 2
Size: 8 1/2 X 7	Saddle stitched	Sample: $10	Sub: $15
Copyright: author	Book reviews: yes	Reviews/year: 4	Translations: yes
Interviews: yes	Fiction: yes	Essays: yes	Copies: yes
Money: no	Time: 1 year		

Authors published: Hugh Alexander, Ron Collings, Becky Dobbs, & David Castleman

Welcomes spiritual poetry with a universal Weltanschaung. Poetry that displays a belief in God. Not only Christian poetry is accepted; comparative religious philosophy in every divine discipline is accepted for intense appreciative evaluation.

CHICKADEE

179 John Street, Suite 500, Toronto, Ontario M5T 3G5
Telephone: (416) 971-5275   Fax: (416) 971-5294
Ed: Carolyn Meredith   Poetry Ed: none

Since: 1979	Circ: 110,000	Pages: 32	Per Year: 10
Size: 8 1/2 X 11	Saddle stitched	Sample: $4.28	Sub: $20.33
Copyright: author	Book reviews: no	Reviews/year: n/a	Translations: no
Interviews: no	Fiction: yes	Essays: yes	Copies: 2
Money: yes	Time: 6-8 weeks		

Authors published: Ellen Bryan Obed, Marilyn Helmer, J. Patrick Lewis, & Goldie Olszyuko Gryu

Pays $3/line for poetry, $250 for fiction. Please send SASE for guidelines. A nature magazine that aims to interest children ages 3 to 9 in the world around them.

CHURCH-WELLESLEY REVIEW

c/o Xtra!, 491 Church Street, Suite 200, Toronto, Ontario M4Y 2C6
Telephone: (416) 925-6665   Fax: (416) 925-6503
Ed: Eleanor Brown

Since: 1984	Circ: 37,000	Pages: 48	Per Year: 24
Size: tabloid	Newspaper	Sample: free	Sub: ?
Copyright: see below	Book reviews: yes	Reviews/year: ?	Translations: no
Interviews: yes	Fiction: no	Essays: yes	Copies: yes
Money: yes	Time: 1-10 months		

Authors published: Timothy Findley, Shyam Selvadurai, David Watmough, & Sandra Haar

Copyright "sort of" reverts to author; the review has to give permission to reprint poems. Only publishes poetry once per year in a special literary issue. This is a gay and lesbian review.

THE CLAREMONT REVIEW

4980 Wesley Road, Victoria, British Columbia V8Y 1Y9
Telephone: (604) 658-5221   Fax: (604) 658-5387
Eds: Bill Stenson, Susan Stenson, & Terence Young

Since: 1992	Circ: 700	Pages: 100	Per Year: 2
Size: 6 X 9	Perfect bound	Sample: $6	Sub: $12
Copyright: author	Book reviews: no	Reviews/year: n/a	Translations: no
Interviews: yes	Fiction: yes	Essays: ?	Copies: 1
Money: maybe	Time: 2-4 weeks		

Authors published: Lori Acker, Julie Lambert, Gillian Roberts, & Erin Boade

We publish literary fiction and poetry from authors aged 13 to 19. We are not interested in science fiction, fantasy, or cliched attempts. Best to show us a slice of life.

COMPENIONS

PO Box 2511, St. Marys, Ontario N4X 1A3
Ed: Jerry Penner   Poetry Ed: Marco Balestrin

Since: 1979	Circ: 30	Pages: 10-12	Per Year: 4

Size: 8 1/2 X 11	Saddle stitched	Sample: $4	Sub: $25
Copyright: author	Book reviews: no	Reviews/year: n/a	Translations: yes
Interviews: no	Fiction: yes	Essays: no	Copies: 2
Money: no	Time: 1-2 months		

Authors published: Carla Murphy, Ian Roger, Lisa Penner, & Marco Balestrin

We like to see poetry and fiction that is out-of-the-ordinary, that challenges the reader to see ordinary things and events with a new perspective. We don't read manuscripts during July & August.

CONFLUENCE
Grant MacEwan Community College, PO Box 1796, Edmonton, Alberta T5J 2P2

CONTEMPORARY VERSE 2
PO Box 3062, Winnipeg, Manitoba R3C 4E5

Telephone: (204) 949-1365

Ed and Poetry Ed: by Collective

Since: 1975	Circ: 500	Pages: 76	Per Year: 4
Size: 9 X 6	Prefect bound	Sample: $6	Sub: $21.98
Copyright: author	Book reviews: yes	Reviews/year: 5-6	Translations: no
Interviews: yes	Fiction: yes	Essays: yes	Copies: yes
Money: $20/poem	Time: 6-8 weeks.		

Authors published: Catherine Hunter, Lori Cayer, Per Brask, & Maara Haas

A feminist poetry journal that publishes work by women and men. Does not accept sexist, homophobic, or racist material.

THE CORMORANT
The University of New Brunswick, Saint John Campus, PO Box 5050, Saint John, New Brunswick E2L 4L5

Ed: William Prouty   Poetry Ed: Thomas Love

Since: 1983	Circ: ?	Pages: 112	Per Year: 2
Size: 6 X 9	Perfect bound	Sample: $4	Sub: ?
Copyright: author	Book reviews: yes	Reviews/year: ?	Translations: ?
Interviews: yes	Fiction: yes	Essays: yes	Copies: ?
Money: no	Time: 1-6 months		

Authors published: Phyllis Rowan, Douglas Lochhead, Liliane Welch, & Robert Gibbs

Interested in emerging writers as well as work by old friends. Fiction editor is Heather Cameron.

DaDaBaBy
382 East Fourth Street, North Vancouver, British Columbia V7L 1J2

Telephone: (604) 980-9361

Ed and Poetry Ed: Jamie Reid

DALHOUSIE REVIEW
Dalhousie University, Sir James Dunn Building, Room 314, Halifax, Nova Scotia B3H 3J5

Telephone: (902) 494-2541   Fax: same

Ed: Alan Andrews   Poetry Ed: J. A Wainwright

Since: 1921	Circ: 700	Pages: 144	Per Year: 3
Size: 6 X 9	Perfect bound	Sample: $10	Sub: $21
Copyright: author	Book reviews: yes	Reviews/year: 40-50	Translations: yes

Interviews: no	Fiction: yes	Essays: yes	Copies: 2
Money: see below	Time: 4-6 months		

Authors published: Glen Sorestad, Margo Button, Michael Thorpe, & Joseph E. Fasciani

Pays $3 for the first poem and $2 per poem thereafter. Pays $1 per page for fiction. Reads manuscripts year round. Subscriptions for institutions are $40/year.

DANDELION
922 9th Avenue S.E., Calgary, Alberta T2G 0S4

Telephone: (403) 265-0524

Eds: Bonnie Benoit, Judy Millar, & Partick Rergant   Poetry Eds: Janeen Werner-King & Gordon Pengilly

Since: 1974	Circ: 750	Pages: 96	Per Year: 2
Size: 6 X 9	Perfect bound	Sample: $7	Sub: $12
Copyright: author	Book reviews: yes	Reviews/year: 2-7	Translations: rarely
Interviews: rarely	Fiction: yes	Essays: no	Copies: 1
Money: $15/poem	Time: 4 months		

Authors published: Monty Reid, Marilyn Dumont, Robbie Newton Drummond, & Calabrese

We consider poetry for our June issue from October to March; for our December issue from April to October. Fiction editor is Judy Millar.

DESCANT
PO Box 314, Station P, Toronto, Ontario M5S 2S8

Telephone: (416) 593-2557

Ed and Poetry Ed: Karen Mulhallen

Since: 1970	Circ: 1,100	Pages: 150	Per Year: 4
Size: 5 3/4 X 8 3/4	Perfect bound	Sample: $8	Sub: $20
Copyright: author	Book reviews: no	Reviews/year: n/a	Translations: yes
Interviews: yes	Fiction: yes	Essays: yes	Copies: 1
Money: $100	Time: 3-4 months		

Authors published: Jan Zwicky, Eric Ormsby, Richard Sanger, & L.R. Berger

Please read the magazine before submitting. Considers submissions year round.

DON'T QUIT YR DAY-JOB
39 Metcalfe Street, #30, Toronto, Ontario M4X 1R7

or

Western address: 1108 Shelburn Street, Winnipeg, Manitoba R3E 2N2

Eds and Poetry Eds: Phil Hall & Andrew Vaisius

DRIFT
Box 40, 90 Shuter Street, Toronto, Ontario M5B 2K6

Telephone: (416) 466-4606 & 462-1741

Ed and Poetry Ed: C.F. Kennedy

Since: 1992	Circ: 50-100	Pages: 12	Per Year: 10-12
Size: 8 1/2 X 11	Stapled	Sample: $1	Sub: ?
Copyright: author	Book reviews: yes	Reviews/year: 4-6	Translations: yes
Interviews: yes	Fiction: yes	Essays: yes	Copies: yes
Money: no	Time: 6 weeks		

Authors published: J.M. Neil, Ruby D. Nash, George Arly, & Audrey Cowan

Associated with Necessary Press, a publisher of chapbooks. More into fiction than poetry, but poets are welcome to submit.

THE ECLECTIC MUSE - POETRY JOURNAL
340 West 3rd Street, #107, North Vancouver, British Columbia V7M 1G4
Eds and Poetry Eds: Joe M. Ruggier & Jeffrey Woodward

EDUCATION FORUM
60 Mobile Drive, Toronto, Ontatio M4A 2P3
Telephone: (416) 751-8300   Fax: (416) 751-3394
Ed: Neil Walker

Since: 1989	Circ: 46,000	Pages: 42	Per Year: 3
Size: 8 1/2 X 11	Saddle stitched	Sample: $6	Sub: ?
Copyright: author	Book reviews: yes	Reviews/year: ?	Translations: no
Interviews: yes	Fiction: ?	Essays: ?	Copies: ?
Money: ?	Time: ?		

ellipse: writers in translation
Université de Sherbrooke, Faculté des letters et sciences humaines, C.P. 10, Sherbrooke, Québec J1K 2R1
Telecopieur: (819) 821-7285
Eds: Charly Bouchara & Monique Grandmangin

EVENT
Douglas College, PO Box 2503, New Westminster, British Columbia V3L 5B2
Telephone: (604) 527-5293   Fax: (604) 527-5095
Ed: David Zieroth   Poetry Ed: Gillian Harding-Russell

Since: 1971	Circ: 1,000	Pages: 144	Per Year: 3
Size: 6 X 9	Perfect bound	Sample: $6.50	Sub: $16
Copyright: author	Book reviews: yes	Reviews/year: 12	Translations: yes
Interviews: no	Fiction: yes	Essays: yes	Copies: 2
Money: $22/page	Time: 1-4 months		

Authors published: Lorna Crozier, Tom Wayman, Sue Wheeler, & Harold Rhenisch

FEEDBACK
Community Relations, Nova Scotia Hospital, PO Box 1004, Dartmouth, Nova Scotia B2Y 3Z9
Ed and Poetry Ed: Jon David Welland

FEUX CHALINS
Université Sainte-Anne, Pointe de l'Église, Nouvelle-Écosse B0W 1M0
Telephone: (902) 769-2114   Fax: (902) 769-2930
Ed: Ollivier Dyens   Poetry Eds: Ollivier Dyens, Yves Cormier, Robert Finley, Maurice Lamothe, Guy Drouin, Norman Godin, & Jean Wilson

Since: 1995	Circ: 500	Pages: 120	Per Year: 1
Size: 6 X 9	Perfect bound	Sample: $8	Sub: $15
Copyright: author	Book reviews: non	Reviews/year: n/a	Translations: non
Interviews: non	Fiction: oui	Essays: non	Copies: oui
Money: non	Time: 2 mois		

Nous accueillons des textes en français et en anglais, ainsi que des paroles de chansons, des photographies, des peintures et des dessins. La date limité d'envoi des oeuvres est le 1er fevrier.

THE FIDDLEHEAD

Campus House, University of New Brunswick, PO Box 4400, Fredericton, New Brunswick E3B 5A3

Telephone: (506) 453-3501   Fax: (506) 453-4599

Ed: Don McKay   Poetry Eds: Robert Gibbs, Robert Hawkes, Eric Hill, & Don McKay

Since: 1945	Circ: 1,000	Pages: 128	Per Year: 4
Size: 6 X 9	Perfect bound	Sample: $8	Sub: $20
Copyright: author	Book reviews: yes	Reviews/year: 12-20	Translations: rarely
Interviews: rarely	Fiction: yes	Essays: rarely	Copies: 1
Money: $10/page	Time: 2-6 months		

Authors published: Susan Downe, Charles Gregory, Roo Borson, & Tom Wayman

Reads throughout the year. Runs an annual writing contest; please send SASE for rules.

FIREWEED: a feminist quarterly

PO Box 279, Station B, Toronto, Ontario M5T 2W2

Telephone: (416) 504-1339

Ed and Poetry Ed: by Collective

Since: 1978	Circ: 2,000	Pages: 88	Per Year: 4
Size: 7 X 10	Perfect bound	Sample: $7	Sub: $20
Copyright: author	Book reviews: yes	Reviews/year: 16	Translations: yes
Interviews: yes	Fiction: yes	Essays: yes	Copies: 2
Money: $30 first page	Time: 6 months		

Authors published: Nancy Chater, Suzette Mayr, Mona Oikawa, & Lynn Crosbie

Foreign subscriptions are $28 (Canadian $).

FIRM NONCOMMITTAL

5 Vonda Avenue, North York, Ontario M2N 5E6

Telephone: (416) 222-8599

Ed: Brian Pastoor   Poetry Eds: Jeff Bersche & Brian Pastoor

Since: 1995	Circ: 200	Pages: 48	Per Year: 1
Size: 6 X 8 1/2	Perfect bound	Sample: $5	Sub: $7
Copyright: author	Book reviews: no	Reviews/year: n/a	Translations: no
Interviews: no	Fiction: yes	Essays: yes	Copies: yes
Money: no	Time: 1-2 months		

Authors published: John & Mike Erskine-Kellie, Libby Scheier, bill bissett, & K.V. Skene

Associated with Pang&deVries, a chapbook publisher. Reads submissions of lighthearted and humorous material every May and June. Prefers poetry under 40 lines, from concrete, dub/Trinislang to villanelle; fiction and non-fiction to 800 words. Seeks writers who find the sunshine in the saturnine.

FreeLance

PO Box 3986, Regina, Saskatchewan S4P 3R9

Telephone: (306) 757-6310   Fax: (306) 565-8554

Ed: April Davies   Poetry Ed: Marie Baker

GARM LU

University of Toronto, St. Michael's College, 81 St. Mary Street, Toronto, Ontario M5S 1J4

Telephone: (416) 944-8781

Eds and Poetry Eds: Sonja Johnston & Deborah Livingston

Since: 1985	Circ: 250-500	Pages: 100+	Per Year: 1
Size: 5 1/2 X 8 1/2	Perfect bound	Sample: $7	Sub: $7
Copyright: author	Book reviews: yes	Reviews/year: ?	Translations: yes
Interviews: yes	Fiction: yes	Essays: yes	Copies: 1
Money: no	Time: ?		

Authors published: Beryl Baigent, Inga Israel, R.L. Cook, & Wayne McNeill

Best time to send poetry is from mid-summer to December. Poetry MUST be Celtic in theme, form, or content (ie. Irish, Scottish, Welsh, Breton, Maritime). Foreign subscriptions are $9 (Canadian $).

GRAFFITO, the poetry poster
University of Ottawa, Department of English, Ottawa, Ontario K1N 6N5
Telephone: (613) 738-2366
Eds and Poetry Eds: Robert Craig, Christal Steck, & b stephen harding

Since: 1994	Circ: 200	Pages: 1-4	Per Year: 12
Size: 14 X 17	Poster	Sample: free	Sub: $10
Copyright: author	Book reviews: yes	Reviews/year: varies	Translations: yes
Interviews: no	Fiction: no	Essays: no	Copies: 3
Money: no	Time: 2 months		

Authors published: Jill Battson, Len Gasparini, rob mclennan, & Joe Blades

Associated with Friday Circle, a small publisher. We are most interested in reviewing chapbooks. Book reviews are limited to one per issue (12 per year). Each issue publishes between 4 to 6 poems. All issues will be on our homepage on the World Wide Web: http://www.cymbiont.ca/graffito

GRAIN
PO Box 1154, Regina, Saskatchewan S4P 3B4
Telephone: (306) 244-2828   Fax: (306) 565-8554
Ed: J. Jill Robinson   Poetry Ed: Tim Lilburn

Since: 1973	Circ: 1,500	Pages: 144	Per Year: 4
Size: 6 X 9	Perfect bound	Sample: $7.50	Sub: $21.35
Copyright: author	Book reviews: no	Reviews/year: n/a	Translations: yes
Interviews: no	Fiction: yes	Essays: yes	Copies: 2
Money: $30-$100	Time: 4-6 months		

Authors published: Monty Reid, Lorna Crozier, John B. Lee, & Barbara Klar

Submissions accepted year round, but no submissions by fax. Preference for work that is fresh, edgy in thought and diction, and skillfully crafted. Open to any form and content. Runs a prose poem contest (Short Grain) as well as a short-short story contest, both with cash prizes. Send SASE for complete contest rules.

GREEN'S MAGAZINE
PO Box 3236, Regina, Saskatchewan S4P 3H1
Ed: David Green

Since: 1972	Circ: 300	Pages: 100	Per Year: 4
Size: 5 1/4 X 8	Saddle stitched	Sample: $4	Sub: $12
Copyright: author	Book reviews: yes	Reviews/year: 4-5	Translations: yes
Interviews: no	Fiction: yes	Essays: no	Copies: yes
Money: no	Time: 2 months		

Authors published: Carl Leggo, Joanna Weston, James Mossman, & John Fell

Plans to start publishing chapbooks. All material must be suitable for family reading.

HECATE'S LOOM

PO Box 5206, Station B, Victoria, British Columbia V8R 6N4

Ed: Yvonne Owens   Poetry Ed: Sylvia Skelton

Since: 1986	Circ: 1,700	Pages: 50	Per Year: 4
Size: 8 1/2 X 11	Perfect bound	Sample: $4.50	Sub: $18
Copyright: author	Book reviews: yes	Reviews/year: 12	Translations: yes
Interviews: yes	Fiction: yes	Essays: yes	Copies: yes
Money: no	Time: 3 months		

Authors published: Robin Skelton, Margaret Blackwood, Don Brennan, & David Ferguson

The magazine exists for the purpose of providing a forum for the creative expression of Paganism, inclusive of Witchcraft, Goddess-Spirituality, Gaia Consciousness, Shamanism, and other Earth-based religious philosophies. We believe that words (and all creative arts) are forms of magic and derive from Shamanistic roots. Poetry about magical/spiritual themes, or magical/transformative in their effect, are welcome. (Must be well-crafted or will not pass our poetry editor.)

HIJ / journal of new writing

31 Northumberland Street, Toronto, Ontario M6H 4G3

Telephone: (416) 532-9568

Eds and Poetry Eds: Hazel & Jay MillAr

Since: 1996	Circ: 15-30	Pages: 15-20	Per Year: 26
Size: 5 1/2 X 8 1/2	Hand sewn	Sample: $5	Sub: n/a
Copyright: ?	Book reviews: maybe	Reviews/year: n/a	Translations: maybe
Interviews: maybe	Fiction: maybe	Essays: maybe	Copies: 1
Money: no	Time: 2-4 weeks		

Authors published: Shannon Bramer, Rob Ruzic, j.a. Love Grove, & John Lepp

Associated with Boondoggle Books. We believe that culture operates on a very small level. People give us new writing and every two weeks we sit down and (hand) make something of it, with whatever materials we have to use. Anyone is invited to send anything; we will publish anything we like.

hole

191 McLeod Street, #22, Ottawa, Ontario K2P 0Z8

Telephone: (613) 237-0969

Eds and Poetry Eds: Louis Cabri & Robert Manery

Since: 1989	Circ: 400	Pages: 60	Per Year: 1-2
Size: 7 X 8 1/2	Saddle stitched	Sample: $4	Sub: $10
Copyright: author	Book reviews: yes	Reviews/year: ?	Translations: yes
Interviews: yes	Fiction: no	Essays: yes	Copies: 2
Money: no	Time: 4-6 months		

Authors published: Steve McCaffery, Hannah Weiner, Alan Davies, & Karen MacCormack

Associated with poetry chapbook publisher hole books. Work that we are interested in recognizes the political and social implications of language practice. Work tends to be formally innovative in its exploration of ways to create meaning.

HOOK & LADDER: Canada's Independent Journal of Poetry and Reviews
PO Box 78, Station B, Ottawa, Ontario K1P 6C3
Telephone: (613) 562-5764   Fax: (613) 562-5990
Ed: Victoria Martin

Since: 1992	Circ: 350-500	Pages: 24-28	Per Year: 2
Size: 5 1/2 X 8 1/2	Saddle stitched	Sample: $2	Sub: $12
Copyright: author	Book reviews: yes	Reviews/year: 6-10	Translations: yes
Interviews: yes	Fiction: no	Essays: yes	Copies: 2
Money: no	Time: 3-6 months		

Authors published: Diana Brebner, John Barton, Tony Cosier, & Colin Morton

Submissions of original poetry always welcome. Prefer contributions from young, unpublished writers, but everyone may submit. No simultaneous submissions or previously published pieces. Reviews must conform to the format laid out in the *MLA Handbook for Writers of Research Papers*.

HOSTBOX
University of Ottawa, Department of English, Ottawa, Ontario K1N 6N5
Eds and Poerty Eds: Stuart Konyer & Chris Pollard

Since: 1992	Circ: 200	Pages: 40	Per Year: 4
Size: 7 X 8 1/2	Saddle stitched	Sample: $2	Sub: $10
Copyright: author	Book reviews: no	Reviews/year: n/a	Translations: no
Interviews: no	Fiction: yes	Essays: no	Copies: 2
Money: no	Time: 3 months		

Authors published: rob mclennan, Lissa Beauchamp, James Spyker, & Tamara Fairchild

Reads all year round. Also publishes cartoons. We are mainly interested in writing nobody else will print, although we are not above publishing first-rate material. And despite the address, rest assured that this is not a university publication.

INK MAGAZINE
Box 52558, 264 Bloor Street West, Toronto, Ontatio M5S 1V0
Ed and Poetry Ed: John Degen

Since: 1993	Circ: 300	Pages: 40	Per Year: 4
Size: digest	Saddle stitched	Sample: $2.50	Sub: $8
Copyright: author	Book reviews: yes	Reviews/year: 4	Translations: yes
Interviews: yes	Fiction: yes	Essays: yes	Copies: yes
Money: no	Time: 3 months		

Authors published: Michael Holmes, Ann Shin, Al Purdy, & Casie Hermansson

Plans to start a chapbook press, Ink Books, soon. All styles of poetry are considered. Looks for poetry that is hard to write, easy to like.

INKSTONE
Box 75009, Hudson Bay Post Office, 20 Bloor Street East, Toronto, Ontario M4W 3T3
Telephone: (416) 920-8686 & 962-6051   Fax: (416) 966-9646
Eds and Poetry Eds: J. Louise Fletcher, Marshall Hryciuk, & Keith Southward

Since: 1982	Circ: 150	Pages: 44	Per Year: 1-2
Size: 5 1/2 X 8	Saddle stitched	Sample: $5	Sub: $15/4 issues
Copyright: author	Book reviews: yes	Reviews/year: 6	Translations: yes

| Interviews: no | Fiction: no | Essays: yes | Copies: I |
| Money: no | Time: 3 months | | |

Authors published: Carol Montgomery, Jim Kacian, Fred Lasser, & Karen Sohne

We are a haiku magazine. Not traditional, but certainly purist. Write the moment of awareness so that it is as sensual and mentally surprising as illumination itself. Remember suchness— jettison the adjectives.

JONES AV.
88 Dagmar Avenue, Toronto, Ontario M4M IWI
Telephone: (416) 461-8739
Ed and Poetry Ed: Paul Schwortz

Since: 1994	Circ: 100	Pages: 24	Per Year: 4
Size: 5 1/2 X 8	Saddle stitched	Sample: $2	Sub: $8
Copyright: author	Book reviews: yes	Reviews/year: 18	Translations: could
Interviews: no	Fiction: no	Essays: no	Copies: I
Money: no	Time: 3 months		

Authors published: LeRoy Gorman, Sophia Kaszuba, Stan Rogal, & Lyn Lifshin

Uses poetry from lyric to ashcan. Likes to keep poems no longer than 30 lines, but this is not an absolute. Interested in prose poetry, also interested in suites of drawings for cover and inside.

KAIROS
Mohawk College, Language Studies, PO Box 2034, Hamilton, Ontario L8N 3T2
Telephone: (905) 575-2001   Fax: (905) 575-2002
Eds and Poetry Eds: R.W. Megens & Royston Tester

Since: 1989	Circ: 500-1,000	Pages: 120	Per Year: I
Size: 5 1/2 X 8 1/2	Perfect bound	Sample: $5	Sub: $5
Copyright: author	Book reviews: yes	Reviews/year: I	Translations: yes
Interviews: yes	Fiction: yes	Essays: yes	Copies: 2
Money: no	Time: ?		

Authors published: John B. Lee, Marilyn Gear Pilling, John Ferns, & Soraya Erian

Published every fall. Submissions accepted all year. Likes computer disc copies of poems on popular IBM or Macintosh programs along with your hard copy.

KICK IT OVER
PO Box 5811, Station A, Toronto, Ontario M5W IP2
Ed: Bob Melcombe

Since: 1981	Circ: 1,600	Pages: 68	Per Year: 4
Size: 8 1/2 X 11	Saddle stitched	Sample: $3	Sub: $12
Copyright: author	Book reviews: yes	Reviews/year: 12	Translations: yes
Interviews: yes	Fiction: yes	Essays: yes	Copies: 3
Money: no	Time: 2 months		

Authors published: J.M. de Moissac, Giovanni Malito, Bob Slaymaker, & Li Min Hua

An anarchist magazine. Poetry should have political/social content. It doesn't have to be didactic, but there should be a sense of political relevance.

KOLA
C.P. 1602, Place Bonaventure, Montréal, Québec H5A IH6
Ed: Horace I. Goddard   Poetry Ed: Shirley Smail

LEGEND
1036 Hampshire Road, Victoria, British Columbia V8S 4S9
Ed and Poetry Ed: Janet Reedman

MADAME BULL'S TAVERN
PO Box 60369, U of A Postal Outlet, Edmonton, Alberta T6G 2S9
Telephone: (403) 469-8464   Fax: same
Eds: Candace Bamber, Jacques Benoit, Dean Hamp, Annette Cannell, & Paul Pearson

Since: 1994	Circ: 300-500	Pages: 128	Per Year: 4
Size: 5 1/2 X 8	Saddle stitched	Sample: $6	Sub: $24
Copyright: author	Book reviews: yes	Reviews/year: 12-16	Translations: no
Interviews: no	Fiction: yes	Essays: yes	Copies: 1
Money: no	Time: 6-9 weeks		

Authors published: Alice Major, Neil Scotten, Jan McLauglin, & C.C. Russell

Looking for work that explores public or "outer" life in a way that exposes and possibly subverts stereotypes, propaganda, and the status quo. Some subjects of interest are: the media, the arts, politics, economics, popular culture, culture and cultural institutions, social movements, and advertising. Satire and humour encouraged. Standard and experimental forms in all genres are welcomed. We are NOT looking for introspection, navel gazing, or personal angst. Fiction and essays to 5,000 words.

THE MALAHAT REVIEW
University of Victoria, PO Box 1700, Victoria, British Columbia V8W 2Y2
Telephone: (604) 721-8524   Fax: (604) 721-7212
Eds: Derk Wynard & Marlene Cookshaw   Poetry Ed: Marlene Cookshaw

Since: 1967	Circ: 1,500	Pages: 125	Per Year: 4
Size: 6 X 9	Perfect bound	Sample: $7	Sub: $19.26
Copyright: author	Book reviews: yes	Reviews/year: 4-5	Translations: yes
Interviews: no	Fiction: yes	Essays: no	Copies: 2
Money: $25/page	Time: 1 month		

Authors published: Don McKay, Lorna Crozier, David Zieroth, & Patricia Young

Runs a long poem contest. Send SASE for rules.

MATRIX
Concordia University, Department of English, LB 501, 1455 de Maisonneuve Blvd. West, Montréal, Québec H3G 1M8
Telephone: (514) 767-7342   Fax: (514) 848-4501
Ed and Poetry Ed: Robert Allen

Since: 1975	Circ: 1,400	Pages: 88	Per Year: 3
Size: ?	Perfect bound	Sample: $6	Sub: $12
Copyright: author	Book reviews: no	Reviews/year: n/a	Translations: yes
Interviews: yes	Fiction: yes	Essays: yes	Copies: 2
Money: varies	Time: ?		

Authors published: Patrick Lane, Erin Mouré, D.G. Jones, & Susan Glickman

Very eclectic mix. Also publishes fine art photography. Interested in work from/about Quebec, but not to the exclusion of other subjects, writers, artists.

McCLUNG'S MAGAZINE
Ryerson Polytechnic University, Oakham House, 63 Gould Street, Toronto,
Ontario M5B 1E9
Telephone: (416) 977-1045   Fax: (416) 977-7709

Since: 1992	Circ: 1,000	Pages: 24-32	Per Year: 2
Size: 8 1/2 X 11	Saddle stitched	Sample: $1	Sub: $2
Copyright: author	Book reviews: yes	Reviews/year: ?	Translations: no
Interviews: yes	Fiction: yes	Essays: yes	Copies: 1
Money: no	Time: 3 months		

Authors published: Rebekah Murdoch, Caroline Outten, Denille Bassels, & Melanie Tinken

Poetry about or written from a woman's perspective welcome. Does not accept work that is vulgar, gratuitously violent, racist, mysogynistic, or in bad taste.

McGILL STREET MAGAZINE
193 Bellwoods Avenue, Toronto, Ontario M6J 2P8
Telephone: (416) 538-0559
Eds: Alexandra Soiseth & Helen Walsh   Poetry Ed: Lisa Schmidt

Since: 1992	Circ: 1,500	Pages: ?	Per Year: 4
Size: 8 1/2 X 11	Saddle stitched	Sample: $5	Sub: $18
Copyright: author	Book reviews: no	Reviews/year: n/a	Translations: not yet
Interviews: yes	Fiction: yes	Essays: yes	Copies: ?
Money: no	Time: 3 months		

Authors published: Janice Kulyk-Keefer, Barry Hammond, nathalic stephens, & Ronna Bloom

Open to poetry of all types from all regions of Canada. We prefer two pages or less, but will consider longer poems on an individual basis.

MINUS TIDES MAGAZINE
Site 50, Box 10, Denman Island, British Columbia V0R 1T0
Telephone: (604) 335-1051
Eds: Hillel Wright & Gisele Charlebois   Poetry Ed: Ruth Terry

Since: 1987	Circ: 200	Pages: 40	Per Year: 2
Size: 8 1/2 X 11	Saddle stitched	Sample: $6	Sub: $12
Copyright: author	Book reviews: yes	Reviews/year: 1-2	Translations: yes
Interviews: yes	Fiction: yes	Essays: yes	Copies: yes
Money: no	Time: 6 months		

Authors published: Carole Chambers, Terry Crane, Alice Tepexcuintle, & bill bissett

Associated with Trabarni Productions, a B.C. poetry publisher. Publishes more fiction than poetry. Interested in narrative, lyric, formal, and experimental poetry.

missing jacket
R.R. 1, Maxville, Ontario K0C 1T0
Telephone: (613) 231-7722
Ed and Poetry Ed: rob mclennan

Since: 1995	Circ: 300-500	Pages: 20-30	Per Year: 2
Size: ?	Binding: ?	Sample: $3	Sub: ?
Copyright: author	Book reviews: yes	Reviews/year: ?	Translations: ?
Interviews: yes	Fiction: yes	Essays: yes	Copies: yes
Money: no	Time: 2-3 months		

Associated with above/ground, a chapbook publisher. Mostly interested in writing on writing and writing on visual arts. Accepts some poetry and short fiction.

THE MITRE
Bishop's University, Box 2133, Lennoxville, Québec J1M 1Z7
Telephone: (819) 822-9697   Fax: (819) 822-9747
Eds: Craig Bowman & Erin McLaughlin

Since: 1893	Circ: 300	Pages: 100	Per Year: 1
Size: 5 X 8	Perfect bound	Sample: $3	Sub: n/a
Copyright: author	Book reviews: no	Reviews/year: n/a	Translations: no
Interviews: no	Fiction: yes	Essays: no	Copies: no
Money: no	Time: 2 weeks		

Authors published: Michael Ondaatje & Ralph Gustafson

Please submit poetry and fiction between January 1st and March 20th. Limited to Bishop's University students, teachers, staff, and alumni. Also interested in fine art and photographs.

M.P.D.
PO Box 53106, Ottawa, Ontario K1N 1C5

Since: 1993	Circ: 400	Pages: 40	Per Year: 2-4
Size: 5 1/2 X 8 1/2	Binding: ?	Sample: $1	Sub: see below
Copyright: author	Book reviews: no	Reviews/year: n/a	Translations: no
Interviews: no	Fiction: yes	Essays: yes	Copies: 5
Money: no	Time: 6 months		

Authors published: Tamara Fairchild, Phoenix, P.C. Chynn, & Trevor Taylor

Cost of subscription: "any donation accepted." Although the primary goal of the magazine is to publish the work of the collective, we will publish 1 or 2 outside submissions per issue. Please note that works published in the magazine will also be electronically published on *M.P.D.*'s WWW site. Multiple submissions are accepted. There is a 2,000 word limit for fiction. E-mail address: ah423@freenet.carleton.ca

THE MUSE JOURNAL
226 Lisgar Street, Toronto, Ontario M6J 3G7
Telephone: (416) 539-9517   Fax: (416) 539-0047
Ed: Manny Goncalves   Poetry Eds: Manny Goncalves & Domenic Scali

Since: 1992	Circ: 1,000	Pages: 24-36	Per Year: 2-4
Size: 8 1/2 X 11	Saddle stitched	Sample: $6.50	Sub: n/a
Copyright: see below	Book reviews: yes	Reviews/year: 4-8	Translations: rarely
Interviews: rarely	Fiction: yes	Essays: yes	Copies: 2
Money: no	Time: 3-6 months		

Authors published: John B. Lee, Phlip Arima, Gail Sidonie Sobat, & Noah Leznoff

Associated with The Muse Journal Press, a literary publisher. Runs an Annual Love Poem Award with three cash prizes. Please send SASE for contest details. Considers submissions all year long. Likes to give young poets a chance. Looks for substance, but doesn't like observational, superficial poetry. Dig deeper. Copyright reverts to author after six months. E-mail address: emanuel.goncalves@ablelink.org

MUSICWORKS MAGAZINE
179 Richmond Street West, Toronto, Ontario M5V 1V3
Telephone: (416) 977-3546   Fax: (416) 204-1084
Ed: Gayle Young

Since: 1978	Circ: 2,000	Pages: 72	Per Year: 3
Size: 8 1/2 X 11	Saddle stitched	Sample: $5	Sub: $14 or $33
Copyright: author	Book reviews: yes	Reviews/year: 6-7	Translations: yes
Interviews: yes	Fiction: no	Essays: yes	Copies: yes
Money: yes	Time: ?		

Authors published: bp Nichol, Paul Dutton, Kurt Schwitters, & The Four Horsemen

Subscriptions are $14 per year (magazine only) or $33 (magazine + CD). Only accepts poetry in relation to music. Special interest in sound poetry.

NEW MUSE OF CONTEMPT

PO Box 596, Station A, Fredericton, New Brunswick E3B 5A6

Telephone: (506) 454-5127   Fax: same

Ed and Poetry Ed: Joe Blades

Since: 1987	Circ: 150	Pages: 36	Per Year: 2
Size: 5 1/2 X 8 1/2	Saddle stitched	Sample: $4	Sub: $7
Copyright: author	Book reviews: yes	Reviews/year: 10-20	Translations: yes
Interviews: yes	Fiction: yes	Essays: yes	Copies: 2
Money: no	Time: 1-6 months		

Authors published: M. Travis Lane, Steven Heighton, Karen Connelly, & James Deahl

Associated with Broken Jaw Press, a publisher of literary books and chapbooks. Runs an annual contest leading to the publication of a first book of poetry. Please send SASE for New Muse contest rules. Interested in visual/concrete poetry. Also publishes homolinguistic poetry. Aims to be an ongoing international forum for mail art. E-mail address: jblades@nbnet.nb.ca

THE NEW QUARTERLY

University of Waterloo, English Language Proficiency Program, P.A.S. 2082, Waterloo, Ontario N2L 3G1

Telephone: (519) 885-1211, Ex. 2837

Ed: Mary Merikle   Poetry Eds: John Vardon, Randi Patterson, & Miriam Maust

Since: 1981	Circ: 400	Pages: 130	Per Year: 4
Size: ?	Perfect bound	Sample: $5.35	Sub: $18
Copyright: author	Book reviews: no	Reviews/year: n/a	Translations: no
Interviews: yes	Fiction: yes	Essays: yes	Copies: 1
Money: $20/poem	Time: 4-6 months		

Authors published: John B. Lee, Diana Brebner, Lorna Crozier, & Dennis Lee

Fiction payment: $100 payment per story. E-mail address: mmerikle@watarts.uwaterloo.ca

NeWest Review

PO Box 394, R.P.O. University, Saskatoon, Saskatchewan S7N 4J8

Telephone: (306) 934-1444

Ed: Gail Youngberg   Poetry Ed: John Lauery

Since: 1975	Circ: 1,000	Pages: 40	Per Year: 6
Size: 8 1/2 X 11	Saddle stitched	Sample: $3	Sub: $16.05
Copyright: author	Book reviews: yes	Reviews/year: 40	Translations: no
Interviews: yes	Fiction: yes	Essays: yes	Copies: yes
Money: yes	Time: 6 weeks		

Authors published: James R. Janz, Steven Whittaker, Stephanie Bolster, & William Nichols

We are a regional magazine and are primarily, although not exclusively, interested in work from western Canadian authors, and especially prairie writers.

NEXUS [is now called *WestWord*]

NORTHERN WOMAN JOURNAL
PO Box 144, Thunder Bay, Ontario P7C 4V5

oh!
Ryerson Polytechnic University, Oakham House, 63 Gould Street, Toronto, Ontario M5B 1E9
Telephone: (416) 977-1045   Fax: (416) 977-7709

Since: 1986	Circ: 1,000	Pages: 24-32	Per Year: 2
Size: 8 1/2 X 11	Saddle stitched	Sample: $1	Sub: $2
Copyright: author	Book reviews: yes	Reviews/year: ?	Translations: no
Interviews: yes	Fiction: yes	Essays: yes	Copies: 1
Money: no	Time: 3 months		

Authors published: C. Grace Kary, Jill Battson, Rob Malich, & Evelyn Hanoski

Please send no more than five poems per submission. Short stories to a 2,000 word limit. Does not accept work that is vulgar, gratuitously violent, racist, misogynistic, or in bad taste.

ON SPEC
PO Box 4727, Edmonton, Alberta T6E 5G6
Telephone: (403) 413-0215
Ed and Poetry Ed: by Collective

Since: 1989	Circ: 2,000	Pages: 96	Per Year: 4
Size: 5 X 8	Perfect bound	Sample: $6	Sub: $19.95
Copyright: author	Book reviews: no	Reviews/year: n/a	Translations: no
Interviews: no	Fiction: yes	Essays: no	Copies: 1
Money: $15/poem	Time: 5 months		

Authors published: Alice Major, Jocko, Sandra Kasturi, & Barry Hammond

Only looks for speculative poetry/fiction, science fiction, fantasy, horror, and magic realism. Pays 2 1/2 cents per word for fiction. Uses 6 to 8 poems per year. No inspirational poetry, does not like rhyming material. Please send SASE for format requirements before submitting. Quarterly deadlines are the end of February, May, August, and November.

OTHER VOICES
Garneau PO Box 52059, 8210 109st Street, Edmonton, Alberta T6G 2T5
Ed and Poetry Ed: by Collective

Since: 1988	Circ: 250	Pages: 120	Per Year: 2
Size: 5 1/2 X 8 1/2	Perfect bound	Sample: $8	Sub: $15
Copyright: author	Book reviews: yes	Reviews/year: 6	Translations: no
Interviews: yes	Fiction: yes	Essays: yes	Copies: yes
Money: yes	Time: up to 6 months		

Authors published: Anne Le Dressay, beth goobie, Anna Mioduchowska, & Norm Sacuta

Submission deadlines are March 15th and September 15th. Interested in black and white prints and artwork.

OUR FAMILY
PO Box 249, Battleford, Saskatchewan S0M 0E0
Telephone: (306) 937-7771   Fax: (306) 937-7644
Ed: Fr. Nestor Gregoire

Since: ?	Circ: ?	Pages: ?	Per Year: 11
Size: ?	Binding: ?	Sample: $2.50	Sub: ?
Copyright: ?	Book reviews: ?	Reviews/year: n/a	Translations: ?
Interviews: ?	Fiction: no	Essays: yes	Copies: ?
Money: yes	Time: 1 month		

Essays/articles should be 1,000 to 3,000 words long. Pays 7 to 12 cents per word. Poetry with a religious flavor/insight is sought. Please send SASE for a list of upcoming themes.

OUT MAGAZINE
359 Davenport Road, Box 5, Toronto, Ontario M5R 1K5
Ed: Shawn Venasse   Poetry Ed: Brian Day

OUTLOOK [is now called *Canadian Jewish Outlook*]

THE OUTREACH CONNECTION
2453 Yonge Street, Suite 3, Toronto, Ontario M4P 2E8
Telephone: (416) 484-1680   Fax: (416) 484-9882
Address for poetry submissions:
c/o I.B. Iskov
31 Marisa Court
Thornhill, Ontario, L4J 6H9
Ed: Dave Mackin   Poetry Ed: I.B. Iskov

Since: 1993	Circ: 6,000-10,000	Pages: 12	Per Year: 50
Size: 15 X 17	Newspaper	Sample: $1.50	Sub: $80
Copyright: author	Book reviews: yes	Reviews/year: n/a	Translations: no
Interviews: yes	Fiction: yes	Essays: yes	Copies: 1
Money: no	Time: 2 weeks		

Authors published: James Deahl, Bernice Lever, Terry Day, & Karen Nelson
Interested in both new and established writers. All styles welcome. Line limit: 32. No lewdness, no foul language, no heavy, preachy religion. Good, humourous pieces are always appreciated.

paperplates
19 Kenwood Avenue, Toronto, Ontario M6C 2R8
Telephone: (416) 651-2551
Ed: Bernard Kelly

Since: 1991	Circ: 350	Pages: 48	Per Year: 4
Size: 8 1/2 X 11	Saddle stitched	Sample: $5	Sub: $26
Copyright: author	Book reviews: yes	Reviews/year: 12	Translations: yes
Interviews: yes	Fiction: yes	Essays: yes	Copies: yes
Money: no	Time: 6-8 weeks		

Authors published: Richard Outram, Colleen Flood, Maja Bannerman, & Jacqueline d'Amtoise
Please send SASE for guidelines. Accepts prose up to 15,000 words and poetry up to 1,500 words. Theatre, film, and book reviews average 2,500 words. E-mail address: beekelly@hookup.net

PARA*phrase
Sheridan Mall, Box 47014, Mississauga, Ontario L5K 2R2
Eds: Jiri Jirasek & Tedy Asponsen   Poetry Ed: George Le Grand

Since: 1984	Circ: 200	Pages: 24	Per Year: 2-3

Size: 7 X 8 1/2	Saddle stitched	Sample: $2	Sub: $6/4 issues
Copyright: author	Book reviews: yes	Reviews/year: 2 or 3	Translations: no
Interviews: yes	Fiction: yes	Essays: yes	Copies: I
Money: n/a	Time: I month		

Authors published: Charles David Rice, Joanna Nealon, Jay Bradford Fowler, Jr., & Iris Litt

Associated with Cosmic Trend. Looks for work that has a New Age slant, sensual and mind-expanding material of any kind. Poems will be preferably unrhymed. Submission fee is $1 for two poems plus $1 for postage. Total fee is $3 for two poems. Submissions accepted any time. Also publishes anthologies.

PARCHMENT, Contemporary Canadian Jewish Writing

445 Hamilton Road, London, Ontario N5Z 1S2

Address for poetry & fiction submissions:

c/o Adam Fuerstenberg

Ryerson Polytechnic University

Department of English

Toronto, Ontario, M5B 2K3

Ed: Adam Fuerstenberg   Poetry Ed: Malca Litovitz

Since: 1991	Circ: 500	Pages: 120	Per Year: I
Size: 5 X 8	Perfect bound	Sample: $12	Sub: $12
Copyright: author	Book reviews: no	Reviews/year: n/a	Translations: yes
Interviews: yes	Fiction: yes	Essays: no	Copies: 2
Money: no	Time: 3 months		

Authors published: Kenneth Sherman, Robyn Sarah, Mick Burrs, & Seymour Mayne

Published every fall. Material limited to the Jewish experience, but writers need not be Jewish.

PECKERWOOD

1465 Lawrence Avenue West, Apt. 1503, Toronto, Ontario M6L 1B2

Eds and Poetry Eds: Ernie Ourique & Ibi Kaslik

PEOPLE'S POETRY LETTER

PO Box 51531, 2060 Queen Street East, Toronto, Ontario M4E 3V7

Eds and Poetry Eds: Ned H. Healey, Jim Aldred, & Ted Plantos

Since: 1993	Circ: 200	Pages: 14	Per Year: 3
Size: 8 1/2 X 11	Stapled	Sample: $5	Sub: $15 minimum
Copyright: author	Book reviews: yes	Reviews/year: 4-5	Translations: no
Interviews: yes	Fiction: no	Essays: yes	Copies: yes
Money: no	Time: 4-6 weeks		

Authors published: Heather Cadsby, Robert Hilles, James Deahl, & John B. Lee

Main focus is commentary on People's Poetry. Most poetry published is from winning entrants in The People's Poem Contest, The People's Political Poem Contest, and the Milton Acorn Memorial People's Poetry Award. Occasionally, poems are solicited for special features. We do invite unsolicited submissions of essays, articles, and commentary on poetry. We are populistic, non-elitest, and non-academic. We favour grassroots, street-level poetry with something to say. Subscriptions go for a minimum donation of $15 (but more dollars are, of course, better).

THE PIG PAPER
70 Cotton Drive, Mississauga, Ontario L5G 1Z9
Ed and Poetry Ed: Gary Pig Gold

THE PLOWMAN
PO Box 414, Whitby, Ontario L1N 5S4
Telephone: (905) 668-7803
Ed and Poetry Ed: Tony Scavetta

Since: 1988	Circ: 15,000	Pages: 56	Per Year: 2
Size: 20 X 13	Newspaper	Sample: free	Sub: $10
Copyright: author	Book reviews: yes	Reviews/year: 100	Translations: no
Interviews: no	Fiction: yes	Essays: yes	Copies: yes
Money: ?	Time: 1-2 weeks		

Authors published: Vassar Smith, John Binns, Fletcher De Wolf, & Richard Ball

Associated with a chapbook press of the same name. All poetry except sardonic and foul language. Submissions considered any time. Special interest in religious poems and articles.

POEMATA
237 Prospect Street South, Hamilton, Ontario L8M 2Z6
Telephone: (905) 312-1779 Fax: (905) 312-8285
Ed and Poetry Ed: James Deahl

Since: 1985	Circ: 160	Pages: 8	Per Year: 6
Size: 8 1/2 X 11	Saddle stitched	Sample: $3	Sub: $15
Copyright: author	Book reviews: yes	Reviews/year: 12-18	Translations: no
Interviews: yes	Fiction: no	Essays: yes	Copies: 2
Money: no	Time: 4 months		

Authors published: Michael Dudley, Joe Blades, Jennifer Footman, & Elizabeth St Jacques

So far all poetry published is by members of the Canadian Poetry Association, but this may change. Book reviews, interviews, and essays can be by anyone. The magazine is associated with Mekler & Deahl, Publishers. M&D publishes chapbooks by C.P.A. members as well as C.P.A. anthologies. *Poemata/C.P.A.* is a major source of poetry market information. E-mail address: ad507@freenet.hamilton.on.ca

POETRY CANADA
PO Box 1061, Kingston, Ontario K7L 4Y5
Telephone: (613) 548-8429 Fax: (613) 548-1556
Poetry Ed: Barry Dempster

Since: 1981	Circ: 1,750	Pages: 40	Per Year: 4
Size: ?	Saddle stitched	Sample: $7.50	Sub: $21.20
Copyright: author	Book reviews: yes	Reviews/year: 16-20	Translations: yes
Interview: yes	Fiction: no	Essays: yes	Copies: 1
Money: $100/page	Time: 3-6 months		

The review features 2 to 6 poems per poet, depending on length. Payment is $100. Associated with Quarry, a major literary press.

POETS' PODIUM
2525-C, Havre des Îles, Suite 211, Chomedey, Québec H7W 4C6
Telephone: (514) 687-4092

Eds and Poetry Eds: Kenneth Elliott, Robert Piquette, & Harry P. Fox

Since: 1993	Circ: 150	Pages: 8	Per Year: 4
Size: 7 X 8 1/4	Stapled	Sample: $2.50	Sub: $10
Copyright: author	Book reviews: no	Reviews/year: n/a	Translations: yes
Interviews: yes	Fiction: no	Essays: no	Copies: 3
Money: no	Time: 3-5 months		

Authors published: P.J. Johnson, Catherine Clayton Elliott Barton, Paul Omeziri, & Elinor Cohen

Associated with a chapbook publisher. Considers all types of poetry; please send SASE for guidelines. Wants poetry depicting nature and its beauty, human conflicts and struggles in life's journey of the years, man in the face of the great questions and challenges in life, God, death, birth, pain, suffering, existence. Seeks to understand man's (and woman's) place in the universe.

POLYGLOT ARMY

71 Thorncliffe Park Drive, Apt. 215, Toronto, Ontario M4H 1L3

Telephone: (416) 696-2350   Fax: same

Ed: Cecil Justin Lam   Poetry Ed: Janet King

Since: 1990	Circ: 1,000	Pages: 16	Per Year: 1
Size: 7 X 8 1/2	Saddle stitched	Sample: $10	Sub: $15
Copyright: author	Book reviews: yes	Reviews/year: 3	Translations: yes
Interviews: yes	Fiction: yes	Essays: yes	Copies: yes
Money: no	Time: 6 months		

Authors published: Nancy L. Dorner, Peter Fusco, E.C. Denhan, Jr., & Doug Draime

With the morale of the Army of God, the polyglot Army united in colourful array. Operated in twelve major languages: English, French, German, Spanish, Italian, Russian, Arabic, Mandarin, Japanese, Hebrew, Greek, & Hindu. The Polyglot reached out for every old culture to proclaim the Glory of Christ Return.

POSSIBILITIES LITERARY ARTS MAGAZINE

2100 Scott Street, #109, Ottawa, Ontario K1Z 1A3

Telephone: (613) 761-1177

Since: 1992	Circ: 600	Pages: 64	Per Year: 4
Size: 8 1/2 X 11	Saddle stitched	Sample: $5	Sub: $18
Copyright: author	Book reviews: yes	Reviews/year: 4	Translations: yes
Interviews: yes	Fiction: yes	Essays: yes	Copies: 4
Money: ?	Time: 4-6 months		

Authors published: George Elliott Clarke, Dionne Brand, Wali A. Shakeen, & Afua Cooper

Please send SASE for submission guidelines. Interested in young emerging and established writers of colour. Seeks to create an exchange of views, tastes, and opinions.

POTTERSFIELD PORTFOLIO

5280 Green Street, PO Box 27094, Halifax, Nova Scotia B3H 4M8

Telephone: (902) 443-9178

Eds: Ian Colford & Karen Smythe   Poetry Eds: Collette Saunders & Gregory Betts

Since: 1979	Circ: 300-400	Pages: 96	Per Year: 3
Size: 6 X 9	Perfect bound	Sample: $7	Sub: $18
Copyright: author	Book reviews: yes	Reviews/year: 12-15	Translations: no

| Interviews: no | Fiction: yes | Essays: yes | Copies: 1 |
| Money: no | Time: 2 months | | |

Authors published: Elizabeth Harvor, Don McKay, M. Travis Lane, & George Elliott Clarke

Will consider any style of poetry on any topic. Fiction editor is Karen Smythe.

PRAIRIE FIRE

100 Arthur Street, Suite 423, Winnipeg, Manitoba R3B 1H3
Telephone: (204) 943-9066   Fax: (204) 942-1555
Ed: Andris Taskans   Poetry Eds: Catherine Hunter & Meira Cook

Since: 1978	Circ: 1,500	Pages: 144	Per Year: 4
Size: 6 X 9	Perfect bound	Sample: $10	Sub: $24
Copyright: author	Book reviews: yes	Reviews/year: 70	Translations: yes
Interviews: yes	Fiction: yes	Essays: yes	Copies: 1
Money: $30/page	Time: 3-6 months		

Authors published: Di Brandt, Patrick Friesen, Lorna Crozier, & Anne Szumigalski

Pays $30 for the first page; $25 per page thereafter to a maximum of $150. Will consider work from all parts of Canada. Plans a number of special issues; please send SASE for complete information. Submissions preferred during the academic year.

THE PRAIRIE JOURNAL

PO Box 61203, Brentwood P.O., Calgary, Alberta T2L 2K6
Ed and Poetry Ed: Anne Burke

Since: 1983	Circ: 400	Pages: 50	Per Year: 2
Size: 8 1/2 X 7	Saddle stitched	Sample: $6	Sub: $6
Copyright: author	Book reviews: yes	Reviews/year: 4	Translations: yes
Interviews: yes	Fiction: yes	Essays: yes	Copies: yes
Money: yes	Time: up to 6 months		

Authors published: Ronnie Brown, Ronald Kurt, Susan Walsh, & John Barton

The journal is associated with a literary press. New and established poets welcomed. Looks for contemporary poetry, not rhymed.

PRESBYTERIAN RECORD

50 Wynford Drive, North York, Ontario M3C 1J7
Telephone: (416) 441-1111   Fax: (416) 441-2825
Ed: John Congram   Poetry Ed: Thomas Dickey

Since: 1876	Circ: 60,000	Pages: 52	Per Year: 11
Size: 10 1/2 X 7	Saddle stitched	Sample: $2	Sub: $13
Copyright: author	Book reviews: yes	Reviews/year: 30-40	Translations: ?
Interviews: yes	Fiction: yes	Essays: yes	Copies: 1
Money: yes	Time: 2-3 months		

Authors published: Frederick Zydek, Joan Bond, Charles Cooper, & Margaret Avison

Wants poetry which is inspirational, Christian, thoughtful, even satiric, but not maudlin. No sympathy card–type verse à la Edgar Guest or Francis Gay. Shorter poems of 10 to 30 lines are preferred. Blank verse OK, if it's not just rearranged prose. "Found poems" also acceptable. Subject matter should have some Christian import, however subtle.

PRISM international

The University of British Columbia, Department of Creative Writing, Buchanan
E462, 1866 Main Mall, Vancouver, British Columbia V6T 1Z1
Telephone: (604) 822-2154   Fax: (604) 822-3616
Eds: Leah Postman & Andrew Gray   Poetry Ed: Jennifer Herbison

Since: 1959	Circ: 1,000	Pages: 85	Per Year: 4
Size: 6 X 9	Perfect bound	Sample: $5.35	Sub: $16
Copyright: author	Book reviews: no	Reviews/year: n/a	Translations: yes
Interviews: no	Fiction: yes	Essays: yes	Copies: 1
Money: $20/page	Time: 3-4 months		

Authors published: Lorna Crozier, Patrick Lane, William Logan, & Karen Connelly

Our only criteria are originality and quality. Would like to see more work that shows a love of the music and the power of words, as well as digging into the heart. Also on the lookout for exciting work in translation. E-mail address: prism@unixg.ubc.ca

PUBLIC WORKS

The University of Western Ontario, Room 33, University College, London, Ontario N6A 3K7
Eds and Poetry Eds: L. Ceaser, S. Bragg, K. Keating, D. Vipperman, D. Campbell, & S. Elmslie

QUARRY

PO Box 1061, Kingston, Ontario K7L 4Y5
Telephone: (613) 548-8429   Fax: (613) 548-1556
Ed and Poetry Ed: Mary Cameron

Since: 1952	Circ: 1,000	Pages: 140	Per Year: 4
Size: 7 X 9	Perfect bound	Sample: $7	Sub: $22
Copyright: author	Book reviews: yes	Reviews/year: 4+	Translations: yes
Interviews: yes	Fiction: yes	Essays: yes	Copies: 1
Money: $10/page	Time: 6-12 weeks		

Authors published: Don Coles, Lynn Crosbie, Don McKay, & Maggie Helwig

Associated with the literary press of the same name. Also welcomes photographic essays.

QUEEN'S QUARTERLY

Queen's University, Kingston, Ontario K7L 3N6
Eds and Poetry Eds: Martha J. Bailey & Boris Castel

QUIT GAWKING

PO Box 84551, 2336 Bloor Street West, Toronto, Ontario M6S 4Z7
Telephone: (416) 767-1545
Eds and Poetry Eds: Natalia Yanchak & Heather Pessione

Since: 1994	Circ: 100	Pages: 20	Per Year: 6
Size: 7 X 8 1/2	Saddle stitched	Sample: 90 cent stamp	Sub: 6 90 cent stamps
Copyright: author	Book reviews: no	Reviews/year: n/a	Translations: no
Interviews: pending	Fiction: yes	Essays: yes	Copies: yes
Money: no	Time: 1 month		

Authors published: Ian Firla, elisabeth oliver, David Simmons, & Biran Pastoor

Contributors get free lifetime subscriptions. There is a 1,000 word limit for prose.

THE RADDLE MOON
2239 Stephens Street, Vancouver, British Columbia V6K 3W5
Ed and Poetry Ed: Susan Clark

RAFFIA MAGAZINE
What's Yer View Productions, PO Box 22, 1450 Johnston Road, White Rock, British Columbia V4B 5E9
Eds and Poetry Eds: Jennifer Cave & Jevon Safarik

Since: 1990	Circ: 250	Pages: 25	Per Year: varies
Size: 8 1/2 X 11	Saddle stitched	Sample: $5.50	Sub: n/a
Copyright: author	Book reviews: yes	Reviews/year: ?	Translations: yes
Interviews: yes	Fiction: yes	Essays: yes	Copies: 1
Money: no	Time: ?		

Authors published: Milton Acorn, Robert Hilles, Annharte, & Allan Safarik
Interested in black and white visuals.

RAW NerVZ HAIKU
67, rue Court, Aylmer, Québec J9H 4M1
Telephone: (819) 684-1345
Ed and Poetry Ed: Dorothy Howard

Since: 1994	Circ: 150	Pages: 48	Per Year: 4
Size: 5 1/2 X 8 1/2	Saddle stitched	Sample: $7	Sub: $20
Copyright: author	Book reviews: yes	Reviews/year: 2-10	Translations: some
Interviews: few	Fiction: some	Essays: few	Copies: no
Money: no	Time: 1-6 weeks		

Authors published: Marlene Mountain, Michael Dudley, LeRoy Gorman, & anne mckay
Associated with proof press, a poetry chapbook publisher. Interested in experimental and traditional haiku and related material (sequences, renga, tanka, graphics, visuals). Canadian & American subscriptions are $20; other foreign subscriptions are $24 (Canadian $).

ROOM OF ONE'S OWN
PO Box 46160, Station D, Vancouver, British Columbia V6J 5G5
Ed and Poetry Ed: by Collective

Since: 1975	Circ: 800	Pages: 96	Per Year: 4
Size: 5 X 7	Perfect bound	Sample: $7	Sub: $20
Copyright: author	Book reviews: yes	Reviews/year: 40	Translations: rarely
Interviews: rarely	Fiction: yes	Essays: yes	Copies: 2
Money: $25	Time: 4-6 months		

Authors published: Sylvia Legris, Sue McLeod, Donna Marsh, & Mina Kumar
Serves as a forum in which women can share their unique perspectives on themselves, each other, and the world.

SCRIVENER CREATIVE JOURNAL
McGill University, 853 Sherbrooke Street West, Montréal, Québec H3A 2T6

Since: 1976	Circ: 500	Pages: 150	Per Year: 1
Size: 6 X 8	Perfect bound	Sample: $5	Sub: $8/2 years
Copyright: author	Book reviews: yes	Reviews/year: 3-5	Translations: no
Interviews: yes	Fiction: yes	Essays: yes	Copies: yes
Money: no	Time: 3-4 months		

Authors published: Leonard Cohen, Ann Diamond, Gary Geddes

Published every May. Submission deadline: end of December.

SEEDS: progressive poetry, thoughts and ideas
Richard Grove, 701 King Street West, Suite 412, Toronto, Ontario M5V 2W7
Telephone: (416) 480-9806
Ed and Poetry Ed: Richard M. Grove (Tai)

Since: 1994	Circ: 300-500	Pages: 14-20	Per Year: 6
Size: 5 1/2 X 8 1/2	Saddle stitched	Sample: SASE (90¢ stamp)	Sub: $10
Copyright: author	Book reviews: yes	Reviews/year: ?	Translations: yes
Interviews: no	Fiction: no	Essays: yes	Copies: yes
Money: no	Time: 1 month		

Authors published: Tanis MacDonald, Dan Goorevitch, Tom Henihan, & A.D. Westman
Associated with Hidden Brook Press. Only interested in reviews of poetry books. Essays must be religious/philosophical in nature. Unpublished poets welcome. Seeks short articles on poets (Canadian preferred) with poetry sample for the "A Look at Poets Past" feature. Send submissions on 3.5 or 5.25 discs as ASCII or WordPerfect. Black and white cover artwork also welcome (4.5 X 4.5 max.); art must be camera ready.

SHARD: A Coupling of Art + Writing
4 Garview Court, Etobicoke, Ontario M9R 4B9
Telephone: (416) 249-5522
Ed and Poetry Ed: Cyril Chen

Since: 1994	Circ: 500	Pages: 48	Per Year: 1
Size: 7 X 10	Perfect bound	Sample: $5	Sub: n/a
Copyright: author	Book reviews: no	Reviews/year: n/a	Translations: yes
Interviews: yes	Fiction: yes	Essays: yes	Copies: 2
Money: ?	Time: ?		

Authors published: Tish P. Sass, Phlip Arima, Jill Battson, & Giovanni Malito
Associated with the literary press of the same name. All submissions should fit at least one of the following descriptions: Seduction through style; Elegance with an edge; the Arena for attitude. Common reference points include Vaughan Oliver, William Gibson, German Expressionism, *Blade Runner*, and '80s alternative music and style. Reads submissions year round.

SKYLARK
2110 Charleroi, #8, Beauport, Québec G1E 3S1
Ed and Poetry Ed: Suzanne Fortin

THE SPECTATOR
44 Frid Street, Hamilton, Ontario L8N 3G3
Address for poetry submissions:
c/o James Deahl, 237 Prospect Street South, Hamilton, Ontario L8M 2Z6
Ed: Rob Austin   Poetry Ed: James Deahl

Since: 1846	Circ: 125,000	Pages: varies	Per Year: 312
Size: tabloid	Newspsper	Sample: ?	Sub: ?
Copyright: author	Book reviews: yes	Reviews/year: 200-250	Translastions: no
Interviews: yes	Fiction: yes	Essays: yes	Copies: no
Money: no	Time: 4 months		

Authors published: Margaret Saunders, John B. Lee, Jeff Seffinga, & Linda Frank

Daily newspaper. Poems appear in the tabloid Ego section. Also publishes short fiction. Poetry is limited to 30 lines; fiction to 1,500 words. All contributors should live in the greater Hamilton area or should be from this area. Poems from current residents are put on the World Wide Web in the poets' own voices. Poets in the general Hamilton area should submit work through one of the local writing groups. Poets from outside this area should mail their work directly to the poetry editor. The fiction editor is R.W. Megens.

STANZAS

R.R. 1, Maxville, Ontario K0C 1T0
Telephone: (613) 231-7722
Ed and Poetry Ed: rob mclennan

Since: 1993	Circ: 750	Pages: 10-15	Per Year: 2-4
Size: 5 1/2 X 8 1/2	Saddle stitched	Sample: $1	Sub: $10/5 issues
Copyright: author	Book reviews: no	Reviews/year: n/a	Translations: no
Interviews: no	Fiction: no	Essays: no	Copies: 25-30
Money: no	Time: 6 months		

Authors published: Joe Blades, Sharon Nelson, rob mclennan, & Kathryn Payne

Associated with above/ground press. Looks for long poems/sequences from 2 to 15 pages in length. Magazine is distributed internationally for free. E-mail address: az421@freenet.carlton.ca

sub-TERRAIN

PO Box 1575, Bentall Centre, Vancouver, British Columbia V6C 2P7
Telephone: (604) 876-8710   Fax: (604) 879-2663
Ed: Brian Kaufman   Poetry Eds: Paul Pitrie & Heidi Greco

Since: 1988	Circ: 2,000-3,000	Pages: 40	Per Year: 4
Size: 7 1/2 X 10 1/2	Saddle stitched	Sample: $5	Sub: $15
Copyright: author	Book reviews: yes	Reviews/year: 10	Translations: no
Interviews: yes	Fiction: yes	Essays: yes	Copies: yes
Money: ?	Time: 2-4 months		

Authors published: Isabella Legosi Mori, Angela McIntyre, Heidi Greco, & Bud Osborn

Associated with Anvil Press, a publisher of full-size poetry and fiction titles. Runs the annual Last Poems Poetry Contest. Please send SASE for contest details.

SURFACE & SYMBOL

Scarborough Arts Council, 1859 Kingston Road, Scarborough, Ontario M1N 1T3
Telephone: (416) 698-7322   Fax: (416) 698-7972
Ed: Vivian Snead

Welcomes submissions of poetry, prose, black and white illustrations, and articles about the arts in Scarborough.

SYMPOSIUM

The University of Western Ontario, Room 33, University College, London, Ontario N6A 3K7
Eds: Lara Navegatsian & Alanna F. Bondar   Poetry Ed: Alanna F. Bondar

tcte Newsletter

Toronto Council of Teachers of English, Royal St. George's College, 120 Howland Avenue, Toronto, Ontario M5R 3B8

Telephone: (416) 944-0662   Fax: (416) 533-0028

Ed and Poetry Ed: Eric Timm

Since: 1980	Circ: 300-400	Pages: 16-20 pages	Per Year: 4
Size: 8 1/2 X 11	Saddle stitched	Sample: free	Sub: $10
Copyright: author	Book reviews: yes	Reviews/year: 6-8	Translations: no
Interviews: yes	Fiction: yes	Essays: yes	Copies: 5
Money: no	Time: 1 month		

Authors published: Brian Pastoor, Elaine Mitchell Matlow, Robin Fulford, & Lorne Kulak

We are interested in poetry that deals with the teaching of English or in any poetry that is written by English teachers at any level. Considers submissions in September, November, March, and May.

TEAK ROUNDUP

9060 Tronson Road, #5, Vernon, British Columbia V1T 6L7

Telephone: (604) 545-4186   Fax: (604) 545-4194

Eds and Poetry Eds: Yvonne & Robert G. Anstey

Since: 1990	Circ: 100-150	Pages: 52	Per Year: 4
Size: 5 1/2 X 8	Saddle stitched	Sample: $5	Sub: $17
Copyright: author	Book reviews: yes	Reviews/year: 8-10	Translations: no
Interviews: no	Fiction: yes	Essays: yes	Copies: no
Money: no	Time: 1 week		

Authors published: Percy Harrison, Doris Rokosh, Robert G. Anstey, & Joan Hamilton

Associated with West Coast Paradise Publishing, a literary press. All prose and poetry styles are considered, but will only consider submissions from subscribers at this time. No uncouth material will be accepted. Please send SASE for submission guidelines.

TESSERA

York University, 350 Stong College, 4700 Keele Street, North York, Ontario M3J 1P3

Address for poetry & fiction submissions: Université de Montréal, Département d'études anglaises, C.P. 6128, Succursale A, Montréal, Québec H3C 3J7

Telephone: (514) 343-7926

Eds: Katherine Binhammer, Jennifer Henderson, Lianne Moyers, & Chantal Vezina

Poetry Ed: Margaret Webb

Since: 1982	Circ: 200	Pages: 120	Per Year: 2
Size: 5 3/4 X 8 3/4	Perfect bound	Sample: $10	Sub: $19.25
Copyright: author	Book reviews: no	Reviews/year: n/a	Translations: yes
Interviews: yes	Fiction: yes	Essays: yes	Copies: 2
Money: $10/page	Time: 2-6 months		

Authors published: Erin Mouré, Louise Dupré, Nicole Brossard, & Suniti Namjoshi

Seeks feminist and experimental poetry by women, especially those residing in Canada. We publish in French and English. Often publishes theme issues; please send SASE for information on upcoming themes. Subscriptions for institutions are $21.40/year.

TEXTSHOP: A Collaborative Journal of Writing
University of Regina, Deptartment of English, Regina, Saskatchewan S4S 0A2
Telephone: (306) 585-4316
Ed and Poetry Ed: Andrew Stubbs

Since: 1993	Circ: 200	Pages: 50	Per Year: 1
Size: 8 1/2 X 11	Saddle stitched	Sample: $2.50	Sub: $4.50
Copyright: author	Book reviews: no	Reviews/year: n/a	Translations: yes
Interviews: yes	Fiction: yes	Essays: yes	Copies: yes
Money: no	Time: 3 months		

Authors published: Rienzi Crusz, Jan Row, Bruce Bond, & Gerald Noonan

Features "Responses" by the editor to published material. Oriented towards rhetorical/creational issues. A kind of writing workshop in print. Interested in experimental forms, multi- & inter-genre approaches. Also "life writing" in any format.

THIS MAGAZINE
16 Skey Lane, Toronto, Ontario M6J 3S4
Telephone: (416) 588-6580   Fax: (416) 588-6638
Eds: Clive Thompson & Anne Bains   Poetry Ed: Clive Thompson

Since: 1966	Circ: 8,000	Pages: 50	Per Year: 8
Size: 8 1/2 X 11	Saddle stitched	Sample: $3.75	Sub: $23.99
Copyright: author	Book reviews: no	Reviews/year: n/a	Translations: no
Interviews: yes	Fiction: yes	Essays: yes	Copies: 1
Money: $100	Time: 6 weeks		

Authors published: Al Purdy, Margaret Atwood, Erin Mouré, & David Donnell

Poetry that doesn't suck! Please send SASE for guidelines.

TickleAce
PO Box 5353, St. John's, Newfoundland A1C 5W2
Telephone: (709) 754-6610   Fax: (709) 754-5579
Ed: Bruce Porter   Poetry Eds: Bruce Porter & Susan Ingersoll

Since: 1977	Circ: 1,000	Pages: 144	Per Year: 2
Size: 6 X 9	Perfect bound	Sample: $8	Sub: $14
Copyright: author	Book reviews: yes	Reviews/year: 12	Translations: yes
Interviews: yes	Fiction: yes	Essays: sometimes	Copies: yes
Money: yes	Time: 3-4 months		

Authors published: Don McKay, Mary Dalton, Patrick Lane, & John Steffler

Reads submissions in March and September. Accepts variety of styles. Focuses largely, but by no means exclusively, on writers based in Newfoundland. Subscriptions for institutions are $17/year.

TICKLED BY THUNDER
7385 129th Street, Surrey, British Columbia V3W 7B8
Telephone: (604) 591-6095   Fax: same
Ed and Poetry Ed: Larry Linder

Since: 1990	Circ: 125	Pages: 16-20	Per Year: 4
Size: 5 1/2 X 8 1/2	Folded	Sample: $2	Sub: $12
Copyright: author	Book reviews: yes	Reviews/year: ?	Translations: no
Interviews: yes	Fistion: yes	Essays: yes	Copies: yes
Money: yes	Time: 1-4 months		

Authors published: Helen Singh, Stephen Gill, Marylin Shaw, & Jo-Ann Godfrey

Associated with Tickled By Thunder Publishing Co., a literary press. Likes poetry packed with original images and ideas— novel ways of looking at life or things. Please send SASE for writers' guidelines. Runs annual contests for poetry, fiction, and articles.

TIME FOR RHYME

General Delivery, Battleford, Saskatchewan S0M 0E0
Telephone: (306) 445-5172
Ed and Poetry Ed: Richard W. Unger

Since: 1995	Circ: less than 100	Pages: 32	Per Year: 4
Size: 3 3/4 X 5 1/2	Sewn	Sample: $3.50	Sub: $12
Copyright: author	Book reviews: yes	Reviews/year: 3-4	Translations: yes
Interviews: not yet	Fiction: no	Essays: no	Copies: 1
Money: ?	Time: 1 month		

Authors published: Sharron R. McMillan, Helen Dowd, J. Alvin Speers, & Gladys Nolan

Associated with Richard W. Unger Publishing, a publisher of poetry books and chapbooks. All poems published (including translations) must rhyme. Considers submissions throughout the year. Rejected poems returned with comments. Especially enjoys light verse. Please send SASE for guidelines.

TORONTO LIFE

59 Front Street East, 3rd floor, Toronto, Ontario M5E 1B3
Ed: Marg de Villiers   Poetry Ed: Ted Whittaker

THE TORONTO REVIEW of Contemporary Writing Abroad

PO Box 6996, Station A, Toronto, Ontario M5W 1X7
Ed: M.G. Vassanji

TOWER POETRY

Tower Poetry Society, Dundas Public Library, 18 Ogilvie Street, Dundas, Ontario L9H 2S2
Telephone: (905) 648-4878
Ed and Poetry Ed: Joanna Lawson

TRANSITION

Canadian Mental Health Association, 2702 12th Avenue, Regina, Saskatchewan S4T 1J2
Telephone: (306) 525-5601 Fax: (306) 569-3788
Ed and Poetry Ed: Lori Allan-Wiens

Since: 1985	Circ: 2,000	Pages: 65	Per Year: 4
Size: 5 1/2 X 8 1/2	Saddle stitched	Sample: n/a	Sub: $10
Copyright: author	Book reviews: no	Reviews/year: n/a	Translations: no
Interviews: rarely	Fiction: yes	Essays: yes	Copies: 2
Money: $15/page	Time: 3-6 months		

Authors published: Arthur Slade, Jennifer Footman, Steve Stapleton, & Greg Button

Pays $15/page to a maximum of $75. Considers short stories of up to 1,200 words. Humour is more than welcome. Also interested in artwork. Most of our works deal with issues like depression, eating disorders, stress, problem gambling, and addictions although we will accept any fiction or poetry that explores the mind and its thought patterns.

THE VOYANT

Box 414, 20384 Fraser Highway, Langley, British Columbia V3A 4G1
Telephone: (604) 533-1559   Fax: (604) 532-0742
Eds: Rob Iuins & Jamie Scott

Since: 1995	Circ: ?	Pages: ?	Per Year: 1
Size: ?	Binding: ?	Sample: ?	Sub: ?
Copyright: ?	Book reviews: no	Reviews/year: n/a	Translations: yes
Interviews: no	Fiction: possibly	Essays: no	Copies: yes
Money: no	Time: 1-6 months		

First issue will be Summer 1996. We will be an avant-garde journal publishing only the freshest, boldest work. Especially interested in receiving poetry and artwork by voyants (see Arthur Rimbaud for definition of voyant).

WASCANA REVIEW of Contemporary Poetry and Short Fiction

University of Regina, Department of English, Regina, Saskatchewan S4S 0A2
Telephone: (306) 585-4302   Fax: (306) 585-4827
Ed: Kathleen Wall   Poetry Ed: Troni Grande

Since: 1966	Circ: 350	Pages: 100	Per Year: 2
Size: 6 X 9	Perfect bound	Sample: $5	Sub: $12
Copyright: author	Book reviews: yes	Review/year: 8	Translations: no
Interviews: yes	Fiction: yes	Essays: yes	Copies: 2
Money: $10/page	Time: 2 months		

Authors published: Mark Cochrane, Sue Neville, & Steven DaGama

Pays $10/page for poetry and $3/page for prose. We welcome new and established voices, and poetry written in a wide variety of styles. Our editorial goal is to cross boundaries of gender, genre, style, and outlook. E-mail address: wallkath@max.cc.uregina.ca

WEST COAST LINE

Simon Fraser University, 2027 East Academic Annex, Burnaby, British Columbia V5A 1S6
Telephone: (604) 291-4287   Fax: (604) 291-5737
Eds and Poetry Eds: Roy Miki & Jacqueline Larson

Since: 1966	Circ: 650	Pages: 144	Per Year: 3
Size: 6 X 9	Perfect bound	Sample: $10	Sub: $20
Copyright: author	Book reviews: yes	Reviews/year: 10-15	Translations: yes
Interviews: yes	Fiction: yes	Essays: yes	Copies: 2
Money: yes	Time: 4-6 months		

Authors published: Erin Mouré, Monty Reid, Nicole Brossard, & Steve McCaffery

Interested in innovation; we almost never publish traditional lyric poems. Looks for writing that experiments with, or expands, the boundaries of conventional forms of poetry, fiction, and criticism. Look at back issues!

WestWord

Simon Fraser University, Department of English, Burnaby, British Columbia V5A 1S6
Eds: Dan Dick, Ace Colhoun, & Derek Cockram   Poetry Ed: Dan Dick

Since: 1985	Circ: 300	Pages: 50-60	Per Year: 3
Size: 5 1/2 X 8 1/2	Binding: ?	Sample: $3	Sub: $8
Copyright: author	Book reviews: no	Reviews/year: n/a	Translations: yes
Interviews: no	Fiction: yes	Essays: yes	Copies: 2

Money: ?   Time: 3 months

Both published and unpublished writers are welcome. Open to new styles and directions. Short-short fiction and creative non-fiction are encouraged.

WHETSTONE

University of Lethbridge, Department of English, 4401 University Drive, Lethbridge, Alberta T1K 3M4

Telephone: (403) 329-2367   Fax: (403) 382-7191

Ed and Poetry Ed: Lori Leister

Since: 1972	Circ: 750	Pages: 120-140	Per Year: 2-3
Size: 15 cm X 22 cm	Perfect bound	Sample: $6.95	Sub: $12
Copyright: author	Book reviews: no	Reviews/year: n/a	Translations: no
Interviews: no	Fiction: yes	Essays: no	Copies: 1
Money: no	Time: 2-5 months		

Authors published: Robert Kroetsch, Lorna Crozier, Patrick Lane, & Susan McMaster

WHITE WALL REVIEW

Ryerson Polytechnic University, Oakham House, 63 Gould Street, Toronto, Ontario M5B 1E9

Telephone: (416) 977-1045   Fax: (416) 977-7709

Since: 1976	Circ: 500	Pages: 144-160	Per Year: 1
Size: 5 3/4 X 8 3/4	Perfect bound	Sample: $8	Sub: $9
Copyright: author	Book reviews: no	Reviews/year: n/a	Translations: yes
Interviews: no	Fiction: yes	Essays: no	Copies: 1
Money: n/a	Time: 6 months		

Authors published: C.M. Buckaway, Terry Watada, Mary Elizabeth Lavzon, & R.W. Thomson

Please send SASE for guidelines. Reserves the right to reprint material in future anthologies. Interested in black and white photography. Work that is gratuitously violent, racist, misogynist, or is in bad taste will not be accepted.

WINDHORSE READER

R.R. 3, Box 3140, Yarmouth, Nova Scotia B5A 4A7

Telephone: (902) 742-7945

Ed and Poetry Ed: John Castlebury

Since: 1982	Circ: 500	Pages: 28	Per Year: 1
Size: varies	Perfect bound	Sample: $10	Sub: n/a
Copyright: author	Book reviews: no	Reviews/year: n/a	Translations: yes
Interviews: no	Fiction: no	Essays: no	Copies: yes
Money: no	Time: 1 month		

Authors published: Raymond Souster, Polly Fleck, Robert Bringhurst, & Susan Musgrave

The annual may change its format/direction in the near future. Please send SASE for up-to-date information.

WINDSOR REVIEW

University of Windsor, Department of English, Windsor, Ontario N9B 3P4

Telephone: (519) 253-4232, Ex. 2332   Fax: (519) 973-7050

Poetry Ed: John Ditsky

Since: 1965	Circ: 250	Pages: 90	Per Year: 2
Size: 6 X 9	Perfect bound	Sample: $6	Sub: $21.35
Copyright: author	Book reviews: no	Reviews/year: n/a	Translations: no
Interviews: yes	Fiction: no	Essays: no	Copies: 1
Money: $15/poem	Time: 2 months		

Authors published: Walter McDonald & Lyn Lifshin

Pays $50 per short story. E-mail address: uwrevu@uwindsor.ca

WOMEN'S EDUCATION DES FEMMES
47 Main Street, Toronto, Ontario M4E 2V6
Telephone: (416) 699-1909   Fax: (416) 699-2145
Ed: Christina Starr   Poetry Ed: Catherine Lake

Since: 1982	Circ: 1,000	Pages: 64	Per Year: 4
Size: 8 1/2 X 11	Saddle stitched	Sample: $2.50	Sub: $17
Copyright: author	Book reviews: yes	Reviews/year: 6	Translations: yes
Interviews: yes	Fiction: no	Essays: yes	Copies: 2
Money: $25/poem	Time: 2-3 months		

Authors published: Susan Ioannou, Sue Nevill, Wilda Kruize, & Annette LeBox

Poetry must be by women and written from a feminist perspective. Poetry focussing on education and learning is appreciated, but submissions are welcome on any topic. Subscriptions for institutions are $30/year.

WRITER'S BLOCK MAGAZINE
Box 32, 9944 33rd Avenue, Edmonton, Alberta T6N 1E8
Telephone: (403) 486-5856   Fax: (403) 444-7504
Ed: Shaun Donnelly   Poetry Ed: Pamela Hegarty

Since: 1994	Circ: 25,000	Pages: 52	Per Year: 4
Size: 5 1/4 X 8	Saddle stitched	Sample: $5	Sub: $12
Copyright: author	Book reviews: yes	Reviews/year: 6-10	Translations: yes
Interviews: yes	Fiction: yes	Essays: yes	Copies: ?
Money: 5 cents/word	Time: 1-2 months		

Authors published: Sandra Mooney-Ellerbeck, John Ballen, Theresa Shea, & Bernice Lever

Please send SASE for writer's guidelines. Pays 5 cents per word but no less than $25 for poems. Runs the Writer's Block Contest. We enjoy a variety of poetry styles and themes. Always responds personally— no form letters. Send only your best poetry.

WRITERS INK.
c/o Strathbarton Postal Outlet, 1565 Barton Street East, Hamilton, Ontario L8H 2Y3
Telephone: (905) 544-9680   Fax: (905) 547-7290
Ed and Poetry Ed: Victoria Miecznikowski

Since: 1995	Circ: 500	Pages: 8	Per Year: 6
Size: 8 1/2 X 11	Folded	Sample: SASE	Sub: $10
Copyright: author	Book reviews: yes	Reviews/year: 6-12	Translations: no
Interviews: yes	Fiction: yes	Essays: yes	Copies: yes
Money: ?	Time: 1 month		

Authors published: Judy Mendelson & Roland Puppa

ZYGOTE MAGAZINE
746 Westminster Avenue, Winnipeg, Manitoba R3G 1A4
Telephone: (204) 775-1432   Fax: (204) 775-7158
Eds: Eva Weidman & Chris Kent

Since: 1993	Circ: 1,000	Pages: 52	Per Year: 4
Size: 8 1/2 X 11	Saddle stitched	Sample: $2.95	Sub: $10
Copyright: author	Book reviews: yes	Reviews/year: 12-20	Translations: no

Interviews: yes   Fiction: yes   Essays: yes   Copies: yes
Money: ?   Time: 3-4 months
Authors published: Lynnette d'Anna, Per Brask, Patrick O'Connell, & Alexis Kienlen
Poetry submissions maximum of 50 lines. Guest poetry editor for each issue.

The following 70 periodicals have ceased publication since the fifth edition of this book, or they no longer publish poetry, or they have asked to be delisted:

After the End
Aggregate
The Alchemist
Alpha Arts Magazine
Anerca/Compost
Ankur
Arts Scarborough
ArtsNews
Atlantis
Babble Ragazine
Bite
Black Apple
Border/Lines Magazine
Breakthrough! Magazine
Briarpatch
can(N)on magazine
Chanticleer
The Conspiracy of Silence
Cumulus
The Dinosar Review
Diva
Existere
(f.)Lip
fly . . .
Georgian Force
Germination
The Harvest
Herspectives
The Idler
Japanese Canadian Cultural Centre Newsletter

The Moosehead Review
{m}Other Tongues
Mr. Magnanmous
New Canadian Review
Next Exit
North Shore Magazine
Parodyse
Piranha
Poetic Justice
Poetry Halifax Dartmouth
Poetry WLU
Probe Post
Proem Canada
Puglia Fruit Market
Quintessence
Rain
Rampike
The Raven Review
SansCrit
Saturday Night
Scat!
Secrets From the Orange Couch
Senary
St. Thomas Chronicles
The Standing Stone
Tabula Rasa Magazine
Taproot
Tenement Magazine
Tidepool
Tyro

Vancouver Sath

the wanderer

what

Wild East

WindScript

Writ

Writing

X-IT

Yak Art & Literature

Zymergy

The following 30 periodicals, believed to still be in existence, have failed to respond to requests for information. This may indicate a lack of interest in unsolicited poetry manuscripts. Or it may mean that the overworked editors can't answer their mail.

Alias
Fred Victor Mission
145 Queen Street East
Toronto, Ontario, M5A 1S1

Black Cat 115
1315 Niagara Street
Suite 4
Windsor, Ontario, N9A 3V8

d'Void
University College of the Fraser Valley
33844 King Road
R.R. 2
Abbotsford, BC, V2S 4N2

Earthkeeper Magazine
PO Box 1649
Guelph, Ontario, N1H 6R7

Exile
PO Box 67, Station B
Toronto, Ontario, M5T 2C0

Geist
1062 Homer Street
Suite 100
Vancouver, BC, V6B 2W9

Generation
University of Windsor
Department of English
Windsor, Ontario, N9B 3P4

The Harpweaver
Brock University
Dept. of English Language & Literature
St. Catharines, Ontario, V8N 4G6

Impulse
16 Skey Lane
Toronto, Ontario, M6J 3S4

Industrial Sabotage
1357 Lansdowne Avenue
Toronto, Ontario, M6H 3Z9

Island
PO Box 256
Lantzville, BC, V0R 2H0

Museum Quarterly
4913 Sea Ridge Drive
Victoria, BC, V8Y 2B4

New Maritimes
6106 Lawrence Street
Halifax, Nova Scotia, B3L 1J6

Paradigm
University College of Cape Breton
PO Box 5300
Sydney, Nova Scotia, B1P 2L6

Pearls
Douglas College
PO Box 2503
New Westminster, BC, V3L 5B2

Poem
20 Prince Arthur Avenue
Apt. 11-C
Toronto, Ontario, M5R 1B1

Portico
Sheridan College
1430 Trafalgar Road
Oakville, Ontario, L6H 2L1

Prison Journal
Simon Fraser University
Institute for the Humanities
Burnaby, BC, V5A 1S6

Scarborough Fair
Scarborough College, Univ. of Toronto
1265 Military Trail
Scarborough, Ontario, M1C 1A4

The Sheaf
University of Saskatchewan
Saskatoon, Saskatchewan, S7N 0W0

Thalia
University of Ottawa
Department of English
Ottawa, Ontario, K1N 6N5

Torque
PO Box 153, Station P
Toronto, Ontario, M5S 2S7

University College Review
University of Toronto
Toronto, Ontario, M5S 1A1

The University of Toronto Review
University of Toronto
12 Hart House Circle
Toronto, Ontario, M5S 1A6

The Ventriloquist
English Student Association
Lakehead University
Thunder Bay, Ontario, P7B 5E1

Western People
PO Box 2500
Saskatoon, Saskatchewan, S7K 2C4

Who Torched Rancho Diablo
PO Box 789, Station F
Toronto, Ontario, M4Y 2N7

Writer's Lifeline
PO Box 1641
Cornwall, Ontario, K6H 5V6

The Yukon Reader
PO Box 4306
Whitehorse, Yukon, Y1A 3T3

Zag
69R Nassau Street
Toronto, Ontario, M5T 1M6

1.6 U.S.A. PERIODICAL LISTINGS

The following 156 American periodicals have expressed interest in Canadian poetry. Unlike other lists in this volume, these American magazines represent the cream of the literary scene. Survey forms were sent only to the top 10% of all U.S. literary journals. It is important to remember that the most prestigious American magazines receive thousands of submissions each year. A number of the periodicals included in this section reject well over 90% of the poetry that shows up in the mail. Many of these editors actively solicit work. Thus, unsolicited poetry may be rarely used.

This does not mean that they won't accept your work. They are, however, a bit of a long shot and, unless you know a journal well, you should start with a query letter or, better yet, you should examine a sample copy. Many of these publications have formal guidelines for contributors, and it is always a good policy to send for these. A university or public library near you may quite possibly subscribe to a number of them.

Make sure that your SASE has U.S. postage or International Reply Coupons with recent dates (some U.S. post offices will not honour IRCs that are more than six months old).

Readers interested in data on less-selective American markets are referred to *The International Directory of Little Magazines and Small Presses*, discussed elsewhere in this guide. But, why not start at the top?

ABRAXAS
2518 Gregory Street, Madison, WI 53711
Telephone: (608) 238-0175
Eds: Ingrid Swanberg & Warren Woessner   Poetry Ed: Ingrid Swanberg

AGNI
Boston University, Creative Writing Program, 236 Bay State Road, Boston, MA 02215
Telephone: (617) 353-5389
Ed and Poetry Ed: Askold Melnyczuk

AIM, America's Intercultural Magazine
7308 South Eberhart Avenue, Chicago, IL 60619
Telephone: (312) 874-6184   Fax: (206) 543-2746
Eds: Myron Apilado & Ruth Apilado   Poetry Ed: Mark Boone

Since: 1973	Circ: 7,000	Pages: 48	Per Year: 4
Size: 8 1/2 X 11	Perfect bound	Sample: $2.50	Sub: $10
Copyright: author	Book reviews: yes	Reviews/year: ?	Translations: no
Interviews: yes	Fiction: ?	Essays: ?	Copies: 1
Money: $25	Time: 1 month		

Authors published: David Appell, Taylor Johnson, Damien-Filer, & Robert Funge
Interested in poetry about racial/social problems.

ALASKA QUARTERLY REVIEW

University of Alaska, Department of English, 3211 Providence Drive, Anchorage, AK 99508-8092
Telephone: (907) 786-4775   Fax: same
Ed and Poetry Ed: Ronald Spatz

Since: 1982	Circ: 1,500	Pages: 200	Per Year: 2
Size: 6 X 9	Perfect bound	Sample: $5	Sub: $10
Copyright: author	Book reviews: yes	Reviews/year: ?	Translations: yes
Interviews: yes	Fiction: yes	Essays: yes	Copies: yes
Money: sometimes	Time: 1-3 months		

Authors published: Hayden Carruth, Lisel Mueller, Stephen Dobyns, & Kim Addonizio
Send SASE for the submission guidelines. Pays money for poetry when grants permit. Reads unsolicited manuscripts between August 15 and May 15. Welcomes both traditional and experimental poetry.

AMERICA

106 West 56th Street, New York, NY 10019
Telephone: (212) 581-4640   Fax: (212) 399-3596
Ed: George Hunt, S.J.   Poetry Ed: Patrick Samway, S.J.

Since: 1909	Circ: 37,000	Pages: 28	Per Year: 45
Size: 8 1/2 X 11	Perfect bound	Sample: $1.25	Sub: $33
Copyright: author	Book reviews: yes	Reviews/year: 150	Translations: no
Interviews: yes	Fiction: no	Essays: yes	Copies: no
Money: $1.40/line	Time: 2 weeks-1 year		

Authors published: Anita Vitacolonna, William Heyen, James Torrens, S.J., and John Frederick Nims
Looks for down home humour. Runs the Foley Poetry Award with a $500 prize. Please send SASE for contest rules/submission guidelines.

THE AMERICAN POETRY REVIEW

1721 Walnut Street, Philadelphia, PA 19103
Telephone: (215) 496-0439   Fax: (215) 569-0808
Eds and Poetry Eds: David Bonanno, Stephen Berg, & Arthur Vogelsang

Since: 1971	Circ: 18,000	Pages: 54	Per Year: 6
Size: tabloid	Newspaper	Sample: $3.50	Sub: $16
Copyright: author	Book reviews: yes	Reviews/year: ?	Translations: yes
Interviews: yes	Fiction: rarely	Essays: yes	Copies: 7
Money: $2/line	Time: 3 months		

Authors published: Adrienne Rich, Galway Kinnell, Louise Glück, & John Ashbery
Welcomes all types of poetry; reads all year long.

THE AMERICAN SCHOLAR

1811 Q Street N.W., Washington, D.C. 20009
Telephone: (202) 265-3808
Ed: Joseph Epstein

Since: 1932	Circ: 26,500	Pages: ?	Per Year: 4
Size: 7 X 10	Binding: ?	Sample: $6.50	Sub: $25
Copyright: ?	Book reviews: yes	Reviews/year: ?	Translations: ?

| Interviews: ? | Fiction: no | Essays: yes | Copies: ? |
| Money: $50 | Time: ? | | |

Please send SASE for writers' guidelines. Pays $50 per poem and up to $500 for articles/essays.

THE AMERICAN VOICE
332 West Broadway, Suite 1215, Louisville, KY 40202
Telephone: (502) 562-0045
Ed and Poetry Ed: Frederick Smock

Since: 1985	Circ: 2,000	Pages: 145	Per Year: 3
Size: 6 X 9	Perfect bound	Sample: $7	Sub: $20
Copyright: author	Book reviews: yes	Reviews/year: 1-2	Translations: yes
Interviews: no	Fiction: yes	Essays: yes	Copies: 2
Money: $100	Time: 2-3 weeks		

Authors published: Jorge Luis Borges, Marge Piercy, Elisabeth Harvor, & Olga Broumas

ANOTHER CHICAGO MAGAZINE
3709 North Kenmore, Chicago, IL 60613
Eds: Barry Silesky, Sharon Solwitz, & Sara Skolnik   Poetry Ed: Barry Silesky

Since: 1977	Circ: 2,000	Pages: 220	Per Year: 2
Size: 5 1/2 X 8 1/2	Perfect bound	Sample: $8	Sub: $15
Copyright: author	Book reviews: yes	Reviews/year: 15	Translations: yes
Interviews: yes	Fiction: yes	Essays: yes	Copies: yes
Money: yes	Time: 3 months		

No special interests. Submit poems in the summer.

THE ANTIOCH REVIEW
PO Box 148, Yellow Springs, OH 45387
Telephone: (513) 767-6389
Ed: Robert S. Fogarty   Poetry Ed: David St. John

Since: 1941	Circ: 4,600	Pages: 128	Per Year: 4
Size: 6 X 9	Perfect bound	Sample: $6 (U.S.)	Sub: $39 (U.S.)
Copyright: author	Book reviews: yes	Reviews/year: 80	Translations: yes
Interviews: no	Fiction: yes	Essays: yes	Copies: 2
Money: $10/page	Time: 2-3 months		

Authors published: Adrian C. Louis, Gillian Conoley, Ellen Bryant Voigt, & Lynn Emanuel

Does NOT read poetry from May 15 to Sept. 1. Does not publish unsolicited book reviews. No "light" verse. Poetry should engage the attention of the intelligent reader. Send SASE for contributors' guidelines.

APPALACHIA
5 Joy Street, Boston, MA 02108
Ed: Sandy Stott   Poetry Ed: Parkman Howe

Since: ?	Circ: 10,000	Pages: 150	Per Year: 2
Size: ?	Perfect bound	Sample: $5	Sub: $10
Copyright: author	Book reviews: yes	Reviews/year: 10	Translations: yes
Interviews: yes	Fiction: no	Essays: yes	Copies: 1
Money: no	Time: ?		

Authors published: Thomas Reiter, Mary Oliver, L.R. Berger, & Jean Hollonder

Please send SASE for submission guidelines. Wants writing of an ecological nature: mountains, rivers, lakes, the sea, animals. Mountaineering is a special interest. Maximum length for poems: 36 lines.

THE ATLANTIC MONTHLY
745 Boylston Street, Boston, MA 02116
Telephone: (617) 536-9500   Fax: (617) 536-3730
Ed: William Whitworth   Poetry Ed: Peter Davison

Since: 1857	Circ: 500,000	Pages: 128	Per Year: 12
Size: 8 1/2 X 11	Binding: ?	Sample: ?	Sub: ?
Copyright: author	Book reviews: yes	Reviews/year: 100	Translations: yes
Interviews: no	Fiction: yes	Essays: yes	Copies: ?
Money: ?	Time: 3 weeks		

Authors published: Margaret Atwood, Richard Wilber, Mark Doty, & Jane Kenyon

ATOM MIND
PO Box 22068, Albuquerque, NM 87154
Ed and Poetry Ed: Gregory Smith

Since: 1968	Circ: 1,000	Pages: 120	Per Year: 4
Size: 8 1/2 X 11	Perfect bound	Sample: $5	Sub: $16
Copyright: author	Book reviews: no	Reviews/year: n/a	Translations: yes
Interviews: yes	Fiction: yes	Essays: yes	Copies: yes
Money: occasionally	Time: 1-2 months		

Authors published: Charles Bukowski, Lawrence Ferlinghetti, Steve Richmond, & Adrian C. Louis

Send several poems at a time, rather than one or two.

AURA LITERARY/ARTS REVIEW
University of Alabama, Box 76, Hill University Center, Birmingham, AL 35294
Telephone: (205) 934-3216   Fax: (205) 934-8070
Ed and Poetry Ed: Steve Mullen

Since: 1974	Circ: 500	Pages: 148	Per Year: 2
Size: 5 X 7	Perfect bound	Sample: $2.50	Sub: $6
Copyright: author	Book reviews: yes	Reviews/year: 2	Translations: no
Interviews: no	Fiction: yes	Essays: yes	Copies: 2
Money: no	Time: 6 months		

Authors published: Miriam Cohen, Lyn Lifshin, Majid Nassiri, & Walker Woods

Interested in all kinds of photos, artwork, and fiction. Fiction should be less than 5,000 words. Deadlines are October 1 and April 1.

THE BELLINGHAM REVIEW
Western Washington University, Mail Stop 9053, Bellingham, WA 98225
Fax: (360) 650-4837
Ed: Robin Hemley   Poetry Eds: Bruce Beasley & Suzanne Paola

Since: 1977	Circ: 500	Pages: 60	Per Year: 2
Size: 5 1/2 X 8	Binding: varies	Sample: $2.50 (U.S.)	Sub: $6 (U.S.)
Copyright: author	Book reviews: yes	Reviews/year: 2	Translations: yes
Interviews: yes	Fiction: yes	Essays: yes	Copies: 1
Money: no	Time: 3 months		

Authors published: Richard Martin, Jim Daniels, Laurel Speer, & James Liddy

Reads submissions from September 15 to May 1. Sometimes magazine is perfect bound and at other times it's saddle stitched. Also runs the annual 49th Parallel

Poetry Contest. Please send SASE for contest rules. Contest address is: The Signpost Press, 1007 Queen Street, Bellingham, WA, 98226

THE BELOIT POETRY JOURNAL
Box 154, RFD 2, Ellsworth, ME 04605
Telephone: (207) 667-5598
Ed and Poetry Ed: Marion K. Stocking

Since: 1950	Circ: 1,700	Pages: 48	Per Year: 4
Size: 5 1/2 X 8 1/2	Saddle stitched	Sample: $4	Sub: $15.20
Copyright: author	Book reviews: yes	Reviews/year: 45	Translations: yes
Interviews: no	Fiction: no	Essays: no	Copies: 3
Money: no	Time: 4 months		

Authors published: Albert Goldbarth, Molly Tenenbaum, & A.E. Stallings

Would rather get Canadian coins than IRCs. 40 cents for 1 ounce, 65 cents for 2 ounces.

BLACK WARRIOR REVIEW
PO Box 2936, Tuscaloosa, AL 35486-2936
Telephone: (205) 348-4518
Ed: Mindy Wilson   Poetry Ed: Madeline Marcotte

Since: 1974	Circ: 3,000	Pages: 200	Per Year: 2
Size: 6 X 9	Perfect bound	Sample: $6	Sub: $11
Copyright: ?	Book reviews: yes	Reviews/year: 8-10	Translations: yes
Interviews: yes	Fiction: yes	Essays: yes	Copies: yes
Money: yes	Time: 1-3 months		

Authors published: Rodney Jones, Tess Gallagher, Gerald Stern, & Dara Wier

Reads submissions year round. Pays $5 to $10/page for fiction; $25 to $35 per poem.

BOGG
Sheila Martindale, Canadian Editor, PO Box 23148, 380 Wellington Street, London, Ontario N6A 5N9
Ed: John Elsberg (USA)   Poetry Ed: Sheila Martindale (Canadian)

Since: 1968	Circ: 800	Pages: 68	Per Year: 2-3
Size: 8 1/5 X 5 1/2	Saddle stitched	Sample: $4	Sub: $10/3 issues
Copyright: author	Book reviews: yes	Reviews/year: 1-3	Translations: no
Interviews: yes	Fiction: no	Essays: yes	Copies: yes
Money: no	Time: 2-3 months		

Authors published: Tim Bowling, Norma West Linder, Barry Dempster, & G.P. Greenwood

Bogg is an Anglo-American journal. Very interested in Canadian poetry; has a Canadian editor. Likes poems that are upbeat, have humour, and are irreverent; nothing stuffy or sanctimonious. Send SASE for guidelines for poets. This journal comes out of Virginia.

BOSTON REVIEW
Massachusettes Institute of Technology, E53-407, 30 Wadsworth Street, Cambridge, MA 02134
Telephone: (617) 253-3642   Fax: (617) 252-1549
Eds: Josh Cohen & John Thompson   Poetry Ed: Kim Cooper

Since: 1975	Circ: 20,000	Pages: 35-40	Per Year: 6

Size: 10 X 14	Perfect bound	Sample: $4.50	Sub: $15
Copyright: author	Book reviews: yes	Reviews/year: 20-24	Translations: yes
Interviews: yes	Fiction: yes	Essays: yes	Copies: yes
Money: varies	Time: 3 months		

Authors published: Josh Weiner, Rachel Hadas, Alfred Corn, & Alan Shapiro

Accepts submissions year round. Institutional subscriptions are $18/year.

BOULEVARD
PO Box 30386, Philadelphia, PA 19103
Telephone: (215) 568-7062
Eds and Poetry Ed: Richard W. Burgin

Since: 1985	Circ: 3,000	Pages: 200+	Per Year: 3
Size: 5 X 7	Perfect bound	Sample: $7 (U.S.)	Sub: $12 (U.S.)
Copyright: author	Book reviews: no	Reviews/year: n/a	Translations: yes
Interviews: yes	Fiction: yes	Essays: yes	Copies: 1
Money: yes	Time: 1-2 months		

Authors published: W.S. Merwin, Eleanor Wilner, Charles Simic, & Donald Hall

Please send SASE for guidelines. Talent is what counts. Interested only in the best work of established writers as well as less experienced writers of exceptional promise. Submit no more than five poems at one time. Pays $25 to $150 for poetry; $50 to $150 for fiction.

THE CAPE ROCK
Southeast Missouri State University, Department of English, Cape Girardeau, MO 63701-4799
Telephone: (314) 651-2500
Ed and Poetry Ed: Harvey Hecht

Since: 1964	Circ: 600	Pages: 64	Per Year: 2
Size: 5 1/2 X 8 1/2	Perfect bound	Sample: $3	Sub: $7
Copyright: see below	Book reviews: no	Reviews/year: n/a	Translations: no
Interviews: no	Fiction: no	Essays: no	Copies: 2
Money: no	Time: 2-4 months		

Does not read between May and August. Pays $200 for the best poem in each issue. Copyright situation is discussed in detail in the guidelines; send SASE for a copy. Prefers poems of under 70 lines. No restrictions on subjects or forms; looks only for quality. Also interested in black and white photos.

THE CAROLINA QUARTERLY
University of North Carolina, CB #3520, Greenlaw Hall, Chapel Hill, NC 27599-3520
Ed: Amber Vogel   Poetry Ed: Carrie Blackstock

Since: 1948	Circ: 1,500	Pages: 88	Per Year: 3
Size: 6 X 9	Perfect bound	Sample: $6	Sub: $12
Copyright: author	Book reviews: yes	Reviews/year: 6-9	Translations: yes
Interviews: yes	Fiction: yes	Essays: yes	Copies: yes
Money: ?	Time: 4-6 weeks		

Authors published: Denise Levertov, Mark Doty, X.J. Kennedy, & Stephen Dunn

Reads manuscripts year round.

THE CENTENNIAL REVIEW

Michigan State University, 312 South Holmes, East Lansing, MI 48824-1044

Telephone: (517) 355-1905

Ed and Poetry Ed: R.K. Meiners

THE CHARITON REVIEW

Truman State University, Kirksville, MO 63501-4221

Telephone: (816) 785-4499   Fax: (816) 785-7486

Ed and Poetry Ed: Jim Barnes

Since: 1975	Circ: 700	Pages: 100	Per Year: 2
Size: 6 X 9	Perfect bound	Sample: $5 (U.S.)	Sub: $9 (U.S.)
Copyright: author	Book reviews: yes	Reviews/year: 1-2	Translations: yes
Interviews: no	Fiction: yes	Essays: yes	Copies: 1
Money: $5/page	Time: 2 weeks		

Authors published: Constance Urdang, Laurance Liebermann, JudyRay, & Samuel Maio

We are prejudiced against literature of fad, such as stories about relatives and bad marriages. We believe that control of tone is essential to good literature and that anything less belongs to another realm.

THE CHATTAHOOCHEE REVIEW

DeKalb College, 2101 Womack Road, Dunwoody, GA 30338-4497

Telephone: (404) 551-3019   Fax: (404) 604-3795

Eds: Lamar York & Jo Ann Yeager Adkins   Poetry Ed: Collie Owens

Since: 1980	Circ: 1,250	Pages: 100	Per Year: 4
Size: 6 X 9	Perfect bound	Sample: $5	Sub: $15
Copyright: see below	Book reviews: yes	Reviews/year: 8-15	Translations: yes
Interviews: yes	Fiction: yes	Essays: yes	Copies: 2
Money: no	Time: 3 months		

Reads all year. Copyrighted in the name of the review, but reprint rights are granted upon written request. Send no more than five poems at one time. Please send SASE for submission guidelines.

CHELSEA

PO Box 773, Cooper Station, New York, NY 10276-0773

Eds: Richard Foerster, Andrea Lockett, & Alfredo de Palchi

Since: 1958	Circ: 1,300	Pages: 130	Per Year: 2
Size: 6 X 9	Perfect bound	Sample: $6	Sub: $15
Copyright: author	Book reviews: yes	Reviews/year: ?	Translations: yes
Interviews: no	Fiction: yes	Essays: yes	Copies: 2
Money: $10/page	Time: 3-6 months		

Authors published: Ruth L. Schwartz, Adrian C. Louis, Mekeel McBride, & D.E. Steward

Runs the Chelsea Awards for Poetry and Short Fiction; send SASE for guidelines. Cash prizes of $500 (U.S.). *Chelsea* always seeks challenging, unusual, original work. No racist or sexist material. Tends to like free verse over formal verse. Submissions are read throughout the year.

CHICAGO REVIEW

The University of Chicago, 5801 South Kenwood Avenue, Chicago, IL 60637

Ed: David Nicholls   Poetry Ed: Angela Sorby

Since: 1946	Circ: 2,600	Pages: 128	Per Year: 4

Size: 6 X 9	Perfect bound	Sample: $5	Sub: $18
Copyright: magazine	Book reviews: yes	Reviews/year: 15	Translations: yes
Interviews: yes	Fiction: yes	Essays: yes	Copies: 3
Money: ?	Time: 2 months		

Authors published: Alice Fulton, Albert Goldbarth, & Adrian C. Louis

Send no more than five poems per submission. Reads all year.

CHIRON REVIEW
522 East South Avenue, St. John, KS 67567-2212
Telephone: (316) 549-3933
Eds: Michael & Jane Hathaway   Poetry Ed: Gerald Locklin

Since: 1982	Circ: 1,000	Pages: 32	Per Year: 4
Size: tabloid	Newspaper	Sample: $4 (U.S.)	Sub: $14 (U.S.)
Copyright: author	Book reviews: yes	Reviews/year: 24-30	Translations: yes
Interviews: yes	Fiction: yes	Essays: yes	Copies: yes
Money: no	Time: 2-4 weeks		

Authors published: Charles Bukowski, Marge Piercy, William Stafford, & Antler

No taboos. Runs a poetry contest and a chapbook contest. Send SASE for contest information.

CIMARRON REVIEW
Oklahoma State University, 205 Morrill Hall, Stillwater, OK 74078-0135
Telephone: (405) 744-9476
Ed: E.P. Walkiewicz

Since: 1967	Circ: 400	Pages: 120	Per Year: 4
Size: 6 X 9	Perfect bound	Sample: $3	Sub: $15
Copyright: magazine	Book reviews: yes	Reviews/year: 10-12	Translations: no
Interviews: no	Fiction: yes	Essays: yes	Copies: 1
Money: $15/poem	Time: 3 months		

Authors published: Walter Bargen, Tim Liardet, Jim Elledge, & Carrie Etter

The review holds copyright, but will grant permission to reprint. Reads year round. Please send no more than six poems per submission. No light verse, no haiku. Looks for strong voices that will appeal to regional as well as international readers.

CINCINNATI POETRY REVIEW
College of Mount St. Joseph, Humanities Department, 5701 Delhi Road, Cincinnati, OH 45233
Ed and Poetry Ed: Jeffrey Hillard

CLOCKWATCH REVIEW
Illinois Wesleyan University, Department of English, Bloomington, IL 61702
Telephone: (309) 556-3352
Ed and Poetry Ed: James Plath

COLLEGE ENGLISH
University of Massachusetts, Department of English, Phillis Wheatley Hall, 100 Morrissey Boulevard, Boston, MA 02125-3393
Telephone: (617) 287-6733
Ed: Louise Z. Smith   Poetry Eds: Helen Davis & Lloyd Schwartz

Since: 1929	Circ: 18,000	Pages: 100	Per Year: 8

Size: 5 1/2 X 9 1/2	Perfect bound	Sample: $6.26	Sub: $40
Copyright: magazine	Book reviews: yes	Reviews/year: 8-10	Translations: no
Interviews: no	Fiction: no	Essays: yes	Copies: 2
Money: no	Time: 2 months		

Authors published: Marjorie Maddox, Julia Kasdorf, & Gerald George

Does not read poetry during the summer. Interested in scholarly articles. E-mail address: collengl@umbsky.cc.umb.edu

CONFRONTATION
C.W. Post Campus of Long Island University, English Department, Brookville, NY 11548
Telephone: (516) 299-2391
Ed and Poetry Ed: Martin Tucker

CORONA, Marking the Edges of Many Circles
Montana State University, Department of History & Philosophy, Bozeman, MT 59717
Telephone: (406) 994-5200
Eds: Lynda Sexson, Michael Sexson, & Sarah Merrill

Since: 1980	Circ: 2,000	Pages: 128	Per Year: ?
Size: 7 X 10	Perfect bound	Sample: $7	Sub: n/a
Copyright: author	Book reviews: yes	Reviews/year: few	Translations: no
Interviews: occasional	Fiction: yes	Essays: yes	Copies: 4
Money: no	Time: 1 month		

Authors published: Frederick Turner, Richard Hugo, Phillip Dacey, & X.J. Kennedy

We are working on an issue on "Book."

COTTONWOOD MAGAZINE
The University of Kansas, 400 Kansas Union, Box J, Lawrence, KS 66045
Telephone: (913) 748-0853
Ed: George F. Wedge   Poetry Ed: Philip Wedge

Since: 1965	Circ: 500	Pages: 108	Per Year: 3
Size: 6 X 9	Perfect bound	Sample: $4 (U.S.)	Sub: $18 (U.S.)
Copyright: author	Book reviews: yes	Reviews/year: 10-15	Translations: no
Interviews: yes	Fiction: yes	Essays: yes	Copies: 1
Money: no	Time: 3-6 months		

Authors published: Rita Dove, William Stafford, Walter McDonald, & Patricia Traxler

Open to both mainstream and experimental work. No academic writing, workshop products, or rhymed couplets. Reads all year. Runs the Alice Carter Awards; send SASE for contest data.

CRAZYHORSE
University of Arkansas, Department of English, 2801 South University, Little Rock, AR 72204
Telephone: (501) 569-3161
Ed: Zabelle Stodola   Poetry Eds: Ralph Burns & Marck L. Beggs

Since: 1960	Circ: 1,000	Pages: 200	Per Year: 2
Size: 6 X 9	Perfect bound:	Sample: $5	Sub: $10
Copyright: author	Book reviews: no	Reviews/year: n/a	Translations: rarely
Interviews: rarely	Fiction: yes	Essays: yes	Copies: 2
Money: $10/page	Time: 4-6 weeks		

Authors published: Roberta Spear, Herbert Morris, Maura Stanton, & Donald Revell
Reads poetry between September and May.

CUMBERLAND POETRY REVIEW
PO Box 120128, Acklen Station, Nashville, TN 37212
Ed and Poetry Ed: by nine member board

Since: 1981	Circ: 500	Pages: 80-100	Per Year: 2
Size: 6 X 9	Perfect bound	Sample: $7	Sub: $14
Copyright: author	Book reviews: no	Reviews/year: n/a	Translations: yes
Interviews: no	Fiction: no	Essays: yes	Copies: 2
Money: no	Time: 3-6 months		

Authors published: Seamus Heaney, X.J. Kennedy, Rachel Hadas, & Lawrence Lerner
No restrictions on form, subject, or style. Work should be perspicuous and compelling. Translations and non-U.S. English-language poetry most welcome. All essays should be about poetry. The review takes special responsibility for reminding American readers that not all excellent poetry in English is written by U.S. citizens.

CutBank
University of Montana, English Department, Missoula, MT 59812
Eds: Allyson Goldin & Lary Kleeman   Poetry Eds: Shan Simmons & Meghan Howes

Since: 1973	Circ: 600	Pages: 100	Per Year: 2
Size: 5 1/4 X 8	Perfect bound	Sample: $5	Sub: $12
Copyright: author	Book reviews: yes	Reviews/year: ?	Translations: yes
Interviews: yes	Fiction: yes	Essays: no	Copies: 2
Money: no	Time: 3-5 weeks		

Authors published: Galway Kinnell, Gerald Stern, Patricia Goedicke, & Mark Levine
Reading period: between August and February. Send SASE for writers' guidelines. Although *CutBank* has not published essays in the past, there is interest in them; please query. Runs the *CutBank* Literary Awards for Fiction and Poetry. Cash prizes. Please send SASE for contest rules.

DEKALB LITERARY ARTS JOURNAL
1135 Gunnison Court, Clarkston, GA 30021
Eds: Frances S. Ellis & Charleise T. Young   Poetry Ed: Eleanor G. Sharp

DENVER QUARTERLY
University of Denver, Department of English, 2140 South Race Street, Denver, CO 80208
Telephone: (303) 871-2892   Fax: (303) 871-2853
Ed and Poetry Ed: Bin Ramke

Since: 1966	Circ: 1,000	Pages: 134	Per Year: 4
Size: 6 X 9	Perfect bound	Sample: $5	Sub: $15
Copyright: author	Book reviews: yes	Reviews/year: 6-10	Translations: yes
Interviews: yes	Fiction: yes	Essays: yes	Copies: yes
Money: $5/page	Time: 1-3 months		

Authors published: John Ashbery, Ann Lauterbach, Herbert Morris, & Michael Palmer
Open to all types of poetry, but most interested in experimentation in form. Also interested in politics. Does not read submissions between May 15 and September 15.

FIELD

Oberlin College, Rice Hall 17, Oberlin, OH 44074-1095

Telephone: (216) 775-8407   Fax: (216) 775-8124

Eds and Poetry Eds: Stuart Friebert & Turner Walker

Since: 1969	Circ: 2,500	Pages: 100	Per Year: 2
Size: 6 X 9	Perfect bound	Sample: $7	Sub: $14
Copyright: author	Book reviews: yes	Reviews/year: 4	Translations: yes
Interviews: yes	Fiction: no	Essays: no	Copies: 2
Money: yes	Time: 2-4 weeks		

Authors published: Margaret Atwood, James Tate, Adrienne Rich, & Rita Dove

Just send poems we can't resist. Very interested in translations. Translator must show evidence of permission to translate and must include original poems. Publishes the Field Translation Series.

FINE MADNESS

PO Box 31138, Seattle, WA 98103-01138

Eds and Poetry Eds: Sean Bentley, Louis Bergsagel, Christine Deavel, John Malek, & John Marshall

THE FLORIDA REVIEW

University of Central Florida, Department of English, Orlando, FL 32816

Telephone: (407) 823-2212   Fax: (407) 823-5156

Ed and Poetry Ed: Russell Kesler

Since: 1972	Circ: 650	Pages: 128	Per Year: 2
Size: 5 1/2 X 8 1/2	Perfect bound	Sample: $4.50	Sub: $7
Copyright: author	Book reviews: yes	Reviews/year: 5-8	Translations: yes
Interviews: rarely	Fiction: yes	Essays: yes	Copies: 3
Money: maybe	Time: 3 months		

Authors published: Ronald Wallace, Katherine Soniat, Walter McDonald, & Sylvia Curbelo

Offers a cash payment when funds are available. Looks for poetry that puts content over form, whether lyric, narrative, or formal-concrete. Likes image-based poetry. Reads all year. Accepts simultaneous submissions.

THE FORMALIST: A Journal of Metrical Poetry

320 Hunter Drive, Evansville, IN 47711

Telephone: (812) 425-7684

Ed: William Baer

Since: 1990	Circ: 1,000	Pages: 128	Per Year: 2
Size: 6 X 9	Perfect bound	Sample: $8 (U.S.)	Sub: $15 (U.S.)
Copyright: author	Book reviews: yes	Reviews/year: 1	Translations: yes
Interviews: yes	Fiction: no	Essays: yes	Copies: 2
Money: no	Time: 2 months		

Authors published: Derek Walcott, Joseph Brodsky, Mona Van Duyn, & Howard Nemerov

Please send SASE for submission guidelines. Reads throughout the year. Send no more than five poems at one time. Looking for well-crafted poetry in a contemporary idiom which uses meter and the full range of traditional poetic conventions in vigorous and interesting ways. Especially interested in sonnets, couplets, tercet, ballads, and the French forms. Sponsors the annual Howard Nemerov Sonnet Award of $1,000; send SASE for complete details.

frogpond
PO Box 767, Archer, FL 32618-0767
Telephone: (904) 495-9482
Ed and Poetry Ed: Kenneth C. Leibman

Since: 1978	Circ: 700	Pages: 56	Per Year: 4
Size: 5 1/2 X 8 1/2	Saddle stitched	Sample: $5 (U.S.)	Sub: $20 (U.S.)
Copyright: author	Book reviews: yes	Reviews/year: 16	Translations: yes
Interviews: no	Fiction: no	Essays: yes	Copies: 1
Money: no	Time: 1 month		

Authors published: anne mckay, LeRoy Gorman, Elizabeth St Jacques, & Jim Force (Nika)

Publishes haiku as well as related genres: tanka, renga, and senryu. Deadlines for seasonally oriented material: Spring, January 1; Summer, April 1; Autumn, July 1, and Winter, October 1. Inquire first for articles, essays, and book reviews. E-mail address: kenneth@freenet.ufi.edu

FUEL MAGAZINE
PO Box 146640, Chicago, IL 60614
Telephone: (312) 935-1706   Fax: (312) 935-1621
Ed and Poetry Ed: (Ms.) Andy Lowry

Since: 1992	Circ: 1,000	Pages: 40	Per Year: 4
Size: 5 1/2 X 8 1/2	Saddle stitched	Sample: $3	Sub: $10
Copyright: author	Book reviews: no	Reviews/year: n/a	Translations: no
Interviews: no	Fiction: yes	Essays: ?	Copies: yes
Money: ?	Time: 4-6 weeks		

Authors published: Lisa Manning, Sesshu Foster, Larry Oberc, & Patrick McKinnon

We shy away from religious, romance, sci-fi, and most rhyme.

A GATHERING OF THE TRIBES
PO Box 20693, Tompkins Sq. Station, New York, NY 10009
Telephone: (212) 674-3778   Fax: (212) 674-5576
Ed and Poetry Ed: Steve Cannon

Since: 1991	Circ: 2,000	Pages: 86	Per Year: 2
Size: 8 1/2 X 11	Saddle stitched	Sample: $10	Sub: $17.50
Copyright: author	Book reviews: yes	Reviews/year: 4	Translations: yes
Interviews: yes	Fiction: yes	Essays: yes	Copies: yes
Money: yes	Time: 3 months		

Authors published: Amiri Baraka, Jessica Hagedorn, Jayne Cortez, & Emily XYZ

GEORGETOWN REVIEW
Georgetown College, 400 East College Street, Box 227, Georgetown, KY 40324
Telephone: (502) 863-8308
Ed: Steve Carter   Poetry Ed: Michael Campbell

Since: 1993	Circ: 1,000	Pages: 96-112	Per Year: 2
Size: 5 1/4 X 8 1/2	Perfect bound	Sample: $5	Sub: $10
Copyright: author	Book reviews: no	Reviews/year: n/a	Translations: yes
Interviews: yes	Fiction: yes	Essays: no	Copies: 2
Money: ?	Time: 2-4 months		

Authors published: William Greenway, X.J. Kennedy, Fred Chappell, & John Tagliabue

Reading period: September 1 to May 1. The review sponsors a poetry contest with cash prizes; please send SASE for details.

THE GEORGIA REVIEW
The University of Georgia, Athens, GA 30602-9009
Telephone: (706) 542-3481   Fax: (706) 542-0047
Eds: Stanley W. Lindberg, Stephen Corey, & Janet Wondra

Since: 1947	Circ: 7,000	Pages: 208	Per Year: 4
Size: 6 3/4 X 10	Perfect bound	Sample: $7 (U.S.)	Sub: $18 (U.S.)
Copyright: author	Book reviews: yes	Reviews/year: 80-100	Translations: no
Interviews: no	Fiction: yes	Essays: yes	Copies: 1
Money: $3/line	Time: 2-4 months		

Authors published: Rita Dove, Stephen Dunn, Linda Pastan, & Charles Simic
Does not accept submissions during June, July, & August. Please send no more than five poems at a time. No length limit on individual poems.

THE GETTYSBURG REVIEW
Gettysburg College, Gettysburg, PA 17325
Telephone: (717) 337-6770
Ed: Peter Stitt

Since: 1988	Circ: 4,000	Pages: 176	Per Year: 4
Size: 6 3/4 X 10	Perfect bound	Sample: $7	Sub: $18
Copyright: author	Book reviews: no	Reviews/year: n/a	Translations: rarely
Interviews: rarely	Fiction: yes	Essays: yes	Copies: 1
Money: $2/line	Time: 1-3 months		

Authors published: Charles Wright, Pattiann Rogers, Donald Hall, & Marilyn Nelson Waniek
Does not read submissions during June, July, and August. Does not publish traditional book reviews, but does publish critical essays on a single book. Pays $25/page for prose.

GRAHAM HOUSE REVIEW
Colgate University, Box 5000, Hamilton, NY 13346
Telephone: (315) 824-1000, Ex. 262
Eds and Poetry Eds: Peter Balakian & Bruce Smith

GRAND STREET
131 Varick Street, Room 906, New York, NY 10013
Telephone: (212) 807-6548   Fax: (212) 807-6544
Ed: Jean Stein   Poetry Ed: Deborah Treisman

Since: 1981	Circ: 7,000	Pages: 272	Per Year: 4
Size: 7 X 9	Perfect bound	Sample: $15	Sub: $40
Copyright: author	Book reviews: no	Reviews/year: n/a	Translations: yes
Interviews: yes	Fiction: yes	Essays: yes	Copies: yes
Money: yes	Time: 2 months		

Authors published: John Ashbery, James Laughlin, Fanny Howe, & Nicholas Christopher

GREEN FUSE POETRY
3365 Holland Drive, Santa Rosa, CA 95404
Telephone: (707) 544-8303
Ed and Poetry Ed: Brian Boldt

Since: 1984	Circ: 750	Pages: 68	Per Year: 2
Size: 5 1/2 X 8 1/2	Perfect bound	Sample: $4	Sub: $17/3 issues
Copyright: author	Book reviews: no	Reviews/year: n/a	Translations: no
Interviews: no	Fiction: no	Essays: no	Copies: yes

Money: ?   Time: 2 months
Authors published: Denise Levertov, Donald Hall, Laurel Speer, & Antler
Publishes high-quality, accessible free verse concerned with political,
environmental, and social justice issues. Doesn't read manuscripts during
February & March and September & October.

GREEN MOUNTAINS REVIEW

Johnson State College, Johnson, VT 05656
Telephone: (802) 635-2356, Ex. 350
Eds: Neil Shepard, Tony Whedon, & Kate Riley   Poetry Ed: Neil Shepard

Since: 1987	Circ: 1,500	Pages: 140-200	Per Year: 2
Size: 6 X 9	Perfect bound	Sample: $7	Sub: $14
Copyright: author	Book reviews: yes	Reviews/year: 5-6	Translations: yes
Interviews: yes	Fiction: yes	Essays: yes	Copies: yes
Money: ?	Time: 2-3 months		

Authors published: Denise Levertov, Derek Walcott, Maxine Kumin, & Donald Hall
Reading period: September 1 to May 1. Publishes well-known as well as
promising new writers.

THE GREENSBORO REVIEW

The University of North Carolina, Department of English, Room 134, McIver
Building, Greensboro, NC 27412-5001
Telephone: (910) 334-5459   Fax: (910) 334-3281
Ed: Margaret Muichead   Poetry Ed: Leigh Ann Couch

Since: 1966	Circ: 600	Pages: 128	Per Year: 2
Size: 6 X 9	Perfect bound	Sample: $4	Sub: $8
Copyright: see below	Book reviews: no	Reviews/year: n/a	Translations: no
Interviews: no	Fiction: yes	Essays: no	Copies: 3
Money: no	Time: 2-4 months		

Authors published: Stephen Dobyns, A. Manette Ansay, Thomas Lux, & Leon Stokesbury
Considers all poetry regardless of subject, theme, or style. Offers *The Greensboro
Review* Literary Awards. Please send SASE for literary award rules. Copyrights for
magazine but can transfer it to the author.

HANGING LOOSE

231 Wyckoff Street, Brooklyn, NY 11217
Telephone: (212) 206-8465
Eds and Poetry Eds: Robert Hershon, Dick Lourie, Mark Pawlak, & Ron Schreiber

Since: 1966	Circ: 2,000	Pages: 100	Per Year: 2
Size: 7 X 8 1/2	Perfect bound	Sample: $8.50 (U.S.)	Sub: $17.50 (U.S.)/3 issues
Copyright: author	Book reviews: yes	Reviews/year: ?	Translations: yes
Interviews: no	Fiction: yes	Essays: rarely	Copies: 3
Money: yes	Time: 2-3 months		

Authors published: Alden Nowlan, Evelyn Lau, Sherman Alexie, & Kimiko Hahn
Please send SASE for guidelines. Also publishes books through Hanging Loose
Press. Book reviews are "short notices." Institutional subscriptions are $21/3
issues.

HAWAI'I REVIEW

University of Hawai'i, Department of English, 1733 Donaghho Road, Honolulu, HI 96822

Telephone: (808) 956-3030   Fax: (808) 956-9962

Ed: Robert Sean MacBeth   Poetry Ed: Maggie Johnson

Since: 1972	Circ: 5,000	Pages: 150-200	Per Year: 3
Size: varies	Perfect bound	Sample: $5 (U.S.)	Sub: $15 (U.S.)
Copyright: author	Book reviews: no	Reviews/year: n/a	Translations: yes
Interviews: yes	Fiction: yes	Essays: yes	Copies: 2
Money: $10-$200	Time: 2 months		

Authors published: W.S. Merwin, Terese Svoboda, Richard Kostelanetz, & Sylvie Bourassa

Interested in Canadian writing. Has published Margaret Atwood, Earle Birney, Steven Heighton, and Michael Ondaatje. Seeks experimental, hard-hitting, brutal verse that leaves you with the sensation that in some unseen topography of your body (along the optic nerve, in the larynx) lightning has just erupted. Wants marginalia of all kinds. Does not want religious or carping, sentimental monologues.

HAYDEN'S FERRY REVIEW

Arizona State Unicersity, Box 871502, Tempe, AZ 85287-1502

Telephone: (602) 965-1243   Fax: (602) 965-8484

Ed: Salima Keegan

Since: 1986	Circ: 600	Pages: 128	Per Year: 2
Size: 6 X 9	Perfect bound	Sample: $6	Sub: $10
Copyright: author	Book reviews: yes	Reviews/year: 2	Translations: yes
Interviews: yes	Fiction: yes	Essays: yes	Copies: yes
Money: no	Time: 2-3 months		

Authors published: Tess Gallagher, Raymond Carver, Rita Dove, & David St. John

Please send SASE for publication guidelines. Send only six poems per submission. Uses eight black and white artworks inside each issue plus one colour artwork on the cover.

HEAVEN BONE

PO Box 486, Chester, NY 10918

Telephone: (914) 469-9018   Fax: (914) 469-7880

Ed and Poetry Ed: Steven Hirsch

Since: 1986	Circ: 2,500	Pages: 96	Per Year: 1
Size: 8 1/2 X 11	Saddle stitched	Sample: $6	Sub: $16.95/4 issues
Copyright: author	Book reviews: yes	Reviews/year: 7-10	Translations: yes
Interviews: yes	Fiction: yes	Essays: yes	Copies: 2
Money: ?	Time: 1-6 months		

Authors published: Diane Di Prima, Charles Bukowski, Michael McClure, & Rene Daumal

Please send SASE for submission guidelines. Editor loves the poetry of Rainer Maria Rilke. The editor also has Buddhist tendencies. The bottom line is inspiration, bringing something of the gods down into the flesh and bone of our normal, spectacularly ordinary experiences. Runs an International Chapbook Competition; send SASE for contest guidelines.

HELLAS, A Journal of Poetry and the Humanities
304 South Tyson Avenue, Glenside, PA 19038
Telephone: (215) 884-1086   Fax: (215) 884-3304
Ed and Poetry Ed: Gerald Harnett

Since: 1989	Circ: 750	Pages: 160	Per Year: 2
Size: 6 X 9	Perfect bound	Sample: $8.75	Sub: $18
Copyright: author	Book reviews: yes	Reviews/year: 6	Translations: no
Interviews: no	Fiction: no	Essays: yes	Copies: 1
Money: no	Time: 3-4 months		

Authors published: Dana Gioia, Molly Peacock, Timothy Steele, & X.J. Kennedy

Metrical poetry preferred. Associated with the Aldine Press, which offers The Lyrica Award for a chapbook manuscript of metrical poetry. Please send SASE for contest data.

HIGH PLAINS LITERARY REVIEW
180 Adams Street, #250, Denver, CO 80206
Telephone: (303) 320-6828
Ed: Robert O. Greer, Jr.   Poetry Eds: Ray Gonzalez & Joy Harjo

Since: 1986	Circ: ?	Pages: 115	Per Year: 3
Size: ?	Perfect bound	Sample: $4	Sub: $20
Copyright: author	Book reviews: yes	Reviews/year: 6	Translations: no
Interviews: yes	Fiction: yes	Essays: yes	Copies: 2
Money: ?	Time: 2-3 months		

Authors published: William Pitt Root, Denise Thomas, Robert Dana, & Pamela Stewart

Pays $10 for essays, $5 for fiction.

INDIANA REVIEW
Indiana University, 316 North Jordan Avenue, Bloomington, IN 47408
Telephone: (812) 855-3439
Eds: Shirley Stephenson & Geoffrey Pollock   Poetry Ed: Shirley Stephenson

Since: 1976	Circ: 2,000	Pages: 200	Per Year: 2
Size: ?	Prefect bound	Sample: $7	Sub: $12
Copyright: author	Book reviews: yes	Reviews/year: 20	Translations: yes
Interviews: yes	Fiction: yes	Essays: yes	Copies: 2
Money: $5	Time: 2-3 months		

Authors published: Charles Simic, Joy Harjo, Alberto Rios, & Taslima Nasreen

Interested in both craft and content. We appreciate writing that addresses relevant social issues without sacrificing form or style. Open to new writers. Reads all year.

INTERIM
University of Nevada, Department of English, 4505 Maryland Parkway, Box 455011, Las Vegas, NV 89154-5011
Eds: A. Wilber Stevens, James Hazen, Joe McCullough, & Timothy Erwin

Since: 1981	Circ: ?	Pages: 48	Per Year: 2
Size: 6 X 9	Perfect bound	Sample: $	Sub: $16
Copyright: ?	Book reviews: no	Reviews/year: n/a	Translations: ?
Interviews: ?	Fiction: yes	Essays: ?	Copies: ?
Money: ?	Time: ?		

Authors published: Gary Sloboda, Ruth Beker, Sean Rima, & Christine Delea

Fiction limit: 8,000 words.

INTERNATIONAL POETRY REVIEW

The University of North Carolina, Department of Romance Languages, Greensboro, NC 27412-5001

Telephone: (910) 334-5655 Fax: (910) 334-5358

Ed and Poetry Ed: Mark Smith-Soto

Since: 1975	Circ: 500	Pages: 100	Per Year: 2
Size: 5 1/2 X 8 1/2	Perfect bound	Sample: $5	Sub: $10
Copyright: author	Book reviews: yes	Reviews/year: 2	Translations: yes
Interviews: no	Fiction: no	Essays: seldom	Copies: yes
Money: no	Time: 3 months		

Authors published: Fred Chappell, Lili Bita, Coleman Barks, & Pierre Chatillon

Two-thirds of each issue is dedicated to poetry in translation with facing originals. One-third is original English-language poetry with an emphasis on international or cross-cultural themes.

THE IOWA REVIEW

University of Iowa, 308 EPB, Iowa City, IA 52242

Telephone: (319) 335-0462 Fax: (319) 335-2535

Eds: David Hamilton & Mary Hussmann

Since: 1970	Circ: 1,500	Pages: 200	Per Year: 3
Size: 6 X 9	Perfect bound	Sample: $6	Sub: $18
Copyright: author	Book reviews: yes	Reviews/year: 2-5	Translations: yes
Interviews: yes	Fiction: yes	Essays: yes	Copies: 2
Money: $1/line	Time: 1-2 months		

Authors published: Chase Twichell, James Laughlin, Jim Daniels, & Marianne Boruch

Submit poems between September 1 and April 1, the earlier in the period the better. Pays $1/line for poetry ($25 min.) and $10/page for prose.

JACARANDA

California State University, English Department, Fullerton, CA 92634

Telephone: (714) 773-3163 Fax: (714) 449-5954

Ed: Cornel Bonca   Poetry Ed: Bruce Kijewski

Since: 1985	Circ: 1,500	Pages: 150	Per Year: 2
Size: 5 1/2 X 8	Perfect bound	Sample: $6	Sub: $10
Copyright: author	Book reviews: yes	Reviews/year: 10	Translations: yes
Interviews: yes	Fiction: yes	Essays: yes	Copies: 3
Money: ?	Time: 2 months		

Authors published: Carolyn Forché, Craig Raine, Charles Bukowski, & Billy Collins

Submissions accepted all year round. Conducts a poetry contest for each issue; send SASE for complete information. E-mail address: jacaranda@edept.fullerton.edu

THE JOURNAL

Ohio State University, Department of English, 164 West 17th Avenue, Columbus, OH 43210

Telephone: (614) 292-4076

Eds: Kathy Fagan & Michelle Herman   Poetry Ed: Kathy Fagan

KANSAS QUARTERLY/ARKANSAS REVIEW
PO Box 1890, Arkansas State University, Department of English & Philosophy,
State University, AR 72467
Ed: Norman Lavers

Since: 1968	Circ: 1,050	Pages: 160	Per Year: 4
Size: ?	Perfect bound	Sample: $6	Sub: $20
Copyright: ?	Book reviews: no	Reviews/year: n/a	Translations: ?
Interviews: no	Fiction: yes	Essays: yes	Copies: 2
Money: no	Time: 3 months		

Focus is almost entirely on fiction and creative non-fiction. Will publish, at most,
two or three poets per issue.

THE KENYON REVIEW
Kenyon College, Gambier, OH 43022
Telephone: (614) 427-3339   Fax: (614) 427-5417
Eds: David H. Lynn & Cy Wainscott

Since: 1939	Circ: 5,000	Pages: 185	Per Year: 3
Size: 7 X 10	Perfect bound	Sample: $8 (U.S.)	Sub: $22 (U.S.)
Copyright: author	Book reviews: yes	Reviews/year: 9	Translations: yes
Interviews: yes	Fiction: yes	Essays: yes	Copies: 2
Money: $15/page	Time: 3-4 months		

Authors published: May Swenson, Tom Disch, Carol Muske, & Robyn Selman
Pays $15 (U.S.)/page for poetry; $10 (U.S.)/page for prose. Does not read
during April to August. Send SASE for information sheet. Considers all genres of
poetry, fiction, and non-fiction. Does not accept unsolicited book reviews.

KUUMBA
PO Box 83912, Los Angeles, CA 90083-0912
Telephone: (310) 410-0808   Fax: (310) 410-9250
Ed and Poetry Ed: Mark Haile

Since: 1991	Circ: 1,000	Pages: 48	Per Year: 2
Size: 8 1/4 X 11	Saddle stitched	Sample: $4.50	Sub: $7.50
Copyright: author	Book reviews: no	Reviews/year: n/a	Translations: yes
Interviews: no	Fiction: no	Essays: no	Copies: yes
Money: no	Time: 1 month		

Authors published: Sabrina Sojourner, Mark Simmons, Karen Augustine, & Richard D. Gore
Dedicated to the celebration of the lives and experiences of Black lesbians and
gay men. An all-verse publication, spiced with an occasional drawing. Welcomes
both new and experienced poets.

THE LAUREL REVIEW
Northwest Missouri State University, Department of English, Maryville, MO 64468
Telephone: (816) 562-1265   Fax: (816) 562-1484
Eds and Poetry Eds: William Trowbridge, David Slater, & Beth Richards

Since: 1960	Circ: 900	Pages: 132	Per Year: 2
Size: 6 X 9	Perfect bound	Sample: $3.50	Sub: $8
Copyright: author	Book reviews: no	Reviews/year: n/a	Translations: no
Interviews: no	Fiction: yes	Essays: yes	Copies: 2
Money: ?	Time: 1-4 months		

Authors published: Howard Nemerov, Patricia Goedicke, Miller Williams, & Nancy Willard

Does not read June through August. Nothing matters except our perception that the poem or story presents something powerfully felt by the writer.

THE LITERARY REVIEW

Fairleigh Dickinson University, 285 Madison Avenue, Madison, NJ 07940
Telephone: (201) 593-8564   Fax: same
Eds and Poetry Eds: Walter Cummins, Martin Green, Harry Keyishian, & William Zander

Since: 1957	Circ: 2,500	Pages: 128	Per Year: 4
Size: 6 X 9	Perfect bound	Sample: $6	Sub: $21
Copyright: author	Book reviews: yes	Reviews/year: 10	Translations: yes
Interviews: yes	Fiction: yes	Essays: yes	Copies: 2
Money: no	Time: 2-3 months		

Authors published: Burton Raffel, Ron deMars, Steve Wilson, & Jeff Wosley

Reads all year. Prefers no more than 5 poems per submission. Open to any format or style, ranging from traditional to experimental.

LONG SHOT

PO Box 6238, Hoboken, NJ 07030
Eds and Poetry Eds: Danny Shot, Nancy Mercado, & Lynn Breifeller

Since: 1982	Circ: 200	Pages: 192	Per Year: 2
Size: 5 1/2 X 8 1/2	Perfect bound	Sample: $8	Sub: $22/4 issues
Copyright: author	Book reviews: no	Reviews/year: n/a	Translations: no
Interviews: no	Fiction: yes	Essays: yes	Copies: 2
Money: no	Time: 3 months		

Authors published: Abbie Hoffman, Sean Penn, Marrianne Faithfull, & Tom Waits

LOUISIANA LITERATURE

Southeastern Louisiana University, SLU 792, Hammond, LA 70402
Telephone: (504) 549-5022   Fax: (504) 549-5021
Ed: David Hanson   Poetry Ed: Jack Bedell

Since: 1984	Circ: 500	Pages: 100-150	Per Year: 2
Size: 6 3/4 X 9 3/4	Perfect bound	Sample: $7.50	Sub: $15
Copyright: author	Book reviews: yes	Reviews/year: 6-10	Translations: yes
Interviews: yes	Fiction: yes	Essays: yes	Copies: 2
Money: no	Time: 1-2 months		

Authors published: Elton Glaser, Judy Longley, Al Maginnes, & Heather Ross Miller

We welcome poetry on any topic; however, we especially seek work related to our regional interests: for example, a topic engaging readers both here and in Canada might be Acadian culture.

LULLWATER REVIEW

Emory University, PO Box 22036, Atlanta, GA 30322
Telephone: (404) 727-6184
Ed: Marci C. Eggers   Poetry Ed: Eric Brignac

Since: 1990	Circ: 2,000	Pages: 100	Per Year: 2
Size: 6 X 9	Perfect bound	Sample: $5	Sub: $12
Copyright: author	Book reviews: no	Reviews/year: n/a	Translations: yes
Interviews: yes	Fiction: yes	Essays: no	Copies: ?
Money: ?	Time: 1-3 months		

Authors published: Colette Inez, Charles Edward Eaton, Harriet Zinnes, & Eve Shelmutt

Accepts submissions throughout the year. Considers all styles and forms. Also interested in drama.

THE MacGUFFIN
Schoolcraft College, 18600 Haggerty Road, Livonia, MI 48152-2696
Telephone: (313) 462-4400, Ex. 5327   Fax: (313) 462-4558
Ed: Arthur J. Lindenberg   Poetry Ed: Elizabeth J. Hebron

Since: 1984	Circ: 500	Pages: 144	Per Year: 3
Size: 5 1/2 X 8 1/2	Perfect bound	Sample: $4	Sub: $12
Copyright: author	Book reviews: no	Reviews/year: n/a	Translations: yes
Interviews: no	Fiction: yes	Essays: yes	Copies: 2
Money: ?	Time: 10-12 weeks		

Authors published: Diane Wakoski, Jim Daniels, Barbara Lefcowitz, & Phillip Sterling
Publishes one theme issue each year; please send SASE for guidelines. Will accept traditional and experimental writing. No pornography, light verse, or concrete poetry.

MĀNOA: A Pacific Journal of International Writing
University of Hawai'i, Department of English, 1733 Donaghho Road, Honolulu, HI 96822
Telephone: (808) 956-3070   Fax: (808) 956-3083
Ed and Poetry Ed: Frank Stewart

Since: 1988	Circ: 2,000	Pages: 240	Per Year: 2
Size: 7 X 10	Perfect bound	Sample: $10 (U.S.)	Sub: $20 (U.S.)
Copyright: author	Book reviews: yes	Reviews/year: 25	Translations: yes
Interviews: yes	Fiction: yes	Essays: yes	Copies: yes
Money: yes	Time: 6 weeks		

Authors published: W.S. Merwin, Robert Creeley, Arthur Sze, & Alberto Rios
Welcomes good poetry from all geographical regions.

THE MASSACHUSETTS REVIEW
University of Massachusetts, Memorial Hall, Amherst, MA 01003
Telephone: (413) 545-2689
Eds: Mary Heath, Jules Chametzky, & Paul Jenkins   Poetry Eds: Paul Jenkins, Anne Halley, & Martin Espada

Since: 1959	Circ: 2,000	Pages: 160	Per Year: 4
Size: 5 X 8	Perfect bound	Sample: $5	Sub: $15
Copyright: author	Book reviews: no	Reviews/year: n/a	Translations: yes
Interviews: yes	Fiction: yes	Essays: yes	Copies: 2
Money: $10	Time: 1-2 months		

Authors published: William Carlos Williams, Adrienne Rich, James Tate, & Amy Clampitt
Pays 35 cents/line for poetry ($10 min.). Poetry submissions welcome September 15 to June 1.

MAYFLY
4634 Hale Drive, Decatur, IL 62526
Telephone: (217) 877-2966
Eds and Poetry Eds: Randy & Shirley Brooks

Since: 1986	Circ: 300	Pages: 16	Per Year: 2
Size: 3 1/2 X 5	Saddle stitched	Sample: $3.50	Sub: $8
Copyright: author	Book reviews: no	Reviews/year: n/a	Translations: no

Interviews: no	Fiction: no	Essays: no	Copies: no
Money: $5/poem	Time: 3-4 months		

Authors published: Michael Dudley, LeRoy Gorman, George Swede, & Jean Jorgensen.

Haiku only; please submit only five haiku per issue.

MICHIGAN QUARTERLY REVIEW
University of Michigan, 3032 Rackham Building, Ann Arbor, MI 48109-1070
Telephone: (313) 764-9265
Ed and Poetry Ed: Laurence Goldstein

Since: 1962	Circ: 2,000	Pages: 160	Per Year: 4
Size: 6 X 9	Perfect bound	Sample: $2.50 (U.S.)	Sub: $18 (U.S.)
Copyright: author	Book reviews: yes	Reviews/year: 16	Translations: yes
Interviews: yes	Fiction: yes	Essays: yes	Copies: yes
Money: $8/page	Time: 1-2 months		

Authors published: Margaret Atwood, Evelyn Lau, Richard Howard, & Philip Levine

Only publishes about twelve pages of poetry per issue, so this is not a market for beginners.

MID-AMERICAN REVIEW
Bowling Green State University, Department of English, Bowling Green, OH 43403
Ed: George Looney, Rebecca Meacham, & Tony Gardner   Poetry Ed: Tony Gardner

Since: 1980	Circ: 600	Pages: 200	Per Year: 2
Size: 5 1/2 X 8 1/2	Perfect bound	Sample: $5	Sub: $12
Copyright: author	Book reviews: yes	Reviews/year: 10-15	Translations: yes
Interviews: no	Fiction: yes	Essays: yes	Copies: 2
Money: $10/page	Time: 1-2 months		

Authors published: Stephen Dunn, Albert Goldbarth, Naomi Shihab Nye, & Greg Pape

Almost never accepts interviews, query first. Does not read poetry between May and September. Poems should emanate from strong, evocative images. Use language with an awareness of how words sound and mean, and have a definite sense of voice. Each line must help carry the poem. An individual vision should be evident. Please send SASE for guidelines.

MIND MATTERS REVIEW
2040 Polk Street, Box 234, San Francisco, CA 94109
Telephone: (415) 775-4545
Ed: Carrie Drake, Lorraine A. Donfor, Benny Williams, & David Castleman   Poetry Ed: Lorraine A. Donfor

Since: 1988	Circ: 1,000	Pages: 58	Per Year: varies
Size: 8 1/2 X 11	Saddle stitched	Sample: $4	Sub: $15
Copyright: author	Book reviews: yes	Reviews/year: 30-40	Translations: no
Interviews: yes	Fiction: no	Essays: yes	Copies: yes
Money: ?	Time: 2-3 months		

Authors published: Rod Farmer, Desoree Thompson, T.N. Turner, & Atar Hadari

Looking for poems that offer inspiration for atheists. Will not consider sexually graphic poems.

the minnesota review
East Carolina University, Department of English, Greenville, NC 27858-4353
Telephone: (919) 328-6388   Fax: (919) 328-4889

Ed: Jeffrey Williams

Since: 1960	Circ: 1,500	Pages: 200	Per Year: 2
Size: 5 1/2 X 8 1/2	Perfect bound	Sample: $7.50 (U.S.)	Sub: $15 (U.S.)
Copyright: author	Book reviews: yes	Reviews/year: 20	Translations: yes
Interviews: yes	Fiction: yes	Essays: yes	Copies: yes
Money: no	Time: 2 months		

Authors published: Anna Leahy, Alvin Greenberg, Elizabeth Hahn, & Kevin Griffith

Often publishes theme issues; please send SASE for information on upcoming special issues. Particularly likes poems that deal with social, political, work, and women's issues.

MISSISSIPPI REVIEW

The University of Southern Mississippi, Box 5144, Hattiesburg, MS 39406-5144

Telephone: (601) 266-4321   Fax: (601) 266-5757

Ed: Frederick Barthelme   Poetry Eds: Angela Ball & D.C. Berry

Since: 1971	Circ: 2,000	Pages: 150	Per Year: 2
Size: 5 X 8	Perfect bound	Sample: $8	Sub: $15
Copyright: author	Book reviews: no	Reviews/year: n/a	Translations: yes
Interviews: yes	Fiction: yes	Essays: yes	Copies: 5
Money: ?	Time: 4-6 weeks		

Authors published: Rita Dove, Guillaume Apollinaire (in trans.), Wendy Bishop, & Michael Waters

THE MISSOURI REVIEW

University of Missouri, 1507 Hillcrest Hall, Columbia, MO 65211

Telephone: (314) 882-4474

Eds: Speer Morgan & Greg Michalson   Poetry Ed: Greg Michalson

Since: 1978	Circ: 6,800	Pages: 208	Per Year: 3
Size: 6 X 9	Perfect bound	Sample: $6	Sub: $15
Copyright: author	Book reviews: yes	Reviews/year: 50-60	Translations: yes
Interviews: yes	Fiction: yes	Essays: yes	Copies: 3
Money: yes	Time: 8-10 weeks		

Authors published: James Tate, Maureen Seaton, Walter McDonald, & Gillian Conoley

Copyright reverts to author upon written request. Each issue features 3 to 5 poets with 6 to 10 pages per poet. Thus, large submissions are required. Pays $125 to $250 for poetry features. Book reviews are very brief.

MODERN HAIKU

PO Box 1752, Madison, WI 53701

Telephone: (608) 233-2738

Ed and Poetry Ed: Robert Spiess

Since: 1969	Circ: 700	Pages: 96	Per Year: 3
Size: 5 1/2 X 8 1/2	Perfect bound	Sample: $5.65 (U.S.)	Sub: $18.50 (U.S.)
Copyright: author	Book reviews: yes	Reviews/year: 28	Translations: yes
Interviews: few	Fiction: no	Essays: yes	Copies: no
Money: $1/haiku	Time: 2 weeks		

Authors published: George Swede, anne mckay, LeRoy Gorman, & Jean Jorgensen

Haiku only. Prefers haiku of insight, depth, intuition and suchness. All essays and articles must relate to haiku. Pays $5/page for prose.

MSS / NEW MYTHS

State University of New York, Binghamton, NY 13902-6000

Ed and Poetry Ed: D. Mooney

THE NATION

72 Fifth Avenue, New York, NY 10011-8046

Ed: Katrina vanden Hewel   Poetry Ed: Grace Schulman

Since: 1865	Circ: ?	Pages: ?	Per Year: 52
Size: ?	Binding: ?	Sample: $5	Sub: $48
Copyright: yes	Book reviews: yes	Reviews/year: ?	Translations: yes
Interviews: no	Fiction: yes	Essays: yes	Copies: ?
Money: $35/poem	Time: ?		

Authors published: W.B. Yeats, D.H. Lawrence, Marianne Moore, & W.S. Merwin

Copyright will be assigned to author upon request. Seeks shorter poems of excellence. As to longer poems, interviews, and essays: anything really good is worth a try.

NATIONAL FORUM

Auburn University, 129 Quad Center, Mell Street, Auburn, AL 36849-5306

Telephone: (334) 844-5200   Fax: (334) 844-5994

Eds: James P. Kaetz, Mary Wood Littleton, & Stephanie Johns Bond

Since: 1920	Circ: 118,000	Pages: 48	Per Year: 4
Size: 8 1/2 X 11	Saddle stitched	Sample: $6.25	Sub: $25
Copyright: author	Book reviews: yes	Reviews/year: n/a	Translations: no
Interviews: yes	Fiction: no	Essays: yes	Copies: 10
Money: ?	Time: 3-4 months		

Authors published: Molly Tamarkin, Stephen Todd Booker, Martha Stainsby, & Dean Kostos

All prose (reviews, interviews, essays) are written in-house or are by invitation only. Accepts short poems (one page long or less) and prints 15 to 25 per year. This quarterly is the journal of the Honor Society of Phi Kappa Phi.

THE NEBRASKA REVIEW

University of Nebraska, Fine Arts Building, 212, Omaha, NE 68182-0324

Telephone: (402) 554-2771   Fax: (402) 554-3436

Eds: Art Homer, Richard Duggin, Susan Aizenberg, & J. Reed   Poetry Ed: Susan Aizenberg

Since: 1972	Circ: 600	Pages: 84	Per Year: 2
Size: 5 1/2 X 8 1/2	Perfect bound	Sample: $2	Sub: $9
Copyright: author	Book reviews: no	Reviews/year: n/a	Translations: no
Interviews: no	Fiction: yes	Essays: no	Copies: yes
Money: no	Time: 3-6 months		

Authors published: David Rivard, Pamela Stewart, Thomas Swiss, & Erin Belieu

Reading period for open poetry submissions: January 1 to April 15. Reading period for the poetry contest: August 15 to November 30. Please send SASE for contest information. Wants lyric poetry from 10 to 200 lines, preference being for under 100 lines. Subject matter is unimportant. Poets should have mastered form, meaning poems should have form, not simply "demonstrate" it. No concrete poetry; no inspirational, didactic, or merely political poetry.

NEGATIVE CAPABILITY

62 Ridgelawn Drive East, Mobile, AL 36608-6116
Telephone: (334) 343-6163   Fax: (334) 344-8478
Ed and Poetry Ed: Sue Walker

Since: 1981	Circ: 1,000	Pages: 200	Per Year: 3
Size: 5 1/2 X 8 1/2	Perfect bound	Sample: $5	Sub: $18
Copyright: author	Book reviews: yes	Reviews/year: 6	Translations: yes
Interviews: yes	Fiction: yes	Essays: yes	Copies: 1
Money: n/a	Time: 6 weeks		

Authors published: Margaret Atwood, W.D. Snodgrass, Marge Piercy, & Jimmy Carter

Has published an issue that featured Canadian writers— Margaret Atwood, Graeme Gibson, Anne Marriott, Leon Rooke, Susan Musgrave, Barbara Wilson. Runs annual competitions for poetry and fiction; send SASE for information. Open in terms of subject matter and form, but no pornography, please.

NEW AMERICAN WRITING

2920 West Pratt, Chicago, IL 60645-4291
Eds and Poetry Eds: Maxine Chernoff & Paul Hoover

NEW ENGLAND REVIEW

Middlebury College, Middlebury, VT 05753
Telephone: (802) 388-3711, Ex. 5075
Eds and Poetry Eds: David Huddle & William Lychack

NEW ORLEANS REVIEW

Loyola University, English Department, New Orleans, LA 70118
Telephone: (504) 865-2295   Fax: (504) 865-2294
Ed and Poetry Ed: Ralph Adamo

Since: 1968	Circ: 700	Pages: 150	Per Year: 4
Size: 6 X 9	Perfect bound	Sample: $7	Sub: $18
Copyright: author	Book reviews: yes	Reviews/year: 10-15	Translations: yes
Interviews: yes	Fiction: yes	Essays: yes	Copies: 5
Money: rarely	Time: 3 months		

Authors published: Rodney Jones, Dave Smith, Jake Berry, & William Matthews

Sometimes publishes special issues; please send SASE for advance information.

THE NEW YORKER

20 West 43rd Street, New York, NY 10036
Telephone: (212) 536-5700
Ed: Tina Brown   Poetry Ed: Alice Quinn

Since: 1925	Circ: 800,000	Pages: 110	Per Year: 50
Size: 8 1/2 X 11	Saddle stitched	Sample: $2.50	Sub: $36
Copyright: author	Book reviews: yes	Reviews/year: many	Translations: yes
Interviews: rarely	Fiction: yes	Essays: yes	Copies: yes
Money: yes	Time: 1 month		

Authors published: Eric Ormsby, W.S. Merwin, Ted Hughes, & Jorie Graham

Very much interested in short stories and essays. Pays top rates. Please send poetry in packets of up to five poems.

NEXUS

Wright State University, Wo16a, Student Union, Dayton, OH 45435
Telephone: (513) 873-5533   Fax: (513) 873-5535
Ed: Tara L. Miller

Since: 1967	Circ: 1,500	Pages: 96-128	Per Year: 3
Size: 7 X 10	Binding: ?	Sample: $5	Sub: $18
Copyright: author	Book reviews: yes	Reviews/year: ?	Translations: yes
Interviews: yes	Fiction: yes	Essays: yes	Copies: 2
Money: no	Time: 2-3 months		

Authors published: Anne Coray-Alaska, Simon Perchik, Scarecrow, & James Graham
Does not usually consider submissions sent during the summer. Most readers are students.

NIMROD

Arts & Humanities Council of Tulsa, 2210 South Main Street, Tulsa, OK
74114-1190
Telephone: (918) 584-3333   Fax: (918) 582-2787
Eds: Francine Ringold, Cheryl Gravis, & Manly Johnson   Poetry Ed: Manly Johnson

Since: 1956	Circ: 3,000	Pages: 160	Per Year: 2
Size: 6 X 9	Perfect bound	Sample: $8 (U.S.)	Sub: $15 (U.S.)
Copyright: author	Book reviews: no	Reviews/year: n/a	Translations: yes
Interviews: yes	Fiction: yes	Essays: yes	Copies: 2
Money: $5-$25	Time: 3-5 months		

Authors published: Lorna Crozier, Gary Geddes, Steven Heighton, & Tess Gallagher
Offers the Pablo Neruda Prize for Poetry. Send SASE for contest rules and guidelines. Is very interested in international poetry and looks for writing that is fresh, vigorous, distinctive, seriously humorous, unflinchingly serious, ironic, whatever— just so long as it is high quality.

NORTH COAST REVIEW

PO Box 103, Duluth, MN 55801-0103
Telephone: (218) 728-3728
Eds and Poetry Eds: Patrick McKinnon, Ellie Schoenfeld, & Andrea McKinnon

Since: 1992	Circ: 1,000	Pages: 56	Per Year: 2-3
Size: 8 1/2 X 7	Saddle stitched	Sample: $3.50 (U.S.)	Sub: $19.50 (U.S.)/6 issues
Copyright: author	Book reviews: no	Reviews/year: n/a	Translations: yes
Interviews: no	Fiction: no	Essays: no	Copies: 3-5
Money: $10	Time: 5 months		

Authors published: Al Hunter, Barton Sutter, Susan Hauser, & Leo Dangel
Looks for quality; looks for poetry that is hard-edged, clear, honest, and grounded in rural values.

NORTH DAKOTA QUARTERLY

University of North Dakota, Department of English, Box 8237, University Station,
Grand Forks, ND 58202-8237
Telephone: (701) 777-2703   Fax: (701) 777-3650
Ed: Robert Lewis   Poetry Ed: Jay Meek

THE NORTH STONE REVIEW

Box 14098, D Station, Minneapolis, MN 55414
Telephone: (612) 721-8011

Eds and Poetry Eds: James Naiden, Jack Jarpe, Allen Topper, & Anne Duggan

Since: 1971	Circ: 2,000	Pages: 250	Per Year: 1-2
Size: 5 1/2 X 8	Perfect bound	Sample: $10	Sub: $20
Copyright: magazine	Book reviews: yes	Reviews/year: ?	Translations: yes
Interviews: ?	Fiction: yes	Essays: yes	Copies: 2
Money: no	Time: 1 month		

Authors published: Robert Bly, David Ignatow, Cynthia Chinelly, & Edward Dyck

Magazine holds copyright, but will grant permission to reprint.

PAINTBRUSH
Northeast Missouri State Universiy, Language & Literature Division, Kirksville, MO 63501
Telephone: (816) 785-4000
Ed and Poetry Ed: Ben Bennani

THE PARIS REVIEW
541 East 72nd Street, New York, NY 10021
Telephone: (212) 861-0016   Fax: (212) 861-4504
Ed: George Plimpton   Poetry Ed: Richard Howard

Since: 1953	Circ: 15,000	Pages: 304	Per Year: 4
Size: 5 1/4 X 8 1/2	Perfect bound	Sample: $11	Sub: $42
Copyright: author	Book reviews: no	Reviews/year: n/a	Translations: yes
Interviews: yes	Fiction: yes	Essays: yes	Copies: yes
Money: yes	Time: 1-2 months		

Authors published: John Ashbery, Carolyn Kizer, A.R. Ammons, & Jorie Graham

PARNASSUS: Poetry in Review
205 West 89th Street, #8F, New York, NY 10024
Telephone: (212) 362-3492   Fax: (212) 875-0148
Ed and Poetry Ed: Herbert Leibowitz

Since: 1972	Circ: 2,500	Pages: 350	Per Year: 2
Size: ?	Perfect bound	Sample: $15	Sub: $29
Copyright: author	Book reviews: yes	Reviews/year: 30+	Translations: rarely
Interviews: no	Fiction: rarely	Essays: yes	Copies: 3
Money: $50-$100	Time: 2 months		

Authors published: Seamus Heaney, Joseph Brodsky, Adrienne Rich, & Richard Howard

The review is primarily dedicated to publishing long essays/reviews in a non-academic style. Almost never publishes unsolicited poetry. Pays $50 to $100 for poetry; $150 to $250 for long reviews.

PARTISAN REVIEW
236 Bay State Road, Boston, MA 02215
Telephone: (617) 353-4260   Fax: (617) 353-7444
Eds: William Phillips & Edith Kurzweil   Poetry Ed: Rosanna Warren

Since: 1934	Circ: 9,000	Pages: 160	Per Year: 4
Size: 6 X 9	Perfect bound	Sample: $6.50	Sub: $22
Copyright: author	Book reviews: yes	Reviews/year: 10-15	Translations: yes
Interviews: yes	Fiction: yes	Essays: yes	Copies: yes
Money: yes	Time: 8-10 weeks		

Authors published: Joseph Brodsky, Charles Simic, Richard Tillinghast, & David Ferry

THE PENNSYLVANIA REVIEW

University of Pittsburgh, English Department, Room 526, Cathedral of Learning, Pittsburgh, PA 15260
Telephone: (412) 624-0026
Ed and Poetry Ed: Julie Parson-Nesbitt

PHOEBE: A Journal of Literary Arts

George Mason University, 4400 University Drive, Fairfax, VA 22030
Telephone: (703) 993-2915
Ed: Graham Foust   Poetry Ed: Kenneth May

Since: 1970	Circ: 1,000	Pages: 85	Per Year: 2
Size: ?	Perfect bound	Sample: $6	Sub: $12
Copyright: author	Book reviews: no	Reviews/year: n/a	Translations: yes
Interviews: yes	Fiction: yes	Essays: yes	Copies: 2
Money: ?	Time: 1 month		

Authors published: C.K. Williams, Bill Knott, Gillian Conoley, & Leslie Scalapino

Considers quality work in both traditional and experimental veins. Wants poetry that makes your hands sweat when you touch it.

PIG IRON

PO Box 237, Youngstown, OH 44501
Telephone: (216) 747-6932   Fax: (216) 747-0599
Ed and Poetry Ed: Jim Villani

Since: 1975	Circ: 1,000	Pages: 128	Per Year: 1
Size: 8 1/2 X 11	Perfect bound	Sample: $5	Sub: $8/annual
Copyright: author	Book reviews: no	Reviews/year: n/a	Translations: yes
Interviews: no	Fiction: yes	Essays: yes	Copies: 2
Money: $5/poem	Time: 4 months		

Authors published: Jennifer Footman, James Bertolino, Laurel Speer, & Warren Woessner

Each issue is a theme issue. Send SASE for information and guidelines. Some themes are: Jazz Tradition (1996); Frontier (1997); the 1960s (1998); Religion in Modernity (1999); the 20th Century (2000). Interested in Canadian writing. Runs the Kenneth Patchen Competition for poetry and fiction book-length manuscripts. Cash prize plus publication.

THE PITTSBURGH QUARTERLY

36 Haberman Avenue, Pittsburgh, PA 15211-2144
Telephone: (412) 431-8885
Canadian mail drop:
c/o James Deahl
237 Prospect Street South
Hamilton, Ontario, L8M 2Z6
Telephone: (905) 312-1779
Ed and Poetry Ed: Frank Correnti

Since: 1991	Circ: 500	Pages: 75	Per Year: 4
Size: 5 1/2 X 8 1/2	Saddle stitched	Sample: $5 (Cdn)	Sub: $20 (Cdn)
Copyright: author	Book reviews: yes	Reviews/year: 12	Translations: yes
Interviews: yes	Fiction: yes	Essays: yes	Copies: 1
Money: no	Time: 1 year		

Authors published: George Amabile, Sheila Hyland, Michael Dudley, & John Castlebury

Payment by Canadians for sample/sub should be sent to the Canadian address. Cheques should be made out to "James Deahl." Publishes Canadian poems and stories in almost every issue. Seeks poems and fictions that bear the handprint of necessity. Open to all forms of writing from epics to haiku. Send only work that demands to be read more than once. Offers the Sara Henderson Hay Prize for Poetry. Please send SASE for contest rules.

PLOUGHSHARES
Emerson College, 100 Beacon Street, Boston, MA 02116-1596
Telephone: (617) 578-8753
Ed: Don Lee   Poetry Ed: David Daniel

Since: 1971	Circ: 6,000	Pages: 250	Per Year: 3
Size: 5 1/2 X 8 1/2	Perfect bound	Sample: $8.95	Sub: $19
Copyright: magazine	Book reviews: yes	Reviews/year: 15-20	Translations: yes
Interviews: no	Fiction: yes	Essays: yes	Copies: yes
Money: $20/page	Time: 3-5 months		

Authors published: Ian Seibles, Maureen Seaton, Martin Espada, & Maurya Simon

Reading period: August 1 to March 31. No longer publishes theme issues. Payment for fiction is $25 to $100.

THE PLUM REVIEW
PO Box 1347, Philadelphia, PA 19105-1347
Ed: Mike Hammer   Poetry Ed: Karen Faul

Since: 1990	Circ: 1,500	Pages: 100-120	Per Year: 2
Size: 6 X 9	Perfect bound	Sample: $7 (U.S.)	Sub: $14 (U.S.)
Copyright: author	Book reviews: yes	Reviews/year: 10	Translations: yes
Interviews: yes	Fiction: no	Essays: yes	Copies: yes
Money: rarely	Time: 2-6 months		

Authors published: Jorge Luis Borges, Mona Van Duyn, Mark Strand, & Jean Valentine

All essays must relate to poetry. Excellence is the only criterion.

POEM
University of Alabama, English Department, Huntsville, AL 35899
Telephone: (205) 895-6320
Ed and Poetry Ed: Nancy Frey Dillard

Since: 1967	Circ: 400	Pages: 70	Per Year: 2
Size: 4 1/2 X 7 1/4	Perfect bound	Sample: $5	Sub: $10
Copyright: author	Book reviews: no	Reviews/year: n/a	Translations: no
Interviews: no	Fiction: no	Essays: no	Copies: 2
Money: no	Time: 1 month		

Authors published: R.T. Smith, Vivian Shipley, Bill Brown, & Betty Greenway

Favours lyric poems. Also accepts some narrative poetry. Open to both traditional forms and free verse. No prose poems. Reads all year; please send SASE for guidelines. Prefers no more than five poems per submission.

POETRY
60 West Walton Street, Chicago, IL 60610
Telephone: (312) 255-3703
Ed and Poetry Ed: Joseph Parisi

Since: 1912	Circ: 7,500	Pages: 64	Per Year: 12

Size: 5 1/2 X 9	Perfect bound	Sample: $3 (U.S.)	Sub: $34 (U.S.)
Copyright: author	Book reviews: yes	Reviews/year: 60	Translations: yes
Interviews: no	Fiction: no	Essays: no	Copies: 2
Money: $2/line	Time: 3 months		

Authors published: Margaret Atwood, John Ashbery, W.S. Merwin, & Billy Collins

Send SASE for guidelines. Awards several annual poetry prizes including the Bess Hokin Prize, the Levinson Prize, the Oscar Blumenthal Prize, the Eunice Tietjens Memorial Prize, the Frederick Bock Prize, the George Kent Prize, the Union League Prize, and the Ruth Lilly Prize. Send up to 6 poems per submission.

POETRY MISCELLANY
3413 Alta Vista Drive, Chattanooga, TN 37411

Telephone: (615) 624-7279

Eds: Richard Jackson & Richard Seehuus   Poetry Eds: Richard Jackson, Richard Seehuus, & Regina Wilkins

Since: 1971	Circ: 600	Pages: ?	Per Year: 1-2
Size: tabloid	Newspaper	Sample: $5	Sub: n/a
Copyright: ?	Book reviews: no	Reviews/year: n/a	Translations: yes
Interviews: no	Fiction: no	Essays: yes	Copies: yes
Money: no	Time: 3-4 months		

Authors published: John Ashbery, Charles Simic, Heather McHugh, & William Matthews

Please inquire before submitting essays. Submit translations (with original poems) to: John DuVal, University of Arkansas, Translation Workshop, Fayetteville, AR, 72701.

POETRY NORTHWEST
University of Washington, 4045 Brooklyn Avenue N.E., JA-15, Seattle, WA 98105

Telephone: (206) 685-4750

Eds: David Wagoner & Robin Seyfried

Since: 1959	Circ: 1,200	Pages: 48	Per Year: 4
Size: 5 1/2 X 8 1/2	Binding: ?	Sample: $4.50	Sub: $15
Copyright: n/a	Book reviews: no	Reviews/year: n/a	Translations: no
Interviews: no	Fiction: no	Essays: ?	Copies: 2
Money: no	Time: 1 month		

Authors published: Theodore Roethke, John Berryman, Philip Levine, & Harold Pinter

The quarterly does not copyright material.

PRAIRIE SCHOONER
University of Nebraska, 201 Andrews Hall, PO Box 880334, Lincoln, NE 68588-0334

Telephone: (402) 472-0911

Eds: Hilda Raz & Kate Flaherty   Poetry Ed: Hilda Raz

Since: 1926	Circ: 3,100	Pages: 176	Per Year: 4
Size: 6 X 9	Perfect bound	Sample: $4 (U.S.)	Sub: $22 (U.S.)
Copyright: author	Book reviews: yes	Reviews/year: 15-20	Translations: yes
Interviews: yes	Fiction: yes	Essays: yes	Copies: 3
Money: no	Time: 3 months		

Authors published: P.K. Page, Jennifer Footman, Susan Musgrave, & Rhea Tregebov

Will transfer copyright to author on request. Has published a special issue on Canadian Women Writers that features the poetry and prose of over thirty-five

Canadian women, among them: Liliane Welch, Lorna Crozier, Patience Wheatley, and Roo Borson. Reads manuscripts from September to May. Send SASE for writer's guidelines. Offers an annual poetry prize.

PROPHETIC VOICES
94 Santa Maria Drive, Novato, CA 94947
Eds and Poetry Eds: Ruth Wildes Schuler, Goldie L. Morales, & Jeanne Leigh Schuler

PUDDING MAGAZINE: The International Journal of Applied Poetry
60 North Main Street, Johnstown, OH 43031
Telephone: (614) 967-6060
Ed and Poetry Ed: Jennifer Bosveld

Since: 1979	Circ: 2,000	Pages: 60	Per Year: 2-3
Size: 8 1/2 X 5 1/2	Saddle stitched	Sample: $10.25 (Cdn.)	Sub: $25 (Cdn.)
Copyright: author	Book reviews: yes	Reviews/year: 6-15	Translations: no
Interviews: no	Fiction: yes	Essays: yes	Copies: 1
Money: no	Time: overnight		

Authors published: Death Waits, Don Rollins, Frank Kooistra, & Lowell Jaeger
Looks for dense, rich, intensive poetry that provides felt experience in the popular culture. Wants daring, deliberate work. Interested in poetry from Poets in the Schools. Runs a poetry publishing workshop; send SASE for details.

PUERTO DEL SOL
New Mexico State University, Box 30001, Las Cruces, NM 88003-0001
Telephone: (505) 646-2345
Ed: Kevin McIlvoy   Poetry Ed: Kathleene West

Since: 1961	Circ: 2,500	Pages: 200	Per Year: 2
Size: 5 X 7	Perfect bound	Sample: $7	Sub: $10
Copyright: author	Book reviews: yes	Reviews/year: 6-8	Translations: yes
Interviews: rarely	Fiction: yes	Essays: yes	Copies: yes
Money: ?	Time: 3-7 months		

Authors published: David Lee, Marilyn Hacker, Colette Inez, & Laurie-Anne Whitt
Translations are usually from Spanish. Essays should be of interest to southwestern readers. Poetry is welcome from all geographical regions. Only reads manuscripts that are postmarked September 1 through April 1.

QUARTERLY WEST
University of Utah, 312 Olpin Union, Salt Lake City, UT 84112
Telephone: (801) 581-3938   Fax: same
Eds: M.L. Williams & Lawrence Coates   Poetry Ed: Margot Schillp

Since: 1971	Circ: 1,400	Pages: 240	Per Year: 2
Size: 6 X 9	Perfect bound	Sample: $6.50 (U.S.)	Sub: $14 (U.S.)
Copyright: author	Book reviews: yes	Reviews/year: 6	Translations: yes
Interviews: yes	Fiction: yes	Essays: yes	Copies: 2
Money: $25-$50	Time: 1-4 months		

Authors published: Philip Levine, Eavan Boland, Albert Goldbarth, & Robert Pinsky
Will assign copyright to author upon request with reprint rights.

RARITAN QUARTERLY
Rutgers University, 165 College Avenue, New Brunswick, NJ 08903
Telephone: (908) 932-7887

Eds and Poetry Eds: Richard Poirier & Suzanne K. Hyman

THE RED CEDAR REVIEW
Michigan State University, Department of English, 17C Morrill Hall, East Lansing, MI 48823

Eds: Tom Bissell & Laura Klynstra   Poetry Ed: Laura Klynstra

Since: 1963	Circ: 500	Pages: 80-150	Per Year: 1-2
Size: 5 1/2 X 8 1/2	Perfect bound	Sample: $2.50	Sub: $10/2 issues
Copyright: author	Book reviews: no	Reviews/year: n/a	Translations: no
Interviews: no	Fiction: yes	Essays: no	Copies: yes
Money: no	Time: 1-4 months		

Authors published: Margaret Atwood, Diane Wakoski, Stuart Dybek, & Allan Peterson

Reads submissions year round.

RIVER CITY
The University of Memphis, Department of English, Memphis, TN 38152

Telephone: (901) 678-4509

Ed and Poetry Ed: Paul Naylor

Since: 1983	Circ: 1,200	Pages: 150	Per Year: 2
Size: 6 X 9	Perfect bound	Sample: $7	Sub: $12
Copyright: author	Book reviews: yes	Reviews/year: few	Translations: yes
Interviews: yes	Fiction: yes	Essays: yes	Copies: 2
Money: no	Time: 3 months		

Authors published: Eavan Boland, Lucille Clifton, Lyn Hejinian, & George Kalamaras

Only occasionally uses book reviews, translations, or interviews. Offers fiction prizes of $2,000, $500, and $300. Please send SASE for guidelines.

RIVER STYX
3207 Washington Avenue, St. Louis, MO 63103-1218

Telephone: (314) 533-4541

Ed and Poetry Ed: Richard Newman

Since: 1975	Circ: 800	Pages: 80	Per Year: 3
Size: 8 1/2 X 5 1/2	Binding: ?	Sample: $7	Sub: $20
Copyright: magazine	Book reviews: no	Reviews/year: n/a	Translations: yes
Interviews: yes	Fiction: yes	Essays: yes	Copies: 2
Money: $8	Time: 2 months		

Authors published: Margaret Atwood, Allen Ginsberg, Adrienne Rich, & Wendy Rose

Right will be given to reprint material at author's request. Only accepts submissions during September and October.

SALT LICK
3530 S.E. Madison, Portland, OR 97214

Telephone: (503) 238-8580

Ed and Poetry Ed: James Haining

Since: 1969	Circ: 1,500	Pages: 70	Per Year: ?
Size: 8 1/2 X 11	Saddle stitched	Sample: $6	Sub: $15
Copyright: magazine	Book reviews: no	Reviews/year: n/a	Translations: yes
Interviews: no	Fiction: ?	Essays: ?	Copies: yes
Money: ?	Time: 2 weeks		

Authors published: Charles Olson, Robert Creeley, David Searcy, & Gerald Burns

SHENANDOAH

Washington & Lee University, 2nd Floor, Troubadour Theatre, Lexington, VA
24450

Telephone: (703) 463-8765

Ed and Poetry Ed: R.T. Smith

Since: 1950	Circ: 2,000	Pages: 120	Per Year: 4
Size: ?	Prefect bound	Sample: $3.50	Sub: $11
Copyright: author	Book reviews: yes	Reviews/year: 3-4	Translations: yes
Interviews: yes	Fiction: yes	Essays: yes	Copies: yes
Money: $2.50/line	Time: 1-2 months		

Authors published: Mary Oliver, Hayden Carruth, Michael Longley, & Rodney Jones

Reads manuscripts September to May.

SLIPSTREAM

PO Box 2071, New Market Station, Niagara Falls, NY 14301

Telephone: (716) 282-2616

Eds and Poetry Eds: Dan Sicoli, Robert Borgatti, & Livio Farallo

Since: 1980	Circ: 500	Pages: 100	Per Year: 1
Size: 7 X 8 1/2	Perfect bound	Sample: $7	Sub: $15
Copyright: author	Book reviews: no	Reviews/year: n/a	Translations: no
Interviews: no	Fiction: yes	Essays: no	Copies: yes
Money: no	Time: 2-8 weeks		

Authors published: Charles Bukowski, Katharine Harer, Gerald Locklin, & Denise Duhamel

Considers work all year. Publishes some theme issues. Send SASE for guidelines and other information. Likes contemporary urban themes. Wants strong writing from the gut that is not afraid to bark or bite. Is not big on pastoral, religious, and rhyming verse. Also publishes chapbooks and produces a series of audiotapes. Runs an annual chapbook contest for manuscripts up to 40 pages long.

SONORA REVIEW

University of Arizona, Department of English, Modern Languages Building, Tucson, AZ 85721

Telephone: (520) 626-8383   Fax: (520) 621-7397

Eds: Julie Newman & Alicia Saposnill   Poetry Ed: Chris Weidenbach

Since: 1980	Circ: 1,000	Pages: 100	Per Year: 2
Size: 6 X 9	Perfect bound	Sample: $6	Sub: $12
Copyright: author	Book reviews: yes	Reviews/year: ?	Translations: yes
Interviews: rarely	Fiction: yes	Essays: yes	Copies: 2
Money: no	Time: 2 months		

Authors published: Tony Hoogland, Allison Deming, Olga Broumas, & Charlie Smith

Considers submissions all year. Runs an annual contest that pays $500.

THE SOUTH CAROLINA REVIEW

Clemson University, Department of English, 801 Strode Tower, Box 341503, Clemson, SC 29634-1503

Telephone: (803) 656-3151   Fax: (803) 656-1345

Ed and Poetry Ed: Frank Day

Since: 1968	Circ: 600	Pages: 208	Per Year: 2
Size: 6 X 9	Perfect bound	Sample: $10 (U.S.)	Sub: $10 (U.S.)
Copyright: author	Book reviews: yes	Reviews/year: 12	Translations: yes
Interviews: yes	Fiction: yes	Essays: yes	Copies: yes

Money: no   Time: 4 months
Authors published: Ron Rash, Mary Youmans, Carl A. Gottesman, & Tom Saya

Prefers poems to be no longer than one manuscript page. Please submit three to six poems at a time. Prefers prose to be less than 4,000 words. Please submit no more than two short stories at one time. Send SASE for contributors' guidelines.

THE SOUTH DAKOTA REVIEW
University of South Dakota, Box 111, University Exchange, Vermillion, SD 57069-2390
Telephone: (605) 677-5979   Fax: (605) 677-6409
Ed: Brian Bedard

Since: 1963	Circ: 500	Pages: 148	Per Year: 4
Size: 6 X 9	Perfect bound	Sample: $3	Sub: $15
Copyright: author	Book reviews: no	Reviews/year: n/a	Translations: no
Interviews: yes	Fiction: yes	Essays: yes	Copies: yes
Money: no	Time: 4-6 weeks		

Authors published: William Stafford, Simon Ortiz, Linda Hasselstrom, & David Allan Evans

Has some western regional bias. Most work accepted is by writers of considerable experience. Please send SASE for guidelines.

SOUTHERN HUMANITIES REVIEW
Auburn University, 9088 Haley Center, Auburn, AL 36849-5205
Telephone: (334) 844-9088   Fax: (334) 844-9027
Eds and Poetry Eds: Dan R. Latimer & Virginia M. Kouidis

Since: 1967	Circ: 700	Pages: 104	Per Year: 4
Size: 6 X 9	Perfect bound	Sample: $7 (U.S.)	Sub: $20 (U.S.)
Copyright: author	Book reviews: yes	Reviews/year: 50	Translations: yes
Interviews: yes	Fiction: yes	Essays: yes	Copies: 2
Money: no	Time: 1-3 months		

Authors published: Donald Hall, Brendan Galvin, Susan Ludvigson, & Reynolds Price

Rarely accepts poems over two pages long. Send three to five poems per submission. Reads all year.

SOUTHERN POETRY REVIEW
University of North Carolina, English Department, Charlotte, NC 28223
Telephone: (704) 547-4309
Ed and Poetry Ed: Ken McLaurin

THE SOUTHERN REVIEW
Louisiana State University, 43 Allen Hall, Baton Rouge, LA 70803
Telephone: (504) 388-5108
Eds and Poetry Eds: James Olney & Dave Smith

SOUTHWEST REVIEW
Southern Methodist University, 307 Fondren Library West, Box 374, Dallas, TX 75275-0374
Telephone: (214) 768-1037   Fax: (214) 768-1408
Eds: Willard Spiegelman & Elizabeth Mills   Poetry Ed: Willard Spiegelman

Since: 1915	Circ: 1,500	Pages: 144	Per Year: 4
Size: 6 X 9	Perfect bound	Sample: $5	Sub: $20
Copyright: author	Book reviews: no	Reviews/year: n/a	Translations: yes

Interviews: yes	Fiction: yes	Essays: yes	Copies: 3
Money: yes	Time: I month		

Authors published: James Merrill, Rachel Hadas, John Burt, & Elizabeth Spires

Please send SASE for guidelines for submissions. Accepts both traditional and experimental poetry. Offers the Elizabeth Matchett Stover Memorial Award for Poetry ($150) and the John H. McGinnis Memorial Award for Fiction ($1,000) and Non-fiction ($1,000). Does not read during June, July, and August.

SOU'WESTER

Southern Illinois University, School of Humanities, Box 1438, Edwardsville, IL 62026-1438
Telephone: (618) 692-3190
Eds: Fred W. Robbins & Allison Funk   Poetry Ed: Nancy Audoian

Since: 1960	Circ: 300	Pages: 120	Per Year: 2
Size: 8 X 10	Perfect bound	Sample: $5	Sub: $10
Copyright: author	Book reviews: no	Reviews/year: n/a	Translations: no
Interviews: no	Fiction: yes	Essays: no	Copies 2
Money: ?	Time: 3 months		

Copyright reverts to author on request. Looks for poems with strong imagery, successful association of images, and skillful, figurative language. Open to longer poems. Does not read submissions during August.

the steelhead special

PO Box 219, Bayside, CA 95524
Telephone: (707) 455-1907
Ed and Poetry Ed: Edward Nelson

Since: 1991	Circ: 3,000	Pages: 40	Per Year: 6
Size: 8 1/2 X 11	Saddle stitched	Sample: $2	Sub: $12
Copyright: author	Book reviews: yes	Reviews/year: 10	Translations: yes
Interviews: yes	Fiction: yes	Essays: yes	Copies: yes
Money: somtimes	Time: 1-2 months		

Authors published: Leonard Cirino, Sharon Doubiago, Kenn Mitchell, & Laura Hasler

Open all year to submissions. Perfers poems rich in images which take the time and care to observe sensual values and give them equal measure. Nothing flat wanted; more dimension rather than less. Interested in the Pacific coast primarily, but other places also.

SULFUR

Eastern Michigan University, English Department, Ypsilanti, MI 48197
Telephone: (313) 483-9787   Fax: same
Ed and Poetry Ed: Clayton Eshleman

Since: 1981	Circ: 2,000	Pages: 255	Per Year: 2
Size: 7 X 9	Perfect bound	Sample: $9	Sub: $18
Copyright: author	Book reviews: yes	Reviews/year: 10	Translations: yes
Interviews: yes	Fiction: no	Essays: yes	Copies: 2
Money: $40	Time: 3 month		

Authors published: Gary Snyder, Allen Ginsberg, Antonin Artaud, & Jayne Cortez

A biannual of the whole art. Wants writing that road-tests the language.

SunDog: The Southeast Review
Florida State University, 406 Williams, Tallahassee, FL 32306
Telephone: (904) 644-4230
Poetry Eds: Nancy Applegate & Karen Janowsky

SYCAMORE REVIEW
Purdue University, Department of English, Heavilon Hall, West Lafayette, IN 47907
Telephone: (317) 494-3783   Fax: (317) 494-3780
Ed: Rob Davidson   Poetry Ed: John Barna

Since: 1988	Circ: 1,000	Pages: 160	Per Year: 2
Size: 6 X 9	Perfect bound	Sample: $8 (U.S.)	Sub: $12 (U.S.)
Copyright: ?	Book reviews: yes	Reviews/year: 4	Translations: yes
Interviews: yes	Fiction: yes	Essays: yes	Copies: 2
Money: no	Time: 1-2 months		

Authors published: Denise Levertov, Ted Kooser, Tom Andrews, & Lee Upton
Manuscripts read from September 1 through April 30. Please send SASE for guidelines. Don't explain your life history or theory of poetics; just let us know who you are and send your best work. No restrictions on style, length, or subject matter.

TALISMAN
PO Box 3157, Jersey City, NJ 07303-3157
Telephone: (201) 938-0698
Ed and Poetry Ed: Edward Foster

Since: 1988	Circ: 1,000	Pages: 268	Per Year: 2
Size: 5 1/2 X 8 1/2	Perfect bound	Sample: $6 (U.S.)	Sub: $11 (U.S.)
Copyright: author	Book reviews: yes	Reviews/year: 4-6	Translations: yes
Interviews: yes	Fiction: no	Essays: yes	Copies: yes
Money: no	Time: 2 months		

Authors published: Anne Waldman, Clark Coolidge, Nathaniel Mackey, & Alice Notley
We tend to publish experimental, innovative work.

TAR RIVER POETRY
East Carolina University, Department of English, Greenville, NC 27858-4353
Telephone: (919) 328-6046 & 328-6041   Fax: (919) 328-4889
Ed: Peter Makuck   Poetry Eds: Peter Makuck & Luke Whisnant

Since: 1968	Circ: 1,000	Pages: 64	Per Year: 2
Size: 6 X 9	Saddle stitched	Sample: $5.50	Sub: $10
Copyright: author	Book reviews: yes	Reviews/year: 10	Translations: yes
Interviews: yes	Fiction: no	Essays: yes	Copies: yes
Money: ?	Time: 6 weeks		

Authors published: A.R. Ammons, Betty Adcock, Brendan Galvin, & Naomi Shihab Nye
Does not consider manuscripts May through August.

THE TENNESSEE QUARTERLY
Belmont University, Department of Literature and Language, 1900 Belmont Boulevard, Nashville, TN 37212-3757
Telephone: (615) 385-6412   Fax: (615) 385-6446
Eds: Anthony Lombardy & J.H.E. Paine   Poetry Ed: Anthony Lombardy

Since: 1994	Circ: 500	Pages: 60-80	Per Year: 3
Size: ?	Perfect bound	Sample: $5	Sub: $15

Copyright: author	Book reviews: yes	Reviews/year: 2	Translations: yes
Interviews: maybe	Fiction: yes	Essays: yes	Copies: 2
Money: ?	Time: 1-2 months		

Authors published: Dana Gioia, Emily Grosholz, Mark Jarman, & Rachel Hadas

Interested in articles on art theory and criticism.

THE TEXAS REVIEW

Sam Houston State University, Department of English & Foreign Languages, Huntsville, TX 77341

Eds: Paul Ruffin & Donald Coers   Poetry Ed: Paul Ruffin

Since: 1979	Circ: 600	Pages: 120-130	Per Year: 2
Size: 6 X 9	Perfect bound	Sample: $5	Sub: $10
Copyright: author	Book reviews: yes	Reviews/year: ?	Translations: yes
Interviews: yes	Fiction: yes	Essays: yes	Copies: 1
Money: ?	Time: 8-10 weeks		

Reads all year. Prefers work that is designed for the general reader rather than for the scholar. Poets should submit five to seven poems at a time.

TriQUARTERLY

Northwestern University, 2020 Ridge Avenue, Evanston, IL 60208-4302

Telephone: (708) 491-7614   Fax: (708) 467-2096

Eds and Poetry Eds: Reginald Gibbons & Susan Hahn

Since: 1964	Circ: 5,000	Pages: 250	Per Year: 3
Size: 6 X 9 1/4	Perfect bound	Sample: $5	Sub: $29
Copyright: author	Book reviews: yes	Reviews/year: 1	Translations: yes
Interviews: yes	Fiction: yes	Essays: yes	Copies: 2
Money: $1.50/line	Time: 2-3 months		

Authors published: Robert Pinsky, Eleanor Wilner, Campbell McGrath, & Alice Fulton

Wants aesthetically informed and inventive poetry and prose. Manuscripts are read from October 1 through March 31. Always interested in translations of contemporary poetry.

TURNING WHEEL

PO Box 4650, Berkeley, CA 94704

Telephone: (510) 525-8596   Fax: (510) 525-7973

Eds: Susan Moon & Denise Caignon

Since: 1984	Circ: 4,500	Pages: 48	Per Year: 4
Size: 8 X 11 1/2	Saddle stitched	Sample: $5	Sub: $20-$35
Copyright: author:	Book reviews: yes	Reviews/year: ?	Translations: yes
Interviews: yes	Fiction: maybe	Essays: yes	Copies: 2
Money: no	Time: 2 months		

Authors published: Gary Snyder, Richard Kostelanetz, Jane Hirshfield, & Stephen Mitchell

We only publish material relating to engaged Buddhism; that is, a Buddhist perspective on issues of social justice, peace work, and ecology. Please do not submit work that has nothing to do with spirituality or activism.

UNMUZZLED OX

105 Hudson Street, New York, NY 10013

Telephone: (212) 226-7170

Ed and Poetry Ed: Michael Andre

| Since: 1971 | Circ: 20,000 | Pages: ? | Per Year: ? |

Size: ?	Binding: ?	Sample: $5 (U.S.)	Sub: $20 (U.S.)/4 issues
Copyright: author	Book reviews: no	Reviews/year: n/a	Translations: yes
Interviews: yes	Fiction: some	Essays: some	Copies: yes
Money: yes	Time: 2 weeks		

Authors published: Al Purdy, Margaret Atwood, Irving Layton, & Allen Ginsberg

Copyright given to author upon request. We're working on a dictionary/encyclopedia on Canada by poets. A–D will be published in the next issue. We're working on E–Z.

UNO MAS MAGAZINE
PO Box 1832, Silver Spring, MD 20915
Telephone: (301) 946-5232   Fax: (301) 949-5590
Eds: Jim Saah & Scott McLemce   Poetry Ed: Ron Saah

Since: 1990	Circ: 3,500	Pages: 50	Per Year: 4
Size: 8 1/2 X 11	Perfect bound	Sample: $3 (U.S.)	Sub: $9 (U.S.)
Copyright: author	Book reviews: yes	Reviews/year: 15-20	Translations: no
Interviews: yes	Fiction: yes	Essays: yes	Copies: yes
Money: no	Time: 1 month		

Authors published: Sparrow, Bill Shields, Errol Miller, & Richard Peabody

Do not send more than five poems at a time.

VERSE
College of William & Mary, English Department, PO Box 8795, Williamsburg, VA 23187-8795
Telephone: (804) 221-3922
Eds: Nancy Schoenberger & Brian Henry   Poetry Ed: Henry Hart

Since: 1984	Circ: 1,000	Pages: 150	Per Year: 3
Size: 6 X 9	Perfect bound	Sample: $6 (U.S.)	Sub: $15 (U.S.)
Copyright: author	Book reviews: yes	Reviews/year: 6-15	Translations: yes
Interviews: yes	Fiction: no	Essays: yes	Copies: 2
Money: ?	Time: 2 months		

Authors published: Margaret Atwood, Robert Bringhurst, Seamus Heaney, & James Merrill

Publishes everything from prose poems to villanelles to long narrative poems. We accept submissions all year. Open to unsolicited reviews, but query about interviews and essays.

VERVE
PO Box 3205, Simi Valley, CA 93093
Telephone: (805) 522-7575
Ed: Ron Reichick   Poetry Ed: Marilyn Hochheiser

Since: 1989	Circ: 750	Pages: 40	Per Year: 2
Size: 8 1/2 X 5 1/2	Saddle stitched	Sample: $3.50 (U.S.)	Sub: $12 (U.S.)/4 issues
Copyright: author	Book reviews: no	Reviews/year: n/a	Translations: no
Interviews: no	Fiction: yes	Essays: no	Copies: 1
Money: no	Time: 4-6 weeks		

Authors published: Denise Levertov, Phillip Levine, Marege Piercy, & Quincy Troupe

Each issue has a special theme. Please send SASE for information. The theme for Fall 1996 is "Out of the Dark"— deadline August 1. Fiction should be short, up to 1,000 words.

WEBER STUDIES
Weber State University, Ogden, UT 84408-1214
Telephone: (801) 626-6473   Fax: (801) 626-7130
Eds: Neila C. Seshachari & Michael Wutz

Since: 1983	Circ: 1,500	Pages: 144	Per Year: 3
Size: 8 1/2 X 5 3/4	Perfect bound	Sample: $7	Sub: $10
Copyright: magazine	Book reviews: yes	Reviews/year: 12-14	Translations: yes
Interviews: yes	Fiction: yes	Essays: yes	Copies: 4
Money: $15-$200	Time: 3-4 months		

Authors published: Katharine Coles, Fred Marchant, Ingrid Werdt, & Shaun T. Griffin
Considers submissions any time. Pays $15 to $200.

WEST BRANCH
Bucknell University, Bucknell Hall, Lewisburg, PA 17837
Telephone: (717) 524-1853   Fax: (717) 524-3760
Eds and Poetry Eds: Karl Patten & Robert Taylor

Since: 1977	Circ: 500	Pages: 108	Per Year: 2
Size: 5 1/2 X 8 1/2	Perfect bound	Sample: $3	Sub: $7
Copyright: author	Book reviews: yes	Reviews/year: 6-8	Translations: yes
Interviews: no	Fiction: yes	Essays: no	Copies: 2
Money: no	Time: 6-8 weeks		

Authors published: Colette Inez, Dave Etter, Denise Duhamel, & Edward Klein Schmidt
Interested in all types of literature that are fresh and exciting. Reads throughout the year.

WHISKEY ISLAND MAGAZINE
Cleveland State University, English Department, Cleveland, OH 44115
Telephone: (216) 687-2056
Ed: Patricia Harusame Leebove   Poetry Ed: Mary E. Weems

Since: 1978	Circ: 1,200	Pages: 90-96	Per Year: 2
Size: 5 X 9	Perfect bound	Sample: $4	Sub: $18
Copyright: author	Book reviews: no	Reviews/year: n/a	Translations: ?
Interviews: yes	Fiction: yes	Essays: yes	Copies: 2
Money: no	Time: 3 months		

Authors published: Adrian C. Louis, Grace Butcher, Frankie Paino, & Marilyn Kallet
Poetry submissions up to ten pages at one time. Fiction up to 6,500 words. Essays up to 4,500 words. Open to submissions all year. All genres of poetry welcome, emphasis on identity, place, transformation, and language. Runs an annual poetry contest; please send SASE for rules.

WILLOW SPRINGS
Eastern Washington University, Pub PO Box 1063, MS-1, Cheney, WA 99004
Telephone: (509) 458-6429
Ed and Poetry Ed: Nance Van Winckel

WIND
PO Box 24548, Lexington, KY 40524
Telephone: (606) 885-5342
Eds: Charlie Hughes & Steven Cope   Poetry Ed: Steven Cope

Since: 1971	Circ: 400	Pages: 100	Per Year: 2
Size: 5 1/2 X 8	Perfect bound	Sample: $3.50	Sub: $14

Copyright: author	Book reviews: yes	Reviews/year: 6	Translations: yes
Interviews: yes	Fiction: yes	Essays: ?	Copies: 1
Money: no	Time: 2 months		

Authors published: Gerald Locklin, Walter McDonald, Jeff Daniel Marion, & Robert Cooperman

Magazine is 40% poetry, 40% fiction, and 20% interviews and book reviews of small press publications.

WISCONSIN REVIEW
University of Wisconsin, Box 158, Radford Hall, Oshkosh, WI 54901
Telephone: (414) 424-2267
Ed and Poetry Ed: Troy Schoultz

THE WORCESTER REVIEW
6 Chatham Street, Worcester, MA 01609
Telephone: (508) 797-4770
Ed and Poetry Ed: Rodger Martin

Since: 1972	Circ: 1,000	Pages: 124-160	Per Year: 1
Size: 6 X 9	Perfect bound	Sample: $8 (U.S.)	Sub: $10 (U.S.)
Copyright: author	Book reviews: yes	Reviews/year: few	Translations: yes
Interviews: yes	Fiction: yes	Essays: yes	Copies: 2
Money: maybe	Time: 6 months		

Authors published: William Stafford, Walter McDonald, Kathleen Spivack, & Chris Gompert

Send SASE for guidelines. Offers cash payment when grants permit. Non-fiction prose (book reviews and essays) should establish a New England connection.

THE WORMWOOD REVIEW
PO Box 4698, Stockton, CA 95204-0698
Telephone: (209) 466-8231
Ed and Poetry Ed: Marvin Malone

Since: 1959	Circ: 700	Pages: 48	Per Year: 4
Size: 5 1/2 X 8 1/2	Saddle stitched	Sample: $4 (U.S.)	Sub: $12 (U.S.)
Copyright: author	Book reviews: yes	Reviews/year: 50	Translations: yes
Interviews: no	Fiction: no	Essays: no	Copies: see below
Money: see below	Time: 1-2 months		

Authors published: Jeff Parsons, David W. Harris, Mary Green, & Brian Gallagher

Will tranfer copyright to author upon request. Offers choice of copies OR cash payment. Has a special fondness for prose poems/fables. Also likes concrete poems, dada, and the extreme avant garde. Work must communicate the temper and the depth of the present and human scene.

The following 50 periodicals have ceased publication since the fifth edition of this book, or they no longer publish Canadian poetry, or they have asked to be delisted:

Acts	**Apalachee Quarterly**
The Amaranth Review	**Berkeley Poetry Review**
Antaeus	**Blue Buildings**

Brussels Sprout	The North America Review
Caesura	Northwest Review
Caliban	Notus New Writing
California Quarterly	Ontario Review
Callaloo	The Painted Bride Quarterly
Central Park	Poet Lore
Colorado Review	Poetry East
Contact II	Poetry/LA
The Cream City Review	Poetry Now
Crosscurrents	The Red Pagoda
Epoch	Salmagundi
Gargoyle	San Jose Studies
Great River Review	Second Coming
Ironwood	Seneca Review
Kentucky Poetry Review	Soundings East
Lips	Stone Country
The Louisville Review	Sunrust Magazine
Loblolly	Temblor
The Midwest Quarterly	Third Rail
The Montana Review	The Virginia Quarterly Review
New Letters	Webster Review
New Mexico Humanities Review	Zone 3

The following 43 periodicals, believed to be still publishing poetry, failed to respond to requests for information. This could indicate a lack of interest in Canadian poetry. They are listed here because some of the very finest American journals— *Hudson Review*, *Poetry USA*, *Yale Review*, for example— belong to this category.

American Writing
4343 Manayunk Avenue
Philadelphia, PA, 19128

Anemone
PO Box 369
Chester, VT, 05143

The Baffler
PO Box 378293
Chicago, IL, 60637

Ball Magazine
PO Box 775
Northampton, MA, 01061

Black Lace
PO Box 83912
Los Angeles, CA, 90083

Blue Light Red Light
496A Hudson Street
Suite F42
New York, NY, 10014

Bomb Magazine
PO Box 2003, Canal Station
New York, NY, 10013

Caution!
PO Box 4694
Richmond, VA, 23220

Cayo
7 Bay Drive
Key West, FL, 33040

Commonweal
15 Dutch Street
New York, NY, 10038

Entelechy
PO Box 1151
Louisville, TN, 37777

Five Fingers Review
PO Box 15426
San Francisco, CA, 94115-0426

The Galley Sail Review
1630 University Avenue
Suite 42
Berkeley, CA, 94703

The Hudson Review
684 Park Avenue
New York, NY, 10021

The Lowell Pearl
University of Masschusetts
South Campus, English Department
1 University Avenue
Lowell, MA, 01854

Manhattan Poetry Review
PO Box 8207
New York, NY, 10150

Mississippi Valley Review
Western Illinois University
Department of English
Macomb, IL, 61455

The New Criterion
850 Seventh Avenue
New York, NY, 10019

The Ohio Review
Ohio University
Athens, OH, 45701

Onthebus
6421 1/2 Orange Street
Los Angeles, CA, 90048

Open Magazine
215 North Avenue
Suite 21
Westfield, NJ, 07090

Passages North
Kalamazoo College
1200 Academy Street
Kalamazoo, MI, 49006-3295

Poetry Flash
PO Box 4172
Berkeley, CA, 94704

Poetry USA
2569 Maxwell Avenue
Oakland, CA, 94601

The River
Mankato State University
University Box #58
PO Box 8400
Mankato, MN, 56002-8400

San Francisco Poetry Journal
18301 Halstead Street
Northridge, CA, 91325

The Santa Monica Review
1900 Pico Boulevard
Santa Monica, CA, 90405

Semiotext(e)
PO Box 568
Brooklyn, NY, 11211

Sequoia
Storke Publications Bldg.
Stanford University
Stanford, CA, 94305

Sewanee Review
University of the South
Sewanee, TN, 37375

Shooting Star Review
7123 Race Street
Pittsburgh, PA, 15208-1424

Slightly West
Evergreen State College
CAB 320, Olympia, WA, 98505

Snake Nation Review
110 West Force Street
Suite 2
Valdosta, GA, 31601

South Coast Poetry Journal
California State University
English Department
Fullerton, CA, 92634

Tampa Review
University of Tampa
401 West Kennedy Boulevard
Tampa, FL, 33606-1490

Tapas
37 Marquette Court
Clayton, CA, 94517-1025

Thinker Review
University of Louisville
SAC W301
Louisville, KY, 40292

The Threepenny Review
PO Box 9131
Berkeley, CA, 94709

Turnstile
175 Fifth Avenue
Suite 2348
New York, NY, 10010

Urbanus/Raizirr
PO Box 192561
San Francisco, CA, 94119-2561

Western Humanities Review
University of Utah
Salt Lake City, UT, 84112

The Yale Review
Yale University
1902A Yale Station
New Haven, CT, 96520

Yellow Silk
PO Box 6374
Albany, CA, 94706

1.7 ENGLAND, SCOTLAND, AND WALES PERIODICAL LISTINGS

The following 121 literary periodicals have indicated an interest in receiving submissions from Canadian poets. Many of these magazines have included poetry from Canada in recent issues.

It is always wise to send for a sample copy before submitting your poetry. Prices here are often stated in British pounds or in U.S. dollars. Since British banks charge very high exchange fees, you should pay for your sample copy with an international money order drawn in British funds.

When submitting poems, you will, of course, require British stamps or International Reply Coupons for the return postage. Please note that dozens of the editors of these magazines report that Canadian and American poets seldom send sufficient IRCs for the return/reply postage.

Surface mail to England is rather slow and air mail is expensive. Thus, to avoid wasting time and money, it is advisable to do complete research. Many British journals maintain a rather narrow editorial policy. Your local university or public library may house some of the better-known magazines on this list. It pays to read before you submit.

The size of many British magazines is shown here as being 6 X 9 inches. The exact dimensions of most British magazines is 5 3/4 X 8 1/4 inches due to the metric paper they are printed on. (Their metric measurement is 14.5 cm X 20.5 cm.)

ABERDEEN LEOPARD

PO Box 222, Aberdeen, AB9 8HA, Scotland
Ed and Poetry Ed: Norman Adams

ACUMEN MAGAZINE

6 The Mount, Higher Furzeham, Brixham, South Devon, TQ5 8QY England
Eds: Patricia Oxley & Glyn Pursglove   Poetry Ed: Patricia Oxley

Since: 1985	Circ: 700	Pages: 100	Per Year: 3
Size: 6 X 8	Perfect bound	Sample: 2.40 pounds	Sub: 10 pounds
Copyright: author	Book reviews: yes	Reviews/year: 75-100	Translations: some
Interviews: yes	Fiction: yes	Essays: yes	Copies: yes
Money: no	Time: 1-3 months		

Authors published: James Deahl, Dannie Abse, Kathleen Raine, & William Oxley

Prefers poetry with feeling and with a strong poetic content. Considers poetry around June and November.

AGENDA
5 Cranbourne Court, Albert Bridge Road, London, SW11 4PE England
Eds: William Cookson & Peter Dale   Poetry Eds: William Cookson, Peter Dale, & Anne Beresford

Since: 1959	Circ: 1,400	Pages: 140	Per Year: 4
Size: 5 X 7	Perfect bound	Sample: 4 pounds	Sub: 20 pounds
Copyright: author	Book reviews: yes	Reviews/year: ?	Translations: yes
Interviews: yes	Fiction: no	Essays: ?	Copies: yes
Money: maybe	Time: 1 month		

Authors published: Geoffrey Hill, Patricia McCarthy, Thom Gunn, & M. Kociejowski
Seeks poetry that has more than usual emotion, more than usual order.

AH POOK IS HERE
96 Brookside Way, West End, Southampton, SO30 3GZ England
Ed and Poetry Ed: Jon Summers

Since: 1994	Circ: 300	Pages: 44	Per Year: 4
Size: 6 X 8	Saddle stitched	Sample: $3	Sub: $11
Copyright: author	Book reviews: no	Reviews/year: n/a	Translations: yes
Interviews: no	Fiction: yes	Essays: yes	Copies: 1 copy
Money: no	Time: 2 weeks		

Authors published: Robert Howington, Steve Sneyd, Andrew Darlington, & Todd Moore
Looking for stuff with Bukowski/Beat influence. Looking for poems about real life and real thought.

AIREINGS
24, Brudenell Road, Leeds, West Yorkshire, LS6 1BD England
Eds: by co-operative   Poetry Ed: Jean Barker

AMBIT
17 Priory Gardens, Highgate, London, N6 5QY England
Eds: Edwin Brock, Carol Ann Duffy, & Henry Graham   Poetry Eds: Carol Anne Duffy

Since: 1959	Circ: 1,250	Pages: 96	Per Year: 4
Size: ?	Perfect bound	Sample: $10	Sub: $45
Copyright: author	Book reviews: yes	Reviews/year: 4	Translations: yes
Interviews: no	Fiction: yes	Essays: no	Copies: yes
Money: yes	Time: 3 months		

Authors published: Earle Birney, James Laughlin, Gavin Ewart, & Peter Porter

AMMONITE
12 Priory Mead, Bruton, Somerset, BA10 0DZ England
Ed and Poetry Ed: John Howard Greaves

Since: 1984	Circ: 200	Pages: 32	Per Year: 1-2
Size: 6 X 8	Saddle stitched	Sample: 2.50 pounds	Sub: 5 pounds
Copyright: author	Book reviews: no	Reviews/year: n/a	Translations: yes
Interviews: yes	Fiction: no	Essays: yes	Copies: 2 copies
Money: no	Time: 6 months		

Authors published: Andrew Darlington, Janet Reedman, Eric Ratcliffe, & John Alan Douglas
Seeks to present myth, image, and words towards the second millenium. Is a seedbed of mythology for our future, potently embryonic... is the power of the ancients generating a new pulse of energy in our culture. Publishes theme issues; please send SASE for information.

AND
89a Petherton Road, London, N5 2QT England
Eds and Poetry Eds: Bob Cobbing & Adrian Clarke

Since: 1954	Circ: 400	Pages: 96	Per Year: erratic
Size: 6 X 8	Perfect bound	Sample: 4 pounds	Sub: n/a
Copyright: author	Book reviews: no	Reviews/year: n/a	Translations: yes
Interviews: no	Fiction: yes	Essays: yes	Copies: yes
Money: no	Time: 2 months		

Authors published: Paul Dutton, Steve McCaffery, Karen McCormack, & sean o huigin

Does not usually publish translations, fiction, and essays. Interested in visual, concrete, sound, performance, and L=A=N=G=U=A=G=E poetry.

ANGEL EXHAUST
Flat 6, Avon Court, Holden Road, London, N12 8HR England
Ed and Poetry Ed: Andrew Duncan

Since: 1977	Circ: 300	Pages: 128	Per Year: 2
Size: 6 X 8	Perfect bound	Sample: 4 pounds	Sub: 9 pounds
Copyright: author	Book reviews: yes	Reviews/year: 30	Translations: yes
Interviews: yes	Fiction: no	Essays: yes	Copies: yes
Money: no	Time: 2 weeks		

Authors published: Maggie Helwig, Denise Riley, Allen Fisher, & Michael Haslam

Magazine is into left modernism, the counterculture, and dissident British poetry.

ANTHEM
36 Cyril Avenue, Bobbers Mill, Nottingham, NG8 5BA England
Eds and Poetry Eds: Howard Roake & Grant Mortimer

Since: 1986	Circ: 500	Pages: 8	Per Year: 1-2
Size: 150 cm X 210 cm	Saddle stitched	Sample: free	Sub: n/a
Copyright: author	Book reviews: no	Reviews/year: n/a	Translations: yes
Interviews: no	Fiction: no	Essays: no	Copies: 1
Money: no	Time: 6-8 weeks		

Authors published: John Light, Christine Michael, Carl Hufton, & Martin Tatham

Open to any type of poetry. We do, however, pay particular attention to individual points of view. For example, issue nine featured poems about homosexuality.

APOSTROPHE
Mr Pillows' Press, 41 Canute Road, Faversham, Kent, ME13 8SH England
Ed and Poetry Ed: Diana Andersson

Since: 1991	Circ: ?	Pages: 32	Per Year: 2
Size: 6 X 8	Saddle stitched	Sample: 2 pounds	Sub: 7 pounds
Copyright: author	Book reviews: yes	Reviews/year: 4	Translations: yes
Interviews: yes	Fiction: no	Essays: no	Copies: yes
Money: no	Time: 1-2 months		

Authors published: Gerald England, George Gott, Tobias Hill, & Eithne Cavanagh

A sample copy can also be had for 1 pound + 3 IRCs; a subscription can also be had for 4.50 pounds + 6 IRCs. Submissions should be sent to England, but subscriptions and inquiries can be sent to Joanna Weston, 1960 Berger Road, Shawnigan Lake, B.C., V0R 2W0. Short poems preferred, forty lines maximum. Wit and humour are two of the qualities the editor is looking for, but doesn't often find. Poetry on any topic is welcomed, but not too much soul-searching. Please do not submit work during August.

AQUARIUS
116 Sutherland Avenue, Flat 10, Room A, Maida Vale, London, W9 England
Ed and Poetry Ed: Eddie S. Linden

ARTERY
34 Waldemar Avenue, Fulham, London, SW6 5NA England
Ed and Poetry Ed: Patricia Scanlan

Since: 1992	Circ: 1,000	Pages: 50	Per Year: 6
Size: 6 X 8	Perfect bound	Sample: 5 pounds	Sub: 25 pounds
Copyright: author	Book reviews: yes	Reviews/year: ?	Translations: yes
Interviews: yes	Fiction: yes	Essays: yes	Copies: yes
Money: maybe	Time: 1 month		

Authors published: Allen Ginsberg, William S. Burroughs, Yoko Ono, & Charles Henri Ford
Pays money when possible. Main interest is in the visual arts. Seeks experimental work. Special interests: international surrealism and 20th century literature and art criticism.

BEAT SCENE
27 Covrt Leet, Binley Woods, Nr. Coventry, Warwickshire, CV3 2JQ England
Ed: Kevin Ring

Since: 1989	Circ: ?	Pages: 50	Per Year: 6
Size: 6 X 8	Saddle stitched	Sample: $8 (U.S.)	Sub: ?
Copyright: author	Book reviews: yes	Reviews/year: lots	Translations: no
Interviews: yes	Fiction: yes	Essays: yes	Copies: 1
Money: no	Time: 2 weeks		

Authors published: Charles Bukowski, Jack Kerouac, Anne Waldman, Jack Micheline.
Primarily a news magazine dealing with American Beat Generation writers. Main interest is in essays and critical pieces, not poetry. When ordering a sample copy please send CASH, not a cheque.

BLITHE SPIRIT
Farnley Gate Farmhouse, Riding Mill, Northumberland, NE44 6AA England
Ed and Poetry Ed: Jackie Hardy

Since: 1990	Circ: 200	Pages: 32	Per Year: 4
Size: 14.5 cm X 21 cm	Perfect bound	Sample: 1.50 pounds	Sub: 12.50 pounds
Copyright: author	Book reviews: yes	Reviews/year: 10	Translations: yes
Interviews: no	Fiction: no	Essays: yes	Copies: no
Money: no	Time: 6 weeks		

Authors published: George Swede, Jim Force (Nika), Ruby Spriggs, & Jean Jorgensen
This is the journal of the British Haiku Society. Publishes haiku, tanka, senryu, and renga by members of the B.H.S. only. Canadian poets are welcomed. To join the Society please contact David Cobb, Sinodun, Shalford, Braintree, Essex, CM7 5HN, England.

BORDERLINES
Nant y Brithyll, Llangynyw, Welshpool, Powys, SY21 0JS Wales
Eds and Poetry Eds: Dave Bingham & Kevin Bamford

Since: ?	Circ: 200	Pages: 48	Per Year: 2
Size: 10 X 7	Binding: ?	Sample: 1.50 pounds	Sub: 4.50 pounds
Copyright: author	Book reviews: no	Reviews/year: n/a	Translations: yes
Interviews: no	Fiction: no	Essays: no	Copies: 1
Money: no	Time: 1 month		

Authors published: Vuyelwa Carlin, Peter Abbs, Eleanor Cooke, & Mike Jenkins

The magazine is the organ of the Anglo-Welsh Poetry Society, but it accepts submissions from anyone anywhere. Seldom accepts poems longer than two pages.

BRADFORD POETRY
9 Woodvale Way, Bradford, West Yorkshire, BD7 2SJ England
Ed and Poetry Ed: Clare Chapman

BRAQUEMARD
20 Terry Street, Hull, Humberside, HU3 1UD England
Ed and Poetry Ed: David Allenby

Since: 1994	Circ: 200	Pages: 40	Per Year: 2
Size: 6 X 8	Saddle stitched	Sample: 3.50 pounds	Sub: 7 pounds
Copyright: author	Book reviews: no	Reviews/year: n/a	Translations: no
Interviews: no	Fiction: ?	Essays: ?	Copies: 1
Money: ?	Time: 2 months		

Authors published: Douglas Houston, Sean O'Brien, & Geoff Hattersley

Shorter poems have a better chance than longer poems. Also interested in small line drawings to go with the poems.

CANDELABRUM POETRY MAGAZINE
9 Milner Road, Wisbech, Cambridge, PE13 2LR England
Ed: Helen Gordon   Poetry Ed: Michael Leonard McCarthy

Since: 1970	Circ: 1,000	Pages: 40	Per Year: 2
Size: 5 X 8	Saddle stitched	Sample: $3 (Cdn)	Sub: $18 (Cdn)
Copyright: author	Book reviews: yes	Reviews/year: few	Translations: yes
Interviews: no	Fiction: no	Essays: no	Copies: 1
Money: no	Time: 10 weeks		

Authors published: Jack Harvey, Ann Keith, Philip Higson, & M.L. McCarthy

Cost of sample and sub quoted above is the cash price. If payment is made by cheque, $8 (Cdn) should be added to cover bank charges. Particularly welcomes traditional poetry (rhymed and metrical). Good quality free verse is not, however, excluded. Will consider any subject, but no racism, sexism, or pornography. Has published a pamphlet by Canadian poet Ian MacLennan.

CASCANDO
PO Box 1499, London, N4 4QA England
Eds and Poetry Eds: Lisa Boardman & Emily Ormond

Since: 1992	Circ: 3,000	Pages: 108	Per Year: 3
Size: 21 cm X 20 cm	Perfect bound	Sample: $15	Sub: $40
Copyright: author	Book reviews: yes	Reviews/year: 30	Translations: yes
Interviews: yes	Fiction: yes	Essays: yes	Copies: yes
Money: no	Time: 4 months		

Authors published: Hal Niedzuiecki, Susan Glover, Scott Andemon, & Martha Perkins

Likes shorter, imagist-influenced poetry with a strong visual language. Also likes poetry with a precise narrative voice. Focus is on work by university students.

CENCRASTUS
Abbeymount Techbase, Unit One, Abbeymount, Edinburgh, EH8 8EJ Scotland
Eds and Poetry Eds: Raymond Ross & Thom Nairn

CHAPMAN
4 Broughton Place, Edinburgh, EH1 3RX Scotland
Ed and Poetry Ed: Joy M. Hendry

Since: 1970	Circ: 2,000	Pages: 104	Per Year: 4
Size: 6 X 8	Perfect bound	Sample: $6 (U.S.)	Sub: $28 (U.S.)
Copyright: author	Book reviews: yes	Reviews/year: 200	Translations: yes
Interviews: yes	Fiction: yes	Essays: yes	Copies: ?
Money: yes	Time: 2 months		

Authors published: Fred Cogswell, James Berry, Sorley MacLean, & Janice Galloway
Looks for the intelligent, the controversial, and the essential in poetry and fiction. Work should be new and creative.

THE COUNTRYMAN
Sheep Street, Burford, Oxford, OX8 4LH England
Ed and Poetry Ed: Chris Hall

DANDELION ARTS MAGAZINE
24 Frosty Hollow, East Hunsbury, Northamptonshire, NN4 0SY England
Ed and Poetry Ed: Jacqueline Gonzalez-Marina

Since: 1978	Circ: 1,000	Pages: 20-30	Per Year: 2
Size: 6 X 8	Binding: ?	Sample: $21	Sub: $38
Copyright: author	Book reviews: yes	Reviews/year: 20	Translations: yes
Interviews: yes	Fiction: yes	Essays: yes	Copies: no
Money: no	Time: 2 weeks		

Authors published: Adrian Henri, Hilda Phillips, Vincente Aleixandre, & Joaquina Gonzalez-Marina
Only considers submissions from subscribers. Does not publish political or religious work.

DELHI LONDON POETRY QUARTERLY
50 Penywern Road, London, SW5 9SX England
Ed and Poetry Ed: Gopi Warrier

DOORS— into and out of Dorset
61 West Borough, Wimborne, Dorset, BH21 1LX England

Since: 1979	Circ: 200	Pages: 36	Per Year: 3
Size: 6 X 8	Saddle stitched	Sample: 1.70 pounds	Sub: 4.65 pounds
Copyright: author	Book reviews: yes	Reviews/year: 6	Translations: yes
Interviews: no	Fiction: ?	Essays: yes	Copies: yes
Money: no	Time: 4 months		

Authors published: Daphne Schiller, Geoff Stevens, Alison Chisholm, & R.G. Gregory
Each issue has a different editor. Half of each issue is made up of work by writers from Dorset and half from elsewhere. Send no more than six poems at one time. Also welcomes short articles on poetry, black and white photos, and illustrations.

EDINBURGH REVIEW
22 George Square, Edinburgh, EH8 9LF Scotland
Eds: Gavin Wallace & Robert Alan Jamieson   Poetry Ed: Robert Alan Jamieson

Since: 1969	Circ: 1,000	Pages: 160-240	Per Year: 2
Size: 6 X 8	Perfect bound	Sample: ?	Sub: $29.50
Copyright: author	Book reviews: yes	Reviews/year: 20	Translations: yes
Interviews: yes	Fiction: yes	Essays: yes	Copies: yes
Money: no	Time: 3 months		

Authors published: Gael Turnbull, Medbh McGuckian, Kenneth White, & Elizabeth Burns

Interested in features on information relating to examples of new Canadian poetry. Also looks for poetry in translation. Would like to forge links with Canadian cultural organizations. Institutional subscriptions are $59.50/year.

ENVOI
44 Rudyard Road, Biddulph Moor, Stoke-on-Trent, ST8 7JN England

EUROPEAN JUDAISM
Leo Baeck College, The Manor House, 80 East End Road, London, N3 2SY England
Eds: Albert H. Friedlander & Jonathan Magonet   Poetry Ed: Ruth Fainlight

Since: 1966	Circ: 1,000	Pages: 60	Per Year: 2
Size: ?	Binding: ?	Sample: ?	Sub: ?
Copyright: author	Book reviews: yes	Reviews/year: 20	Translations: yes
Interviews: no	Fiction: no	Essays: yes	Copies: yes
Money: no	Time: 2 months		

Authors published: George Szirtes, Dannie Abse, Linda Pastan, & Grace Schulman

Poetry should have some relevance to Judaism.

EXILE
8 Snow Hill, Clare, Suffolk, CO10 8QF England
Eds and Poetry Eds: Ann Elliott-Marr & John Marr

Since: 1989	Circ: 800	Pages: 40	Per Year: 4
Size: 6 X 8	Binding: ?	Sample: 2 pounds	Sub: 8 pounds
Copyright: author	Book reviews: yes	Reviews/year: ?	Translations: no
Interviews: no	Fiction: no	Essays: no	Copies: 1
Money: no	Time: 2 weeks		

Authors published: Sidney Moreleigh, Crystal Indiankhana Candy, Mark Beevers, & Debbie Nicholson

Poetry should be less than forty lines. Runs a yearly poetry contest.

EXTRANCE
33 Meredith Street, Great Lever, Bolton, Lancashire, BL3 2DD England
Eds and Poetry Eds: Peter Overton & Anne McGrath

FIRST OFFENSE
"Syringa," Stodmarsh, Canterbury, Kent, CT3 4BA England
Ed and Poetry Ed: Tim Fletcher

Since: 1987	Circ: 200	Pages: 40-60	Per Year: ?
Size: 6 X 8	Binding: ?	Sample: 2.50 pounds	Sub: ?
Copyright: author	Book reviews: yes	Reviews/year: ?	Translations: yes
Interviews: no	Fiction: yes	Essays: yes	Copies: no
Money: ?	Time: ?		

Only publishes contemporary, experimental work such as L=A=N=G=U=A=G=E poetry. Traditional poetry is never accepted.

FIRST TIME
Burdett Cottage, 4 Burdett Place, George Street, Old Town, Hastings, East Sussex, TN34 3ED England
Ed and Poetry Ed: Josephine Austin

Since: 1981	Circ: 600	Pages: 80-90	Per Year: 2
Size: 6 X 9	Saddle stitched	Sample 2 pounds	Sub: 9 pounds
Copyright: author	Book Reviews: no	Reviews/year: n/a	Translations: no
Interviews: no	Fiction: no	Essays: no	Copies: 1
Money: no	Time: 1 month		

Authors published: James Deahl, Peter Sherry, Andy Robson, & Pauline Hawksworth
Often accepts Canadian poetry. Poems should be thirty lines or less. Runs an annual poetry contest, the Hastings National Poetry Competition, with cash prizes. Send IRC for details. Welcomes all types of poetry.

FOOLSCAP MAGAZINE
78 Friars Road, East Ham, London, E6 1LL England
Ed and Poetry Ed: Judi Benson

Since: 1987	Circ: 200	Pages: 80	Per Year: 2
Size: 6 X 8	Perfect bound	Sample: $6 (U.S.)	Sub: $15 (U.S.)
Copyright: author	Book reviews: no	Reviews/year: n/a	Translations: yes
Interviews: no	Fiction: yes	Essays: yes	Copies: 1
Money: ?	Time: 3 months		

Authors published: Rhona McAdam, Carol Ann Duffy, Matthew Sweeny, & Ken Smith
Looks for poetry and prose that says something and says it well. Not keen on the new formalism or trite rhymes. Please submit no more than six poems per submission. Interested in black and white drawings.

FREELANCE WRITING & PHOTOGRAPHY
Tregeraint House, Zennor, St. Ives, Cornwall, TR26 3DB England
Ed and Poetry Ed: John T. Wilson

GLOBAL TAPESTRY JOURNAL
Spring Bank, Longsight Road, Copster Green, Blackburn, Lancashire, BB1 9EU England
Ed and Poetry Ed: Dave Cunliffe

GREY SUIT Video for Art & Literature
21 Augusta Street, Adamsdown, Carfiff, CF2 1EN Wales
Eds: Anthony Howell, Simon Sawyer, & Nicola Schauerman   Poetry Ed: Anthony Howell

Since: 1992	Circ: ?	Pages: n/a	Per Year: 4
Size: n/a	Video cassette	Sample: $70 (Cdn.)	Sub: $165 (Cdn.)
Copyright: author	Book reviews: no	Reviews/year: n/a	Translations: yes
Interviews: no	Fiction: no	Essays: no	Copies: 2-6
Money: 30-80 pounds	Time: 1 month		

Authors published: John Ashbery, Les Murry, F.T. Prince, & Anne-Marie Albiach
Interested in seeing poetry from all around the world ON VIDEO. That is, live video recordings by poets. Video "magazine" will publish a paper translation of

poems not read in English. Always open to submissions. E-mail address: gs@greysuit.demon.co.uk

HEADLOCK
Old Zion Chapel, The Triangle, Somerton, Somerset, TA11 6QP England
Ed and Poetry Ed: Tony Charles

Since: 1994	Circ: 200	Pages: 66	Per Year: 2
Size: 6 X 8	Perfect bound	Sample: 4 pounds	Sub: 6.50 pounds
Copyright: author	Book reviews: no	Reviews/year: n/a	Translations: yes
Interviews: no	Fiction: no	Essays: no	Copies: 1
Money: no	Time: 1 month		

Authors published: Iain Crichton Smith, Kerry Sowerby, john alan douglas, & Gordon Wardman

Magazine is wall-to-wall poetry, nothing else. Canadian submissions should be non-returnable copies, with bio note included, and one IRC for response.

THE HONEST ULSTERMAN
102 Elm Park Mansions, Park Walk, London, SW10 0AP England
Eds and Poetry Eds: Ruth Hooley & Robert Johnstone

HQ: The Haiku Quarterly
39 Exmouth Street, Swindon, Wiltshire, SN1 3PU England
Ed and Poetry Ed: Kevin Bailey

Since: 1990	Circ: 1,000	Pages: 60	Per Year: 3-4
Size: 6 X 8	Perfect bound	Sample: 2.40 pounds	Sub: 11 pounds
Copyright: author	Book reviews: yes	Reviews/year: 15-20	Translations: yes
Interviews: yes	Fiction: no	Essays: yes	Copies: yes
Money: no	Time: 6 months		

Authors published: Lucien Stryk, James Kirkup, Peter Redgrove, & Adrian Henri

No limit on number of haiku submitted; send a good sample of your work.

HRAFNHOH
32 Stryd Ebeneser, Pontypridd, CF37 5PB Wales
Ed and Poetry Ed: Joseph Biddulph

INKSHED
387 Beverley Road, Hull, North Humberside, HU5 1LS England
Eds: Anthony Smith, Sue Wilsea, Bernard Young, & Lesli Markham   Poetry Ed: Lesli Markham

INTERACTIONS
PO Box 250, St. Helier, Jersey, Channel Islands, JE4 8TZ Great Britain
Ed and Poetry Ed: Diane M. Moore

Since: 1989	Circ: 1,000	Pages: 74	Per Year: 2
Size: 6 X 8	Saddle stitched	Sample: $4 (U.S.)	Sub: 11 pounds
Copyright: author	Book reviews: no	Reviews/year: n/a	Translations: yes
Interviews: no	Fiction: no	Essays: no	Copies: 1
Money: no	Time: 1 month		

Authors published: Dannie Abse, Gavin Ewart, Michael Hamburger, & Leopold Sedar Senghor

Publishes poetry in English, French, German, & Spanish. Short poems preferred, maximum of thirty lines. Tends to accept postmodern work. Runs an annual open poetry contest.

iota
67 Hady Crescent, Chesterfield, Derbyshire, S41 0EB England
Ed and Poetry Ed: David Holliday

Since: 1988	Circ: 350	Pages: 40	Per Year: 4
Size: 6 X 8	Saddle stitched	Sample: $2 cash	Sub: $10 cash
Copyright: author	Book reviews: yes	Reviews/year: 30	Translations: yes
Interviews: no	Fiction: no	Essays: no	Copies: 2
Money: no	Time: 1 month		

Authors published: James Deahl, Carolyn Raney, David Rhine, & David Starkey

If payment for sub not made in cash, please add $5 to cover bank charges. Will consider everything except concrete poetry. Shorter poems have the edge.

IRON
5 Marden Terrace, Cullercoats, North Shields, Tyne and Wear, NE30 4PD England
Eds and Poetry Eds: Peter Mortimer, Kitty Fitzgerald, & David Stephenson

ISSUE ONE
2 Tewkesbury Drive, Grimsby, South Humberside, DN34 4TL England
Ed and Poetry Ed: Ian Brocklebank

JOE SOAP'S CANOE
30 Quilter Road, Felixstowe, Suffolk, IP11 7JJ England
Ed and Poetry Ed: Martin Stannard

THE KEROUAC CONNECTION
76 Calderwood Square, East Kilbride, Glasgow, G74 3BQ Scotland
Ed and Poetry Ed: James Morton

KRAX MAGAZINE
63 Dixon Lane, Leeds, West Yorkshire, LS12 4RR England
Eds: Andy Robson & Dave Pruckner   Poetry Ed: Andy Robson

Since: 1971	Circ: 450	Pages: 64	Per Year: 1
Size: 6 X 8	Saddle stitched	Sample: $1 (Cdn)	Sub: $12/3 issues
Copyright: author	Book reviews: no	Reviews/year: n/a	Translations: yes
Interviews: yes	Fiction: no	Essays: no	Copies: 1
Money: no	Time: 6 weeks		

Authors published: Herb Batty, Dianne Chow, Robert Trudel, & Mary R. Stanko

Payment for sample/sub should be in cash; no cheques please. Favours light-hearted and humorous material. Some simple graphic or concrete items accepted.

LONDON MAGAZINE
30 Thurloe Place, London, SW7 England
Ed and Poetry Ed: Alan Ross

Since: 1954	Circ: 5,000	Pages: 160	Per Year: 6
Size: ?	Perfect bound	Sample: 6 pounds	Sub: 33.50 pounds
Copyright: author	Book reviews: yes	Reviews/year: ?	Translations: yes
Interviews: yes	Fiction: yes	Essays: yes	Copies: yes

Money: yes   Time: 3 weeks
Authors published: Seamus Heaney, Derek Walcott, Tony Harrison, & Hugo Williams
Open to both traditional and avant-garde work.

MAELSTROM
58 Malvern, Coleman Street, Southend-on-Sea, Essex, SS2 5AD England
Ed and Poetry Ed: Malcolm E. Wright

Since: 1987	Circ: 250	Pages: 60	Per Year: 2
Size: 6 X 8	Saddle stitched	Sample: 1.80 pounds	Sub: 6.50 pounds
Copyright: author	Book reviews: yes	Reviews/year: ?	Translations: yes
Interviews: maybe	Fiction: yes	Essays: maybe	Copies: 1
Money: no	Time: 3 months		

Authors published: Steve Sneyd, Andrew Darlington, Malcolm E. Wright, & J.P.V. Stewart
All poetry accepted must be related to science fiction, fantasy, or horror. Cash only, no foreign cheques please.

MEMES
38 Molesworth Road, Plympton, Plymouth, Devon, PL7 4NT England
Ed and Poetry Ed: Norman Jope

MOMENTUM
Almere Farm, Rossett, Wrexham, Clwyd, LL12 0BY Wales
Ed: Jeff Bell   Poetry Ed: Pamela Goodwin

MOONSTONE
BM Moonstone, London, WC1N 3XX England
Eds and Poetry Eds: Talitha Clare & Robin Brooks

NEVER BURY POETRY
30 Beryl Avenue, Tottington, Bury, Lancashire, BL8 3NF England
Poetry submission address: 12a Kirkstall Gardens, Radcliffe, Manchester, M26 0QJ England
Ed and Poetry Ed: Eileen Holroyd

Since: 1988	Circ: 120	Pages: 48	Per Year: 4
Size: 8 X 12	Saddle stitched	Sample: $3 (U.S.)	Sub: 7 pounds
Copyright: author	Book reviews: no	Reviews/year: n/a	Translations: no
Interviews: no	Fiction: no	Essays: no	Copies: no
Money: no	Time: 1-2 months		

Authors published: Thomas Kretz, Ann Rutherford, R.L. Cook, & Linda Chui

NEW HOPE INTERNATIONAL
20 Werneth Avenue, Gee Cross, Hyde, Cheshire, SK14 5NL England
Ed and Poetry Ed: Gerald England

Since: 1980	Circ: 1,500	Pages: 52	Per Year: varies
Size: 6 X 8	Saddle stitched	Sample: 3 pounds	Sub: 20 pounds
Copyright: author	Book reviews: yes	Reviews/year: 500	Translations: yes
Interviews: no	Fiction: yes	Essays: yes	Copies: 1
Money: ?	Time: 3 months		

Authors published: Jean Jorgensen, Mary R. Stanko, B.Z. Niditch, & Joanna M. Weston
Publishes 2 to 6 issues per year. Accepts all styles of poetry from the traditional to the avant-garde. Likes fiction to be under 2,000 words. Send SASE (IRC) for

guidelines. Publishes a special all-book-review issue every now and then. Always welcomes books for review.

NEW POETRY QUARTERLY
5, Stockwell, Colchester, Essex, CO1 1HP England
Eds: S.C. Brittan, N.S. Thompson, B. Gibbons, J. Cook, & C. Hart   Poetry Ed: N.S. Thompson

Since: 1994	Circ: 600	Pages: 60-70	Per Year: 4
Size: 17 cm X 24.5 cm	Saddled stitched	Sample: 5 pounds	Sub: 22 pounds
Copyright: author	Book reviews: yes	Reviews/year: 6	Translations: yes
Interviews: yes	Fiction: no	Essays: yes	Copies: 3
Money: 10-50 pounds	Time: 2 weeks		

Authors published: Peter Porter, Andrew Motion, Tom Paulin, & Bernard O'Donoghue

Focus is on academic essays that relate to poetry from all periods. Publishes only about a dozen poems per issue.

NEW PROSPECTS POETRY MAGAZINE
Prospect House, Snowshill, Broadway, Worcestershire, WR12 7JU England
Ed and Poetry Ed: Tony Sims

NEW SPOKES
The Orchard House, 45 Clophill Road, Upper Gravenhurst, Bedfork, MK45 4JH England
Ed and Poetry Ed: Donald Atkinson

THE NEW WELSH REVIEW
Saint David's University College, Department of English, Lampeter, Dyfed SA48 7ED Wales
Eds and Poetry Eds: Belinda Humfrey & Robin Reeves

NEW WRITING SCOTLAND
University of Stirling, Department of English Studies, Stirling, FK9 4LA Scotland
Ed and Poetry Ed: Maggie Beveridge

NINETIES POETRY
33 Lansdowne Place, Hove, Sussex, BN3 1HF England
Ed and Poetry Ed: Graham Ackroyd

Since: 1994	Circ: 200	Pages: 88	Per Year: 4
Size: 8 1/2 X 5 1/2	Binding: ?	Sample: 5 pounds	Sub: ?
Copyright: author	Book reviews: yes	Reviews/year: 4	Translations: yes
Interviews: no	Fiction: no	Essays: no	Copies: no
Money: no	Time: 1 day		

Authors published: Al Purdy, Rosemary Sullivan, Gary Snyder & David Gascoyne

THE NORTH
51 Byram Arcade, Westgate, Huddersfield, HD1 1ND England
Eds and Poetry Eds: Peter Sansom & Janet Fisher

OASIS
12 Stevenage Road, London, SW6 6ES England
Ed and Poetry Ed: Ian Robinson

OBJECT PERMANENCE
121 Menock Road, Kingspark, Glasgow, G44 5SD Scotland
Eds and Poetry Eds: Robin Purves & Peter Manson

Since: 1993	Circ: ?	Pages: 72	Per Year: 3
Size: 6 X 8	Binding: ?	Sample: 2.50 pounds	Sub: 9 pounds
Copyright: author	Book reviews: yes	Reviews/year: 18	Translations: yes
Interviews: no	Fiction: no	Essays: no	Copies: yes
Money: no	Time: 1 month		

Authors published: Charles Bernstein, Clarke Coolidge, Edwin Morgan, & Norma Cole

Publishes experimental/modernist poetry. Loves Steve McCaffery's poetry. Interested in Canadian concrete/visual poets.

ONE
48 South Street
Colchester, Essex, CO2 7BJ England
Ed and Poetry Ed: Wendy Cardy

Since: 1980	Circ: 200	Pages: 34	Per Year: ?
Size: 6 X 8	Perfect bound	Sample: $2 (Cdn.)	Sub: $8 (Cdn.)
Copyright: author	Book reviews: yes	Reviews/year: ?	Translations: yes
Interviews: yes	Fiction: yes	Essays: yes	Copies: yes
Money: no	Time: 1 month		

Authors published: Queenie Barker, Ken Miles, John Drinkwater, & Steve Powell

Christian magazine. Publishes poetry, travel, crafts, pets, gardening, visions, and personalities. Interested in material for children.

ORBIS
199 The Long Shoot, Nuneaton, Warwickshire, CV11 6JQ England
Ed and Poetry Ed: Mike Shields

Since: 1968	Circ: 1,000	Pages: 64	Per Year: 4
Size: 6 X 8	Perfect bound	Sample: $3 (Cdn.)	Sub: $28 (U.S.)
Copyright: author	Book reviews: yes	Reviews/year: 80	Translations: yes
Interviews: no	Fiction: no	Essays: rarely	Copies: 3
Money: yes	Time: 2 months		

Authors published: Earle Birney, Erin Mouré, Anne Szumigalski, Christopher Wiseman

Payment for sample/sub should be in cash, not by cheque. Publishes a wide variety of poetry, especially work in traditional forms. Supports rhyming poetry with a major annual competition— Rhyme Revival. Send SASE (IRC) for rules and guidelines. Haiku and other Japanese forms are rarely accepted. Interested in Canadian literature and has published a special Canadian issue.

OUTPOSTS POETRY QUARTERLY
22, Whitewell Road, Frome, Somerset, BA11 4EL England
Ed and Poetry Ed: Roland John

Since: 1944	Circ: 2,000	Pages: 85	Per Year: 4
Size: 6 X 8	Perfect bound	Sample: $8	Sub: $22
Copyright: author	Book reviews: yes	Reviews/year: 50	Translations: yes
Interviews: yes	Fiction: no	Essays: no	Copies: yes
Money: yes	Time: 2 weeks		

Authors published: Seamus Heaney, John Heath-Stubbs, Elizabeth Jennings, & Alan Brownjohn

Runs an annual poetry competition. Send SASE (IRC) for rules. One of the first, if not the first, English quarterlies to do a Canadian issue. Publishes a translation issue every year.

OWL MAGAZINE
Oxford University, Magdalen College, Oxford, OX1 4AU England
Eds and Poetry Eds: Jane Griffiths & Giles Scupham

PAGAN AMERICA
18 Chaddesley Road, Kidderminster, Worcestershire, DY10 3AD England
Ed and Poetry Ed: Jeremy Robinson

Since: 1991	Circ: 200	Pages: 60	Per Year: 2
Size: 6 X 8	Saddle stitched	Sample: $5 (U.S.)	Sub: $17 (U.S.)
Copyright: author	Book reviews: ?	Reviews/year: ?	Translations: yes
Interviews: ?	Fiction: yes	Essays: ?	Copies: 1
Money: no	Time: 3-4 months		

Authors published: Peter Redgrove, Penelope Shuttle, Jeremy Reed, D.J. Enright
We prefer non-rhyming and free verse. Welcomes gay and lesbian poetry. Also welcomes passionate, erotic, religious, and manic poetry.

PASSION
18 Chaddesley Road, Kidderminster, Worcestershire, DY10 3AD England
Ed and Poetry Ed: Jeremy Robinson

Since: 1994	Circ: 200	Pages: 60	Per Year: 4
Size: 6 X 8	Saddle stitched	Sample: $6 (U.S.)	Sub: $22 (U.S.)
Copyright: author	Book reviews: yes	Reviews/year: 50-100	Translations: yes
Interviews: yes	Fiction: yes	Essays: yes	Copies: 1
Money: no	Time: 3-4 months		

Authors published: Andrea Dworkin, V.S. Naipaul, Colin Wilson, & Alan Bold
Interested in politics, philosophy, media, and feminism. Poetry ranges from the passionate and erotic to the humorous.

PAUSE
27 Mill Road, Fareham, Hampshire, PO16 0TH England
Eds and Poetry Eds: Johnathon Clifford & Helen Robinson

PEACE & FREEDOM
17 Farrow Road, Whaplode Drove, Spalding, Lincolnshire, PE12 0TS England
Ed and Poetry Ed: Paul Rance

PEN & KEYBOARD MAGAZINE
526 Fulham Palace Road, London, SW6 6JE England
Ed and Poetry Ed: David Stern

Since: 1992	Circ: 200	Pages: 60	Per Year: 2
Size: 21 cm X 14.5 cm	Saddle stitched	Sample: 3 pounds	Sub: 12 pounds
Copyright: author	Book reviews: yes	Reviews/year: 6	Translations: yes
Interviews: yes	Fiction: yes	Essays: yes	Copies: yes
Money: maybe	Time: 1 month		

Authors published: Lynette Wadiow, Ray Wilson, Gregory Robb, & Tom McFaddon
Seeks poetry that has a sense of wonder. Doesn't like to agonize over hidden and subtle meanings. Avoids the infantile and the sickly sweet. Short stories should fall within the 2,000 to 2,500 word range.

PENNINE PLATFORM
Ingmanthorpe Hall Farm Cottage, Wetherby, West Yorkshire LS22 5EQ, England
Ed and Poetry Ed: Brian Merrikin Hill

Since: 1966	Circ: 300	Pages: 40	Per Year: 3
Size: 6 X 8	Saddle stitched	Sample: 2.30 pounds	Sub: 7 pounds
Copyright: author	Book reviews: yes	Reviews/year: 15	Translations: yes
Interviews: no	Fiction: no	Essays: no	Copies: 2
Money: no	Time: 2 months		

Authors published: Peter Russell, John Ward, & Ann Adams

Payment for sample/sub should be by British cheque or in cash. Favours poems of spiritual, religious, or socio-political awareness. (But no agitprop.) Prefers formalist poetry although well-crafted free verse is accepted.

THE PEOPLE'S POETRY
71 Harrow Crescent, Romford, Essex, RM3 7BJ England
Ed and Poetry Ed: P.G.P. Thompson

Since: 1991	Circ: 500	Pages: 32	Per Year: 4
Size: ?	Saddle stitched	Sample: 1.50 pounds	Sub: 5 pounds
Copyright: author	Book reviews: no	Reviews/year: n/a	Translations: no
Interviews: no	Fiction: no	Essays: no	Copies: 1
Money: no	Time: 1-2 months		

Authors published: Gerald England, Peter Russell, Pamela Constantine, & Peter Geoffrey Paul Thompson

Poetry of the Romantic school— Shelleyan. Poetry should be accessible. Looks for soulful, spiritual, inspirational poetry.

PHOENIX BROADSHEETS
78 Cambridge Street, Leicester, LE3 0JP England
Ed and Poetry Ed: Toni Savage

PLANET— The Welsh Internationalist
PO Box 44, Aberystwyth, Dyfed Wales
Ed and Poetry Ed: John Barnie

Since: 1970	Circ: 1,400	Pages: 120	Per Year: 6
Size: 6 X 8	Perfect bound	Sample: 3.50 pounds	Sub: 13 pounds
Copyright: author	Book reviews: yes	Reviews/year: 80	Translations: yes
Interviews: yes	Fiction: yes	Essays: yes	Copies: 1
Money: 25 pounds/poem	Time: 4-6 weeks		

Authors published: R.S. Thomas, Les Murray, Sarah Kirsch, & Randolph Stow

Only publishes 6 to 8 poems per issue. Pays 40 pounds/1,000 words for prose.

POETRY DURHAM
University of Durham, School of English, Elvet Riverside, New Elvet, Durham DH1 3JT England
Eds and Poetry Eds: David Hartnett, Michael O'Neill, & Gareth Reeves

POETRY LIFE
14 Pennington Oval, Lymington, Hampshire, SO41 8BQ England
Eds and Poetry Eds: Adrian Bishop & Anna Markey

Since: 1993	Circ: 1,400	Pages: 30	Per Year: 3
Size: 6 X 8	Saddle stitched	Sample: 2 pounds	Sub: 6 pounds

Copyright: author	Book reviews: yes	Reviews/year: 4-5	Translations: no
Interviews: yes	Fiction: no	Essays: no	Copies: yes
Money: yes	Time: 1 month		

Authors published: Caroil Ann Duffy, Les Murray, Michael Donaghy, & Kamau Braithwaite

Poems published are the winners of the Poetry Life Open Poetry Competition. There are cash prizes from 500 pounds to 50 pounds. Please send SAE (IRC) for contest rules.

POETRY NOTTINGHAM INTERNATIONAL
39 Cavendish Road, Long Eaton, Nottingham, NG10 4HY England
Ed: Martin Holroyd   Poetry Eds: Cathy Grindrod & Jeremy Duffield

Since: 1941	Circ: 250	Pages: 44	Per Year: 4
Size: 15 cm X 21 cm	Saddle stitched	Sample: 3 pounds	Sub: 14 pounds
Copyright: author	Book reviews: yes	Reviews/year: 4	Translations: yes
Interviews: ?	Fiction: no	Essays: yes	Copies: 1
Money: no	Time: 3-6 months		

Authors published: Barry Butson, Ian Gough, Margaret Colebrook Pearce, & Joseph Epstein

We do not publish any poetry that discriminates between one social group or another or poems that incite hatred between races or religions.

POETRY REVIEW
Poetry Society, 21 Earls Court Square, London, SW5 9DE England
Ed and Poetry Ed: Peter Forbes

Since: 1909	Circ: 5,000	Pages: 96	Per Year: 4
Size: 6 1/2 X 9 1/2	Perfect bound	Sample: 6.50 pounds	Sub: 23 pounds
Copyright: author	Book reviews: yes	Reviews/year: 120	Translations: yes
Interviews: yes	Fiction: no	Essays: yes	Copies: 1
Money: 15 pounds/poem	Time: 3 months		

Authors published: Fleur Adcock, Tony Harrison, U.A. Fanthorpe, & R.S. Thomas

Considers a wide range of poetry, but good, fat, longish-lined poems are preferred. This is the quarterly of the Poetry Society, but North American poets are often published.

POETRY WALES
26 Andrew's Close, Heolgerrig, Merthyr Tydfil, Mid Glamorgan, CF48 1SS Wales
Eds and Poetry Eds: Mike Jenkins & Richard Poole

PREMONITIONS
13 Hazely Combe, Arreton, Isle of Wight, PO30 3AJ England
Ed and Poetry Ed: Tony Lee

Since: ?	Circ: ?	Pages: 80	Per Year: 1
Size: 6 X 8	Saddle stitched	Sample: $9 (U.S.)	Sub: $35 (U.S.)
Copyright: author	Book reviews: no	Reviews/year: n/a	Translations: yes
Interviews: no	Fiction: yes	Essays: no	Copies: yes
Money: no	Time: 3 weeks		

Authors published: Steve Sneyd, Bruce Boston, Wayne Edwards, & Don Webb

A subscription covers four annual issues. Science fiction poems and stories only. Uses a dozen short stories per issue.

PSYCHOPOETICA

University of Hull, Department of Psychology, Hull, HU6 7RX England

Eds and Poetry Eds: Geoff Lowe & Trevor Millum

Since: 1981	Circ: 300	Pages: 50	Per Year: 3-4
Size: 8 X 12	Perfect bound	Sample: 1.50 pounds	Sub: $16 (U.S.)
Copyright: author	Book reviews: yes	Reviews/year: 36	Translations: no
Interviews: no	Fiction: no	Essays: no	Copies: 1
Money: no	Time: 1 month		

Authors published: Dylan Pugh, Jeffrey Hanson, Charlie Mehrhoff, & D.F. Lewis

Wants psychologically-based poetry.

PURPLE PATCH

8 Beaconview House, Charlemont Farm, West Bromwich, West Midlands, B71 3PL England

Ed and Poetry Ed: Geoff Stevens

Since: 1976	Circ: ?	Pages: 14	Per Year: 3-6
Size: 11 1/2 X 8	Saddle stitched	Sample: $3 (Cdn.)	Sub: $10 (Cdn.)
Copyright: author	Book reviews: yes	Reviews/year: 150	Translations: no
Interviews: yes	Fiction: yes	Essays: yes	Copies: no
Money: no	Time: 2 weeks		

Authors published: James Michael Robbins, R.G. Bishop, R.D. Black, & Maureen Weldon

Payment should be in cash, not by cheque. Payment for sample ($3) can be in Canadian postage stamps. All fiction and essays must be very short. Reads submissions year round.

REFLECTIONS

PO Box 70, Sunderland, Tyne and Wear, SR1 1DU England

Since: 1991	Circ: 100	Pages: 20	Per Year: 4
Size: 6 X 8	Saddle stitched	Sample: 1 pound	Sub: 6.20 pounds
Copyright: author	Book reviews: no	Reviews/year: n/a	Translations: yes
Interviews: no	Fiction: yes	Essays: yes	Copies: 1
Money: no	Time: 3 months		

Limit for essays is 1,500 words maximum. Also wants black and white artwork/photos.

THE REID REVIEW

8 Mendip Court, Avonley Village, Avonley Road, London, SE14 5EU England

Ed and Poetry Ed: Nick Reid

THE RIALTO

32 Grosvenor Road, Norwich, Norfolk, NR2 2PZ England

Eds and Poetry Eds: Michael Mackmin & John Wakeman

Since: 1984	Circ: 1,500	Pages: 48	Per Year: 3
Size: 8 X 12	Perfect bound	Sample: 6 pounds	Sub: 16 pounds
Copyright: author	Book reviews: no	Reviews/year: n/a	Translations: yes
Interviews: ?	Fiction: no	Essays: yes	Copies: yes
Money: 10 pounds/poem	Time: 3 months		

Authors published: Carol Ann Duffy, Les Murray, Fleur Adcock, & Brendan Kennelly

A RIOT OF EMOTIONS

PO Box HK31, Leeds, West Yorkshire, LS11 9XN England

Ed and Poetry Ed: Andrew Cocker

Since: 1989	Circ: 1,000	Pages: 40	Per Year: 1-2
Size: 5 1/2 X 8	Saddle stitched	Sample: $3	Sub: n/a
Copyright: author	Book reviews: yes	Reviews/year: ?	Translations: ?
Interviews: maybe	Fiction: yes	Essays: maybe	Copies: yes
Money: no	Time: 3 weeks		

Authors published: Steve Sneyd, Lainie Duro, Andrew Darlington, & Crystal Indiankhana Candy

Favours the bizarre, the strange, and the esoteric as well as science fiction. Please send SAE (IRC) for full contributors' guidelines. Welcomes short stories of up to 2,000 words.

RUSTIC RUB

14 Hillfield, Selby, North Yorkshire, YO8 0ND England

Ed and Poetry Ed: (Mrs.) Jay Woodman

Since: 1993	Circ: 300	Pages: 80	Per Year: 2
Size: 6 X 8	Perfect bound	Sample: 4 pounds	Sub: 7 pounds
Copyright: author	Book reviews: no	Reviews/year: n/a	Translations: yes
Interviews: yes	Fiction: no	Essays: yes	Copies: 1
Money: no	Time: 2 weeks		

Authors published: John Alan Douglas, Sheila E. Murphy, & David Caddy

Open to all types of poetry. Reads submissions all year.

SEPIA

Knill Cross House, Knill Cross, Millbrook, Nr. Torpoint, Cornwall, PL10 1DX England

Ed and Poetry Ed: Colin Webb

Since: 1977	Circ: 125	Pages: 32	Per Year: 3
Size: 6 X 8	Saddle stitched	Sample: 50 pence	Sub: 2 pounds
Copyright: author	Book reviews: yes	Reviews/year: 20	Translations: yes
Interviews: no	Fiction: yes	Essays: yes	Copies: yes
Money: no	Time: 10 days		

Authors published: Jesse Glass, Jr., Frank Minogue, Jacques du Lumiere, & Serge le Comte

Accepts non-traditional poetry— no rhymes, avoid strict metre— and stories. Prefers a more prosaic approach to a lyrical approach.

SKELETON GIRLS

Ty Fraen, The Park, Blaenavon, Gwent, NP4 9AG Wales

Eds and Poetry Eds: Em, Ali, Princess Spider, Sekhmet, Black Countess, Cyrthia, & Paola

Since: 1991	Circ: ?	Pages: 40	Per Year: ?
Size: 6 X 8	Saddle stitched	Sample: 3 pounds	Sub: n/a
Copyright: author	Book reviews: yes	Reviews/year: ?	Translations: yes
Interviews: yes	Fiction: yes	Essays: yes	Copies: no
Money: no	Time: ?		

Authors published: Andrew Darlington, Steve Sneyd, D.F. Lewis, & Jon Summers

Special interests include: the Gothic, Goddesses, Princess Spider, female revenge, Black Countess, Circe/witches, and male angels. *Skeleton Girls* is also called *Roisin Dubh* and *Knochenmädchen In Pelze Mit Peitsche.*

SLOW DANCER
U.S. address: Box 149A, RFD 1, Lubec, ME 04652
Eds: John Harvey & Alan Brooks   Poetry Ed: Alan Brooks (N. American)

SMITHS KNOLL
49 Church Road, Little Glemham, Woodbridge, Suffolk, IP13 0BJ England
Eds and Poetry Eds: Roy Blackman & Michael Laskey

Since: 1991	Circ: 300	Pages: 60	Per Year: 3
Size: 14 cm X 21 cm	Perfect bound	Sample: 3 pounds	Sub: 8 pounds
Copyright: author	Book reviews: no	Reviews/year: n/a	Translations: yes
Interviews: no	Fiction: no	Essays: no	Copies: 1
Money: 5 pounds/poem	Time: 2 weeks		

Authors published: Carole Satyamurti, Robert Etty, Patricia Pogson, & John Latham
Very seldom accepts poems of less than eight lines or more than two pages. Seldom finds rhymed poems good enough. Very seldom interested in poems about writing poetry. Very seldom prints concrete poems. Please send no more than five poems at one time.

SMOKE
40 Canning Street, Liverpool, L8 7NP England
Eds and Poetry Eds: Dave Ward & Dave Calder

Since: 1974	Circ: 1,000	Pages: 24	Per Year: 2
Size: 6 X 8	Saddle stitched	Sample: $2	Sub: $5
Copyright: author	Book reviews: no	Reviews/year: n/a	Translations: rarely
Interviews: no	Fiction: some	Essays: no	Copies: yes
Money: no	Time: 2 months		

Authors published: Miroslav Holub, Carol Ann Duffy, Douglas Dunn, & Libby Houston
Prefers short poems and short fiction in the modern style. Payment for sample/sub should be in cash.

SOL MAGAZINE
58 Malvern, Coleman Street, Southend-on-Sea, Essex, SS2 5AD England
Ed and Poetry Ed: Malcolm E. Wright

Since: 1969	Circ: 250	Pages: 60	Per Year: 2
Size: 6 X 8	Saddle stitched	Sample: 1.50 pounds	Sub: 6.50 pounds
Copyright: author	Book reviews: yes	Reviews/year: ?	Translations: maybe
Interviews: maybe	Fiction: yes	Essays: yes	Copies: 1
Money: no	Time: 3 months		

Authors published: Gavin Ewart, Roger McGough, Ian Macmillan, & Rupert Mallin
Subscriptions run for two years; payment should be by cash, not cheque. Considers all types of poetry all year.

SOUTH
61 West Borough, Wimborne, Dorset, BH21 1LX England
Ed and Poetry Ed: by Committee

Since: 1990	Circ: 250	Pages: 56	Per Year: 2
Size: 6 X 8 1/2	Saddle stitched	Sample: 2.25 pounds	Sub: 6 pounds
Copyright: author	Book reviews: no	Reviews/year: n/a	Translations: ?
Interviews: ?	Fiction: no	Essays: no	Copies: 1
Money: no	Time: ?		

Authors published: R.G. Gregory, David Orme, Brian Hinton, & Terry Diffey

Submit six poems at a time. Also interested in black and white graphics if they relate to the poetry. While the focus is on the south of England, poems are chosen for their quality.

SOUTHFIELDS
98 Gressenhall Road, London, SW18 5QJ England
Eds and Poetry Eds: Raymond Friel & Richard Price

Since: 1994	Circ: 300	Pages: 180	Per Year: 1
Size: 6 X 8	Perfect bound	Sample: 7 pounds	Sub: 13 pounds
Copyright: author	Book reviews: yes	Reviews/year: 6	Translations: yes
Interviews: maybe	Fiction: yes	Essays: yes	Copies: 1
Money: no	Time: 6-8 weeks		

Authors published: Edwin Morgan, Tom Paulin, John Burnside, & David Kinloch

Subscriptions cover two annual issues. Every issue has a theme; please send SAE (IRC) for information. This is a London magazine with a Scottish accent. Interested in all art forms, with a particular interest in poetry.

SPECTACULAR DISEASES
83 (b) London Road, Peterborough, Cambridgeshire, PE2 9BS England
Ed and Poetry Ed: Paul Green

Since: 1974	Circ: 500	Pages: 80	Per Year: ?
Size: 6 X 8	Perfect bound	Sample: $5	Sub: $20/4 issues
Copyright: author	Book reviews: no	Reviews/year: n/a	Translations: yes
Interviews: yes	Fiction: maybe	Essays: yes	Copies: yes
Money: no	Time: 2 weeks		

Authors published: Allen Fisher, Jackson MacLow, Don David, & Bernard Noël

Open to experimental poetry only. Good long poems are sought after. Work is read at any time. Essays should be relevant to experimental poetry/poets. Please inquire about interviews and forty-page poems.

STAPLE MAGAZINE
Tor Cottage, 81 Cavendish Road, Matlock, Derbyshire, DE4 3HD England
Eds and Poetry Eds: Donald Measham & Bob Windsor

Since: 1982	Circ: 500-800	Pages: 90	Per Year: 3
Size: 6 X 8	Perfect bound	Sample: 3 pounds	Sub: 15 pounds
Copyright: author	Book reviews: no	Reviews/year: n/a	Translations: yes
Interviews: maybe	Fiction: yes	Essays: ?	Copies: 3
Money: no	Time: ?		

Authors published: Michael J. Bakerpearce, Jennifer Olds, James Brockway, & Christopher Oliver

Best times for submission: February/March, July/September, and December. A mainstream poetry magazine— emphasis on craft, though not necessarily tradition. Runs an open poetry competition; please send SAE (IRC) for contest rules.

SUNK ISLAND REVIEW
PO Box 74, Lincoln, LN1 1QG England
Ed and Poetry Ed: Michael Blackburn

Since: 1989	Circ: 1,000	Pages: 100	Per Year: 2
Size: 13 cm X 20 cm	Perfect bound	Sample: 7 pounds	Sub: 14 pounds

Copyright: author	Book reviews: yes	Reviews/year: ?	Translations: yes
Interviews: maybe	Fiction: yes	Essays: yes	Copies: 2
Money: 10-20 pounds	Time: 4-6 weeks		

Authors published: Elisaviztta Ritchie, Sean O'Brien, Penelope Shuttle, & Ken Smith

Mainly a fiction magazine, but always contains 6 to 8 poems per issue. E-mail address: 100074.140@compuserve.com for information, writers' guidelines plus submissions. Also publishes poetry on floppy computer disc (The Electronic Poetry Pack)— send 3 IRCs. Runs a poetry contest with 1,000 pounds in prizes.

SUPER TROUPER AUDIOZINE
81 Castlerigg Drive, Burnley, Lancashire, BB12 8AT England
Ed and Poetry Ed: Andrew Savage

Since: 1985	Circ: 100	Pages: n/a	Per Year: 4
Size: n/a	Audio cassette	Sample: $5 (U.S.)	Sub: $16 (U.S.)
Copyright: author	Book reviews: yes	Reviews/year: 60	Translations: yes
Interviews: yes	Fiction: no	Essays: no	Copies: 1
Money: ?	Time: 1-3 months		

Authors published: Steve Sneyd, Lovely Ivor, Ian Sawicki, & Mathew Dalby

Submissions of up to four poems should be sent on audiotape. Each poem should be no longer than three minutes. Prefers comedy. Poems set to music or weird sounds are most welcome. Also accepts songs, comedy sketches, short reviews, short interviews, friendly chat and laughter.

TABLA
7 Parliament Hill, London, NW3 2SY England
Ed and Poetry Ed: Stephen James Ellis

Since: 1991	Circ: 300	Pages: 100	Per Year: 1
Size: 6 X 8	Perfect bound	Sample: 2.50 pounds	Sub: n/a
Copyright: author	Book reviews: yes	Reviews/year: 3	Translations: yes
Interviews: no	Fiction: no	Essays: no	Copies: 1
Money: no	Time: 1 month		

Authors published: David Constantine, Kathleen Raine, Peter Redgrove, & Jeremy Reed

The annual issue is published in the spring. ALL work accepted is work entered in the annual poetry competition. Please send SAE (IRC) for full details.

TALUS
King's College, Department of English, Strand, London, WC2R 2LS England
Eds: Marzia Balzani & Stephen Want

Since: 1987	Circ: 200	Pages: 130	Per Year: 1
Size: ?	Perfect bound	Sample: 5 pounds	Sub: 10 pounds
Copyright: author	Book reviews: no	Reviews/year: n/a	Translations: yes
Interviews: yes	Fiction: yes	Essays: yes	Copies: 2
Money: no	Time: 1 year		

Authors published: Anne Waldman, Jerome Rothenberg, Robert Kelly, & Eric Mottram

Particularly welcomes articles on inter-cultural issues.

TANDEM
13 Stephenson Road, Barbourne, Worcester, WR1 3EB England
Ed and Poetry Ed: Michael J. Woods

| Since: 1993 | Circ: 700 | Pages: ? | Per Year 3: |
| Size: 6 X 8 | Perfect bound | Sample: 3.75 pounds | Sub: 12 pounds |

Copyright: author	Book reviews: yes	Reviews/year: 3	Translations: yes
Interviews: yes	Fiction: yes	Essays: ?	Copies: 1
Money: no	Time: 2 weeks		

Authors published: Seamus Heaney, Carol Ann Duffy, Jo Shapcott, & Benjamin Zephaniah

All types of poetry welcome; very catholic outlook. Mostly poetry; very limited amount of fiction used.

TEARS IN THE FENCE
38 Hod View, Stourpaine, Nr. Blandford Forum, Dorset, DT11 8TN England
Ed and Poetry Ed: David Caddy

Since: 1984	Circ: 500	Pages: 80	Per Year: 3
Size: 6 X 8	Perfect bound	Sample: $5 (U.S.)	Sub: $15 (U.S.)
Copyright: author	Book reviews: yes	Reviews/year: 70	Translations: yes
Interviews: yes	Fiction: yes	Essays: yes	Copies: yes
Money: ?	Time: 1 month		

Authors published: Gerald Locklin, Donna Hilbert, Martin Stannard, & Mary Maher

Payment for sample/sub should be in U.S. currency, not by cheque. Poetry and fiction should communicate the temper and range of lived experience. Runs an annual chapbook contest for manuscripts of up to 24 pages of poetry. Please send SAE (IRC) for competition rules.

10th MUSE
33 Hartington Road, Southampton, Hampshire, SO14 0EW England
Ed and Poetry Ed: Andy Jordan

Since: 1990	Circ: 250	Pages: 48	Per Year: 2
Size: 6 X 8	Saddle stitched	Sample: $5 (Cdn.)	Sub: $10 (Cdn.)
Copyright: author	Book reviews: yes	Reviews/year: ?	Translations: no
Interviews: no	Fiction: yes	Essays: yes	Copies: yes
Money: no	Time: 3 months		

Authors published: Peter Redgrove, Steve Sneyd, Vittoria Vaughan, & Norman Jope

Payment for sample/sub should be in Canadian bills, not by cheque. The limit for fiction and essays is 2,000 words. Most American poetry I get sent is about screwing and it is very sad. I hope Canadian poets have something more to say.

TERRIBLE WORK
21 Overton Gardens, Mannamead, Plymouth, Devon, PL3 5BX England
Eds: Tim Allen & Alexis Kirke

Since: 1993	Circ: 250	Pages: 92	Per Year: 2
Size: 6 X 8	Perfect bound	Sample: $7 (U.S.)	Sub: $20 (U.S.)
Copyright: author	Book reviews: yes	Reviews/year: ?	Translations: yes
Interviews: no	Fiction: yes	Essays: yes	Copies: 1
Money: no	Time: 1-3 months		

Authors published: Sheila E. Murphy, Peter Redgrove, Roy Fisher, & Spencer Selby

Tries to be left-field and eclectic. With overseas contributors we are more interested in innovative poetry. Subscriptions run for three issues.

THE THIRD ALTERNATIVE
5 Martins Lane, Witcham, Ely, Cambridgeshire, CB6 2LB England
Ed and Poetry Ed: Andy Cox

Since: 1994	Circ: 1,000	Pages: 60	Per Year: 4
Size: 6 X b	Saddle stitched	Sample: $9 (Cdn.)	Sub: $30 (Cdn.)

Copyright: author	Book reviews: yes	Reviews/year: ?	Translations: yes
Interviews: yes	Fiction: yes	Essays: yes	Copies: yes
Money: yes	Time: 1 month		

Authors published: Sheila E. Murphy, Bruce Boston, David Chorlton, & Albert Russo

Open to submissions year round. Publishes modern poetry from the fields of fantasy, horror, and science fiction, but does NOT use genre cliches. Not keen on rhyming poetry or haiku.

THE THIRD HALF LITERARY MAGAZINE
16, Fane Close, Stamford, Lincolnshire, PE9 1HG England
Ed and Poetry Ed: Kevin Troop

Since: 1987	Circ: ?	Pages: 100	Per Year: 2-3
Size: 6 X 8	Perfect bound	Sample: 3 pounds	Sub: n/a
Copyright: author	Book reviews: no	Reviews/year: n/a	Translations: yes
Interviews: maybe	Fiction: yes	Essays: maybe	Copies: yes
Money: no	Time: ?		

Authors published: Steve Sneyd, Pauline Kirk, Michael Newman, & Isabel Cortan

Send up to six poems at one time. All styles welcome.

THREADS
32 Irvin Avenue, Saltburn, Cleveland, TS12 1QH England
Ed and Poetry Ed: Geoff Lynas

Since: 1993	Circ: 100	Pages: 56	Per Year: 4
Size: 6 X 8	Binding: ?	Sample: 3.50 pounds	Sub: 12.50 pounds
Copyright: author	Book reviews: yes	Reviews/year: ?	Translations: no
Interviews: no	Fiction: yes	Essays: no	Copies: 1
Money: no	Time: 9 weeks		

Authors published: Steve Sneyd, Andy Darlington, Mike Hoy, & Sidney Morleigh

Mostly a short story magazine; usually no more than six poems per issue. Focus is on science fiction and fantasy. Runs the BSPG Poetry Competition; SAE (IRC) for details. As a rule is overstocked with poetry; it can be a very long wait between acceptance and publication.

UNDER SURVEILLANCE
60 Arnold Street, Brighton, East Sussex, BN2 2XT England
Ed and Poetry Ed: Eddie Harriman

Since: 1994	Circ: 500	Pages: 32-36	Per Year: 2-3
Size: 14 cm X 20 cm	Saddle stitched	Sample: $5 (U.S.)	Sub: $15 (U.S.)
Copyright: author	Book reviews: yes	Reviews/year: ?	Translations: yes
Interviews: no	Fiction: no	Essays: no	Copies: 2
Money: no	Time: 1-2 months		

Authors published: Lee Harwood, Laurel Speer, Brian Patten, & Mary Rudbeck

Poetry preferably with a socio-political bias "investigating" the strengths and weaknesses, the beauty and ugliness, of the culture and environment, both historically and futuristically, the writers inhabit, or foresee to be their fate. All year round submissions considered.

VARIOUS ARTISTS
65 Springfield Avenue, Horfield, Bristol, Avon, BS7 9QS England
Ed and Poetry Ed: Tony Lewis Jones

Since: 1992	Circ: 250	Pages: 24	Per Year: 1
Size: 6 X 8	Saddle stitched	Sample: 1 pound	Sub: 3 pounds
Copyright: author	Book reviews: yes	Reviews/year: ?	Translations: yes
Interviews: no	Fiction: no	Essays: no	Copies: 2
Money: no	Time: 1 week		

Authors published: Dylan Pugh, Vittoria Vaughan, Barry Butson, & Mary Maher

Open to poetry in all shapes and sizes, formal or free verse. Best time to submit is autumn.

VERSE
University College, Oxford, OX1 4BH England
Eds and Poetry Eds: Nancy Schoenberger & Brian Henry

Since: 1984	Circ: 1,000	Pages: 135	Per Year: 3
Size: 6 X 9	Perfect bound	Sample: $6	Sub: $15
Copyright: author	Book reviews: yes	Reviews/year: 15-25	Translations: yes
Interviews: yes	Fiction: no	Essays: yes	Copies: 2
Money: no	Time: 1-2 months		

Authors published: Seamus Heaney, Czeslaw Milosz, John Ashbery, & Margaret Atwood

Considers submissions all year. Has published a special Canadian feature. Has also published an issue with 26 poets interviewed— "Talking Verse." Very interested in translations and critical articles.

WEST COAST MAGAZINE
Unit F8, Festival Business Centre, 150 Brand Street, Glasgow, G51 1DH Scotland
Ed: Joe Murray   Poetry Ed: Brian Whittingham

Since: 1988	Circ: 800	Pages: 44	Per Year: 3-4
Size: 8 X 12	Saddle stitched	Sample: 3.50 pounds	Sub: 20 pounds
Copyright: author	Book reviews: yes	Reviews/year: 20	Translations: yes
Interviews: yes	Fiction: yes	Essays: yes	Copies: yes
Money: 10-15 pounds	Time: 2 months		

Authors published: Julie Brittain, Carol Mgt. Davidson, Denise Duhamel, & Sharon Cumberland

Open to all types of writing all year. Focus is mainly on new writing in Scotland, but accepts good work wherever it comes from.

WORKS
12 Blakestones Road, Slaithwaite, Huddersfield, West Yorkshire, HD7 5UQ England
Ed and Poetry Ed: Dave W. Hughes

Since: 1988	Circ: 2,000	Pages: 40	Per Year: 2
Size: 6 X 8	Saddle stitched	Sample: 4 pounds	Sub: 8 pounds
Copyright: author	Book reviews: no	Reviews/year: n/a	Translations: no
Interviews: no	Fiction: yes	Essays: yes	Copies: yes
Money: ?	Time: 2 weeks		

Authors published: Steve Sneyd, Andy Darlington, Bruce Boston, & Winter Damon

Seeks science fiction poetry of no more than fifty lines.

WRITERS VIEWPOINT
PO Box 514, Eastbourne, East Sussex, BN23 6RE England
Ed and Poetry Ed: Belinda Rance

Since: 1993	Circ: 1,000	Pages: 30	Per Year: 4

Size: 6 X 8	Binding: ?	Sample: 3.50 pounds	Sub: 20 pounds
Copyright: author	Book reviews: yes	Reviews/year: 10	Translations: yes
Interviews: yes	Fiction: yes	Essays: yes	Copies: yes
Money: no	Time: 1 day		

Authors published: Sam Smith, R.L. Cook, Kenneth Stevens, & Marion Primrose

All work published is by subscribers to the magazine. Runs quarterly literary competitions. Please send SAE (IRC) for complete details. Interested in traditional, contemporary, and/or experimental material, but not keen on religious or didactic poetry. Poems must not exceed forty lines.

X-CALIBRE
Nemeton Publishing, PO Box 780, Bristol, BS99 5BB England
Eds and Poetry Eds: Juli & Ken Taylor

ZIMMERFRAMEPILEUP
54 Hillcrest Road, Waltnamstow, London, E17 4AP England
Ed and Poetry Ed: Stephen Jessener

Since: 1994	Circ: 150	Pages: 22	Per Year: 12
Size: ?	Stapled	Sample: 1.30 pounds	Sub: 17 pounds
Copyright: author	Book reviews: yes	Reviews/year: 12	Translations: yes
Interviews: yes	Fiction: yes	Essays: yes	Copies: 1
Money: no	Time: 1-2 weeks		

Authors published: Brian Pastoor, Bashō, & Bob Black

Anything considered. Only publishes silly book reviews. Will consider interviews with normal people. Fiction must be short— storiettes.

THE ZONE
13 Hazely Combe, Arreton, Isle of Wight, PO30 3AJ England
Ed and Poetry Ed: Tony Lee

Since: 1994	Circ: ?	Pages: 40	Per Year: 2-3
Size: 6 X 8	Saddle stitched	Sample: $9 (U.S.)	Sub: $45 (U.S.)
Copyright: author	Book reviews: yes	Reviews/year: ?	Translations: yes
Interviews: yes	Fiction: yes	Essays: yes	Copies: yes
Money: $10	Time: 1 month		

Authors published: Bruce Boston & J.P.V. Stewart

Science fiction only. Showcases one poet per issue by invitation only, so please inquire with SAE (IRC). Subscriptions run for five issues. Cheques/I.M.O.s should be payable to "Tony Lee."

The following 24 periodicals have ceased publication since the fifth edition of this book, or they are no longer interested in Canadian poetry, or they have asked to be delisted:

Boundary Magazine	**The Frogmore Papers**
Casablanca	**Label**
Corpus Journal	**The Last Ever Melodic Scribble**
Dada Dance Magazine	**Lines Review**
The Echo Room	**Margin**

The Old Police Station (TOPS)
Ordinance
Quest
Rock Drill
Spanner
Stand Magazine
Steppin Out

Stride
Tak Tak Tak
Ver Poets Voices
Westwords
Weyfarers
The White Rose
Writing

The following 22 periodicals, believed to be still publishing poetry, failed to respond to requests for information. This could indicate a lack of interest in Canadian poetry. They are listed here because a number of the leading journals published in England, Scotland, and Wales— *Bete Noire* and *Oxford Poetry*, for example— are in this category.

Bestings
19 Southminster Road
Roath, Cardiff, CF2 5AT, Wales

Bete Noire
American Studies Department
The University, Cottingham Road
Hull, HU6 7RX, England

The Bound Spiral
Open Poetry Conventicle
72 First Avenue, Bush Hill Park
Enfield, EN1 1BW, England

Brimstone Signatures
St. Lawrence Cottage
Sellman Street
Gnosall, Stafford, ST20 0EP, England

Distaff
London Women's Centre
Wesley House, 4 Wild Court
Kingsway, London, WC2, England

Fragmente
8 Hertford Street
Oxford, OX4 3AJ, England

Grim Humour
PO Box 63, Herne Bay
Kent, CT6 6YU, England

Magpie's Nest
176 Stoney Lane, Sparkhill
Birmingham, B12 8AN, England

New Departures
Piedmont
Bisley, near Stroud
Gloucestershire, GL6 7BU, England

Ostinato
PO Box 522
London, N8 7SZ, England

Oxford Poetry
Oxford University
Magdalen College
Oxford, OX1 4AU, England

Pages
239 Lessingham Avenue
London, SW17 8NQ, England

Paladin
66 Heywood Court
Tenby, Dyfed, SA70 8DE, Wales

P.N. Review
402 - 406 Corn Exchange
Manchester, M4 3BY, England

Poetry Digest
28 Stainsdale Green
Whitwick
Leicester, LE67 5PW, England

Poetry London Newsletter
PO Box 4LF
London, W1A 4LF, England

The Printer's Devil
Top Offices, 13A Western Road
Hove, East Sussex
BN3 IAE, England

Scratch
9 Chestnut Road, Eaglescliffe
Stockton-on-Tees, TSI6 OBA, England

Tees Valley Writer
57 The Avenue
Linthorpe, Middlesborough
Cleveland, TS5 6QU, England

The Wide Skirt
28 St. Helen's Street
Elsecar, Barnsley
South Yorkshire, S74 8BH, England

Working Titles
The Hollies, 29 St. Martin's Road
Knowle, Bristol, BS4 2NQ, England

Writing Women
Unit 14, Hawthorn House, Forth Banks
Newcastle upon Tyne, NEI 3SG, England

1.8 OTHER INTERNATIONAL PERIODICAL LISTINGS

The following 61 periodicals publish poetry in English and all have expressed interest in considering the work of Canadian poets. Some of them are located in English-speaking countries like Australia, others in non-English-speaking countries like France, Italy, and Japan.

Because few of these journals will be found at your local public library, you may have to purchase sample copies to get to know them. Prices quoted tend to be in local currencies— Australian dollars, Japanese yen— or in U.S. dollars. (Indeed, you might assume that all Australian prices are in Australian funds, and that the rest that use the dollar sign ($) are in U.S. funds.) This is not a knock against the Canuck buck. The American currency just happens to function as international money. When sending for sample copies, it is best to use international money orders because many countries have odd exchange policies.

Remember to supply sufficient return postage in the form of International Reply Coupons. Replies may take up to six months (or even a year) due to the slowness of surface mail.

AUSTRALIA

BLAST
PO Box 3514, Manuka, Australian Capital Territory, 2603 Australia
Eds: Bill Tully & Ann Nugent   Poetry Ed: Ann Nugent

EDDIE THE MAGAZINE
PO Box 199, Newtown, New South Wales, 2042 Australia
Ed: Eddie Greenaway

Since: 1991	Circ: 5,000	Pages: 90	Per Year: 3
Size: 13.5 cm X 21 cm	Perfect bound	Sample: $6 (U.S.)	Sub: $20 (U.S.)
Copyright: author	Book reviews: yes	Reviews/year: 30	Translations: no
Interviews: yes	Fiction: yes	Essays: yes	Copies: 1
Money: no	Time: ?		

Authors published: Mikol Furneaux, Thoddeus Rutkowski, Leanne Formica, & Michelle Zintschenko

Magazine retains anthology rights; all others stay with author. Bias towards local poets, but will consider Canadian work. Prefers gritty, social realist, and punk writing. Nothing overtly political, but social satire and humour welcome.

GOING DOWN SWINGING
PO Box 24, Clifton Hill, Victoria, 3068 Australia
Eds and Poetry Eds: Louise Craig & Lyn Boughton

Since: 1980	Circ: 1,000	Pages: 190	Per Year: 1
Size: 27.5 cm X 20 cm	Saddle stitched	Sample: $10 (Aus)	Sub: $20 (Aus)
Copyright: author	Book reviews: yes	Reviews/year: 3-5	Translations: yes
Interviews: yes	Fiction: yes	Essays: yes	Copies: 1

Money: maybe   Time: 3-4 months
Authors published: Billie Livingston, Coral Hull, Eric Beach, & Peter Bakowski

No sexist or racist material. All types of writing welcome. Aims to encourage new and innovative poets; also interested in new work from more established poets. Accepts submissions from June to November.

HERMES
University of Sydney, Publications Centre, Manning House, Sydney, New South Wales, 2006 Australia
Eds: Thomas Clark & Sue Bower

Since: 1884	Circ: 500	Pages: 108	Per Year: 2
Size: 6 X 8	Perfect bound	Sample: $6 (Aus)	Sub: $20 (Aus)
Copyright: author	Book reviews: yes	Reviews/year: 8	Translations: yes
Interviews: yes	Fiction: yes	Essays: yes	Copies: 1
Money: no	Time: ?		

Authors published: John Tranter, Kate Lewellyn, Robert Adamson, & Coral Hull

Canadian writers may submit work if they have published in Australian publications before, or if they intend to continue to publish in Australian magazines. Interested in black and white artistic material as well as commentary on the arts. Seeks to be flexible and innovative, if a little (self-consciously) posh.

IMAGO: new writing
University of Queensland, School of Media & Journalism, Faculty of Arts, GPO 2434, Brisbane, Queensland, 4001 Australia
Eds and Poetry Eds: Philip Neilsen & Helen Horton

Since: 1989	Circ: 750	Pages: 112	Per Year: 3
Size: 6 X 8	Perfect bound	Sample: $10 (Aus)	Sub: $28 (Aus)
Copyright: author	Book reviews: yes	Reviews/year: 30	Translations: yes
Interviews: yes	Fiction: yes	Essays: yes	Copies: 1
Money: $40 (Aus)/poem	Time: 2-4 months		

Authors published: Tom Shapcott, Nancy Cato, David Malouf, & Bruce Dawe

Book reviews, interviews, and essays are usually commissioned and the content must be relevant to Australian writers. Query first. Only publishes a small number of translations.

ISLAND
PO Box 207, Sandy Bay, Tasmania, 7005 Australia
Ed: Cassandra Pybus   Poetry Ed: Stephen Edgar

LINQ
James Cook University, Department of English, Townsville, Queensland, 4811 Australia
Eds and Poetry Eds: Elizabeth Perkins & Cheryl Taylor

MATTOID
Deakin University, Centre for Research in Cultural Communication, Geelong, Victoria, 3217 Australia
Eds and Poetry Eds: Brian Edwards & Robyn Gardner

Since: 1975	Circ: 600	Pages: 250	Per Year: 3
Size: ?	Perfect bound	Sample: $20 (Aus)	Sub: $40 (Aus)

Copyright: author	Book reviews: yes	Reviews/year: 30	Translations: yes
Interviews: yes	Fiction: yes	Essays: yes	Copies: 2
Money: no	Time: 3 months		

Authors published: George Bowering, Douglas Barbour, Daphne Marlatt, & Betsy Warland

Interested in high quality poetry and in work that is experimental.

MEANJIN
99 Barry Street, Carlton, Victoria, 3053 Australia
Ed: Christina Thompson   Poetry Ed: Laurie Duggan

Since: 1940	Circ: 2,500	Pages: 192	Per Year: 4
Size: 14 cm X 21 cm	Perfect bound	Sample: $13 (Aus)	Sub: $40 (Aus)
Copyright: author	Book reviews: yes	Reviews/year: 20	Translations: yes
Interviews: rarely	Fiction: yes	Essays: yes	Copies: 2
Money: yes	Time: 3 months		

Authors published: Gael Turnbull, Dorothy Hewett, John Forbes, & Elizabeth Smither

Pays Australian Authors' Society rates for work published.

OTIS RUSH
Experimental Art Foundation, PO Box 21, North Adelaide, South Australia, 5006 Australia
Ed and Poetry Ed: Ken Bolton

Since: 1987	Circ: 500	Pages: 220	Per Year: 1-2
Size: 16 cm X 21 cm	Perfect bound	Sample: $12 (Aus)	Sub: $60 (Aus)
Copyright: author	Book reviews: yes	Reviews/year: 4	Translations: yes
Interviews: yes	Fiction: yes	Essays: yes	Copies: yes
Money: maybe	Time: 2-3 months		

Authors published: Ron Padgett, Pam Brown, Tony Towle, & Michele Leggott

Subscriptions run for four issues.

THE PHOENIX REVIEW
University of Sydney, Department of English, Sydney, New South Wales, 2006 Australia
Eds: David Brooks, Nicolette Stasko, & Craig Powell   Poetry Ed: David Brooks

POETRY AUSTRALIA
The Market Place, Berrima, New South Wales, 2577 Australia
Ed and Poetry Ed: John Millett

QUADRANT
PO Box 1495, Collingwood, Victoria, 3066 Australia
Eds: Robert Manne   Poetry Ed: Les Murray

Since: 1956	Circ: 6,000	Pages: 96	Per Year: 10
Size: 27 cm X 20 cm	Saddle stitched	Sample: $7 (Aus)	Sub: $54 (U.S.)
Copyright: author	Book reviews: yes	Reviews/year: 60	Translations: yes
Interviews: yes	Fiction: yes	Essays: yes	Copies: 2
Money: $40 (Aus)	Time: 4 months		

Authors published: Robert Crawford, Bruce Dawe, Les Murray, & Graham Walker

Pays minimum of $90 (Aus) for articles and short stories, $60 (Aus) for reviews, and $40 (Aus) for poems. Publishes around two hundred poems each year.

REDOUBT: stories - poetry - art - reviews - issues

University of Canberra, Faculty of Communication, PO Box 1, Belconnen,
Australian Capital Territory, 2616 Australia

Eds: Ruth Sless & Ron Miller   Poetry Eds: Gillian Ferguson & Maureen Bettle

Since: 1988	Circ: 300	Pages: 130	Per Year: 2
Size: 17.5 cm X 25 cm	Saddle stitched	Sample: $5 (Aus)	Sub: $16 (Aus)
Copyright: author	Book reviews: yes	Reviews/year: 6-10	Translations: yes
Interviews: yes	Fiction: yes	Essays: yes	Copies: 1
Money: yes	Time: 5 months		

Authors published: Charles Bukowski, C.E. Hull, Tim Liardet, John Miles

We prefer short poems, i.e., less than forty lines. Looks for fresh imagery and unusual viewpoints.

SCARP— new arts & writing

University of Wollongong, Faculty of Creative Arts, Northfields Avenue,
Wollongong, New South Wales, 2522 Australia

Ed and Poetry Ed: Ron Pretty

Since: 1982	Circ: 1,000	Pages: 64	Per Year: 2
Size: A4	Perfect bound	Sample: $6 (Aus)	Sub: $20 (Aus)
Copyright: author	Book reviews: yes	Reviews/year: 10-12	Translations: yes
Interviews: yes	Fiction: yes	Essays: yes	Copies: yes
Money: no	Time: 4 months		

Authors published: Opal Adisa, Deb Westbury, Shane McAuley, & Jill Jones

Please send SAE (IRC) for guidelines. Interested in any length or style of poetry. Looks for poetry with a sense of rhythm. Prose should be under 2,000 words. Black and white artwork and photography is also welcome. Reads all year but prefers submissions in February/March or June/July.

SOUTHERLY

The University of Sydney, Department of English, Sydney, New South Wales, 2006
Australia

Eds: Ivor Indyk & Elizabeth Webby

Since: 1939	Circ: 1,000	Pages: 195	Per Year: 4
Size: ?	Perfect bound	Sample: $12 (Aus)	Sub: $50 (Aus)
Copyright: ?	Book reviews: yes	Reviews/year: 12	Translations: yes
Interviews: yes	Fiction: yes	Essays: yes	Copies: 1
Money: $50 (Aus)/poem	Time: 4-6 weeks		

Authors published: Les Murry, Gwen Harwood, John Tranter, & Bruce Dawe

Contributors from Canada must be Australian born. Reads all year. Will consider all types of poetry.

SOUTHERN REVIEW

University of Adelaide, English Department, Adelaide, South Australia, 5001
Australia

Eds: Cathy Greenfield & Barbara Milech   Poetry Ed: Anne Brewster

STUDIO— a journal of christians writing

727 Peel Street, Albury, New South Wales, 2640 Australia

Ed and Poetry Ed: Paul Grover

Since: 1980	Circ: 300	Pages: 36	Per Year: 4

Size: 15 cm X 21 cm	Saddle stitched	Sample: $8 (Aus)	Sub: $40 (Aus)
Copyright: author	Book reviews: yes	Reviews/year: 20	Translations: yes
Interviews: yes	Fiction: yes	Essays: yes	Copies: yes
Money: no	Time: 3-6 weeks		

Authors published: Les Murry, Luci Shaw, & Kevin Hart

Please send SAE (IRC) for guidelines. Experimental work welcome. Poems should be under 200 lines; prose pieces should be under 5,000 words. Has a special interest in poetry and fiction that reflects something of Christian identity and values.

WESTERLY
University of Western Australia, Department of English, Nedlands, Western Australia, 6009 Australia
Eds: Bruce Bennett, Peter Cowan, & Dennis Haskell

WOMANSPEAK
PO Box 103, Spit Junction, New South Wales, 2088 Australia
Ed and Poetry Ed: by collective

BARBADOS

BIM MAGAZINE
Ferney, Atlantic Shores, Christ Church Barbados
Eds and Poetry Eds: Andy Taitt, John Gilmore, & John Wickham

Since: 1942	Circ: 300	Pages: ?	Per Year: 2
Size: ?	Binding: ?	Sample: ?	Sub: ?
Copyright: author	Book reviews: yes	Reviews/year: ?	Translations: yes
Interviews: yes	Fiction: yes	Essays: yes	Copies: yes
Money: no	Time: ?		

Authors published: Derek Walcott, Frank Collymore, & Kamau Brathwaite

Emphasis is on Caribbean work, but the only criterion is quality. Tries to publish in June and December, but financial hardship has interrupted this schedule.

BELGIUM

HORIZON
Stationsstraat 232A, B-1770 Liedekerke Belgium
Ed and Poetry Ed: Johnny Haelterman

Since: 1985	Circ: 200	Pages: 36	Per Year: 4
Size: 21 cm X 30 cm	Saddle stitched	Sample: $8 (U.S.)	Sub: $18 (U.S.)
Copyright: author	Book reviews: yes	Reviews/year: 40	Translations: yes
Interviews: no	Fiction: yes	Essays: yes	Copies: 1
Money: no	Time: ?		

Authors published: Anthony Walstorm, Simon Jackson, Ann Keith, & Tim Meinbresse

Please send SAE (IRC) for guidelines. Preference is given to poems with metre and rhyme, but this is not a hard and fast rule. Stories should be short, up to 1,000 words. This is a Flemish magazine (in Dutch) with a few English-language pages in each issue.

POSTFLUXPOSTBOOKLETS
Grote Nieuwedijkstraat 411, B-2800 Mechelen Belgium
Ed and Poetry Ed: Luce Fierens

Since: 1987	Circ: 100	Pages: 8	Per Year: ?
Size: 15 cm X 10.5 cm	Saddle stitched	Sample: 2 IRCs	Sub: $70 (U.S.)
Copyright: author	Book reviews: no	Reviews/year: n/a	Translations: no
Interviews: no	Fiction: no	Essays: no	Copies: yes
Money: no	Time: ?		

Authors published: Ken Friedman, Robin Crozier, Pete Spence, & Serge Segay

Subscription covers 34 issues. Only uses visual poetry. Especially interested in alternative art, collage, and mail art. Material should be in black and white, maximum size: 9 X 12 cm. Please send SAE (IRC) for guidelines. Booklets are in unlimited editions and are distributed world-wide.

EIRE

CYPHERS
3, Selskar Terrace, Dublin 6 Eire
Eds and Poetry Eds: Leland Bardwell, Eiléan Ní Chuilleanáin, Pearse Hutchinson, & Macdara Woods

ECO-RUNES
Monascriebe, Faughart, Dundalk, County Louth Eire
Ed and Poetry Ed: D. O'Ruié

Since: 1988	Circ: 1,500	Pages: 30	Per Year: ?
Size: 6 X 8	Saddle stitched	Sample: $3	Sub: n/a
Copyright: author	Book reviews: no	Reviews/year: n/a	Translations: yes
Interviews: yes	Fiction: yes	Essays: yes	Copies: yes
Money: no	Time: quick		

Authors published: Mike Johnson, G. Stevens, Dick Lucas, D.F. Lewis

Is switching from a periodical format to the production of limited edition paperback books (anthologies). Please send SAE (IRC) for details of this new direction. *Eco-Runes* is a non-profit escapade into creativity for the sake of it. Interested in poetry, graphics, and occasional short stories. We concentrate on social and ecological comment. No sexist, racist, and homophobic material.

FLAMING ARROWS
Co. Sligo VEC, Riverside, County Sligo Erie
Ed: Leo Regan

Since: 1989	Circ: 1,000	Pages: 90	Per Year: 1
Size: 6 X 8	Perfect bound	Sample: 5 pounds	Sub: n/a
Copyright: author	Book reviews: no	Reviews/year: n/a	Translations: no
Interviews: yes	Fiction: yes	Essays: yes	Copies: yes
Money: yes	Time: ?		

Authors published: Medbh McGuckian, Sydney Bernard Smith, James Liddy, & Francis Harvey

Poetry should be well-structured, concise, cogent, have vivid imagery and precise feeling. Looks for moments of spiritual epiphany in well-lived and mature existence expressed lyrically in simplicity. Special interest: mystical psychology. Autumn is the best time to submit work.

LIMERICK POETRY BROADSHEET

Cragbeg, Clarina, County Limerick Eire

Ed and Poetry Ed: Noel Bourke

POETRY IRELAND REVIEW

Bermingham Tower, Dublin Castle, Dublin 2 Eire

Since: 1978	Circ: 1,000	Pages: 132	Per Year: 4
Size: 6 X 8	Perfect bound	Sample: $8 (U.S.)	Sub: 36 pounds
Copyright: author	Book reviews: yes	Reviews/year: 80	Translations: yes
Interviews: yes	Fiction: no	Essays: yes	Copies: 1
Money: ?	Time: 3 months		

Authors published: Seamus Heaney, Sharon Olds, Galway Kinnell, & Eavan Boland

Reads submissions all year. Open to all types of poetry, but strongly dislikes sexism and racism. Sometimes will publish a special issue. Uses about fifty poems per issue. Payment for sample/sub. should be in Irish pounds or U.S. dollar equivalent.

RIVERINE

Chapel Street, Mooncoin, Waterford, County Waterford Eire

Ed and Poetry Ed: Edward Power

STUDIES

35 Lower Leeson Street, Dublin 2 Eire

Ed and Poetry Ed: Rev. Noel Barber, S.J.

WINDOWS

"Auburn." Stragella, County Cavan Eire

or: "Monkey's Rest," Drumcrow, Carrickaboy, County Cavan Eire

Eds and Poetry Eds: Heather Brett & Noel Monahan

Since: 1992	Circ: 1,000	Pages: 144	Per Year: see below
Size: n/a	Binding: ?	Sample: n/a	Sub: n/a
Copyright: author	Book reviews: no	Reviews/year: n/a	Translations: yes
Interviews: no	Fiction: yes	Essays: no	Copies: yes
Money: no	Time: 1-3 months		

Authors published: Carol Rumens, Thomas Lynch, Fabio Doplicher, & Mariana Marin

We publish three types of thing: 1) poetry broadsheets with space for fourteen poems, mainly for emerging writers; 2) an annual poetry book featuring the work of two visual artists (8 reproductions each), a few poets (8 poems each), a short story or extract from a novel; 3) a big literary biannual (poetry and prose). Broadsides cost 2 pounds, the annual book (50 pages) costs 4 pounds, the biannual volume (144 pages) costs 7 Irish pounds. All publications are international in scope and all focus on emerging writers although major poets like John Montague, Nuala Ní Dhómhnaill, and Medbh McGuckian are also published.

FINLAND

BRIO CELL— Visual And Experimental Poetry Portfolio
Stenbocksv 24, 02860 Esbo Finland
Ed and Poetry Ed: J. Lehmus

Since: 1994	Circ: 20	Pages: 15-20	Per Year: 4-6
Size: 8 1/2 X 12	Unbound sheets	Sample: $10 (U.S.)	Sub: n/a
Copyright: author	Book reviews: no	Reviews/year: n/a	Translations: ?
Interviews: no	Fiction: no	Essays: no	Copies: 1
Money: no	Time: few weeks		

Authors published: Dick Higgins, Fernando Aquiar, Serge Segay, & John M. Bennett
Visual poetry only. Each participant is invited to send twenty copies (originals or duplicates); thus, each copy of the portfolio is unique. Please send sample of work before submitting your twenty copies. Focus is on experimental language art. Copyright reverts to author on request.

SIVULLINEN
Kaarelantie 86 B 28, 00420 Helsinki Finland
Ed and Poetry Ed: Jouni Väaräkangas

Since: 1985	Circ: 500	Pages: 32	Per Year: 2
Size: varies	Saddle stitched	Sample: $3 (U.S.)	Sub: n/a
Copyright: author	Book reviews: no	Reviews/year: n/a	Translations: no
Interviews: no	Fiction: yes	Essays: yes	Copies: 1
Money: no	Time: 1-2 months		

Authors published: Scott C. Holstad, Bob Zark, Trebor, & Robert Howington
When ordering a sample copy please send $3 (U.S.) in cash. Size varies; some issues are 6 X 8 1/2, others are 8 1/2 X 12. Please send no more than five poems at a time.

FRANCE

REVUE POLYPHONIES
85, rue de la Santé, 75013 Paris France
Ed: Pascal Culerrier

Since: 1985	Circ: ?	Pages: 112	Per Year: 2
Size: 16 cm X 14 cm	Perfect bound	Sample: 65 (Fr)	Sub: 100 (Fr)
Copyright: author	Book reviews: yes	Reviews/year: ?	Translations: yes
Interviews: yes	Fiction: no	Essays: yes	Copies: no
Money: no	Time: 2 months		

Authors published: Joseph Brodsky, L. Gaspar, Mario Luzi, & S. Stétié

ZOOM-ZOUM
4, rue des Carmes, 75005 Paris France

Since: 1993	Circ: ?	Pages: ?	Per Year 3:
Size: ?	Binding: ?	Sample: $3 (U.S.)	Sub: ?
Copyright: magazine	Book reviews: ?	Reviews/year: ?	Translations: yes
Interviews: no	Fiction: yes	Essays: ?	Copies: ?
Money: ?	Time: 2 months		

Authors published: Hubert Lucot, Michelle Grengout, & J. Desjardins
Fiction pieces should be short. Work should be highly experimental.

GERMANY

miniature obscure

Landrain 143, D-06118 Halle/Saale Germany
Eds and Poetry Eds: Gerhild Ebel & Cornelia Ahnert

Since: 1991	Circ: 88	Pages: 50	Per Year: 1-2
Size: 11 cm X 11 cm	Binding: ?	Sample: 280 (DM)	Sub: ?
Copyright: author	Book reviews: no	Reviews/year: n/a	Translations: no
Interviews: no	Fiction: no	Essays: no	Copies: yes
Money: no	Time: 3 months		

Authors published: Guillermo Deisler, Heinz Gappmayr, Friederike Mayröcker, & Uwe Warnke

Graphic art and visual poetry only; only the most experimental literature and art is accepted. Each issue is handmade and contains the work of thirty to forty participants.

PIPS-DADA-CORPORATION

Prinz-Albert-Strabe 31, D-53113 Bonn Germany
Ed: Claudia Pütz   Poetry Ed: Katharina Eckart

Since: 1986	Circ: 95	Pages: 40-60	Per Year: 3
Size: n/a	Box	Sample: $50	Sub: $150
Copyright: author	Book reviews: yes	Reviews/year: few	Translations: yes
Interviews: yes	Fiction: yes	Essays: yes	Copies: 1
Money: no	Time: 4 months		

Authors published: Anna Banana, Theo Breuer, Karen-Susan Fessel, & Mascha Grüne

Every issue is a theme issue. Please send SAE (IRC) for upcoming themes and guidelines. Work accepted is limited to extremely experimental/conceptual mail art and Dada literary texts. Original pieces are packed loose in a box for international distribution. Maximum size is 21 cm X 29.7 cm.

SILHOUETTE, Literatur-International

Laurinsteig 14a, 13 465 Berlin Germany
Ed and Poetry Ed: Tilly Boesche-Zacharow

Since: 1980	Circ: 200	Pages: ?	Per Year: ?
Size: 8 X 12	Saddle stitched	Sample: $2.50	Sub: n/a
Copyright: author	Book reviews: yes	Reviews/year: ?	Translations: yes
Interviews: yes	Fiction: yes	Essays: yes	Copies: 1
Money: no	Time: ?		

Authors published: Mazo de la Roche, James Deahl, Ella Bobrow, & Schalom Ben-Chorin

Number of pages changes greatly issue to issue. Magazine is published irregularly. Reads submissions through the year. Special interests: Israel and Judaism. English-language works are translated into German by the editor.

GUYANA

KYK-OVER-AL

c/o Ian McDonald, Guysuco, 22 Church Street, Georgetown Guyana
Ed and Poetry Ed: Ian McDonald

Since: 1945	Circ: 1,000	Pages: 96	Per Year: 2
Size: 5 1/2 X 8	Saddle stitched	Sample: $7 (U.S.)	Sub: n/a

Copyright: author	Book reviews: yes	Reviews/year: 6	Translations: no
Interviews: yes	Fiction: yes	Essays: yes	Copies: yes
Money: no	Time: ?		

Authors published: David Dabydeen, Kamau Brathwaite, Lorna Goodison, & Cecil Gary

Publishes poetry, fiction, reviews, and articles by Caribbean authors wherever they may live.

INDIA

THE INDIAN WRITER
C-23, Anna Nagar East, Madras - 600 102, Tamilnadu State South India
Ed and Poetry Ed: P.K. Joy

Since: 1986	Circ: 750	Pages: 16	Per Year: 4
Size: 6 X 8	Saddle stitched	Sample: free	Sub: $20
Copyright: author	Book reviews: yes	Reviews/year: 4	Translations: no
Interviews: rarely	Fiction: no	Essays: no	Copies: 4
Money: no	Time: 2 months		

Prefers short poems. Also seeks scholarly notes on the mechanics of writing as well as news about national and international literary activities.

MANUSHI— A Journal About Women and Society
C-202 Lajpat Nagar - 1, New Delhi, 110024 India
Ed and Poetry Ed: Madhu Kishwar

Since: 1979	Circ: 10,000	Pages: 44	Per Year: 6
Size: ?	Saddle stitched	Sample: $4 (U.S.)	Sub: $28 (Cdn)
Copyright: author	Book reviews: yes	Reviews/year: 6	Translations: yes
Interviews: yes	Fiction: yes	Essays: yes	Copies: 2
Money: no	Time: 2-3months		

Authors published: A. Varma, Kamla Iovo, Indu Jain, & A. Pritam

Interested in women's issues and women, especially South Asian women. Publishes in both English and Hindi.

PRAKALPANA LITERATURE
P40 Nandana Park, Calcutta, 700034, West Bengal India
Ed and Poetry Ed: Vattacharja Chandan

Since: 1977	Circ: 1,000	Pages: 120	Per Year: 1
Size: 5 1/2 X 8 1/2	Saddle stitched	Sample: 6 IRCs	Sub: 6 IRCs
Copyright: n/a	Book reviews: yes	Reviews/year: n/a	Translations: yes
Interviews: no	Fiction: yes	Essays: yes	Copies: 1
Money: no	Time: ?		

Authors published: Richard Kostelanetz, Winter Damon, Dillp Gupta, & Susan Smith Nash

Only interested in experimental, avant–garde, Sarbangin poetry (poetry of language with typographic visuals) and in Prakalpana (a mixed composition of prose + poetry + drama + essay, all in one, with typographic visuals). Writing must be experimental yet accessible. Also will consider black and white art photography and artwork. Contributors should submit a photo and a 5–line bio note. All material should be able to fit into a 4 X 7 inch text-box. Global in scope and concerns. Reads submissions all year. Publishes in English and Bengali. Magazine is not copyrighted.

ISRAEL

HOOPOE INTERNATIONAL LITERARY REVIEW
North American Editor, 601 North Santa Rosa, Suite E-8, San Antonio, TX 78207
Ed and Poetry Ed: Caryl Bulmer

Since: 1988	Circ: 790	Pages: 60	Per Year: 2
Size: 6 X 9	Perfect bound	Sample: $3 (U.S.)	Sub: $16 (U.S.)
Copyright: author	Book reviews: yes	Reviews/year: 4-6	Translations: yes
Interviews: yes	Fiction: yes	Essays: yes	Copies: 3
Money: no	Time: 3 weeks		

Authors published: John Tugliabue, Roger White, Avraham Sutzkever, & Ada Aharoni
Has U.S. representative. (Head office: 14 Hanassi Street, Jerusalem 92188, Israel.)
Admires Canadian poets. Not much interested in traditional forms although an
exceptional villanelle may be considered. Likes universal, non-parochial,
non-judgmental poetry. Ethnic-folk tales are encouraged. Submissions from
minority poets are welcome. No taboos except gratuitous vulgarisms.

VOICES ISRAEL
PO Box 5780, 46157, Herzlia Israel
Eds and Poetry Eds: Mark L. Levinson, Gretti Izak, & Luiza Carol

Since: 1972	Circ: 350	Pages: 120	Per Year: 1
Size: 16.5 cm X 23 cm	Saddle stitched	Sample: $10 (U.S.)	Sub: $15 (U.S.)
Copyright: author	Book reviews: no	Reviews/year: n/a	Translations: yes
Interviews: no	Fiction: no	Essays: no	Copies: no
Money: no	Time: up to 1 year		

Authors published: Irving Layton, Donia Blumenfeld Clenman, Yehuda Amichai, Evelyne
Voldeng
Poetry on all themes and in all styles welcome. Deadline is March 1st. Requires
7 copies of each poem sent. Poems should be no longer than 40 lines and poets
should submit only four pieces at one time. Does not welcome hard-to-
reproduce typographical shenanigans. Copyright reverts to author, but the
magazine reserves the non-exclusive right to reprint in an anthology.

ITALY

LO STRANIERO
via Chiaia 149/A, 80121 Napoli Italy
Ed and Poetry Ed: Ignazio Corsaro

Since: 1985	Circ: 10,000	Pages: 16	Per Year: 2
Size: 25 cm X 35 cm	Binding: ?	Sample: $15	Sub: $50
Copyright: author	Book reviews: yes	Reviews/year: ?	Translations: yes
Interviews: yes	Fiction: no	Essays: yes	Copies: ?
Money: ?	Time: 6 months		

Authors published: Richard Kostelanetz, Irén Kiss, Peter Hugo McClure, & Sam Smith
Subscription includes insertion in the Network Directories. Official language of
publication is English, but French- and Italian-language work is also accepted.
The goal of the magazine is to document people's difficulty in living within their
own human environment where everybody increasingly feels a stranger.

TRAPANI NUOVA
Via Argenteria KM-4, 91100 Trapani, Sicilia Italy
Eds: Nina Di Giorgio & Stefano Schifano   Poetry Ed: Nat Scammacca

JAMAICA

JAMAICA JOURNAL
2A Suthermere Road, Kingston 10, Jamaica West Indies
Ed: Leeta Hearne   Poetry Ed: Eddie Bough

Since: 1967	Circ: 5,000	Pages: 64	Per Year: 3
Size: 8 1/2 X 11	Saddle stitched	Sample: free	Sub: $25 (U.S.)
Copyright: magazine	Book reviews: yes	Reviews/year: 3-6	Translations: yes
Interviews: yes	Fiction: yes	Essays: yes	Copies: yes
Money: yes	Time: 2-3 month		

Authors published: Edward Kamau Brathwaite, Lorna Goodison, Tony McNeill, M. Morris

Welcomes submissions from Canadian authors if there is a clear association with Jamaica or the Caribbean. Considers submissions any time of the year. Copyright usually stays with the magazine, but this can be negotiated.

JAPAN

ABIKO QUARTERLY
8-1-8 Namiki, Abiko-shi, Chiba-ken 270-11 Japan
Eds: Biddy the hen & Laurel Sicks   Poetry Ed: Jesse Glass, Jr.

Since: 1988	Circ: 500	Pages: 500	Per Year: 2
Size: B-5	Perfect bound	Sample: $15	Sub: ?
Copyright: author	Book reviews: yes	Reviews/year: ?	Translations: yes
Interviews: yes	Fiction: yes	Essays: yes	Copies: 1
Money: ?	Time: 1 month		

Authors published: Jon Silkin, Cid Corman, Vivian Shipley, & Burton Raffel

Runs an annual poetry contest and most of the poems used in this semi-annual review were entered in the contest. For information on the contest please send SAE (IRC).

BLUE JACKET/BLUE BEAT JACKET
1-5-54 Sugue-cho, Sanjo-shi, Niigata-ken 955 Japan
Ed and Poetry Ed: Yusuke Keida

Since: 1971	Circ: 400	Pages: 70	Per Year: 1
Size: 8 1/2 X 10	Binding: ?	Sample: $4 (U.S.)	Sub: $10 (U.S.)
Copyright: author	Book reviews: yes	Reviews/year: 1	Translations: yes
Interviews: yes	Fiction: yes	Essays: yes	Copies: 3
Money: no	Time: ?		

Authors published: Michael Bullock, Sam Hamill, Rod Austee, & Trevor Carolan

Independent Beat and post-Beat magazine.

KŌ
1-36-7 Ishida-cho, Mizuho-ku, Nagoya, 467 Japan
Ed and Poetry Ed: Kōko Katō

Since: 1986	Circ: 1,000	Pages: 40	Per Year: 2
Size: 6 X 8	Perfect bound	Sample: $5	Sub: $10

Copyright: author	Book reviews: yes	Reviews/year: ?	Translations: yes
Interviews: no	Fiction: no	Essays: yes	Copies: 1
Money: yes	Time: ?		

Authors published: James Kirkup, H.F. Noyes, Alexis Rotella, & Gusta van Gulick

Payment for sample/sub can be made in cash (U.S.) or by IRC. You can send 5 IRCs for a sample or 10 IRCs for a subscription. Interested only in haiku. Essays, book reviews, and translations must relate to haiku poetry.

THE LONSDALE: The International Quarterly of the Romantic Six
VIP Meguro 802, 4-1-16 Shimo-meguro, Meguro-ku, Tokyo 153 Japan
Ed and Poetry Ed: Michael L. Jabri-Pickett

Since: 1993	Circ: 4,000	Pages: 16	Per Year: 4
Size: 8 1/2 X 11	Saddle stitched	Sample: free	Sub: $19 (Cdn)
Copyright: author	Book reviews: yes	Reviews/year: ?	Translations: yes
Interviews: yes	Fiction: yes	Essays: yes	Copies: 30
Money: no	Time: 4-6 weeks		

Authors published: Paula Anne Sharkey Lemire & James R. Heron

All work accepted must be about or relate to William Blake, William Wordsworth, Samuel Taylor Coleridge, Lord Byron, Percy Bysshe Shelley, and/or John Keats. Essays should be between 1,200 and 1,500 words. Black and white artwork that relates to the six Romantic poets is also considered.

MAINICHI DAILY NEWS
1-1-1 Hitotsubashi, Chiyoda-ku, Tokyo, 100 Japan
Poetry Ed: Kazuo Sato

POETRY KANTO
Kanto Gakuin University, 1641 Kamariya-cho, Kanazawa-ku, Yokohama, 236 Japan
Eds and Poetry Eds: William I. Elliott & Kazuo Kawamura

Since: 1984	Circ: 700	Pages: 55	Per Year: 1
Size: 20 cm X 25 cm	Saddle stitched	Sample: SASE	Sub: n/a
Copyright: author	Book reviews: no	Reviews/year: n/a	Translations: yes
Interviews: no	Fiction: no	Essays: no	Copies: 5
Money: no	Time: 2 weeks		

Authors published: Seamus Heaney, Les Murray, W.S. Merwin, & Denise Levertov

Interested in modern English and Japanese poems. Uses translations, Japanese to English. Prefers short poems. Each issue has a special theme, so a query letter is vital; send SAE (IRC) for information on future issues. Submissions should be sent between March 1st and May 15th.

POETRY NIPPON
5-11-2, Nagaike-cho, Showa-ku, Nagoya, 466 Japan
Ed: Atsuo Nakagawa   Poetry Ed: Yorifumi Yaguchi

NEW ZEALAND

SPIN
7 Megan Avenue, Pakuranga, Auckland 1706 New Zealand
Ed and Poetry Ed: P.N.W. Donnelly

| Since: 1986 | Circ: 150 | Pages: 75 | Per Year: 3 |

Size: 15 cm X 21 cm	Saddle stitched	Sample: $5 (N.Z.)	Sub: $21 (N.Z.)
Copyright: author	Book reviews: yes	Reviews/year: 5-6	Translations: no
Interviews: no	Fiction: no	Essays: no	Copies: no
Money: no	Time: 3 months		

Authors published: John O'Connor, Catherine Maur, John Alan Douglas, & June Owens

Preference given to submissions from subscribers, but will consider all. Likes haiku and short poems.

SPORT
PO Box 11-806, Wellington New Zealand
Eds and Poetry Eds: Fergus Barrowman & James Bronon

Since: 1988	Circ: 600	Pages: 160	Per Year: 2
Size: 6 X 8	Perfect bound	Sample: $16 (N.Z.)	Sub: $37 (N.Z.)
Copyright: author	Book reviews: no	Reviews/year: n/a	Translations: rarely
Interviews: no	Fiction: yes	Essays: yes	Copies: 1
Money: yes	Time: ?		

Authors published: Phyllis Webb, Les Murray, Bill Manhire, Allen Curnow

The priority is writers with a New Zealand connection, but will consider all.

NORTHERN IRELAND

FORTNIGHT
7 Lower Crescent, Belfast, BT7 1NR Northern Ireland
Ed: Robin Wilson   Poetry Ed: Medbh McGuckian

THE HONEST ULSTERMAN
14 Shaw Street, Belfast, BT4 1PT Northern Ireland
or: 159 Lower Braniel Road, Belfast, BT5 7NN Northern Ireland
Eds and Poetry Eds: Ruth Hooley, Tom Clyde, & Robert Johnstone

POLAND

MANDRAKE POETRY MAGAZINE
ul. Wielkiej Niedzwiedzicy 35/8, 44-117 Gliwice Poland
Ed and Poetry Ed: Leo Yankevich

Since: 1993	Circ: 250	Pages: 32	Per Year: 2
Size: 6 X 8	Perfect bound	Sample: $3 (U.S.)	Sub: $10 (U.S.)
Copyright: author	Book reviews: yes	Reviews/year: 4-10	Translations: yes
Interviews: yes	Fiction: rarely	Essays: yes	Copies: 1
Money: no	Time: 1 month		

Authors published: David Castleman, Mary Rudbeck Stanko, M.A. Schaffner, & Stephen Todd Booker

Subscriptions cover two years (4 issues). Considers all kinds of poetry.

SWITZERLAND

EN PLEIN AIR
Gerbegasse 18, 3210 Kerzers Switzerland
Ed: Aida Ghanim   Poetry Ed: Ghanim-Hedjazi

Since: 1993	Circ: 265	Pages: 20	Per Year: 2

Size: varies	Binding: ?	Sample: $6	Sub: $20
Copyright: author	Book reviews: no	Reviews/year: n/a	Translations: yes
Interviews: no	Fiction: no	Essays: no	Copies: 2
Money: no	Time: 6-8 weeks		

Authors published: Celestine Frost, Carol Gunther, Zahira El-Biali, & Nathalie Monsour
An enviromentally friendly magazine. Prefers imagism and beauty in poetry.
Leans toward surrealism. Sentimental, didactic, and vulgar poetry is unwelcome.

VIRGIN ISLANDS

THE CARIBBEAN WRITER
Caribbean Research Institute, University of the Virgin Islands, RR 02, Box 10,000,
Kingshill, St. Croix, Virgin Islands 00850
Ed and Poetry Ed: Erika J. Smilowitz Waters

The following 14 periodicals have ceased operations since the fifth edition of
this guide, or they no longer accept Canadian poetry, or they have asked to be
delisted.

Adelaide Review (Australia)	**The Salmon (Eire)**
Brave New World (Australia)	**Frank (France)**
Hecate (Australia)	**Poet (India)**
P76 (Australia)	**Carn (Isle of Man)**
Prints (Australia)	**Z Magazine (Isle of Man)**
Refractory Girl (Australia)	**NE-europa (Luxembourg)**
Scripsi (Australia)	**The New Voices (Trinidad and Tobago)**

The following 67 periodicals, believed to be still publishing poetry, failed to
respond to requests for information. This could indicate a lack of interest in
Canadian poetry. They are listed here because a number of very fine journals—
Chinese Literature and *The Irish Review*, for example— are in this category.

The Australian Literary Quarterly
2 Holt Street, Sydney
New South Wales, 2000, Australia

Grass Roots
PO Box 242
Euroa, Victoria, 3666, Australia

Fine Line Journal
PO Box 1178
North Richmond, 3121, Australia

Heartland
PO Box 435
Annerley, Queensland, 4103, Australia

The Glarn Trap
PO Box 202
Applecross, Western Australia, 6153,
Australia

Idiom 23
University College of Central Queensland
Rockhampton, Queensland, 4702, Australia

Luna
PO Box 18
Hampton, 3188, Australia

Migrant
Box 2430 V, GPO
Melbourne, Victoria, 3001, Australia

Overland
PO Box 14146
Melbourne, Victoria, 3000, Australia

Salt
PO Box 202, Applecross
Western Australia, 6153, Australia

Taboo Jadoo
GPO Box 994/H
Melbourne, Victoria, 3001, Australia

Union Recorder
University of Sydney Union
Level One, Manning House
Sydney, New South Wales, 2006
Australia

Verandah
TAS, Deakin University
Toorak Campus
336 Glenterrie Road
Malvern, Victoria, 3144, Australia

The Washingmachine
15 - 47 Progress Drive
Nightcliff, Northern Territories, 0810
Australia

Webber's
15 McKillop Street
Melbourne, Victoria, 3000, Australia

XY
PO Box 26, Ainslie, Canberra
Australian Capital Territory, 2602
Australia

Banja
National Cultural Foundation
West Terrace
St. James, Barbados

The Plum Review
28a rue de l'Abbaye
150 Brussels, Belgium

Gorham
30-32 Macaw Avenue
PO Box 279
Belmopan, Belize

The Vortex
30-32 Macaw Avenue
PO Box 279
Belmopan, Belize

Made in U.S.A.
PO Box 7024
Limassol, Cyprus

Trafika
Janovskeho 14
17000 Prague, Czech Republic

The Irish Review
Cork University Press
University College
Cork, County Cork, Eire

Krino
PO Box G5
Dun Laoghaire
County Dublin, Eire

Silver Wolf and Little People
46 Balbutcher Lane
Ballymun
Dublin 11, Eire

The Steeple
Three Spires Press
Killeen, Blackrock Village
Cork City, County Cork, Eire

Books From Finland
PO Box 15 (Unioninkatu 36)
SF-00014, University of Helsinki, Finland

Doc(k)s
Le Moulin de Ventabren
13122 Ventabren, France

Fig
Jean Davie
3bi rue Fessart
75019 Paris, France

If
Jean-Jacques Viton
12 Place Castellane
13006 Marseille, France

MOHS
8 rue Chaptal
44100 Nantes, France

Numero
5 rue des Tulipes
44120 Vertou, France

**Paris/Atlantic International
Magazine of Creative Work**
31 Avenue Bosquet
75007 Paris, France

Souterrains & Lola Fish
Bruno Pommey
10 Residence Jean Mace
28300, Mainvilliers, France

**Sphinx— Women's International
Literary/Art Review**
175 Avenue Ledru-Rollin
75011 Paris, France

Empty Times
Muggenhoferstr 39
Numberg 8500, Germany

Non(+)Ultra
Matthias Schamp
Grosse-Weischede-Strasse 1
44803 Bochum, Germany

Uni/Vers(;)
Guillermo Deisler
Kirchnerstrabe 11
06112 Halle (Salle), Germany

Ex-Symposium
8200 Veszprem
Anyos u. 1-3, Hungary

Manx Graffiti
Flat 2, 32 Derby Square
Douglas Isle of Man

Viewpoint
PO Box 1777
Tel Aviv, 61016, Israel

Au/Art Unidentified
1-1-10-301 Koshiengu-chi
Nishinomiya
Hyogo 663, Japan

Lizzengreasy
Dai Ni Kuroda Kopo #203
Funabashi 5-30-6
Setagaya-ku
Tokyo-to 156, Japan

New Cicada
40 - 11 Kubo
Hobara
Fukushima, 960-06, Japan

Tels Press
407 Shibuya Co-op
14 - 10 Sakuragaoka-machi
Shibuya-ku
Tokyo, 150, Japan

Plural
Paseo de la Reforma 18.1 piso
Deleg. Cuauthemoc
DF 06600, Mexico

San Miguel Writer
Apdo. 989
San Miguel de Allende
GTO 37700, Mexico

Broadsheet
PO Box 68-026
Newton, Auckland, New Zealand

Islands
4 Sealy Road
Torbay, Auckland 10, New Zealand

Rashi
Box 1198
Hamilton, New Zealand

Takahe
PO Box 13-335
Christchurch, New Zealand

Gay Star
PO Box 44
Belfast, BT1 1SH, Northern Ireland

Gown Literary Supplement
Queen's University
Belfast, Northern Ireland

Grotesque
24 Hightown Drive
Newtownabbey, BT36 7TG
County Antrim, Northern Ireland

Mere Pseud
PO Box 148
Belfast, Northern Ireland

North Magazine
10 Stranmillis Park
Belfast, BT9 5AU, Northern Ireland

Rhinoceros
120 Soudan Street
Belfast, BT12 6LD, Northern Ireland

Scorched Earth
Flat 1, 2 Magdalen Street
Belfast, BT7 1PU, Northern Ireland

Chinese Literature
24 Baiwanzhuang Road
Beijing 100037
People's Republic of China

New Contrast
PO Box 3841
Cape Town, 8000
Republic of South Africa

Romanian Review
Piata Presei Libere 1
Bucharest, Romania

Double
Rea Nikonova
Sverdlova 175
Eysk 353660, Russia

Russian Letter
PO Box 30
St. Petersburg 192282, Russia

The Lundian
PO Box 722
220 07 Lund, Sweden

Transnational Perspectives
CP 161
1211 Geneva 16, Switzerland

2Plus2: A Collection of International Writing
Case Postale 35
1000 Lausanne, 25, Switzerland

Graffiti
Horacio Versi
Colonia 815
of. 105
Montevideo, Uruguay

TWO: GETTING PUBLISHED: BOOKS AND CHAPBOOKS

If you are like the vast majority of poets, your thoughts will turn to books and chapbooks once you have seen your poems in the pages of a few of the better literary quarterlies.

For the purposes of this discussion, a chapbook is a collection of poems in which there are fewer than 48 pages of poetry. Poetry publications commonly have 10 to 16 pages of supporting material (half-title page, title page, contents, introduction, colophon, etc.); therefore, a volume can have over 60 pages and still count as a chapbook if its actual literary contents come to only 47 pages. "Chapbook" originally referred to any pamphlet or small book of tales or ballads sold by a chapman (a street vendor). The chapbook was the start of popular printed literature in a form that was affordable for the masses.

A book is a publication that contains 48 or more pages of poetry. As a general rule, a book will be perfect-bound, or folded in signatures and then sewn. A chapbook, on the other hand, is usually stapled. There are exceptions: *Whiskey Jack* by Milton Acorn is perfect-bound, but with only 35 pages of poetry, it counts as a chapbook. By the same token, *Soy*, by the feminist poet Zelima, a full-length book with 77 pages of poetry and art, is merely stapled.

While there have been some notable exceptions, many poets have started with one or two chapbooks before moving on to full-sized books. Some of the publishers covered below produce only chapbooks, some are limited to books, while others publish both. You should not shun the seemingly humble chapbook. Chapbooks have a long and noble history and, since the very early 1800s, have been a major vehicle of publication.

There are, nonetheless, some drawbacks to chapbook publication. For one thing, only literary bookshops will take chapbooks. This means that your poetry will see only limited distribution in large cities. Arts councils and government funding bodies may not recognize them. The mass media will seldom, if ever, review a chapbook. And public libraries don't much like them because they are difficult to shelve and, because they are often stapled, they do not stand up with use. Chapbooks, initially a product designed for the masses (the first adventure in mass–market publishing), now tend to be specialty products that circulate primarily among the members of the literary scene.

Almost all Canadian publishers who accept poetry are small presses or literary presses. Very few major commercial houses will consider poetry manuscripts. This is because there is no real profit in most poetry publishing. Only a handful of poets are so popular that their books can return even a modest profit: Margaret Atwood, Milton Acorn, Al Purdy, Dorothy Livesay, etc. For most poets, and even for some who have won Governor General's Awards, the best they can hope for is that their books will break even. Thus, it is the non-profit houses that publish the bulk of the poetry books in this country.

Including limited-edition publications, there are about 200 poetry books and chapbooks published in Canada each year. There are at least 1,000 poetry manuscripts in circulation at any point in time. Here are some ways to improve your chances of publication.

2.1 HOW TO SUBMIT POETRY TO BOOK PUBLISHERS

Here are seven tips to getting published.

1. Always send a professional-looking submission: a clean and neatly typed copy of the proposed book. Always double space your poems.

2. Include a self-addressed stamped envelope (SASE). Be sure that you supply adequate postage for the return of your manuscript.

3. Along with the poems include a complete bibliography setting forth all of your publishing credits (journal and anthology appearances, as well as books and chapbooks). In particular, clearly note which poems in the manuscript under consideration have been previously published, and where. (The more journal appearances the better.)

4. You may also wish to include a brief bio note, but do not go on too long about yourself. The focal point of a submission should be the poems, not the poet.

5. Along with your manuscript should be a covering letter offering the poems for publication and thanking the editors for their time and consideration.

6. Even with a proper SASE, some manuscripts will go astray. Thus, you should always keep a copy in a safe place.

7. Try to remain calm when your work is rejected. It is quite difficult to win acceptance of a book-length manuscript. There are at least ten times as many manuscripts in circulation as there are spaces on publishers' lists. Every poet has a collection of rejection slips. In one interesting case an exceptional manuscript was turned back over 60 times. It eventually was published and won the Gardner Poetry Award. As long as you believe in your manuscript, don't give up.

As with submitting to periodicals, doing market research plays a major role. There are over one hundred presses in Canada that publish poetry books or chapbooks. It is never wise to submit blindly. Rather, you should become familiar with the type of material published by a press BEFORE you send off your manuscript. This will save you a great deal of time, money, and frustration.

Before mailing your manuscript, it is often a sound idea to query the publisher as to preferences in manuscript format, length, and submission times. The query letter should describe your manuscript and may include a half-dozen sample poems. Always send an SASE with your query letter. This will help establish a good impression, an important objective when there are far more poets than publishers. It can be frustrating to have a completed manuscript just sitting in a desk drawer while the letters of inquiry are out. It seems that nothing is happening, but you will, in the long run, save time. And if the editor is not favourably impressed with your sample pieces, it is highly unlikely that the manuscript would have succeeded.

2.2 NEGOTIATING A CONTRACT

When a manuscript is accepted, for a chapbook or a full-sized book, you will require a contract. It is never wise to proceed without a proper contract. You will wish to ensure that your rights are fully protected. The history of publishing is littered with the sad tales of authors who thought that a handshake was sufficient. Don't make the same mistake yourself. Many publishers have a standard contract that is more or less like the one developed by The Writers' Union. Most important: do not agree to terms with which you are not happy.

If you do, you will be sorry later. Also, do not sign any contract unless you completely understand its terms.

The relationship between a poet and a publisher is a business arrangement. Your book is not considered accepted until a signed agreement exists between you and the publishing house. Do not let a publisher sit on a manuscript to be published without establishing a contractual agreement. Remember, while verbal agreements can be binding, they do not possess the clarity and precision of written contracts. You may want to have a lawyer or copyright agent examine the terms of a contract before you sign it.

2.3   THE EDITORIAL PROCESS

All manuscripts require editing. Your manuscript requires editing. There is no way around this. The editorial process can be long and painful or short and happy. (It can also be short and painful or long and happy.) The end result should be the best possible book. This is what you want, and it is what your publisher wants.

The relationship between poet and editor is beyond the scope of this guide. The reader is directed to a wonderful booklet (indeed, a chapbook) from The Book and Periodical Council. *Author & Editor: A Working Guide* is packed with useful information (distributed by Prentice Hall of Canada, 1870 Birchmount Road, Scarborough, Ontario, M1P 2J7), and first-time authors should study it.

2.4   BOOK PROMOTION

One of the topics to be discussed with your publisher is how the book will be promoted. There are two sides to this coin. What will the publisher do? What will the author do? (Books, sad to say, do not sell themselves.)

The most economical way for publishers to promote books is to seek book reviews as soon as your book is in print. The publisher, not the author, should look after this by sending review copies to a mixture of literary magazines and daily newspapers. Copies should always go to the leading critical journals (listed elsewhere in this guide).

Some publishers are shockingly lax when it comes to sending out review copies. You should make sure that copies are sent out: you want people to know about and read your book.

If you are dealing with a publisher who is inexperienced in the field of poetry, you might wish to suggest places that may review your book. This is especially true if your book might appeal to special-interest periodicals, if you have contacts with newspaper and/or magazine editors, or if you know of new or international publications that might review your work.

You could also discuss with your publisher (keeping in mind the limited budgets of literary presses) the possibility of advertising in appropriate quarterlies and in places like *Books in Canada* and *Quill & Quire*.

You and/or your publisher may be able to set up radio interviews. You have probably heard other authors being interviewed and there is no reason why you cannot be on the air, too. And you need not be well known to connect with a radio or television program. All you need is a couple of contacts, and most publishers can supply these. Many local cable TV companies and independent or university radio stations carry local information and interview shows. They are usually eager to welcome a "home-town" or visiting author. The same is true for community newspapers. A bit of good luck will also help, but hard work in making and following up contacts will usually carry the day.

The truth is that poets have to bear more of the burden of book promotion than other writers. You may wish to do a series of poetry readings soon after publication. It can also help sales if you make yourself known to local librarians and booksellers. Do not assume that your local library will automatically order your book. Do not assume that bookstore managers will mount window displays on your behalf. Upon occasion they need a little push.

Many poets have no qualms about promoting their books and developing their promotional skills. Others feel reluctant to do certain kinds of marketing. The choice is yours: but remember that promotion is an important way to reach new readers and that it will help your publisher sell more copies of your book.

2.5 LITERARY AGENTS

In other fields of literature and the arts, agents can be of great assistance in securing exposure for one's work. Unfortunately, very few literary agents in Canada will handle poetry, and those few who do will take on only a handful of very highly respected poets. This is because agents normally work on a commission basis, taking perhaps 15% of a publisher's payments to the author. However, publishing poetry in Canada, even for the most famous, usually brings little more than artistic satisfaction; and agents cannot live on a percentage of this intangible.

In the United States, however, published poets often have agents. Indeed, most American commercial publishing houses will not consider poetry that is not represented by an agent. If you wish to publish in New York you will find it most useful to secure the services of a U.S. literary agent. Several American book publishers suggest *The Literary Market Place* as a source of data on U.S. agents.

2.6 SELF-PUBLISHING

Though prior editions of this guide have tried to discourage poets from self-publication, times and circumstances change; one can no longer reject self-publishing out of hand.

Throughout the history of Canadian literature more than one author who could not find a publisher, or who found a publisher who was demanding or unsympathetic, has thought: Why don't I just bring the book out myself? There are stories of books published by their authors that went on to win fame and glory. There have been titles that sold so well in underground editions that major publishers picked up the reprint rights. This is a very, very rare event. It is not likely something that will happen for you. Then again, it might.

Unless a poet has expert knowledge of production and marketing (or expert help), self-publishing can result in several cartons of expensive, and often unattractive, bound paper lodged permanently in various corners of the poet's apartment. Nonetheless, there is far less poetry publishing in Canada by literary presses than there was during the 1970s and 1980s; most publishers have cut back sharply as government and arts council grants have dried up. Self-publishing can today be viewed as a viable option.

2.7 SUBSIDY PRESSES

Subsidy publishing can be a way to get your poetry into print. It is a type of self-publishing in that the author pays for the production of the book. As with literary presses, there are almost as many business deals as there are presses and you, the consumer, should ensure that you fully understand the terms before you agree to anything. You will, of course, require a contract with the subsidy press just as you would with a literary press. Do not agree to a bad deal.

While it is clearly preferable to avoid all forms of self-publication for a number of reasons, there are some distinct advantages to this route. You will (or should) have complete control over your book. You can have as much say in the decision-making process as you want. You will not only be able to control the literary content of your book, you will also control the cover, paper stock, internal illustrations, press run, retail price, and publication date.

A limited survey of the self-publishing scene was undertaken and the results indicate that self-published books can return the cost of production if the author works hard at marketing and if the costs of publication are kept down. Some recently self-published titles have even returned a profit. There are a number of subsidy presses that can help you get your poetry into print at a reasonable cost, but you must be warned that there are also some people who charge outrageous fees for their work, or who collect all the costs in advance but return only a small portion of the revenue to the author. You should shop around for the best deal. And don't forget to ask to see samples of a press's work before you sign a contract.

You should also understand what services are being offered. You will need editorial help, proofreading, book design, typesetting, printing and binding, sales, and maybe storage and distribution. You may also need help deciding on cover stock, press run, printing process, and marketing plans. You can get these services from several independent people or you can buy them all at the same place. The key thing to know is what the press will do for you and your book and what the press will not do.

2.8   TRADE OR LITERARY BOOK PUBLISHERS

There are several reasons for dealing only with trade book publishers. Although there are notable exceptions, literary presses will do a better job than subsidy presses in the following areas:

1. *Editing.* One of the most important services offered by a publisher is the objective eye of an editor. The editor will normally provide detailed critical comments and advice on individual poems as needed. The editor may also help with the organization of the collection itself. And, with a professional publisher, you can expect proper copyediting and proofreading. (You should, nevertheless, ask for a set of author's galleys to proofread yourself. This is important because even the best proofreaders are fallible.)

2. *Production and Design.* Book production is a trade, with a body of technical knowledge, much like house construction. A publisher, as a rule, will have a solid understanding of items like typesetting, page layout and design, kinds of

text paper and cover stock, and methods of binding. Most literary presses do a far better job at production and design than the subsidy presses. It is important that your book look good.

3. *Marketing, Promotion, and Distribution.* A regular publisher will be able to get your book into shops and libraries. The publishing house will issue an annual catalogue in which your book will be listed. People will read your book. Indeed, a house's record in the areas of marketing and distribution can be an important factor in the choice of a publisher.

4. *And, of course, money.* A literary publisher will pay the entire cost of producing and marketing your book. With a subsidy publisher, you advance the funds and then try to recover your costs through sales.

2.9 CANADIAN POETRY BOOK PUBLISHERS

The following 99 Canadian publishers are interested in reading poetry manuscripts. Some focus on famous poets; others seek new talent. Some are well known and get their books into the major bookstore chains; others are underground and only distribute to a handful of literary bookshops.

It would be best if you made yourself familiar with a few of a publisher's titles before you submit your work.

Note: Not all publishers listed below meet the professional standards advocated by the League of Canadian Poets. The goal here was to cover ALL publishers in Canada who have issued poetry books or chapbooks. Thus, it may happen that some of the presses on this list conduct their business in a way that is unfair to poets. You must ensure that a publisher meets your standards before you strike any sort of business arrangement.

AARDVARK ENTERPRISES

204 Millbank Drive S.W., Calgary, Alberta T2Y 2H9

Telephone: (403) 256-4639

Poetry Ed: J. Alvin Speers

Since: 1978	Press run: 100	Pages: 100	Poetry titles: 5
Fiction: yes	Drama: yes	Art: no	Children's: yes
Textbooks: no	Non-fiction: yes	TWUC contract: no	Royalties: $1 per copy

Authors published: W. Ray Lundy, Aubrey G. (Duffy) Bebout, Susan J. Davidson, & Tom McFadden

Publishes both full-size books and chapbooks. We publish for hire at economical rates, and also consult to assist do-it-yourselfers. Inquiries welcome. Strongly prefer rhyme due to proven success with it. Also publishes how-to manuals. Please send SASE for guidelines.

AB collector publishing

5835 Grant Street, Halifax, Nova Scotia B3H 1C9

Telephone: (902) 429-1712   Fax: (506) 385-1981

Poetry Eds: Astrid Brunner, Norval Balch, & Richard Messum

Since: 1991	Press run: 800-1,000	Pages: 80-100	Poetry titles: 2
Fiction: yes	Drama: yes	Art: yes	Children's: no
Textbooks: no	Non-fiction: no	TWUC contract: yes	Royalties: 10-20%

Authors published: Jason Holt, Norval Balch, Kristine Power, & Willeen Keough

Publishes only full-size books (although their anthology series is called the "AB Chapbook Series"). Initial royalty payment is 50 free books. Cash royalties are 10 to 20% after the cost of publishing is recovered. Interested in anything from lyrical to epic; content philosophical, mythological, suited for musical adaptation; aphoristic satire. Editorial policy: suggesting, guiding rather than steamrolling.

above/ground press
R.R. I, Maxville, Ontario K0C IT0
Telephone: (613) 231-7722
Poetry Ed: rob mclennan

Since: 1993	Press run: 300	Pages: 30	Poetry titles: 3
Fiction: no	Drama: no	Art: no	Children's: no
Textbooks: no	Non-fiction: no	TWUC contract: ?	Royalties: yes

Authors published: Sharon H. Nelson, Joe Blades, David Collins, & Stan Rogal

Publishes only poetry chapbooks and broadsheets. Royalties are in copies: one-quarter to one-third of the press run. Looking for long poems, experimental, etc. Any kind of good writing that forms a coherent manuscript. Enjoys publishing first chapbooks by new, unpublished poets. E-mail address: az42l@freenet.carleton.ca

ANVIL PRESS
175 East Broadway, Suite 204-A, Vancouver, British Columbia V5T IW2
Telephone: (604) 876-8710   Fax: (604) 879-2667
Poetry Eds: Paul Pitre & Heidi Greco

Since: 1988	Press run: 1,000	Pages: 92	Poetry titles: I
Fiction: yes	Drama: yes	Art: no	Children's: no
Textbooks: no	Non-fiction: possibly	TWUC contract: yes	Royalties: 15% of sales final

Authors published: Bud Osborn, Angela McIntyre, Isabella Legosi Mori, & Heidi Greco

Publishes full-size collections only. Focus is on contemporary urban material that is attempting to deal with issues of importance to the modern world. Not interested in rhyming, nostalgic, pastoral, vague-word-association-language-centred-post-post-modernist types of poetry, but rather work that has an accessible entry point of departure that is truly trying to say something to the reader.

ARSENAL PULP PRESS
1014 Homer Street, Suite 103, Vancouver, British Columbia V6B 2W9
Telephone: (604) 688-6320   Fax: (604) 669-8250

Since: 1971	Press run: 1,000	Pages: ?	Poetry titles: 2
Fiction: yes	Drama: no	Art: no	Children's: no
Textbook: no	Non-fiction: yes	TWUC contract: yes	Royalties: 15% of Net

Authors published: Douglas Fetherling, Michael Turner, Sheri D. Wilson, & Dennis Denisoff

Publishes only full-size books. Publishes very little poetry. Does NOT read unsolicited poetry manuscripts; query (with SASE) first. Please send SASE for guidelines.

AURORA EDITIONS
1184 Garfield Street North, Winnipeg, Manitoba R3E 2PI
Telephone: (204) 783-7113   Fax: (204) 786-6188
Poetry Ed: Roma Quapp

Since: 1993	Press run: 200	Pages: 36	Poetry titles: 2
Fiction: yes	Drama: no	Art: no	Children's: no
Textbooks: no	Non-fiction: yes	TWUC contract: yes	Royalties: 10%

Authors published: Roma Quapp & Joan McKay

Publishes only chapbooks when it comes to poetry. Fiction can be full-length.

Also publishes chapbook biographies. Send SASE for fiction/biography guidelines. Only pays royalties on full-size books. Do NOT send unsolicited poetry manuscripts; query (with SASE) first.

BEACH HOLME PUBLISHERS
4252 Commerce Circle, Victoria, British Columbia V8Z 4M2
Telephone: (604) 727-6514 Fax: (604) 727-6418
Poetry Ed: Antonia Banyard

Since: 1971	Press run: 600	Pages: 112	Poetry titles: 2
Fiction: yes	Drama: no	Art: no	Children's: young adult
Textbooks: no	Non-fiction: yes	TWUC contract: yes	Royalties: yes

Authors published: Evelyn Lau, Marilyn Bowering, Robin Skelton, & Joe Rosenblatt
Full-size collections only. Please send query plus sample poems first. Looking for new writing from serious poets, new and experienced. Replies in 4 to 6 months. Manuscripts will not be returned without SASE. No fax or E-mail submissions. Please send SASE for guidelines.

BLACK MOSS PRESS
PO Box 143, Station A, Windsor, Ontario N9A 6L7
Telephone: (519) 252-2551
Poetry Ed: Rod Willmot

BOONDOGGLE BOOKS
31 Northumberland Street, Toronto, Ontario M6H 4G3
Telephone: (416) 532-9568
Poetry Ed: Jay & Hazel MillAr

Since: 1991	Press run: 1-50	Pages: 10-40	Poetry titles: ?
Fiction: maybe	Drama: no	Art: maybe	Children's: no
Textbooks: no	Non-fiction: no	TWUC contract: ?	Royalties: yes

Authors published: Rob Ruzic, Jay MillAr, & Stefan Lehmann
The editors will publish anything they like, but please send a query letter first. Publications are handcrafted. Attention is paid to the materials at hand.

BOREALIS PRESS LIMITED
9 Ashburn Drive, Nepean, Ontario K2E 6N4
Telephone: (613) 224-6837 Fax: (613) 829-7783
Poetry Eds: Glenn Clever & Frank Tierney

Since: 1972	Press run: 500	Pages: 80	Poetry titles: 2
Fiction: yes	Drama: yes	Art: no	Children's: yes
Textbooks: yes	Non-fiction: yes	TWUC contract: yes	Royalties: 10%

Authors published: Carol Shields, Pier Giorgio di Cicco, Fred Cogswell, & John Ferns
Publishes only full-size books. Please send SASE for guidelines. Due to cut-backs, Borealis is not looking for poetry at this time. When things return to normal please do NOT send complete poetry manuscript; send a few sample poems first. Normally takes 3 to 4 months to reply to submissions.

BREAKWATER BOOKS LTD.
PO Box 2188, St. John's, Newfoundland A1C 6E6
Telephone: (709) 722-6680 Fax: (709) 753-0708

Poetry Eds: Kyran Pittman & Sherry Doyle

BRICK BOOKS

PO Box 20081, 431 Boler Road, London, Ontario N6K 4G6
Telephone: (519) 657-8579   Fax: same
Poetry Eds: Don McKay, Jan Zwicky, John Donlan, Marnie Parsons, Sheila Deane, & Gary Draper

Since: 1975	Press run: 500	Pages: 80	Poetry titles: 5
Fiction: no	Drama: no	Art: no	Children's: no
Textbooks: no	Non-fiction: no	TWUC contract: ?	Royalties: 10% of copies

Authors published: P.K. Page, Dennis Lee, Karen Connelly, & Michael Ondaatje

Publishes only full-size poetry books. Do NOT send complete manuscript; start with query letter and fifteen sample poems. Pays royalties in copies. Please send SASE for guidelines.

BROKEN JAW PRESS

PO Box 596, Station A, Fredericton, New Brunswick E3B 5A6
Telephone: (506) 454-5127   Fax: same
Poetry Ed: Joe Blades

Since: 1985	Press run: varies	Pages: ?	Poetry titles: 3
Fiction: yes	Drama: yes	Art: yes	Children's: no
Textbooks: no	Non-fiction: yes	TWUC contract: yes	Royalties: 10%

Authors published: Robin Skelton, James Deahl, Beth Jankola, & Eric Folsom

Accepts unsolicited manuscripts. Runs the annual NEW MUSE Manuscript Award (1994 winner: pj flaming; 1995 winner: Tom Schmidt) to publish a poet's first book of poems. Send SASE for contest information. Publishes both full-size collections and chapbooks. The BOOK RAT imprint publishes chapbooks of visual poetry and found/homolinguistic translation poetry. Broken Jaw also publishes audiotapes. E-mail address: jblades@nbnet.nb.ca

BS POETRY SOCIETY

PO Box 596, Sataion A, Fredericton, New Brunswick E3B 5A6
Telephone: (506) 454-5127   Fax: same
Poetry Ed: Joe Blades

Since: 1986	Press run: 100-500	Pages: 36	Poetry titles: 3
Fiction: no	Drama: no	Art: no	Children's: no
Textbooks: no	Non-fiction: no	TWUC contract: no	Royalties: 10%

Authors published: John Tranquilla, Corie MacKinnon, Jessica Campbell, & Owen Diamond

Publishes book and chapbook anthologies. All publishing projects are BSPS generated. Some projects involve membership in the BS Poetry Society or entry fees. No unsolicited manuscripts, please. Query with SASE for information on current projects. E-mail address: jblades@nbnet.nb.ca

THE CAITLIN PRESS

PO Box 2387, Station B, Prince George, British Columbia V2N 2S6
Poetry Ed: Cynthia Wilson

CAPERS AWEIGH SMALL PRESS
PO Box 96, Sydney, Nova Scotia B1P 6G9
Telephone: (902) 567-1449
Poetry Ed: John MacNeil

Since: 1992	Press run: 500	Pages: 52	Poetry titles: 10
Fiction: yes	Drama: no	Art: no	Children's: no
Textbooks: no	Non-fiction: no	TWUC contract: ?	Royalties: 10-20%

Authors published: Shirley Kiju Kawi, J.M. Weil, Joan of Arc, James Seminal

Publishes both books and chapbooks. Send SASE for information on the publishing program. Regional press; considers only Cape Breton Island writers. Pays royalties in copies only.

CHILDE THURSDAY
29 Sussex Avenue, Toronto, Ontario M5S 1J6
Telephone: (416) 979-2544
Poetry Eds: David & M.L. Knight

Full-size books only. Over-committed, so no submissions until 1997.

THE COACH HOUSE PRESS INC.
760 Bathurst Street, 2nd floor, Toronto, Ontario M5S 2R6
Telephone: (416) 588-8999   Fax: (416) 588-3615

Since: 1964	Press run: 1,000	Pages: 96	Poetry titles: 6
Fiction: yes	Drama: yes	Art: no	Children's: no
Textbooks: no	Non-fiction: no	TWUC contract: ?	Royalties: yes

Authors published: Sharon Thesen, Robin Blaser, Evelyn Lau, & Lynn Crosbie

Does NOT accept unsolicited poetry manuscripts. Query first with SASE. Publishes full-size books only. Also publishes screenplays.

CORMORANT BOOKS
[NO longer publishes poetry]

COSMIC TREND
Sheridan Mall Box 47014, Mississauga, Ontario L5K 2R2
Poetry Eds: George Le Grand & Jiri Jirasek

Since: 1984	Press run: 100	Pages: 55	Poetry titles: 5
Fiction: yes	Drama: no	Art: no	Children's: no
Textbooks: no	Non-fiction: no	TWUC contract: no	Royalties: no

Authors published: Jay Bradford Fowler, Jr., Joanna Nealon, Susan Benischek, & Iris Litt

Publishes both books and chapbooks. Considers unsolicited poetry. Interested in New Age and Post-New Age, mind expanding and sensual material of any kind. Prefers unrhymed poems. Please send SASE for guidelines. There is a submission fee of $1 for each two poems plus $1 for postage. The minimum fee is, however, $3. Submissions accepted any time and submissions are also considered for the audiotape and anthology projects. Interested in audiotapes with both poetry and music.

COTEAU BOOKS
2206 Dewdney Avenue, Suite 401, Regina, Saskatchewan S4R 1H3
Telephone: (306) 777-0170   Fax: (306) 522-5152

Since: 1975	Press run: 750	Pages: 64-136	Poetry titles: 4

Fiction: yes	Drama: yes	Art: rarely	Children's: yes
Textbooks: no	Non-fiction: rarely	TWUC contract: yes	Royalties: 10%

Authors published: Patrick Lane, Anne Szumigalski, Louise B. Halfe, & Barbara Klar

Will consider unsolicited manuscripts, but would rather see a query letter first. No multiple submissions. Reports in 3 to 4 months. Only publishes full-size books.

DaDaBaBy Enterprises
382 East Fourth Street, North Vancouver, British Columbia V7L 1J2
Telephone: (604) 980-9361
Poetry Ed: Jamie Reid

Since: 1994	Press run: 150-500	Pages: 16	Poetry titles: 2
Fiction: no	Drama: no	Art: yes	Children's: no
Textbooks: no	Non-fiction: no	TWUC contract: ?	Royalties: 10% +

Authors published: bill bissett, Gerry Gilbert, Kedrick James, & Adeena Karasick

Will sometimes consider unsolicited submissions. Publishes only chapbooks. Interested in Dadaist poetry, prose, and black & white graphics/art.

disOrientation chapbooks
312 12th Street N.W., Calgary, Alberta T2N 1Y5
also 224 15th Street N.W., Calgary, Alberta T2N 2A7
Telephone: (403) 283-6802   Fax: same
Poetry Eds: Nicole Markotic & Ashok Mathur

Since: 1991	Press run: 300	Pages: 15	Poetry titles: 3
Fiction: no	Drama: no	Art: no	Children's: no
Textbooks: no	Non-fiction: no	TWUC contract: no	Royalties: 10%

Authors published: Suzette Mayr, Roy Miki, Yasmin Ladha, & Meira Cook

Publishes poetry chapbooks only. Seeks "disoriented" poetry— writing that deliberately does not fit into the conventions of contemporary poetry. Do NOT send unsolicited manuscripts; query first with SASE.

ECW PRESS
2120 Queen Street East, Toronto, Ontario M4E 1E2
Telephone: (416) 694-3348   Fax: (416) 698-9906
Poetry Ed: Michael Holmes

Since: 1979	Press run: 500	Pages: 80	Poetry titles: 3
Fiction: no	Drama: no	Art: yes	Children's: no
Textbooks: no	Non-fiction: yes	TWUC contract: no	Royalties: 10%

Authors published: Stan Rogal, John Newlove, Michael Holmes, & Nelson Ball

Publishes only full-size books. Sometimes considers unsolicited poetry.

EDICIONES CORDILLERA
c/o Girol Books, PO Box 5473, Station F, Ottawa, Ontario K2C 3M1
Telephone: (613) 234-3677   Fax: (613) 567-1568
Poetry Ed: Leandro Urbina

Since: 1979	Press run: 1,000	Pages: 150	Poetry titles: 2
Fiction: ?	Drama: ?	Art: ?	Children's: ?
Textbooks: ?	Non-fiction: yes	TWUC contract: no	Royalties: no

Authors published: Jorge Etcheverry, Eric Martínez, Naín Nómez, & Gonzalo Millan

Publishes both full-size books and chapbooks. Publishes Chilean contemporary poets as well as essays about poetry. In general, we solicit manuscripts from Chilean poets living in Chile or abroad. Has published authors living in Chile, France, the Netherlands, and Canada.

ee.no books
PO Box 1347, Station F, Toronto, Ontario M4Y 2V9
Telephone: (416) 960-1317
Poetry Eds: David Fujino & Robert Willson

Since: 1991	Press run: 300	Pages: 130	Poetry titles: ?
Fiction: no	Drama: no	Art: no	Children's: no
Textbooks: no	Non-fiction: no	TWUC contract: ?	Royalties: ?

Authors published: David Fujino

Self-publisher at present. For the future, interested in concrete poetry texts and postmodern L=A=N=G=U=A=G=E poetry. Query first.

EMPYREAL PRESS
PO Box 1746, Place Du Parc, Montréal, Québec H2W 2R7
Poetry Ed: Sonja Skarstedt

Since: 1990	Press run: 500	Pages: 90	Poetry titles: 1
Fiction: yes	Drama: no	Art: no	Children's: no
Textbooks: no	Non-fiction: yes	TWUC contract: yes	Royalties: 10%

Authors published: Yuki Hartman, David Lawson, Patricia Renée Ewing, & Stephen Morrissey

Publishes only full-size books. Poetry is not a business, unless one is writing greeting card interiors or advertising copy. Read the work of poets you admire, let their music percolate in your ear— an ignition device for your own voice. Does NOT want unsolicited poetry; send query letter with SASE first.

EXILE EDITIONS LIMITED
PO Box 67, Station B, Toronto, Ontario M5T 2C0
Fax: (416) 969-9556
Poetry Ed: B. Callaghan

Since: 1972	Press run: 1,000	Pages: 96	Poetry titles: 4
Fiction: yes	Drama: yes	Art: yes	Children's: no
Textbooks: no	Non-fiction: no	TWUC contract: yes	Royalties: 10%

Authors published: Patrick Lane, Diane Keating, Joe Rosenblatt, & Death Waits

Publishes only full-size books. Accepts unsolicited manuscripts. Read *Exile* (the quarterly) to see what the editor is looking for.

FIFTH HOUSE PUBLISHERS
[NO longer publishes poetry]

THE FOLKS UPSTAIRS PRESS
51 Dewson Street, Suite 5, Toronto, Ontario M6H 1G6
Poetry Eds: Ben & Julie Phillips

Since: 1968	Press run: 500	Pages: ?	Poetry titles: none
Fiction: no	Drama: no	Art: no	Children's: no
Textbooks: no	Non-fiction: no	TWUC contract: no	Royalties: in theory

Authors published: Verne Schultz, Steven Burdick, Rob Chick, & Lynette Seator

Publishes only poetry chapbooks and poetry postcards. Once in a great while we publish something. We NEVER invite submissions, but accidents do happen. We are slackers of the first order.

FREI PRESS
953 Frei Street, Cobourg, Ontario K9A 5L5
Telephone: (905) 373-1677
Poetry Ed: Eric Winter

Since: 1995	Press run: ?	Pages: ?	Poetry titles: ?
Fiction: no	Drama: no	Art: no	Children's: no
Textbooks: no	Non-fiction: no	TWUC contract: ?	Royalties: no

Authors published: n/a

Preference is for poetry with good sound, good sense, good language, and good timing. Add to these the requirements that the poetry should be fairly scholarly and in the modern idiom. So far has published only poetry chapbooks.

ga press
3997, ave. Coloniale, Montréal, Québec H2W 2B9
Telephone: (514) 286-9950
Poetry Ed: Colin Christie & Corey Frost

Since: 1994	Press run: 200	Pages: 52	Poetry titles: 4
Fiction: yes	Drama: not yet	Art: not yet	Children's: not yet
Textbooks: no	Non-fiction: no	TWUC contract: yes	Royalties: 10%

Authors published: Steve Edgar, Ian Stephens, Michelle Power, & Catherine Kidd

Publishes both full-size poetry collections and chapbooks. Also issues sound recordings. Focus is on interesting, innovative fun.

GOOSE LANE EDITIONS
469 King Street, Fredericton, New Brunswick E3B 1E5
Telephone: (506) 450-4251
Poetry Ed: Laurel Boone

Since: 1957	Press run: 500	Pages: 112	Poetry titles: 3
Fiction: yes	Drama: no	Art: yes	Children's: no
Textbooks: no	Non-fiction: yes	TWUC contract: yes	Royalties: 10%

Authors published: Sheree Fitch, Kwame Dawes, Claire Harris, & Heather Browne Prince

Publishes only full-size books. Send SASE for guidelines. We will be publishing only two poetry titles in 1996 and don't know yet what our plans for 1997 will be. We publish regional guidebooks in addition to fiction.

GORSE PRESS
1420 Gorse Street, Prince George, British Columbia V2L 1G3
Telephone: (604) 563-3495
Poetry Ed: Barry McKinnon

Since: 1982	Press run: 126	Pages: 40	Poetry titles: 2
Fiction: no	Drama: no	Art: no	Children's: no
Textbooks: no	Non-fiction: no	TWUC contract: no	Royalties: no

Authors published: George Bowering, Victoria Walker, George Stanley, & Ken Belford

Publishes only poetry chapbooks and broadsides. Does not pay royalties but gives poets free copies. Does NOT welcome unsolicited manuscripts; query with SASE first.

GREEN'S MAGAZINE CHAPBOOKS
PO Box 3236, Regina, Saskatchewan S4P 3H1
Poetry Ed: David Green

Since: 1972	Press run: 300	Pages: 48	Poetry titles: 1
Fiction: yes	Drama: no	Art: no	Children's: no
Textbooks: no	Non-fiction: no	TWUC contract: no	Royalties: ?

Authors published: Sheila Hyland, L.A.A. Harding, D.L. Tucker, & John Fell

Chapbooks only. Send SASE for guidelines. Interested in the general run of topics, but work must be suitable for family reading.

GUERNICA EDITIONS INC.
PO Box 117, Station P, Toronto, Ontario M5S 2S6
Telephone: (416) 658-9888
Poetry Ed: Antonio D'Alfonso

Since: 1978	Press run: 1,000	Pages: 128	Poetry titles: 5
Fiction: yes	Drama: yes	Art: no	Children's: no
Textbooks: no	Non-fiction: yes	TWUC contract: yes	Royalties: 10%

Authors published: Pasquale Verdicchio, Gianna Patriarca, Raymond Filip, & Daphne Marlatt

Publishes only full-size books. A very active publisher of translations. NO unsolicited manuscripts; query first. Our books deal with pluriculturalist issues. We want works that offer a new vision of the world we live in. We want books that bridge various cultures but that do not sell out to false notions of the melting pot or any other nationalistic dogmas. Please send SASE for guidelines.

HAMILTON HAIKU PRESS
237 Prospect Street South, Hamilton, Ontario L8M 2Z6
Telephone: (905) 312-1779   Fax: (905) 312-8285
Eds: James Deahl & Jeff Seffinga

Offers the annual Herb Barrett Haiku Prize. Please write for contest details.
E-mail address: ad507@freenet.hamilton.on.ca

HARBOUR PUBLISHING
PO Box 219, Madeira Park, British Columbia V0N 2H0
Telephone: (604) 883-2730   Fax: (604) 883-9451

Since: 1972	Press run: 1,000	Pages: 80	Poetry titles: 3
Fiction: yes	Drama: no	Art: no	Children's: yes
Textbooks: no	Non-fiction: yes	TWUC contract: yes	Royalties: 15% of net

Authors published: Tom Wayman, Patrick Lane, John Pass, & Howard White

NO unsolicited manuscripts. Please query first with 10 to 15 pages of poetry. Only publishes full-size books. Emphasis is on authors from British Columbia. Please send SASE for guidelines.

HEARTHSTONE BOOKS
Small House, 136 Nelson Street, Stratford, Ontario N5A 2J7

Since: 1994	Press run: varies	Pages: varies	Poetry titles: 4
Fiction: yes	Drama: no	Art: no	Children's: no
Textbooks: no	Non-fiction: yes	TWUC contract: no	Royalties: no

Publishes only full-size books. Contract publisher specializing in beautiful, exceptionally well-designed editions. Manuscripts (with SASE) are welcomed for assessment; publishes a small number of books per year.

HIGH GROUND PRESS
R.R. 1, S 15, C 5, Madeira Park, British Columbia V0N 2H0
Telephone: (604) 883-2377
Poetry Eds: John Pass & Theresa Kishkan

Since: 1986	Press run: 100	Pages: 1	Poetry titles: 3
Fiction: no	Drama: no	Art: no	Children's: no
Textbooks: no	Non-fiction: no	TWUC contract: no	Royalties: yes

Authors published: Don Domanski, Sharon Thesen, Michael Ondaatje, & Jan Zwicky
Publishes only poetry broadsheets with the very occasional poetry chapbook. Query with SASE for current projects/format. We publish only limited, letterpress editions. Payment in copies. All work to date has been solicited. Poems in forthright public voice which lend themselves to visual (esp. typographical) design work best in broadsheet format.

HIGHWAY BOOK SHOP
[NO longer publishes poetry]

HMS PRESS
PO Box 340, London, Ontario N6A 4W1
Telephone: (519) 433-8994
Poetry Ed: Wayne Ray

Since: 1982	Press run: n/a	Pages: n/a	Poetry titles: 1
Fiction: yes	Drama: no	Art: no	Children's: no
Textbooks: no	Non-fiction: yes	TWUC contract: ?	Royalties: ?

Authors published: Sheila Dalton, Jennifer Footman, Milton Acorn, & Bruce Ross
Books on Disk; electronic publishing only. "Book" size between 9k (chapbook size) to 2,317k (monster novel size). E-mail address: resource.center@onlinesys.com or wayne.ray@onlinesys.com

HOUNSLOW PRESS
2181 Queen Street East, Suite 301, Toronto, Ontario M4E 1E5
Telephone: (416) 698-0454   Fax: (416) 698-1102
Poetry Ed: Tony Hawke

Since: 1972	Press run: 1,000	Pages: 112	Poetry titles: 1
Fiction: yes	Drama: no	Art: yes	Children's: no
Textbooks: no	Non-fiction: yes	TWUC contract: yes	Royalties: 10%

Authors published: George Faludy, Doug Fetherling, Janis Rapoport, & R.A.D. Ford
NO unsolicited manuscripts; send query letter (with SASE) first with a small sample of your work plus a complete resume. We tend to prefer traditional, lyric poetry. Publishes only full-size books.

HOUSE OF ANANSI PRESS LIMITED
1800 Steeles Avenue West, Concord, Ontario L4K 2P3
Telephone: (905) 660-0611   Fax: (905) 660-0676
Poetry Ed: Martha Sharpe

Since: 1969	Press run: 1,000	Pages: 96-160	Poetry titles: 3
Fiction: yes	Drama: no	Art: no	Children's: no

Textbooks: no   Non-fiction: yes   TWUC contract: yes   Royalties: 8-10%

Authors published: Patricia Young, John Barton, Esta Spalding, & Steven Heighton

Full-size books only. Do NOT send complete manuscript. Send a proposal letter first with sample poems and a literary resume. Work submitted without SASE will not be returned. We consider all kinds of poetry. The only "type" we prefer is excellent! As far as advice goes, I would suggest that poets build up their publication records by submitting poems to literary journals and magazines before trying to get a complete collection published. While we publish first books of poetry, it is highly unlikely that we would publish a poet who has never been published anywhere.

INSOMNIAC PRESS
378 Delaware Avenue, Toronto, Ontario M6H 2T8
Telephone: (416) 536-4308   Fax: (416) 588-4198
Poetry Ed: Mike O'Connor

Since: 1992	Press run: 1,000-1,500	Pages: 96	Poetry titles: 3
Fiction: yes	Drama: no	Art: no	Children's: no
Textbooks: no	Non-fiction: no	TWUC contract: yes	Royalties: 7%

Authors published: Stan Rogal, Jill Battson, Mary Elizabeth Grace, & Phlip Arima

Publishes both full-size books and chapbooks. Send sample of ten poems rather than full manuscript. Interested in poetry that works well with illustration, photography, and graphic design. See existing Insomniac books.

KING'S ROAD PRESS
148 King's Road, Pointe Claire, Québec H9R 4H4
Poetry Ed: Marco Fraticelli

Since: ?	Press run: 500	Pages: 16	Poetry titles: 1
Fiction: no	Drama: no	Art: no	Children's: no
Textbooks: no	Non-fiction: no	TWUC contract: no	Royalties: yes

Authors published: George Swede, Alexis Rotella, Betty Drevniok, & LeRoy Gorman

Publishes only haiku chapbooks. NOT accepting unsolicited manuscripts; query first with SASE. Pays royalties in copies.

LAUGHING RAVEN PRESS
PO Box 89, Silverton, British Columbia V0G 2B0
Telephone: (604) 358-7167   Fax: (604) 358-2767
Poetry Eds: David Badke & Diana Hartog

Since: 1994	Press run: 200	Pages: 40	Poetry titles: 2
Fiction: yes	Drama: no	Art: maybe	Children's: yes
Textbooks: no	Non-fiction: maybe	TWUC contract: no	Royalties: 10-15%

Authors published: Diana Hartog, Jenna White, & Kamegaya Chie

Publishes both books and chapbooks.

letters
77 Florence Street, Studio 104, Toronto, Ontario M6K 1P4
Telephone: (416) 537-5403
Poetry Ed: Nicky Drumbolis

Since: 1982	Press run: 100	Pages: 16	Poetry titles: 31
Fiction: some	Drama: once	Art: with poetry	Children's: a few

Textbooks: no   Non-fiction: yes   TWUC contract: no   Royalties: yes

Authors published: Victor Coleman, jwcurry, Gerry Gilbert, & Charles Baudelaire

Pays authors in copies (25% of press run). Does both chapbooks and full-size books. Interested in poetry that moves, not because of its facility, but because the poet allows language to absorb him/her. (I'm also a sucker for a fine sentiment.) Advice: join the fun, make your own books: ecology of artifactual reality as much as economy of language the operative dynamic.

MEKLER & DEAHL, PUBLISHERS
237 Prospect Street South, Hamilton, Ontario L8M 2Z6
Telephone: (905) 312-1779   Fax: (905) 312-8285
Poetry Ed: James Deahl

Since: 1994	Press run: 300-500	Pages: varies	Poetry titles: 1
Fiction: yes	Drama: yes	Art: yes	Children's: yes
Textbooks: maybe	Non-fiction: yes	TWUC contract: no	Royalties: sometimes

Authors published: Jeff Seffinga, Judge Mazebedi, Audrey Duncan Major, & Albert W.J. Harper

Publishes both books and chapbooks. Contract publisher; please write for information on our publishing program or send complete manuscript for evaluation. Provides editorial, production, and marketing services. Will consider all projects except racist, sexist, or pornographic material. Interested in anthologies of up to six poets and/or short story writers. Has an American operation, Unfinished Monument Press (Pittsburgh), and can publish books in the U.S., Canada, or both. Authors are paid annually for books sold. E-mail address: ad507@freenet.hamilton.on.ca

MELLEN POETRY PRESS
PO Box 67, Queenston, Ontario L0S 1L0
Telephone: (716) 754-2266   Fax: (716) 754-4056
Poetry Ed: Patricia Schultz

Since: 1980	Press run: 200	Pages: 64	Poetry titles: 20
Fiction: no	Drama: no	Art: no	Children's: no
Textbooks: no	Non-fiction: no	TWUC contract: no	Royalties: no

Authors published: Eugene Combs, Mary Angela Nangini, Georges Duquette, & Robert Carter

Publishes only full-size books. Send SASE for guidelines. In addition to poetry, publishes scholarly books through The Edwin Mellen Press. Submit 30 to 60 poems for appraisal by editorial board. Unified in tone, mood, or theme. Entire volume should be encompassable within one reading. Upon acceptance, author must provide camera-ready copy. Author works with marketing department to actively promote pre-publication sales of the book. Author receives two free copies.

THE MERCURY PRESS
137 Birmingham Street, Stratford, Ontario N5A 2T1
Poetry Ed: Beverley Daurio

Since: 1978	Press run: 750	Pages: 112	Poetry titles: 2
Fiction: yes	Drama: no	Art: no	Children's: no
Textbooks: no	Non-fiction: yes	TWUC contract: yes	Royalties: 10%

Authors published: bpNichol, Margaret Christakos, Libby Scheier, & Gerry Shikatani
Publishes only full-size books. NOT accepting unsolicited poetry at this time.
Send query letter with SASE. Editorial policy is eclectic, favouring
non-traditional practice. Writers should research houses to whom they submit;
work hard to publish in journals; always present work professionally; and always
enclose an adequately sized SASE for return of their materials.

MINI MOCHO PRESS
PO Box 57424, Jackson Station, Hamilton, Ontario L8P 4X2
Telephone: (905) 523-1518
Poetry Eds: James Strecker, Gerard Dion, & Margaret Strecker

Since: 1989	Press run: 1,000	Pages: 80	Poetry titles: none
Fiction: yes	Drama: not yet	Art: no	Children's: not yet
Textbooks: yes	Non-fiction: yes	TWUC contract: no	Royalties: 8-10%

Authors published: John Rives, Richard Standen, Diane Mattiussi, & Ronald Rice
To date only full-size books have been published. Accepts unsolicited poetry.
We have published individual titles that deal with incest, animal rights, prison
life, and black jazz; so, I guess we tend to do books on specific, and often
avoided, topics. We also do anthologies to promote unknown but quality writers.

MOONPRINT PRESS
PO Box 293, Winnipeg, Manitoba R3C 2G9
Poetry Eds: Diane Driedger & Cecile Guillemot

Since: 1994	Press run: 200	Pages 35	Poetry titles: 4
Fiction: yes	Drama: yes	Art: no	Children's no
Textbooks: no	Non-fiction: yes	TWUC contract: yes	Royalties: 10%

Authors published: Annharte, Sylvia Legris, Diane Driedger, & Cecile Brisebois Guillemot
Publishes only chapbooks. Send SASE for guidelines. Accepts unsolicited poetry
manuscripts. Publishes poetry by women about issues concerning women. Also
publishes essays. Submissions from minority authors welcome.

MOONSTONE PRESS
167 Delaware Street, London, Ontario N5Z 2N6
Telephone: (519) 659-5784   Fax: (519) 659-6278
Poetry Ed: Peter Baltensperger

Since: 1984	Press run: 500	Pages: 100	Poetry titles: none
Fiction: yes	Drama: no	Art: no	Children's: no
Textbooks: no	Non-fiction: yes	TWUC contract: yes	Royalties: 10%

Authors published: James Deahl, James Reaney, Colleen Thibaudeau, & Henry Beissel
Publishes only full-size books. Will consider unsolicited poetry; send samples or
complete manuscript. Please send SASE for guidelines. No multiple submissions.
Please include author bio and publishing credits. Prefers symbolistic, imagistic,
mystical poetry. Manuscripts will not be returned without SASE.

{m}Öthêr Tøñgué Press
290 Fulford-Ganges Road, Saltspring Island, British Columbia V8K 2K6
Fax: (604) 537-4725
Poetry Ed: Mona Fertig
Publishes only limited edition chapbooks. Send SASE for information.

THE MUSE JOURNAL PRESS
226 Lisgar Street, Toronto, Ontario M6J 3G7
Telephone: (416) 539-9517   Fax: (416) 539-0047
Poetry Ed: Manny Goncalves

Since: 1994	Press run: 500	Pages: 34-46	Poetry titles: none
Fiction: yes	Drama: maybe	Art: no	Children's: yes
Textbooks: no	Non-fiction: no	TWUC contract: no	Royalties: yes

Authors published: Nik Beat, Jack Pollock, Marjorie Rebeiro, & Phlip Arima
Chapbooks only. Publishes *The Time is Write!* (information & inspiration for poets).

THE MUSES' COMPANY/LA COMPAGNIE DES MUSES
51 rue de l'Eglise, Dorion, Québec J7V 1W5
Telephone: (514) 455-2943   Fax: same
Poetry Ed: Endre Farkas

Since: 1980	Press run: 500	Pages: 112	Poetry titles: 4
Fiction: no	Drama: no	Art: no	Children's: no
Textbooks: no	Non-fiction: no	TWUC contract: yes	Royalties: 10%

Authors published: Bruce Whiteman, Ruth Taylor, Elias Leteuer-Ruz, & Sharon H. Nelson
Publishes only full-size poetry collections. Quality is what counts. Accepts unsolicited manuscripts; SASE is a must.

NATURAL HERITAGE/NATURAL HISTORY INC.
PO Box 95, Station O, Toronto, Ontario M4A 2M8
Telephone: (416) 694-7907   Fax: (416) 690-0819
Poetry Ed: Nancy Penhale-Mayer

Since: ?	Press run: 3,000	Pages: 50-70	Poetry titles: none
Fiction: no	Drama: no	Art: yes	Children's: yes
Textbooks: yes	Non-fiction: yes	TWUC contract: ?	Royalties: 10%

Authors published: Linda Stitt, Robert Nero, Peter Jailall, & James Savage
Publishes poetry only occasionally. Query before sending manuscript. Publishes both books and chapbooks. Focus is on non-fiction works dealing with culture, art, history, and environmental issues.

NC PRESS LIMITED
345 Adelaide Street West, Suite 400, Toronto, Ontario M5V 1R5
Telephone: (416) 593-6284   Fax: (416) 593-6204
Poetry Ed: Caroline Walker

Since: 1970	Press run: 2,000	Pages: 120	Poetry titles: 1
Fiction: no	Drama: no	Art: maybe	Children's: no
Textbooks: no	Non-fiction: yes	TWUC contract: yes	Royalties: 10%

Authors published: Art Solomon, Milton Acorn, & David Waltner-Toews
Publishes only full-size books. Considers unsolicited poetry but publishes very few poetry titles. Looks for social or political work; left-wing, progressive.

NETHERLANDIC PRESS
PO Box 396, Station A, Windsor, Ontario N9A 6L7
Telephone: (519) 944-2171
Poetry Ed: Hendrika Ruger

Since: 1980	Press run: 750	Pages: ? Poetry titles: 3

Fiction: yes	Drama: no	Art: no	Children's: no
Textbooks: no	Non-fiction: yes	TWUC contract: yes	Royalties: 10%

Authors published: Pleuke Boyce, Diana Brebner, Maria Jacobs, & John Terpstra

NIETZSCHE'S BROLLY
30 Brunswick Avenue, Toronto, Ontario M5S 2L7
Telephone: (416) 920-8686   Fax: (416) 966-9646
Poetry Ed: Marshall Hryciuk

Since: 1985	Press run: ?	Pages: 60	Poetry titles: 4
Fiction: no	Drama: no	Art: yes	Children's: no
Textbooks: no	Non-fiction: no	TWUC contract: ?	Royalties: ?

Authors published: Greg Evason, Yves Troendle, jwcurry, & LeRoy Gorman

Publishes both chapbooks and full-size books. Experimental, language-centred poetry and haiku.

NIGHTWOOD EDITIONS
PO Box 411, Madeira Park, British Columbia V0N 2H0
Telephone: (604) 885-0212   Fax: same

Since: 1963	Press run: ?	Pages: ?	Poetry titles: none
Fiction: no	Drama: no	Art: no	Children's: yes
Textbooks: no	Non-fiction: no	TWUC contract: yes	Royalties: yes

Authors published: bill bissett, Daniel David Moses, Tim Bowling, & Sally Ito

Full-size books only. Please send SASE for guidelines. Do NOT send complete manuscript, rather send a 10 to 15 page sample. Responds in 3 to 6 months.

OOLICHAN BOOKS
PO Box 10, 7190 Lantzville Road, Lantzville, British Columbia V0R 2H0
Telephone: (604) 390-4839   Fax: same
Poetry Ed: Ron Smith

Since: 1974	Press run: 750	Pages: 80	Poetry titles: 4
Fiction: yes	Drama: no	Art: no	Children's: yes
Textbooks: no	Non-fiction: yes	TWUC contract: yes	Royalties: 6-10%

Authors published: Linda Rogers, Aaron Bushkowsky, George McWhirter, & John O'Neill

Full-size books only. Will consider unsolicited poetry. Prefers to receive query letter and twenty pages of poetry rather than entire manuscript. Interested in contemporary poetry. Poets should be aware of current aesthetics. Please send SASE for guidelines. Attempts to maintain a balance between established and unknown poets. The poetry list is booked through the end of 1998.

OUTLAW EDITIONS
721 Powderly Avenue, Victoria, British Columbia V9A 2Z3
Poetry Eds: John Harley & Jay Ruzesky

Since: 1993	Press run: 100-150	Pages: 20	Poetry titles: 2
Fiction: yes	Drama: yes	Art: yes	Children's: yes
Textbooks: yes	Non-fiction: yes	TWUC contract: no	Royalties: yes

Authors published: Marlene Cookshaw, Derk Wynand, Jay Ruzesky, & Michael Kenyon

Publishes only chapbooks. Query with SASE before submitting manuscript. The goal: to present outstanding writing particularly suited to chapbook format: i.e., long poems, short collections of stories, essays, etc. Pays royalties in copies.

OWL'S HEAD PRESS

PO Box 57, Alma, New Brunswick E0A 3C0

Telephone: (506) 887-2073

Poetry Ed: Allan Cooper

Since: 1985	Press run: 500	Pages: 50-60	Poetry titles: none
Fiction: ?	Drama: ?	Art: ?	Children's: ?
Textbooks: no	Non-fiction: ?	TWUC contract: ?	Royalties: 10%

Authors published: Leigh Faulkner, Robert Bly, Francis Ponge, Edward Gates

Owl's Head is currently over-committed. Not looking at unsolicited manuscripts at this time.

OXFORD UNIVERSITY PRESS CANADA

70 Wynford Drive, Don Mills, Ontario M3C 1J9

Telephone: (416) 441-2941

Since: 1904	Press run: ?	Pages: 96	Poetry titles: 2
Fiction: no	Drama: no	Art: no	Children's: no
Textbooks: yes	Non-fiction: yes	TWUC contract: ?	Royalties: yes

Authors published: n/a

We only publish full-size, "selected" volumes of poetry, consisting of previously published poetry by a single poet, and reflecting that poet's career so far. We are not considering new work, even by established poets, at this time.

THE PLOWMAN

PO Box 414, Whitby, Ontario L1N 5S4

Telephone: (905) 668-4425

Poetry Ed: Anthony Scavetta

Since: 1988	Press run: 50	Pages: 28	Poetry titles: 50
Fiction: yes	Drama: yes	Art: yes	Children's: yes
Textbooks: no	Non-fiction: no	TWUC contract: no	Royalties: 20%

Authors published: Richard Ball, Fletcher DeWolf, Beecher Smith, & Randy Ball

Publishes only chapbooks. Send SASE for guidelines. Considers unsolicited manuscripts. Likes religious, comedy— basically all except satanic and/or rude words.

THE POEM FACTORY

PO Box 1658, Huntingdon, Québec J0S 1H0

Telephone: (514) 264-4304

Poetry Ed: Carolyn Zonailo

Since: 1991	Press run: 100	Pages: 24	Poetry titles: 2
Fiction: no	Drama: no	Art: no	Children's: no
Textbooks: no	Non-fiction: yes	TWUC contract: no	Royalties: 10%

Authors published: David McFadden, Beth Jankola, Stephen Morrissey, & Ken Norris

Publishes only chapbooks and broadsides of poetry and literary criticism. Work must be of an original and well-crafted calibre. Originality is of great importance. We publish mainly small pamphlets and broadsides plus the occasional chapbook. We may publish full-size books in the future. Pays poets in copies. NO unsolicited manuscripts; query with SASE first.

POLESTAR PRESS
1011 Commercial Drive, 2nd Floor, Vancouver, British Columbia V5L 3X1
Telephone: (604) 251-9718   Fax: (604) 251-9738
Poetry Ed: Michelle Benjamin

Since: 1982	Press run: 1,200	Pages: 76	Poetry titles: 14
Fiction: yes	Drama: no	Art: no	Children's: no
Textbooks: no	Non-fiction: yes	TWUC contract: yes	Royalties: 10%

Authors published: George Elliott Clarke, Paulette Jiles, Kate Braid, & Greg Scofield

Publishes only full-size books. Also publishes young adult fiction and sports books. Please send SASE for guidelines. Manuscripts must be typed and double spaced. A resume including writing experience should accompany the work. No computer discs or fax submissions accepted. We do not consider any material that is racist, sexist, or homophobic. SASE is a must. Responds to submissions in three to six months.

pooka press
PO Box 1302, Station B, Ottawa, Ontario K1P 5R4
Telephone: (613) 241-9066
Poetry Ed: Warren D. Fulton

Since: 1994	Press run: 200-500	Pages: 25-30	Poetry titles: 8
Fiction: yes	Drama: yes	Art: comics	Children's: ?
Textbooks: no	Non-fiction: maybe	TWUC contract: ?	Royalties: 20-30%

Authors published: rob mclennan, Jeffrey Mackie, Joe Blades, & Tamara Fairchild

To date only chapbooks have been published. Could start doing full-size books in 1996. Accepts unsolicited poetry. Our editorial policy is no policy. We will consider many styles of poetry, poetry that speaks, poetry that lives, poetry that raises its hand in class, or poetry that is/was the class clown. The way the poem communicates is important. I like poetry of the experience, Beat, Confessional, witty, entertaining, etc. Free verse and traditional; like haiku, sonnets, and others. E-mail address: al714@freenet.carleton.ca

THE PORCUPINE'S QUILL, INC.
68 Main Street, Erin, Ontario N0B 1T0
Telephone: (519) 833-9158   Fax: same
Poetry Ed: John Metcalf

Since: 1974	Press run: 800	Pages: 160	Poetry titles: 1
Fiction: yes	Drama: yes	Art: yes	Children's: yes
Textbooks: no	Non-fiction: yes	TWUC contract: yes	Royalties: 10%

Authors published: Irving Layton, Don Coles, John Newlove, & Richard Outram

Publishes only full-size books. Does NOT welcome unsolicited manuscripts; send query letter with SASE first.

PRESS GANG PUBLISHERS
603 Powell Street, Vancouver, British Columbia V6A 1H2
Telephone: (604) 253-2537
Poetry Ed: Barbara Kuhne

PRISE DE PAROLE
111, rue Elm, Sudbury, Ontario P3C 1T3
Telephone: (705) 675-6491   Fax: (705) 673-1817

Since: 1975	Press run: ?	Pages: ?	Poetry titles: 3
Fiction: oui	Drama: oui	Art: oui	Children's: oui
Textbooks: oui	Non-fiction: oui	TWUC contract: oui	Royalties: 10%

Authors published: Patrice Desbiens. Andreé Lacelle, Robert Dickson, & Yolande Jimenez

Uses a standard contract similar to the one suggested by The Writers' Union of Canada; French version UNEQ. Publishes full-size books only. Please send SASE for guidelines.

proof press
67, rue Court, Aylmer, Québec J9H 4M1
Telephone: (819) 684-1345
Poetry Ed: Dorothy Howard

Since: 1993	Press run: 160	Pages: 12-40	Poetry titles: 4
Fiction: maybe	Drama: no	Art: no	Children's: no
Textbooks: no	Non-fiction: no	TWUC contract: ?	Royalties: yes

Authors published: Marco Fraticelli, Michael Dudley, Karen Sohne, & LeRoy Gorman

Pays writers in books (10% of press run). Chapbooks only. Interested in haiku, sequences, and renga.

QUARRY PRESS INC.
PO Box 1061, Kingston, Ontario K7L 4Y5
Telephone: (613) 548-8429   Fax: (613) 548-1556
Poetry Ed: Bob Hilderley

Since: 1965	Press run: 1,000	Pages: 104	Poetry titles: 8
Fiction: yes	Drama: no	Art: yes	Children's: yes
Textbooks: no	Non-fiction: yes	TWUC contract: yes	Royalties: 10%

Authors published: Douglas LePan, Vivian Marple, Gary Geddes, & Gillian Robinson

Publishes only full-size books. Publishes New Canadian Poets Series. Does NOT welcome unsolicited manuscripts. Read our books before making a query. Due to recent cut-backs in funding, Quarry has cut its poetry publishing in half.

RAGWEED PRESS INC.
PO Box 2023, Charlottetown, Prince Edward Island C1A 7N7
Telephone: (902) 566-5750   Fax: (902) 566-4473

Since: 1980	Press run: 500-750	Pages: 96	Poetry titles: none
Fiction: yes	Drama: no	Art: no	Children's: yes
Textbooks: no	Non-fiction: yes	TWUC contract: ?	Royalties: 10%

Authors published: Rita Joe, Marlene Nourbese Philip, John Smith, & M.F. White

Full-size books only. Please send SASE for guidelines. Interested in feminist, lesbian non-fiction for its gynergy books imprint.

RED DEER COLLEGE PRESS
PO Box 5005, Red Deer, Alberta T4N 5H5
Telephone: (403) 342-3321
Poetry Ed: Dennis Johnson

REFERENCE WEST
2450 Central Avenue, Victoria, British Columbia V8S 2S8
Telephone: (604) 598-0096
Poetry Eds: Charles Lillard, Rhonda Batchelor, & Robin Skelton

Since: 1990	Press run: 150	Pages: 24-32	Poetry titles: 11
Fiction: yes	Drama: yes	Art: no	Children's: no
Textbooks: no	Non-fiction: no	TWUC contract: no	Royalties: yes

Authors published: Linda Rogers, Mike Doyle, Marilyn Bowering, & Patrick Lane

Publishes only chapbooks. Will consider unsolicited poetry manuscripts, but are booked up for about a year in advance. Pays royalties in copies. Each chapbook in our "Hawthorne Series" is launched with a public reading at the Hawthorne Bookshop in Victoria. Since we are not subsidized by any grants we cannot pay our authors. Poets submitting manuscripts should be willing to be here in Victoria for the reading/launch at their own expense. We're only interested in previously unpublished, quality work that is suitable for our chapbook/reading format.

RIVER BOOKS
10405 Jasper Avenue, Suite 214-21, Edmonton, Alberta T5J 3S2
Telephone: (403) 448-0590   Fax: (403) 448-0192

Since: 1992	Press run: 1,000	Pages: 100	Poetry titles: ?
Fiction: yes	Drama: not yet	Art: yes	Children's: maybe
Textbooks: no	Non-fiction: maybe	TWUC contract: yes	Royalties: 5-12%

Authors published: Dianne Linder, Candas J. Dorsey, Timothy Anderson, & Mary Woodbury

Please send SASE for guidelines. Do NOT send complete manuscript, but queries are welcomed. Publishes quality books in a variety of genres.

RIVER CITY PRESS
PO Box 752, Sarnia, Ontario N7T 7J7
Poetry Ed: Carol Vainio

Since: 1978	Press run: ?	Pages: ?	Poetry titles: 1
Fiction: yes	Drama: ?	Art: ?	Children's: no
Textbooks: no	Non-fiction: yes	TWUC contract: yes	Royalties: 10%

Authors published: Norma West Linder, Peggy Fletcher, Carmen Ziolkowski, & Hope Morritt

Publishes both full-size collections and chapbooks.

RONSDALE PRESS
3350 West 21st Avenue, Vancouver, British Columbia V6S 1G7
Telephone: (604) 738-1195   Fax: (604) 731-4548
Poetry Ed: Ronald B. Hatch

Since: 1988	Press run: 500	Pages: 100	Poetry titles: 4
Fiction: yes	Drama: yes	Art: no	Children's: yes
Textbooks: no	Non-fiction: yes	TWUC contract: yes	Royalties: 10%

Authors published: Robin Skelton, anne mckay, Keith Maillard, & Zoë Landale

Publishes only full-size collections. Accepts unsolicited poetry; prefers to see the whole manuscript. We recommend strongly that poets have published a goodly number of poems in magazines before any attempt at book publication. We publish both classical and experimental work. The editor looks for strong images and a clearly defined voice. We struggle to return manuscripts within one month. Poets should always enclose a letter-size SASE for an initial reply and also a large SASE for the return of the manuscript. Send SASE for guidelines. Ronsdale Press used to be called Cacanadadada Press.

ROSEWAY PUBLISHING COMPANY LTD.
R.R. 1, Lockeport, Nova Scotia B0T 1L0
Telephone: (902) 656-2223 Fax: same
Poetry Eds: K. Tudor, Brenda Conroy, & Tanya Mars

Since: 1990	Press run: 500	Pages: 80	Poetry titles: none
Fiction: yes	Drama: would	Art: would	Children's: yes
Textbooks: no	Non-fiction: yes	TWUC contract: yes	Royalties: 10%

Authors published: Margaret Hammer & Sue MacLeod

Only publishes full-size books. Will reluctantly consider unsolicited poetry manuscripts. We publish what we like and can afford; all three editors have similar tastes. Does not publish religious poetry nor folk poetry; does not publish amateur poetry except in a historical/social context. Prefers good, contemporary work. Looks for accessible poetry. All submissions should be typed. SASE a must.

ROWAN BOOKS
10405 Jasper Avenue, Suite 214-21, Edmonton, Alberta T5J 3S2
Telephone: (403) 448-0590 Fax: (403) 448-0192

Since: 1992	Press run: 1,000	Pages: 100	Poetry titles: ?
Fiction: yes	Drama: no	Art: no	Children's: maybe
Textbooks: no	Non-fiction: no	TWUC cotract: yes	Royalties: 5-12%

Authors published: Alice Major, Shirley Serviss, Anne Swannell, & Lorna Crozier

Full-size books only. Welcomes queries from established poets. Focus is on anthologies of poetry/prose on specific themes.

SERAPHIM EDITIONS
PO Box 98174, 1000 Gerrard Street East, Toronto, Ontario M4M 3L9
Telephone: (416) 465-1901 Fax: same
Poetry Ed: Tanya Nanavati

Since: 1994	Press run: 1,000	Pages: 80-100	Poetry titles: none
Fiction: yes	Drama: yes	Art: yes	Children's: no
Textbooks: no	Non-fiction: yes	TWUC contract: yes	Royalties: 10%

Authors published: Steve McCabe & Michael J. Paul-Martin

Publishes only full-size books.

SHORELINE
23 Ste-Anne, Ste-Anne-de-Bellevue, Québec H9X 1L1
Telephone: (514) 457-5733 Fax: same

Since: 1991	Press run: 500-1,000	Pages: 66-118	Poetry titles: none
Fiction: no	Drama: no	Art: yes	Children's: no
Textbooks: no	Non-fiction: yes	TWUC contract: yes	Royalties: 10%

Authors published: Vi Bercovitch & Judith Isherwood

Only publishes full-size collections. Also publishes biographies and history. Will consider unsolicited poetry, but we are very small and have a long waiting list of manuscripts to be published.

SISTER VISION PRESS

PO Box 217, Station E, Toronto, Ontario M6H 4E2

Telephone: (416) 595-5033

Poetry Ed: Makeda Silvera

Since: 1985	Press run: 2,000	Pages: 120-180	Poetry titles: 2
Fiction: yes	Drama: yes	Art: no	Children's: yes
Textbooks: no	Non-fiction: yes	TWUC contract: yes	Royalties: 10%

Authors published: Himani Bannerji, Afua Cooper, Ramabai Espinet, & Ahdri Zhina Mandiela

Will consider unsolicited manuscripts. Work must be typed, double spaced, and on 8.5 x 11 paper. Publishes work by black women, Native women, Asian women, and mixed-race women.

SNOWAPPLE PRESS

PO Box 66024, Heritage Postal Outlet, Edmonton, Alberta T6J 6T4

Telephone: (403) 437-0191   Fax: same

Poetry Ed: Vanna Tessier

Since: 1991	Press run: 300-500	Pages: 130-140	Poetry titles: 2
Fiction: yes	Drame: no	Art: no	Children's: yes
Textbooks: no	Non-fiction: no	TWUC contract: no	Royalties: 10%

Authors published: Vanna Tessier, Paolo Valesio, Peter Prest, & Gilberto Finzi

Publishes both books and chapbooks. Also publishes anthologies. Will consider unsolicited poetry; send SASE for guidelines. Replies in 4 to 8 weeks. Please include a C.V., publishing credits, notes/bibliography, SASE, and an indication as to what parts, if any, of the manuscript have been previously published.

SONO NIS PRESS

1725 Blanshard Street, Victoria, British Columbia V8W 2J8

Telephone: (604) 382-1024   Fax: (604) 382-0775

Poetry Ed: Ann J. West

Since: 1968	Press run: 600	Pages: 80-100	Poetry titles: 4
Fiction: no	Drama: no	Art: yes	Children's: no
Textbooks: no	Non-fiction: yes	TWUC contract: ?	Royalties: 10%

Authors published: Linda Rogers, Liliane Welch, Ralph Gustafson, & Brian Brett

Publishes only full-size collections. Please send SASE for guidelines. Unsolicited manuscripts are accepted but we prefer a query letter first. No type of poetry is preferred but our reputation is for avant-garde work— if such a thing still exists.

SpareTime Editions

PO Box 596, Station A, Fredericton, New Brunswick E3B 5A6

Telephone: (506) 454-5127   Fax: same

Poetry Ed: Joe Blades

Since: 1990	Press run: 100-500	Pages: 32-60	Poetry titles: 5
Fiction: no	Drama: no	Art: no	Children's: no
Textbooks: no	Non-fiction: no	TWUC contract: no	Royalties: 10%

Authors published: Milton Acorn, Joe Blades, & Madison Shadwell

Publishes poetry chapbooks and books. Pays royalties in money or books. This imprint of HMS Press (HMS itself no longer prints books on paper, but is 100% electronic publishing) also publishes selected audio and book works. Query with SASE for current information. E-mail address: jblades@nbnet.nb.ca

SPLIT/QUOTATION

PO Box 71037, L'Esplanade Postal Outlet, Ottawa, Ontario K2P 0R3
Telephone: (613) 567-1567   Fax: (613) 567-1568
Poetry Ed: Jorge Etcheverry

Since: 1986	Press run: 500	Pages: 120	Poetry titles: 1
Fiction: yes	Drama: no	Art: no	Children's: no
Textbooks: no	Non-fiction: no	TWUC contract: no	Royalties: 10%

Authors published: Louis Lama, Paulette Turcotte, Gonzalo Millan, & Luciaro Diaz

Pays writers 10% in cash or books. Publishes both chapbooks and full-size collections. Interested in Latin-American/Canadian and/or Latin-American poetry in Spanish or in translation. Looks for Chilean poetry, hyper-poetry, and anti-poetry, meaning multitextual, pluriformal, non-lyric poetry within the experimental, surrealistic tradition.

TALONBOOKS LTD.

1019 East Cordova Street, Suite 201, Vancouver, British Columbia V6A 1M8
Telephone: (604) 253-5261   Fax: (604) 255-5755
Poetry Ed: Karl H. Siegler

Since: 1967	Press run: 1,000	Pages: 125	Poetry titles: 3
Fiction: yes	Drama: yes	Art: some	Children's: no
Textbooks: no	Non-fiction: yes	TWUC contract: yes	Royalties: yes

Authors published: bill bissett, Adeena Karasick, Jeff Derksen, & David McFadden

NO unsolicited poetry. Query with SASE first. Publishes only full-size books. Interested in non-fiction; interested in literary criticism, ethnography, and social issues.

TESSERACT BOOKS

10405 Jasper Avenue, Suite 214-21, Edmonton, Alberta T5J 3S2
Telephone: (403) 448-0590   Fax: (403) 448-0192

Since: 1984	Press run: 5,000	Pages: 300	Poetry titles: n/a
Fiction: yes	Drama: no	Art: maybe	Children's: no
Textbooks: no	Non-fiction: no	TWUC contract: yes	Royalties: yes

Authors published: Eileen Kernaghan, Robert Zend, Judith Merril, & Dorothy Corbett Gentleman

Full-size books only. Tesseract is primarily a publisher of speculative fiction (science fiction, fantasy, magic realism, and horror). Our annual anthology is open to submissions of poetry that falls within this category. Send SASE for guidelines.

THIRD EYE

31 Clarke Side Road, London, Ontario N5W 5W5
Telephone: (519) 453-6151   Fax: (519) 453-3746
Poetry Ed: Navtej S. Bharati

Since: 1979	Press run: 600	Pages: 80	Poetry titles: 1
Fiction: yes	Drama: no	Art: no	Children's: no
Textbooks: yes	Non-fiction: yes	TWUC contract: yes	Royalties: 10%

Authors published: Paul Cameron Brown, Michael Bullock, Cyril Dabydeen, & Nellie McClung

Considers unsolicited poetry manuscripts. Publishes full-size books. Seeks work that has a liberating sensibility.

THISTLEDOWN PRESS LTD.
633 Main Street, Saskatoon, Saskatchewan S7H 0J8
Telephone: (306) 244-1722 Fax: (306) 244-1762
Poetry Eds: Patrick O'Rourke, Sean Virgo, & Glen Sorestad

Since: 1975	Press run: 750	Pages: 80	Poetry titles: 4
Fiction: yes	Drama: no	Art: no	Children's: yes
Textbooks: no	Non-fiction: no	TWUC contract: yes	Royalties: 10%

Authors published: Robert Hilles, Eva Tihanyi, Patrick Lane, & John V. Hicks
Full-size books only. Will consider unsolicited poetry, but prefers query letter first. Send SASE for guidelines. Equal opportunity— talent and brilliance count. Also publishes books for young adults.

TICKLED BY THUNDER
7385 129th Street, Surrey, British Columbia V3W 7B8
Telephone: (604) 591-6095 Fax: same
Poetry Ed: Larry Lindner

Since: 1990	Press run: 150	Pages: 20	Poetry titles: 2
Fiction: yes	Drama: yes	Art: yes	Children's: yes
Textbooks: yes	Non-fiction: yes	TWUC contract: no	Royalties: no

Authors published: Marylin Shaw, Alicia De Leon, Helen Michiko Singh, & Tracey Goldfinch
Subsidy press. Publishes both chapbooks and books. Considers unsolicited manuscripts. Please send SASE for guidelines. We publish the best of what we receive, whatever style or length. We like poetry with strong images, appealing to a wide audience.

TURNSTONE PRESS
100 Arthur Street, Suite 607, Winnipeg, Manitoba R3B 1H3
Telephone: (204) 947-1555

TYRO PUBLISHING
194 Carlbert Street, Sault Ste. Marie, Ontario P6A 5E1
Telephone: (705) 253-6402 Fax: (705) 942-3625
Poetry Ed: George R. Hemingway

Since: 1984	Press run: 500	Pages: 150	Poetry titles: 1
Fiction; yes	Drama: no	Art: no	Children's: no
Textbooks: yes	Non-fiction: yes	TWUC contract: yes	Royalties: yes

Authors published: Nancy M. Fisher, Anna Livia, & Bruce W. Bedell
Publishes only full-size books so far, but will consider chapbooks. Send SASE for guidelines. Will accept unsolicited poetry manuscripts, but prefer a query letter with a few sample poems (about 10 pages). We consider almost any type of quality poetry. If we find the work saleable, we send the writer a proposal which involves the writer in all stages of the project, including sales. With only one exception, all of our writers have made some money. Pays royalties on a "profit-share" basis.

UNDERWHICH EDITIONS
PO Box 262, Adelaide St. Station, Toronto, Ontario M5C 2J4
Poetry Eds: Paul Dutton, Karl Jirgens, Lucas Mulder, Jill Robinson, & Steven Ross Smith

Since: 1979	Press run: 300	Pages: 64	Poetry titles: 2

| Fiction: yes | Drama: no | Art: yes | Children's: no |
| Textbooks: no | Non-fiction: no | TWUC contract: yes | Royalties: 10% |

Authors published: Gerry Gilbert, Paul Dutton, Victor Coleman, & John Riddell

NO unsolicited manuscripts. Query one of the editors first. A publisher of distinctive editions— books, chapbooks, broadsides, boxed, tubed, and other unusually formed literary items, including audiotapes and the occasional CD. We issue new works by contemporary creators, focusing on formal invention and encompassing the expanded frontiers of literary endeavous. Almost all our projects are by invitation. Pays royalties in cash or books (the smart choice).

UNFINISHED MONUMENT PRESS

237 Prospect Street South, Hamilton, Ontario L8M 2Z6
Telephone: (905) 312-1779   Fax: (905) 312-8285
Poetry Ed: James Deahl

Since: 1978	Press run: 300	Pages: 40	Poetry titles: none
Fiction: maybe	Drama: yes	Art: no	Chidlren's: no
Textbooks: no	Non-fiction: yes	TWUC contract: yes	Roylaties: 10%

Authors published: Chris Faiers, Mark McCawley, Leslie Webb, & David Allen Greene

Publishes mostly chapbooks. Currently overstocked with projects. We hope to resume looking at poetry manuscripts in 1997. U.S. address is: PO Box 4279, Pittsburgh, PA, 15203. Our UnMon Northland imprint publishes chapbooks and books in Canada and our UnMon America imprint publishes in the U.S. Runs two poetry contests: the Sandburg-Livesay Anthology Contest and the Acorn–Rukeyser Chapbook Contest. Please send SASE for complete contest rules. E-mail address: ad507@freenet.hamilton.on.ca

RICHARD W. UNGER PUBLISHING

General Delivery, Battleford, Saskatchewan S0M 0E0
Telephone: (306) 445-5172
Poetry Ed: Richard W. Unger

Since: 1995	Press run: 120-160	Pages: ?	Poetry titles: ?
Fiction: no	Drama: no	Art: no	Children's: yes
Textbooks: no	Non-fiction: yes	TWUC contract: ?	Royalties: yes

Authors published: none to date.

Has not published a book as of summer 1995, but plans books by the end of the year. Send SASE for guidelines. Intends to publish both books and chapbooks. Royalties will be 25% of the press run. Do NOT send unsolicited manuscripts. Send a query letter with a few samples. Prefers rhyming poetry with metre (any traditional or even a created form). Feels that poetry books and chapbooks are best when the poems have a common theme and a title to reflect that. Keep it "family viewing"... touch my heart or tickle my "funny-bone" and you could well find your name as author on one of my books. Will consider and comment on all submitted proposals with an SASE. I plan to publish limited editions on a handpress with handset, letterpress type, with type illustrations or woodcuts/lino–cuts/rubber stamps. Books will be hand-bound.

VÉHICULE PRESS
PO Box 125, Place du Parc Station, Montréal, Québec H2W 2M9
Telephone: (514) 844-6073   Fax: (514) 844-7543
Poetry Ed: Michael Harris

Since: 1975	Press run: 500-750	Pages: 96	Poetry titles: 3
Fiction: yes	Drama: no	Art: no	Children's: no
Textbooks: no	Non-fiction: yes	TWUC contract: yes	Royalties: 10%

Authors published: Peter Dale Scott, Rhea Tregebov, Ann Diamond, & John Reibetanz
Publishes only full-size books. Will consider unsolicited poetry manuscripts but the press is booked up through 1996.

WOLSAK AND WYNN PUBLISHERS LTD.
PO Box 316, Don Mills Post Office, Don Mills, Ontario M3C 2S7
Telephone: (416) 445-7498   Fax: (416) 445-1816
Poetry Eds: Maria Jacobs & Heather Cadsby

Since: 1982	Press run: 500	Pages: 80	Poetry titles: 5
Fiction: no	Drama: no	Art: no	Children's: no
Textbooks: no	Non-fiction: no	TWUC contract: yes	Royalties: 10%

Authors published: Heather Spears, Robert Hilles, Richard Harrison, & Nicole Markotic
Publishes only full-size collections. Send SASE for guidelines. Welcomes unsolicited manuscripts. Please send query first with 15 to 20 sample poems. Open to any type of poetry. Our hope is to continue to publish five poetry books per year, but government cut-backs could have an impact on W and W in future years.

WOMEN'S PRESS
517 College Street, Suite 233, Toronto, Ontario M6G 4A2
Telephone: (416) 921-2425   Fax: (416) 921-4428
Poetry Eds: Ann Decter & Martha Ayim

Since: 1972	Press run: 1,200-2,000	Pages: 90	Poetry titles: 1
Fiction: yes	Drama: yes	Art: no	Children's: yes
Textbooks: no	Non-fiction: yes	TWUC contract: ?	Royalties: 10%

Authors published: Lillian Allen, Lydia Kwa, Betsy Warland, & Carmen Rodriguez
Publishes only full-size books; send SASE for guidelines. Will consider unsolicited poetry. Query first with a few sample poems. We look for dynamic political work which addresses new issues, challenges perceived wisdom, and is committed to women. Welcomes writing by politicised women of colour and lesbians.

The following book and chapbook publishers do NOT wish to receive unsolicited poetry manuscripts. They do, however, tend to be open to new work. You should send a query letter (with SASE) and perhaps five to ten sample poems first.

Anvil Press

Arsenal Pulp Press

Aurora Editions

Beach Holme Publishers

Black Moss Press

Borealis Press

Brick Books
Childe Thursday
The Coach House Press
Coteau Books
disOrientation chapbooks
Ediciones Cordillera
ee.no books
Empyreal Press
Ergo Productions
The Folks Upstairs
Gorse Press
Green's Magazine Chapbooks
Guernica Editions
Harbour Publishing
HMS Press
Hounslow Press
House of Anansi
Insomniac Press
King's Road Press
Laughing Raven Press
letters
The Mercury Press
Mosaic Press

Natural Heritage/Natural History
Nightwood Editions
Oolichan Books
Outlaw Editions
Oxford University Press
The Poem Factory
Polestar Press
The Porcupine's Quill
Quarry Press
River Books
River City Press
Rowan Books
Sono Nis Press
SpareTime Editions
Split/Quotation
Talonbooks
Tesseract Books
Thistledown Press
Tyro Publishing
Underwhich Editions
Richard W. Unger, Publishing
Wolsak and Wynn Publishers
Women's Press

The following publishers do not consider poetry at this time:

Cormorant Books
Doubleday Canada
Fifth House Publishers
Irwin Publishing

Highway Book Shop
Macmillan of Canada
Penguin Books Canada
Some Bees Press

The following publishers have ceased operation since the fifth edition of this book:

Brook Farm Books
Burro Books
Dollarpoems
Page Publications

Stubblejumper Press
Wild East Publishing Co-operative
Word-Fires

The following 16 book and chapbook publishers, who seem to still publish poetry, failed to respond to requests for information. This may indicate a lack of interest in unsolicited poetry manuscripts. They are listed here because some very major houses— McClelland and Stewart and Stoddart, for example— are in this category. Query first (with SASE).

Curvd H&Z
1357 Lansdowne Avenue
Toronto, Ontario, M6H 3Z9

DC Books
Box 662, 1495 rue de l'Eglise
Ville St. Laurent, Québec, H4L 4V9

Ekstasis Editions Canada Ltd.
PO Box 8474
Main Postal Outlet
Victoria, British Columbia, V8W 3S1

Lancelot Press
PO Box 425
Hantsport, Nova Scotia, B0P 1P0

Lugus Productions Ltd.
48 Falcon Street
Toronto, Ontario, M4S 2P5

McClelland & Stewart
481 University Avenue
Toronto, Ontario, M5G 2E9

Mosaic Press
PO Box 1032
Oakville, Ontario, L6J 5E9

Oberon Press
400 - 350 Sparks Street
Ottawa, Ontario, K1R 7S8

Penumbra Press
PO Box 40062
Ottawa, Ontario, K1V 0W8

Pottersfield Press
R.R. 2
Porters Lake, Nova Scotia, B0J 2S0

Prairie Journal Press
PO Box 61203, Brentwood Postal Services
3630 Brentwood Road N.W.
Calgary, Alberta, T2L 2K6

Proper Tales Press
PO Box 789, Station F
Toronto, Ontario, M4Y 2N7

Stoddart Publishing Co. Limited
34 Lesmill Road
Don Mills, Ontario, M3B 2T6

TSAR Publications
PO Box 6996, Station A
Toronto, Ontario, M5W 1X7

Vesta
PO Box 1641
Cornwall, Ontario, K6H 5V6

Window Press
20 Prince Arthur Avenue, Suite 11-C
Toronto, Ontario, M5R 1B1

2.10   U.S. POETRY BOOK PUBLISHERS

The American literary market is hard to crack. Yet it's been done. One thinks of Irving Layton (New Directions) and Margaret Avison (W.W. Norton), or of Robert Bringhurst (Copper Canyon) and Robert Allen (Ithaca House). It can, and does, happen. There are Canadian poets who have books out in the U.S. and England in addition to their Canadian titles.

Many American publishers, such as Doubleday and Harcourt Brace & Company, will deal only with literary agents. (Many of the largest American publishers suggest that writers consult *The Literary Market Place* for listings of literary agents as well as other information on how to approach commercial publishing houses.) Others, such as Macmillan and HarperCollins, do not reply to requests for their submission guidelines (even when an SASE is provided). Still others, such as Atheneum and Knopf, will consider manuscripts only from poets who have already published with them. A few, like New Directions and Random House, will accept unsolicited, unrepresented poetry.

The leading 27 American commercial houses to publish single-author poetry books in recent years were contacted. Their data are in the first list below.

The second list covers 30 literary and university presses that have published books by Canadian poets or that are interested in reading Canadian manuscripts. This list is drawn from my personal knowledge and is far from complete. No survey of U.S. book publishers was done. The list is provided to show what kinds of presses are interested in Canadian poetry. Some focus on chapbooks (Bogg), while others publish only full-size collections (Princeton University). A few do both chapbooks and full-size books (Slipstream Productions). Some specialize in haiku (High/Coo), while others are willing to consider just about anything (White Pine).

It should be noted that most university presses have very detailed guidelines, as well as limited submission periods. Reading fees are not unknown in the United States. Therefore, you should always start with a letter of inquiry (with an SASE with U.S. stamps or an IRC) for best results. Some publishers only want about 15 sample poems, while others wish to view your entire manuscript. Indeed, American poetry publishers in general have more rules and special procedures, as well as narrower time periods, than is common in Canada.

You should also be aware of the type of poetry published by these presses.

Your local public library or literary book store will likely have samples of their titles.

27 commercial trade publishers:

ATHENEUM PUBLISHERS
866 Third Avenue, New York, NY 10022
Telephone: (212) 702-2000
Karen Petroski, Editorial Department

Atheneum's poetry list is currently closed to new submissions. Atheneum is part of the Macmillan group but maintains a separate editorial operation.

BOA EDITIONS, LTD.
92 Park Avenue, Brockport, NY 14420
Telephone: (716) 637-3844 and 473-1896
A. Poulin, Jr., Poetry Editor

GEORGE BRAZILLER, INC.
60 Madison Avenue, Suite 1001, New York, NY 10010
Telephone: (212) 889-0909
Adrienne Baxter, Editor

DOUBLEDAY PUBLISHING GROUP
1540 Broadway, New York, NY 10036-4094

Doubleday, as well as Bantam and Dell, does not like to be listed in directories.

E.P. DUTTON
375 Hudson Street, New York, NY 10014-3657

Dutton only considers manuscripts represented by literary agents. Dutton is part of the Penguin group but may maintain a separate editorial operation. Dutton did not reply to our inquiry.

THE ECCO PRESS
100 West Broad Street, Hopewell, NJ 08525-1919
Telephone: (212) 645-2214
Daniel Halpern, Editor

Open to new work. Likes query letter first.

FARRAR, STRAUS & GIROUX, INC.
19 Union Square West, New York, NY 10003
Telephone: (212) 741-6900

FSG includes Noonday Books. No reply to requests for guidelines.

HARCOURT BRACE & COMPANY
525 B Street, Suite 1900, San Diego, CA 92101
Telephone: (619) 699-6810

Includes Holt, Rinehart & Winston.

HarperCollins Publishers
10 East 53rd Street, New York, NY 10022
HarperCollins does not like to be listed in directories.

HENRY HOLT AND COMPANY, INC.
115 West 18th Street, New York, NY 10011
Telephone: (212) 886-9200
Jennifer Silverman, Editorial Assistant
Henry Holt is extremely selective and publishes very few poetry collections.

HOLT, RINEHART & WINSTON
see Harcourt Brace & Company, above

HOUGHTON MIFFLIN COMPANY
222 Berkeley Street, Boston, MA 02116
Peter Davison, Poetry Editor
Houghton Mifflin is open to inquiries.

ALFRED A. KNOPF INCORPORATED
201 East 50th Street, New York, NY 10022
Telephone: (212) 751-2600
Harry Ford, Poetry Editor   Ann Kraybill, Assistant Poetry Editor
Knopf's poetry list is currently closed to new submissions. Knopf is part of the Random House group but maintains a separate editorial operation.

LITTLE, BROWN AND COMPANY
34 Beacon Street, Boston, MA 02106
also Time-Life Building, 1271 Avenue of the Americas, New York, NY 10020
Telephone: (212) 522-8700
Little, Brown does not like to be listed in directories.

MACMILLAN PUBLISHING COMPANY, INC.
866 Third Avenue, New York, NY 10022
No reply to requests for guidelines.

WILLIAM MORROW & COMPANY INC.
1350 Avenue of the Americas, New York, NY 10019
Telephone: (212) 261-6500
No reply to requests for guidelines.

NEW DIRECTIONS PUBLISHING CORPORATION
80 Eighth Avenue, New York, NY 10011
Telephone: (212) 255-0230
Peter Glassgold, Poetry Editor   Stephen Moran, Editorial Department
New Directions is open to new submissions. Replies take 3 to 4 months.

NOONDAY BOOKS
see Farrar, Straus & Giroux, above. No reply to requests for guidelines.

W.W. NORTON & COMPANY
500 Fifth Avenue, New York, NY 10110
Telephone: (212) 354-5500
Jill Bialosky, Poetry Editor

Norton is open to new submissions. Send SASE for guidelines and the dates of their submission periods.

THE OVERLOOK PRESS
149 Wooster Street, New York, NY 10012
Telephone: (212) 477-7162

PENGUIN USA
375 Hudson Street, New York, NY 10014-3657
Telephone: (212) 366-2000

Penguin, Signet, Mentor, and NAL Books only consider manuscripts represented by literary agents.

PERSEA BOOKS
60 Madison Avenue, New York, NY 10010
Telephome: (212) 779-7668
Michael Braziller, Editor

RANDOM HOUSE, INC.
201 East 50th Street, 22nd floor, New York, NY 10022
Telephone: (212) 751-2600

Random House does not like to be listed in directories.

CHARLES SCRIBNER'S SONS
866 Third Avenue, New York, NY 10022

No reply to requests for guidelines. Scribner's is part of the Macmillan group but may maintain a separate editorial operation.

ELISABETH SIFTON BOOKS
201 East 50th Street, 22nd floor, New York, NY 10022
Telephone: (212) 751-2600
George Andreou, Editor

Sifton does not like to be listed in directories.

VIKING PENGUIN
375 Hudson Street, New York, NY 10014-3657
Telephone: (212) 366-2000
Christine Pevitt, Publisher

Viking only considers manuscripts represented by literary agents. Viking is part of the Penguin group but maintains a separate editorial operation.

VINTAGE BOOKS
see Random House, above

Dutton, Farrar, Straus & Giroux, HarperCollins, Macmillan, William Morrow, Noonday Books, and Charles Scribner's Sons failed to respond to requests for information even when an SASE was supplied. These seven houses may have no interest in unsolicited, unrepresented maunscripts. They are in the above list because they are important publishers of poetry.

The following 30 American literary and university presses have published books and/or chapbooks by Canadian poets or are on occasion willing to consider Canadian submissions. Many require reading fees, so you should always write for guidelines with SASE or IRC. Please keep in mind that these fees are in U.S. funds; submitting to these presses can be very expensive.

BkMk Press
University of Missouri, 5216 Rockhill Road, Room 204, Kansas City, MO 64110-2499
Telephone: (816) 276-2558
Dan Jaffe, Director

BLACK SPARROW PRESS
24 Tenth Street, Santa Rosa, CA 95401
Telephone: (707) 579-4011
Michele Filshie, Editor

BLACK SWAN BOOKS LTD.
PO Box 327, Redding Ridge, CT 06876
Telephone: (203) 938-9548
Pat Walsh, Editor

BOGG PUBLICATIONS
422 North Cleveland Street, Arlington, VA 22201
John Elsberg, Editor

CITY LIGHTS BOOKS
261 Columbus Avenue, San Francisco, CA 94133
Telephone: (415) 362-1901
Lawrence Ferlinghetti & Nancy J. Peters, Editors

CLEVELAND STATE UNIVERSITY PRESS
Poetry Center, Rhodes Tower, Room 1815, Cleveland, OH 44115
Telephone: (216) 687-3986 and 687-3950
David Evett & Leonard Trawick, Editors

COPPER CANYON PRESS
PO Box 271, Port Townsend, WA 98368
Telephone: (206) 385-4925
Sam Hamill, Editor

THE FIGURES
5 Castle Hill Avenue, Great Barrington, MA 01230-1552
Telephone: (413) 528-2552
Geoffrey Young, Editor

HIGH/COO PRESS
4634 Hale Drive, Decatur, IL 62526-1117
Telephone: (217) 877-2966
Randy and Shirley Brooks, Editors

LOUISIANA STATE UNIVERSITY PRESS
PO Box 25053, Baton Rouge, LA 70894-5053
Telephone: (504) 388-6294
E.L. Phillabaum, Poetry Editor

OHIO STATE UNIVERSITY PRESS
180 Pressey Hall, 1070 Carmack Road, Columbus, OH 43210-1002
Telephone: (614) 292-6930
David Citino, Poetry Editor

THE ONTARIO REVIEW PRESS
9 Honey Brook Drive, Princeton, NJ 08540
Raymond J. Smith, Editor

PRINCETON UNIVERSITY PRESS
41 William Street, Princeton, NJ 08540
Telephone: (609) 452-4900 and 258-4900
Robert E. Brown, Literary Editor

PURDUE UNIVERSITY PRESS
Building D, South Campus Courts, West Lafayette, IN 47907-1532
Telephone: (317) 494-2035 and 494-2038
Verna Emery, Managing Editor

THE SHEEP MEADOW PRESS
PO Box 1345, Riverdale-on-Hudson, NY 10471
Telephone: (212) 548-5547
Stanley Moss, Editor

SLIPSTREAM PRODUCTIONS
PO Box 2071, New Market Station, Niagara Falls, NY 14301
Telephone: (716) 282-2616
Dan Sicoli, Robert Borgatti, & Livio Farallo, Editors

SWAMP PRESS
323 Pelham Road, Amherst, MA 01002
Ed Rayher, Editor

THE UNIVERSITY OF ARKANSAS PRESS
201 Ozark, Fayetteville, AR 72701
Scot Danforth, Acquisition Editor

UNIVERSITY OF CENTRAL FLORIDA CONTEMPORARY POETRY SERIES
English Department, University of Central Florida, Orlando, FL 32816-1346
Telephone: (407) 823-2212
Judith Hemschemeyer, Poetry Editor

THE UNIVERSITY OF GEORGIA PRESS
Athens, GA 30602
Telephone: (706) 369-6140 and 542-2830
Bin Ramke, Poetry Series Editor

UNIVERSITY OF ILLINOIS PRESS
1325 South Oak Street, Champaign, IL 61820-6903
Telephone: (217) 333-0950
Laurence Lieberman, Editor

UNIVERSITY OF IOWA PRESS
Iowa City, IA 52242-1000

THE UNIVERSITY OF MASSACHUSETTS PRESS
PO Box 429, Amherst, MA 01004-0429
Telephone: (413) 545-2217

UNIVERSITY OF MISSOURI PRESS
2910 LeMone Blvd., Columbia, MO 65201
Telephone: (314) 882-7641
Clair Wilcox, Editor

UNIVERSITY OF PITTSBURGH PRESS
127 North Bellefield Avenue, Pittsburgh, PA 15260
Telephone: (412) 624-4110
Ed Ochester, Poetry Editor

UNIVERSITY OF WISCONSIN PRESS
114 North Murray Street, Madison, WI 53715-1199
Ronald Wallace, Poetry Editor

UTAH STATE UNIVERSITY PRESS
Logan, UT 84322-7800
Telephone: (801) 750-1362
John R. Alley, Editor

WAYNE STATE UNIVERSITY PRESS
5959 Woodward Avenue, Detroit, MI 48202
Telephone: (313) 577-4606   Fax: (313) 577-6131
Arthur B. Evans, Director

WESLEYAN UNIVERSITY PRESS
110 Mt. Vernon, Middleton, CT 06459
Telephone: (203) 344-7918
Susanna Tammenin, Editor

WHITE PINE PRESS
10 Village Square, Suite 28, Fredonia, NY 14063
Telephone: (716) 672-5743
Dennis Maloney, Editor

THREE: POETRY READINGS: THE ORAL TRADITION

Until recent times, most people became acquainted with poetry through live readings. It was only after mass education and the achievement of mass literacy that ordinary people could deal with written, or printed, texts. This created a need for cheap, mass-produced publications that all could afford. The chapbook and the broadside (or broad sheet) answered this requirement. During the early 1800s, chapmen (street vendors of literary works) popularized these small publications. They also got people used to the idea that a poem or ballad could be read from the page as well as listened to. But, up until 150 years ago, poetry was, for most people, oral poetry.

Some would say that the poetry book is merely a substitute for the reading. In this way it is similar to the record album or audiotape of a musical performance. Most people prefer to attend a live concert. Owning a recording is the next best thing.

The Canada Council funds public readings by poets. A host can apply directly to the Canada Council, or can apply to the League of Canadian Poets or the Writers' Union of Canada for a Council-funded reading. There are limitations on the number of readings any one poet can obtain in a three-year period. The Canada Council is currently revising its readings program but will continue to provide a reading fee and travel expenses to eligible writers. For more information on this program, contact the League of Canadian Poets, the Writers' Union, or the Canada Council at P.O. Box 1047, Ottawa, Ontario, K1P 5V8, or at its web site: www.ffa.ucalgary.ca/cc

In Canada there exists a large audience for the live reading/performance. Many of these people would never purchase a book. (It is my personal opinion that at least half of all people who attend poetry readings seldom, if ever, buy poetry books.) You may wish to tap this market.

Of course, one's career as a poetry performer is restricted by the availability of reading places. The Ontario poet has 100 to choose from. The poet in Newfoundland has far fewer.

3.1 HOW TO LOCATE READING VENUES

In the fourth edition of this book the names and addresses of 312 professional poetry reading venues were listed. No such comprehensive list is offered this time. The turnover of reading hosts is such that our list was out of date by the time it was in print. A survey of the Toronto poetry reading scene revealed that one-quarter of the listed venues were dead within one year of publication. In London there were six venues. One year after the fourth edition was issued, two were dead and three of the remaining four had different hosts! While some poetry reading places closed up shop, new ones started up. The big published list was pointless.

At any point in time there are about 300 reading hosts in Canada. One-quarter of these will be at universities or colleges. Just about one-half of all Canadian universities and colleges run readings. Another quarter of the venues will be found at public libraries. Most large library systems have at least one branch where readings take place.

The other half of the poetry venues (about 150) is made up of art galleries, bookshops, writers' clubs, bars, cafes, and social clubs.

Most communities will have at least one reading venue. For example, Hamilton offers a choice of five major venues: a university, a community college, the public library, a book store, and a cafe. It is fairly easy to find out about poetry readings in your area.

The League of Canadian Poets publishes *Poetry Spoken Here*, a bi-monthly calendar of readings by members across the country. It is available for $10 per year. The Canada Council also keeps track of where Council-funded readings are held, and posts these on its web site: wwa.ffa.ucalgary.ca/cc. You can also check the League's home page at http://www.swifty. com/lc for information. The LCP will also sell copies of its current reading venues list at a nominal charge of $5.

Professional writers' associations like the League of Canadian Poets and The Writers' Union of Canada have networks of provincial reps. These people keep up to date on readings in their areas. News of poetry readings in any part of Canada is usually just one telephone call away.

Now, a few tips on readings.

3.2 HOW TO DO A POETRY READING

A live reading is first and foremost a performance. How a poet reads is every bit as important as what is read. Thus, a run-of-the-mill poet with an excellent presentation will likely be a hit with most audiences, whereas a fine poet with a poor reading style will tend to flop. The skills required to write a good poem are not the same as those required to give a good reading. Richard Burton, for example, was a great reader of poetry; I don't recall that he ever wrote any of his own. Reading skills, like all skills, can be learned and/or improved.

The most important tip is: Keep it short. A solo reading might consist of two parts. The first set should be no more than 25 minutes long. After an intermission of about 15 minutes there could be a second set of perhaps 20 minutes (a maximum of 45 minutes reading time).

If two poets are sharing a reading they should read for about 30 minutes each, with a short break in between.

In the case of a group reading (five or more poets), each reader should be limited to 10 to 15 minutes. Poets who exceed their allotted reading time win no friends. People may be quite happy to listen to a two-and-a-half-hour Bruce Springsteen concert, but poetry requires greater concentration, and the listener needs time to absorb what you are saying. The audience will likely revolt if you try to read your poems (no matter how great they may be) for an hour straight. In the case of poetry, too little is better than too much.

There are two ways to learn how to do a good reading. One way is to attend other poets' readings. Study what works as well as what does not. Try to judge the reading as a performance, and note what the audience responds to. The other way to learn about readings is to do some yourself. Ask friends in the audience for feedback. Like many things, one learns most by doing.

Because you face a real audience you should try to establish a positive relationship straightaway. You should speak to the people. Eye contact is also important. Never stare at your feet or mumble. Speak clearly and do not go too fast. A poetry reading is not a race; far better to read a few poems well than to read many poems badly.

An easy way to start giving poetry readings is to participate in the open sets that precede or follow quite a few readings. You might also tape-record your readings. The results may surprise you. Remember, you can be serious and high-minded, or you can be light as the air and funny. Just never be boring. Let the location dictate the way you read. A reading in a library will be a quiet affair.

It can also be overly formal and stuffy. A poetry reading in a cafe or bar will be more relaxed but there may be considerable background noise. You should always try to do readings where you will feel comfortable. There can be a formal dais and podium arrangement or there can be a round-table set-up. Some places allow smoking, some don't. Not every venue will suit you, your work, and your personality. As with literary periodicals and book publishers, you must study the market.

The best way to approach reading hosts is to send a letter of inquiry accompanied by a half a dozen sample poems. Due to the fact that most poets enjoy doing several readings per year, the competition can be fierce, especially for the better venues.

One final bit of advice. Before you agree to do an out-of-town reading make sure that the arrangements are acceptable. This will include travel plans, accommodation (if you are to stay overnight), reading fee, meals, etc. The Canada Council literary reading tours program for published writers pays a fee of $200 per solo reading or $100 per shared reading, and covers some travel costs— up to $400 for a solo reading and up to $200 for a shared reading. To justify expensive travel costs (ie. airfare between provinces), the Council prefers— and may soon require— that the writer read at more than one venue. For instance, a Vancouver poet might arrange readings in Toronto, Hamilton, and London, and claim airfare and rail fare between these cities. Under this program, the host is responsible for providing accommodation for the night of the reading. Some hosts offer lavish hospitality. Others can afford very little. A reading engagement is like any other business deal. The terms should be clearly understood before a commitment is made.

3.3   RADIO BROADCASTS AND CASSETTE TAPES

Another way to present poetry in performance is the radio broadcast. Most large cities in Canada have at least one radio station with a poetry program. Often this will be a nonprofit station affiliated with a university or community college. Radio is the best way to reach a big audience. A top-of-the-line Canadian poet may, over several years, sell 1,000 to 2,000 copies of a poetry book. Such a poet may do six live readings per year to audiences that average 100 to 150 each (or 600 to 900 in total). Yet a single radio broadcast can, and does, reach thousands of listeners.

The best way to find out about radio opportunities is from your provincial writers' association (listed elsewhere in this directory). Radio readings require special skills. For instance, you cannot see your audience. When doing a public reading there is real contact with the audience. You actually see the people you are addressing, and you receive immediate emotional feedback. By contrast, a radio reading involves sitting alone in a small room and looking at one or two technicians through a thick glass window. You have to imagine the audience.

When one gives a reading to a live audience the relationship between poet and listener is immediate and direct. The radio reading is, by contrast, abstract and vague. The poet must supply all of the emotional energy. Again, one learns by doing.

Cassette tapes and CDs offer yet another possibility. There is a good market for high-quality tape recordings of poetry. This market has not, to date, been effectively tapped. In the future we can expect this situation to improve. Eventually, audiotape sales may equal book sales.

Some publishers, such as Underwhich Editions and Broken Jaw Press, have issued tapes as well as books and chapbooks. Other publishers, like Pyramid Associates, produce only tapes. The LCP offers audiotapes for sale by Alfred Bailey, Earle Birney, Elizabeth Brewster, Fred Cogswell, Gwladys Downes, Ron Everson, R.A.D. Ford, Eldon Grier, George Johnston, Leo Kennedy, Douglas LePan, Dorothy Livesay, A.J.M. Smith, Kay Smith, Raymond Souster, and George Woodcock. Several other poets recorded by the LCP have seen their editions sell out.

Finally, there has been some recent activity in the area of poetry videos. So far, marketing activities have been directed at institutions such as schools, universities, and libraries. As the whole video market is fairly new, it is too early to tell anything about the potential for poetry videos.

FOUR: GETTING HELP

There is more to writing and publishing poetry than meets the eye. Even the most widely published poets need advice on matters of craft and markets. Poets can also use financial help from time to time.

Sources of assistance and encouragement include writers' organizations (national, provincial, and local), government agencies, arts councils (national, provincial, and municipal), books, and periodicals. Some of these are detailed below.

4.1 YOUR FELLOW POETS

Other writers are a key source of help. They can give you feedback on your writing, tips about new magazines or other publishing opportunities, and emotional support and friendship.

There are several ways to meet other poets. A sure-fire way to find poets is to attend poetry readings. Poets also tend to be found at the meetings of writers' federations. Most Canadian cities have active poetry circles or workshops. For example, Hamilton, Ontario, offers no less than six workshops open to the public as well as a few "by invitation only" groups. Many universities and community colleges offer poetry classes or creative writing workshops. A list of university and college workshops is found elsewhere in this directory. Public libraries may also house writing circles. There is no shortage of people who write poetry in Canada. And people count. You may read books such as this one and get all sorts of fine advice, but books are not people. The making of poetry is a lonely, often frustrating, affair. A book, even a great book, is a poor companion when you are feeling the frustrations of writer's block.

You may wish to join a workshop as a formal and regular way to enjoy the good fellowship of other poets. Or you may be happier with a small, informal network. Few poets can develop their craft without feedback, and you will find that your relationships with other poets will be an important source of encouragement and new ideas.

4.2 WRITERS' ASSOCIATIONS

Writers' associations are a great source of help. They provide encouragement, advice, and marketing information. Many host poetry readings and workshops. Almost all issue newsletters and other types of publications.

Perhaps even more important than the above, they make it possible to meet and get to know other poets. Writing is a solitary calling. It is done alone. The friendship and support of fellow poets can be extremely valuable. There is no better place to meet other writers than at a gathering of a local or national association.

The growth of writers' associations has gone hand in hand with a broadening of public awareness of, and interest in, Canadian literature.

CANADA - NATIONAL

CANADIAN AUTHORS ASSOCIATION
27 Doxsee Avenue North, Campbellford, Ontario K0L 1L0
Telephone: (705) 653-0323   Fax: (705) 653-0593
Administrator: Alec McEachern
Number of members: 900
Membership fees: $107
Writers Helping Writers is the motto. The CAA exists to foster and develop a climate favourable to the creative arts and to promote recognition of writers and their works. It has active branches in Halifax, Montreal, Ottawa, Kingston, Peterborough, Toronto, Oakville, Hamilton, St. Catharines, Kitchener-Waterloo, London, Sarnia, Winnipeg, Edmonton, Kelowna, Vancouver, and Victoria.

The CAA publishes a national newsletter and a magazine, *Canadian Author*. It also puts together *The Canadian Writer's Guide* (published by Fitzhenry & Whiteside). The CAA runs workshops and literary readings and holds an annual conference attended by authors from across the nation.

Four major literary awards are offered by the CAA for works of poetry, fiction, drama, and non-fiction. Also, the CAA administers two literary awards: the Air Canada Award (for writers under 30) and the Vicky Metcalf Award for children's literarure.

CANADIAN POETRY ASSOCIATION
PO Box 22571, St. George Postal Outlet, Toronto, Ontario M5S 1V0
Telephone: (905) 451-4258 or (416) 944-3985   Fax (for newsletter): (905) 312-8285
Membership Secretary: Jennifer Footman
National Secretary: Allan Briesmaster
President: Joe Blades
Number of members: 130
Membership fee: $25 regular; students & seniors: $15
The goal of the CPA is to promote the writing and appreciation of poetry in Canada.

It also provides a means for groups and individuals to communicate on a national level. There are active branches in several cities including: Toronto, Hamilton, London, Sarnia, Kitchener/Waterloo, and Vancouver.

The CPA issues a national news and poetry magazine, *Poemata*. The CPA organizes poetry readings and social events for its members, including two major group readings in Toronto every year. It administers two literary awards: the Shaunt Basmajian Chapbook Award and the Herb Barrett Haiku Award.

Membership is open to all who are interested in poetry: poets, teachers, booksellers, librarians, and readers of poetry.

The association publishes a chapbook series of members' poetry. It also publishes an anthology of members' work.

The CPA has established a literary archive for research purposes at York University. It also operates a poetry resource centre in London, Ontario. A small press poetry library is being established by the CPA at McMaster University. E-mail address for CPA: cpa@wwdc.com — E-mail address for CPA newsletter: ad507@freenet.hamilton.on.ca

CANADIAN SOCIETY OF CHILDREN'S AUTHORS, ILLUSTRATORS AND PERFORMERS/LA SOCIÉTÉ CANADIENNE DES AUTEURS, ILLUSTRATEURS ET ARTISTES POUR ENFANTS
35 Spadina Road, Toronto, Ontario M5R 2S9
Telephone: (416) 515-1559
Office Manager: Nancy Prasad
President: Paul Kropp
Number of members: 1,160
Membership fees: $60 (Full Member); $25 (Friend)
CANSCAIP seeks to promote interest in writing, illustration, and performing for children across Canada. This is done on two fronts. Members visit schools and libraries to give readings and performances, or to conduct workshops in creative writing, story-telling, illustrating, and/or drama. Promoters of children's literature are encouraged to use Canadian materials. Writers and people interested in writing careers encourage each other in their writing endeavours.

Membership criteria: Full membership is open to published writers in the field of children's literature; "Friends" are people interested in the work of CANSCAIP or writing for children.

CANSCAIP publishes a quarterly bulletin. There is also CANSCAIP Travels, an annotated list of members who visit schools and libraries. A major biographical record of Canadian children's authors, illustrators, and performers is also published. The current edition provides data on 346 artists and writers.

Regular meetings and workshops take place. Administers the EBEL Award.

EDITORS' ASSOCIATION OF CANADA
35 Spadina Road, Toronto, Ontario M5R 2S9
Telephones: Toronto: (416) 975-1379, Montréal: (514) 849-9886, Ottawa: (613) 820-5731, British Columbia: (604) 681-7184, Newsletter: (360) 945-3387

HAIKU CANADA
51 Graham West, Napanee, Ontario K7R 2J6

THE CANADIAN CENTRE, INTERNATIONAL P.E.N.
24 Ryerson Avenue, Suite 309, Toronto, Ontario M5T 2P3

THE LEAGUE OF CANADIAN POETS
54 Wolseley Street, Suite 204, Toronto, Ontario M5T 1A5
Telephone: (416) 504-1657   Fax: (416) 703-0059
Executive Director: Edita Petrauskaite
Assistant: Sandie Drzewiecki
Number of members: 350
Membership fees: Full - $175 (+ GST); Associate - $60 (+ GST)
The LCP is a national organization of professionally published and performing poets in Canada. The objectives of the LCP are to develop the art of poetry; to enhance the status of poets and nurture a professional poetic community; to facilitate the teaching of Canadian poetry at all levels of education; to enlarge the audience for poetry by encouraging publication, performance, and recognition of Canadian poetry nationally and internationally; and to uphold freedom of expression.

Full membership generally requires the authorship of at least one full-sized book, two chapbooks, or one audiotape of poetry performance. Associate members are required to show that they have been publishing poetry in literary periodicals.

The LCP runs Canada Council funded reading tours from coast to coast. It also runs the Poets in the Schools program of the Ontario Arts Council.

The LCP offers two literary awards— the Gerald Lampert Award, for the best first book of poetry by a Canadian, published in the preceding year, and the Pat Lowther Award, for the best book of poetry by a Canadian woman, published in the preceding year. The LCP also runs the annual National Poetry Contest, which offers three cash prizes plus publication of the best fifty entries in an anthology.

Among the publications of the LCP are: *Who's Who in the League of Canadian Poets*; *Poetry Markets for Canadians* (co-published with The Mercury Press); *Poets in the Classroom* (Pembroke Press); *Vintages*, an annual anthology of poetry contest winners (Quarry Press); and the *Living Archives Series* of feminist poetics.

The LCP has also produced cassette tape recordings of senior poets. An extensive library of books, recordings, periodicals, and biographical material is maintained for research purposes.

To facilitate the development of the poetry writing community, the LCP issues a newsletter (6 issues per year) as well as the *Museletter* (twice per year) and a calendar of poetry readings across the country (6 times per year). E-mail address: league@io.org— Web site: http://www.swifty.com/lc

PERIODICAL WRITERS ASSOCIATION OF CANADA
54 Wolseley Street, Toronto, Ontario M5T 1A5

PLAYWRIGHTS UNION OF CANADA
54 Wolseley Street, 2nd Floor, Toronto, Ontario M5T 1A5
Telephone: (416) 703-0201   Fax: (416) 703-0059

Executive Director: Angela Rebeiro
Information Officer: Jodi Armstrong
Number of members: 345
Membership fee: $135
The Union's goal is the promotion of professionally produced Canadian plays and playwrights. The Union can act as an agent on behalf of members' amateur productions. Membership is open to Canadian playwrights who have had a play professionally produced.

The Union publishes and distributes plays under the Playwrights Canada Press imprint. The Union provides the most comprehensive selection of scripts by Canadian authors. In addition to publishing plays, the Union issues a news magazine, *CanPlay*, six times per year.

National (Canada Council) and provincial reading tours are organized. Contract advice is available from the head office staff.

THE WRITERS' UNION OF CANADA

24 Ryerson Avenue, Toronto, Ontario M5T 2P3
Telephone: (416) 703-8982   Fax: (416) 703-0826
Executive Director: Penny Dickens
Assistant/Information: Siobhan O'Connor
Number of members: 925
Membership fee: $180 (+ GST)
The Union is an association of professional writers. Its goal is to assist and advance the interests of book authors in Canada. The Union maintains relations with Canadian publishers (both book and periodical), works to safeguard the freedom to write and publish, and establishes good relations with other writers and their organizations within Canada and in all parts of the world. To be eligible for membership, you must be a Canadian citizen or landed immigrant and have had a book published by a commercial or university press in the last seven years or have a book currently in print.

The Union runs Canada Council-funded reading tours from coast to coast. It also runs Ontario Arts Council-funded readings in the school system of Ontario.

To establish and maintain contact among its members, the Union publishes a newsletter nine times per year. The Union also publishes books and chapbooks of value to professional authors: *Help Yourself to a Better Contract*; *Writers' Guide to Electronic Publishing Rights*; *Writers' Guide to Canadian Publishers*; *Writers' Guide to Grants*; *Awards, Competitions, and Prizes*; *Author & Editor*, *Author and Literary Agent*; and a directory of its members, among other titles.

The Union has developed a standard trade book contract that serves as an excellent model. Many Canadian book publishers use this contract or one like it.

It sponsors the Short Prose Competition for Developing Writers. (Please send SASE for contest rules.)

The Union runs a Manuscript Evaluation Service and Contract Services (for non-members). There is also a Contract Negotiation Service. E-mail address: twuc@the-wire.com

ALBERTA

WRITERS GUILD OF ALBERTA
Percy Page Centre, 3rd Floor, 11759 Groat Road, Edmonton, Alberta T5M 3K6
Telephone: (403) 422-8174   Fax: (403) 422-2663, Red Deer office: (403) 342-1146, Calgary office: (403) 265-2226
Executive Director: Miki Andrejevic
Information Officer: Darlene Diver
Number of members: 750
Membership fee: $55 regular; students & seniors: $20
The purpose of the Guild is to provide a meeting ground and common voice for the writers of Alberta. Membership is open to any writer who is a current, or former, resident of Alberta.

The Guild offers writers' retreats (both guided and non-guided), workshops, a manuscript-reading service, a newsletter, several publications of use to authors, and an awards program to recognize writing excellence in every genre, including the Stephan G. Stephansson Award for Poetry.

The Guild's newsletter is published six times a year and features plenty of market information.

General meetings and local gatherings of Guild members provide direct contact between writers and provide encouragement to writers of every level of expertise.

The Guild organizes the Stroll of Poets in Edmonton.

BRITISH COLUMBIA

BURNABY WRITERS' SOCIETY
6584 Deer Lake Avenue, Burnaby, British Columbia V5G 2J3
Telephone: (604) 435-6500
Information officer: Eileen Kernaghan
Number of members: 300
Membership fee: $25 regular; students & seniors: $15
The Society is open to anyone who has an interest in writing (any genre). It hosts a regular series of monthly events and public readings. It runs an annual writing contest that is open to all B.C. writers.

A monthly newsletter is published that provides market and workshop information and advance notice of public literary events.

The Society awards an annual scholarship to a promising young writer through the University of British Columbia's Creative Writing Department.

THE FEDERATION OF BRITISH COLUMBIA WRITERS
905 West Pender Street, Suite 400, Vancouver, British Columbia V6C 1L6
Telephone: (604) 683-2057   Fax: (604) 683-8269
Executive Director: Corey Van't Haaff
Number of members: 600
Membership fees: Full – $50; Associate – $25
The Federation is open to professional and aspiring B.C. writers of all genres (technical and business, as well as literary writing). Several publications assist or

promote local writers. These include their *Literary Arts Directory*, an important resource manual.

The Federation hosts readings, workshops, and other writer-related events. The Federation sponsors an annual writing competition, Literary Rites. (Please write for contest details.) It also organizes the literary component of the B.C. Festival of the Arts.

It will assist members with valid grievances with editors and publishers.

MANITOBA

MANITOBA WRITERS' GUILD INC.
100 Arthur Street, Suite 206, Winnipeg, Manitoba R3B 1H3
Telephone: (204) 942-6134   Fax: (204) 942-5754
Executive Director: Robyn Maharas
Information Officer: Kathie Axtell
Number of members: 500
Membership fee: $40; students, seniors, & fixed income: $20
The Guild is open to anyone with an interest in the art of writing. It works to advance and promote literature, in all its forms, in the province of Manitoba. Several prizes are offered via the Manitoba Literary Awards for both English and French books and writers.

The Guild issues a monthly newsletter, *WordWrap*, that includes market information. It hosts poetry readings (the Cafe Reading Series), workshops, and an annual conference. A manuscript reading service is available. Also available is a Mentor Program that links promising new writers and experienced writers.

Resource manuals, such as *The Writers' Handbook*, are available through the Guild office.

NEW BRUNSWICK

THE WRITERS' FEDERATION OF NEW BRUNSWICK
PO Box 37, Station A, Fredericton, New Brunswick E3B 4Y2
Telephone: (506) 459-7228   Fax: same
Project Coordinator: Anna Mae Snider
Number of members: 230
Membership fee: $15
The Federation seeks to promote the works of New Brunswick authors. It also works to encourage greater public recognition of N.B. writers. Membership is open to those who have an interest in writing. A newsletter, *New Brunswick ink*, provides literary market information.

The Federation holds a yearly literary competition for N.B. writers. There are two poetry prizes, one for single poems and one for a collection of poems. The Federation also hosts public readings by N.B. and Canadian authors.

Workshops are held at the Federation's fall book fair and at its AGM, held in the spring. A manuscript reading service is available. Other activities include literary salons, book launches, and a writers-in-the-schools program.

NEWFOUNDLAND

WRITERS' ALLIANCE OF NEWFOUNDLAND & LABRADOR
PO Box 2681, St. John's, Newfoundland A1C 5M5
Telephone: (709) 739-5215   Fax: same
Executive Director: Patricia Warren
Number of members: 200
Membership fee: $25, $45, & $60
Membership is open to all with an interest in writing. The Alliance offers monthly
readings which feature many poets. Writing workshops are held at the AGM,
including poetry writing.

Publishes *Word*, a newsletter of market information and advice. The Alliance
works to promote the literary arts in Newfoundland and Labrador. It does so through
its ongoing program of meetings, readings, workshops, retreats, and contacts with
educational institutions.

NOVA SCOTIA

WRITERS' FEDERATION OF NOVA SCOTIA
1809 Barrington Street, Suite 901, Halifax, Nova Scotia B3J 3K8
Telephone: (902) 423-8116   Fax: (902) 422-0881
Executive Director: Jane Buss
Number of members: 395
Membership fee: $30 regular; $15 for students
The Federation was established to foster creative writing and the profession of
writing in Nova Scotia; to provide advice and assistance to writers at all stages of their
careers; to encourage greater public recognition of N.S. writers and their
achievements; and to enhance the literary arts in both the regional and the national
culture.

The Federation organizes workshops, conferences, retreats, and educational
programs. It publishes *Eastword*, a newsletter, and maintains a permanent collection of
N.S. books.

It administers the Evelyn Richardson Memorial Literary Trust and Award and
the Thomas Raddall Atlantic Fiction Award. It also holds the annual Atlantic Writing
Competition, for unpublished manuscripts.

The Federation offers a manuscript reading service at a modest cost. It administers
the N.S. Writers in the Schools Program. Membership is open to anyone who writes.

ONTARIO

OTTAWA INDEPENDENT WRITERS/LES ÉCRIVAINS INDÉPENDENTS D'OTTAWA
265 Elderberry Terrace, Orléans, Ontario K1E 1Z2
Telephone: (613) 841-0572   Fax: (613) 841-0775
Executive Director: Maureen Moyes
OIW offers the Archibald Lampman Poetry Award, currently worth $400. It is
presented during an annual literary awards night.

TOWER POETRY SOCIETY
Dundas Public Library, 18 Ogilvie Street, Dundas, Ontario L9H 2S2

PRINCE EDWARD ISLAND

P.E.I. Writers' Guild
PO Box 2234, Charlottetown, Prince Edward Island C1A 8B9

QUEBEC

FEDERATION OF ENGLISH-LANGUAGE WRITERS OF QUEBEC
1200 ave. Atwater, Suite 3, Montréal, Québec H3Z 1X4
Telephone: (514) 934-2485   Fax: same
President: Linda Ghan
Communications: Guy Rodgers
Number of members: 170
Membership fee: $20
The FEWQ's purpose is to bring together English-language writers of all genres for
idea-sharing and book promotion. It also serves as an advocate for English writers
vis-à-vis the federal and provincial governments and vis-à-vis publishers and editors
in the cases of conflict/dispute.

There are three membership categories: full membership (for book authors or
authors with substantial periodical publications); associate membership (for
unpublished writers); and supporting membership (for people who may not be
writers but who wish to support and encourage English-language writing in Quebec).

The FEWQ publishes a quarterly newsletter. Its programs include poetry
workshops, writers-in-the-schools, writers-in-libraries, public poetry readings, and a
manuscript reading service.

SASKATCHEWAN

THE SASKATCHEWAN POETRY SOCIETY
3104 College Avenue, Regina, Saskatchewan S4T 1V7
Telephone: (306) 522-6321
President: Keith Foster
Secretary: Joan Hamilton
Treasurer: Vesta Pickel
Number of Members: 40
Membership fee: $1
The Society, now sixty years old, hopes to further the writing of poetry by its
members. Poets who wish to join must live in Saskatchewan at the time they apply
for membership. They can, however, keep their membership if they move to
another province.

The Society holds regular meetings on the first Friday of each month to hear and
discuss poems. Occasional workshops are organized, as are lectures and readings.

The Society publishes a bi-annual anthology, *The Saskatchewan Poetry Book.* Each member has a page in the book.

SASKATCHEWAN WRITERS GUILD
PO Box 3986, Regina, Saskatchewan S4P 3R9
Telephone: (306) 757-6310   Fax: (306) 565-8554
Membership fee: $50; students and seniors: $30
Introductory first year rates are $40 and $25.
The SWG seeks to improve the status of writers in Saskatchewan. It also seeks to establish liaison with others who are concerned with writing and writing standards. Membership is open to all who are interested in writing.

The SWG publishes three periodicals: *Grain,* a literary quarterly; *FreeLance,* a market news and literary magazine (ten issues per year); and *WindScript,* a high-school literary magazine. The SWG also publishes one of the best resource manuals around, the *Saskatchewan Literary Arts Handbook,* as well as other valuable titles on book publishing contracts and the electronic media.

The SWG provides a wide range of programming to serve its members, other writers, and the general public. Programming for writers includes annual conferences and general meetings, writers' colony programs (at Emma Lake and St. Peter's Abbey), public readings (in Regina and Saskatoon), a workshop program, funding for local literary events, and annual literary awards and competitions, such as the City of Regina Writing Award and the Saskatchewan Book Awards. Several scholarships are available.

The SWG maintains a large research library of literary works and periodicals. It also operates an electronic bulletin board service (BBS) that offers an on-line resident writer program for students in Saskatchewan.

FOREIGN

THE ACADEMY OF AMERICAN POETS
584 Broadway, Suite 1208, New York, NY 10012-3250
Telephone: (212) 274-0343   Fax: (212) 274-9427
Executive Driector: William Wadsworth
Program Director: Matthew Brogan
Number of members: 4,200
Membership fee: $45 (U.S.) for associate membership
Membership in the Academy can be useful to Canadian poets who publish and/or present public readings in the U.S. Associate members receive copies of the winners of the Walt Whitman Award and the Lamont Poetry Selection every year. In addition to those two prizes, the Academy administers the Tanning Prize ($100,000), the Lenore Marshall Poetry Prize ($10,000), the Harold Morton Landon Translation Award ($1,000), the Peter I.B. Lavan Younger Poet Awards (three $1,000 prizes), and the annual University & College Poetry Prizes.

The Academy is the coordinator of National Poetry Month and the organizer of public poetry readings in New York, Washington, Philadelphia, Los Angeles, and San Francisco.

THE HAIKU SOCIETY OF AMERICA
Japan Society Inc., 333 East 47th Street, New York, NY 10017

POETRY SOCIETY
National Poetry Centre, 22 Betterton Street, London, WC2H 9BU England
Telephone: 0171-240-4810   Fax: 0171-240-4818
Executive Director: Chris Meade
Information Officer: Rachel Bourke
Number of members: 2,800
Membership fee: 40 pounds (airmail) for Canadian poets
The Society works to promote poets and poetry through public events, publication in magazine, and education. Membership is open to all who enjoy poetry, readers as well as writers.

The Society publishes *Poetry Review*, a major quarterly, as well as a newsletter, *Poetry News*. It runs a poetry bookshop and one of the finest poetry libraries in the world. The Society holds a series of public readings and lectures in London. Cassette tape recordings of senior British poets are available from the Society.

The Society administers the Dylan Thomas Award, the Alice Hunt Bartlett Award, and the European Poetry Translation Prize. It also runs the National Poetry Competition.

The Society has numerous publications that are of use to poets everywere. It can help foreign poets with public readings in Britain. E-mail address: poetrysoc@bbcnc.org.uk

POETRY SOCIETY OF AMERICA
15 Gramercy Park, New York, NY 10003
Telephone: (212) 254-9628   Fax: (212) 673-2352
Executive Director: Elise Paschen
Information Officer: Diana Burnham
Number of members: 2,700
Membership fee: $40 (U.S.)
The Society, founded in 1910, exists to raise public awareness of poetry, to deepen the understanding of it, and to encourage more people to read, listen to, and write poetry. To help attain these goals, the Society offers the Frost Medal, the Shelley Memorial Award, the William Carlos Williams Award, the Norma Farber First Book Award, and the Alice Fay Di Castagnola Award among many others.

The Society run a poetry reading series, peer workshops, and a series of poetry contests. It also publishes a newsletter. While most of its public events take place in New York, it also hosts readings in Chicago, Los Angeles/Hollywood, and Cambridge.

Membership would be useful to Canadian poets active in the New York scene or who want to be up-to-date on U.S. poetry happenings.

POETS & WRITERS, INC.
72 Spring Street, New York, NY 10012
Telephone: (212) 226-3586   Fax: (212) 226-3963
Executive Director: Elliot Figman

Poets & Writers is not a membership organization in the usual sense of the term. There is a $5 application fee for a listing in the Directory of American Poets and Fiction Writers, the major publication of P & W. Over 6,600 authors are listed in the P & W directory. To be in this directory a writer must, upon occasion, publish work in American periodicals or have a book with an American publishing house. (Thus, many Canadians would be eligible.)

P & W publishes a bimonthly journal, *Poets & Writers Magazine*, with news of grants, awards, and periodicals seeking manuscripts. The magazine contains interviews with and/or articles by poets and other authors. This is one of the two or three most important sources of poetry market information in the U.S.

Among other useful publications are: *Literary Agents: A Writer's Guide*; *Author & Audience: A Readings and Workshops Guide*; *Writers Conferences*; and *Into Print: A Guide to the Writing Life*. P & W runs a reading program and a workshop program. E-mail address: PWSubs@aol.com

POETS HOUSE
72 Spring Street, New York, NY 10012
Telephone: (212) 431-7920   Fax: (212) 431-8131
Executive Director: Lee Ellen Briccetti
Dir. of Public Relations: Carolyn Peyser
Number of members: 550
Membership fee: $40 (U.S.) for basic membership
Poets House is a comfortable, accessible place for poetry. It is a library and meeting place which invites poets and the public to step into the living tradition of poetry. The library has over 30,000 poetry books, literary journals, and audiotapes.

Anyone can join Poets House and be part of its events in New York. Poets House is very friendly to Canadian poets.

Year-round programs include Passwords (featuring distinguished poets), Parallel Lines (exploring the connections between poetry and other art forms), the Sunset Reading Series (summer readings at Hudson River Park), and Poetry in The Branches (workshops. seminars, and poetry readings in the New York Public Library system).

Hosts the Poetry Publication Showcase (October 28 to December 2) to promote recently published books to the New York market.

4.3   GOVERNMENT RESOURCES

In Canada very few literary writers (perhaps a dozen or so) are able to earn a living by putting words on paper. No one makes a living at writing poetry exclusively. Government departments and arts councils provide important financial support to all types of authors. Indeed, it is common for senior Canadian authors to receive far more from grants than from royalties.

Below is a list of the agencies that give money to support Canadian literature. Some, like the Canada Council, are "arm's length" bodies. Others, like the

Ontario Ministry of Citizenship, Culture, and Recreation are part of the government.

I have tried to report on as many granting agencies as possible: national, provincial, and municipal. There are, unfortunately, many omissions on the municipal level. Your provincial writers' federation may be a good source of this local information.

Only brief summaries of activities and programs are given here. Because grants almost always require the completion of formal applications, you should write for complete information.

While established professionals certainly get their share of the funding, many unpublished writers apply for grants, and every year some receive them.

One important tip: keep photocopies of your grant applications. Often several applications are required before one is accepted. It is important to keep the applications going. All too often poets give up after one or two rejections. You should apply frequently.

Because of recent cutbacks in funding for the Canada Council and for most, if not all, provincial arts councils, granting programs are currently under review. Some councils, such as the North York Arts Council, have actually disbanded since the last edition of this book. Much of the information below may no longer be accurate by the time it reaches you. Please check with the relevant organizations for the latest data.

CANADA - NATIONAL

THE CANADA COUNCIL

Arts Awards Service, PO Box 1047, Ottawa, Ontario K1P 5V8
Telephone: 1-800-263-5588; (613) 566-4414, Ex. 5537   Fax: (613) 566-4410
Application forms: Silvie Bernier

Grants to writers: Robert Richard

The Council offers Work-in-Progress grants for writers of up to $10,000 and Special Projects grants of up to $15,000. Deadlines are March 1 and September 1.

The Council offers A and B Grants for creative writing. A Grants are for up to $24,000; B Grants for up to $17,000. Three deadlines each year for A Grants: April 1, May 15, October 1. Deadlines for B Grants: April 1, May 15, November 15.

The Council provides Short Term Grants of up to $4,000 and Travel Grants of up to $2,800. Please contact the Council for application forms and guidelines. E-mail address: silvie_bernier%canada_council@mcimail.com

Government of Canada — DEPARTMENT OF COMMUNICATIONS

Arts and Culture, 300 Slater Street, 20th Floor, Ottawa, Ontario K1A 0C8

Government of Canada — DEPARTMENT OF FOREIGN AFFAIRS AND INTERNATIONAL TRADE

Cultural Division, 125 Sussex Drive, Ottawa, Ontario K1A 0G2

Telephone: (613) 992-5726   Fax: (613) 992-5965

Literary Officer: René Picard

Provides travel grants to Canadian writers. Also provides counselling by cultural agents in foreign missions. Requires up to six months to consider requests for grants.

The goal is to promote Canadian literature abroad in collaboration with foreign editors. Can assist with promotion of books and with promotional tours. Can also help with the sale of foreign reprint rights.

ALBERTA

ALBERTA COMMUNITY DEVELOPMENT

Arts & Cultural Industries Branch, 3rd Floor, Beaver House, 10158 103 Street, Edmonton, Alberta T5J 0X6

ALBERTA CULTURE AND MULTICULTURALISM

Arts Branch, 10004 - 104 Avenue, 11th Floor, CN Tower, Edmonton, Alberta T5J 0K5

ALBERTA FOUNDATION FOR THE ARTS

5th Floor, Beaver House, 10158 103 Street, Edmonton, Alberta T5J 0X6

Telephone: (403) 427-6315

Provides grants to assist qualified writers in Alberta to undertake writing projects. Three levels of grants: Junior (up to $4,000), Intermediate (up to $11,000), and Senior (up to $25,000). These grants are intended for major writing projects.

Also offered are Special Project Grants of up to $5,000. Special grants are intended for projects in the literary arts that do not consist primarily of original writing.

BRITISH COLUMBIA

BRITISH COLUMBIA MINISTRY OF SMALL BUSINESS, TOURISM & CULTURE

Cultural Services Branch, 800 Johnson Street, 5th Floor, Victoria, British Columbia V8V 1X4

Telephone: (604) 356-1718 & 356-1728   Fax: (604) 387-4099

Coordinator, Arts Awards: Walter K. Quan

Writers with at least two published books may apply for assistance to a maximum of $5,000 for specific writing projects. Applicants must have lived in B.C. for at least one year and be Canadian citizens or landed immigrants. Application deadline: October 15, 1994

The Ministry also supports a Writers-in-Libraries Program featurung public readings and workshops.

COMMUNITY ARTS COUNCIL OF VANCOUVER

837 Davie Street, Vancouver, British Columbia V6Z 1B7

OFFICE OF CULTURAL AFFAIRS

Social Planning Department, City of Vancouver, City Square, Box 96, 455 West 12th Avenue, Vancouver, British Columbia V5Z 3X7

Telephone: (604) 871-6000   Fax: (604) 871-6048

Arts/Culture Officer: Teresa Wang

Offers the City of Vancouver Book Award of $2,000 to the author of a book that contributes to understanding Vancouver.

The Department also funds literary arts events and festivals.

MANITOBA

MANITOBA ARTS COUNCIL/CONSEIL DES ARTS DU MANITOBA

525 - 93 Lombard Avenue, Winnipeg, Manitoba R3B 3B1

Telephone: (204) 945-2237   Fax: (204) 945-5925

Literary Officer: Pat Sanders

Offers grants to individual writers, grants to literary and writers' organizations, and funds to support public readings.

Major Arts Grants are to support personal creative projects of 6 to 10 months duration ($25,000 max.). A Grants are for concentrated work on a major writing project ($10,000 max.). Writers must have two books published to apply for an A Grant. B Grants are also for concentrated work on a major writing project ($5,000 max.). Writers must have one book published to apply. C Grants ($2,000 max.) are for emerging writers. Deadlines are April 15 and September 15.

Short-Term Project Grants are also available for up to $1,000. Apply 4 weeks prior to start of project.

NEW BRUNSWICK

NEW BRUNSWICK DEPARTMENT OF MUNICIPALITIES, CULTURE & HOUSING

Arts Branch, PO Box 6000, Fredericton, New Brunswick E3B 5H1

NEW BRUNSWICK DEPARTMENT OF TOURISM, RECREATION & HERITAGE/NOUVEAU-BRUNSWICK TOURISME, LOISIRS & PATRIMOINE

Arts Branch, PO Box 12345, Fredericton, New Brunswick E3B 5C3

NEWFOUNDLAND

THE NEWFOUNDLAND AND LABRADOR ARTS COUNCIL

PO Box 98, Station C, St. John's, Newfoundland A1C 5H5

Telephone: (709) 726-2212   Fax: (709) 726-0619

Executive Director: Randy Follett

Literary Officer: Reg Winsor

Information Officer: Jean K. Smith

Applicants for grants must be Canadian citizens or landed immigrants and must have lived in Newfoundland or Labrador for one year. Deadlines are: January 15, April 15, & September 15. Evaluation criteria: originality, growth potential, permanence, access, ability, and feasibility.

NEWFOUNDLAND AND LABRADOR DEPARTMENT OF TOURISM & CULTURE

Cultural Affairs Division, PO Box 1854, St. John's, Newfoundland A1C 5P9

NORTHWEST TERRITORIES

NORTHWEST TERRITORIES ARTS COUNCIL

Department of Education, Culture and Employment, Government of the Northwest Territories, PO Box 1320, Yellowknife, Northwest Territories X1A 2L9

NOVA SCOTIA

NOVA SCOTIA DEPARTMENT OF EDUCATION AND CULTURE

Cultural Affairs Division, PO Box 578, Halifax, Nova Scotia B3J 2S9

Telephone: (902) 424-6389   Fax: (902) 424-0710

Cultural Industries Officer: Peggy Walt

The Assistance to Established Writers program provides grants to Nova Scotia writers working on projects for which there is serious trade publisher interest. Maximum grant at any one time: $2,000. Such a grant can be used for research or for manuscript preparation. Deadlines are April 1 and October 1.

ONTARIO

ARTS ETOBICOKE
PO Box 222, Etobicoke, Ontario M9C 4V3

ARTS YORK
City of York, Parks and Recreation Department, 2700 Eglinton Avenue West, City of York, Ontario M6M IVI

CITY OF ETOBICOKE
Parks & Recreation Services, 399 The West Mall, Etobicoke, Ontario M9C 2Y2

CITY OF NORTH YORK
Arts Unit, Culture Branch, Parks and Recreation Department, 5100 Yonge Street, North York, Ontario M2N 5V7
Telephone: (416) 395-6193 or 395-6194   Fax: (416) 395-7886
Asst. Arts Officer: Jyoti Sapra-Shannon
The Arts Unit's mandate is to make the people of North York aware of arts programs in the city. We are able to re-direct individual writers to organizations and service organizations that can provide assistance. Programs are currently under review. Please phone for information.

CITY OF SCARBOROUGH
Recreation, Parks and Culture Department, Arts and Heritage Services Division, 150 Borough Drive, Scarborough, Ontario MIP 4N7
Telephone: (416) 396-7766
Program Coordinator: John Anderson
Scarborough Arts and Heritage Services was established to work with community arts groups and the Scarborough Arts Council. It tries to support community development and education in the arts.

Grants are available to non-profit community arts organizations whose activities take place within the City of Scarborough.

The city publishes the *Scarborough Arts Directory*.

GUELPH ARTS COUNCIL
147 Wyndham Street North, Suite 404, Guelph, Ontario N1H 4E9
Telephone: (519) 836-3280   Fax: (519) 766-9212
Executive Director: Sally Wismer
The Council runs a resource centre and is a source of grant and contest/awards information. It publishes a newsletter nine times per year and helps facilitate co-operation among artists and arts groups in Guelph.

HAMILTON & REGION ARTS COUNCIL
116 King Street West, Hamilton, Ontario L8P 4V3
Telephone: (905) 529-9485   Fax: (905) 529-0238
Administrator: Patti Beckett
ARTSbeat editor: Ivan Jurakic
Organizes a salon (called Lit Chat) where writers can discuss the issues of the day and

literary theory. Publishes poetry in *ARTSbeat*, its tabloid newsletter. Organizes book launches and public readings for local writers. Helps writers with book promotions.

The Council offers the Hamilton Book Awards and the Hamilton Short Piece Awards with cash prizes. Awards are presented for poetry, fiction, non-fiction, and children's literature.

A team of mentors is a major source of information on publishing opportunities (both periodical and book) and regional creative writing groups. E-mail address: harac@freenet.hamilton.on.ca

THE MUNICIPALITY OF METROPOLITAN TORONTO

Culture Division, Metro Hall, 55 John Street, Stn. 1240, 24th Floor, Toronto, Ontario M5V 3C6

Telephone: (416) 392-4218   Fax: (416) 392-3355

Cultural Affairs Officer: Irene Bauer

Has a Cultural Grants Program. This supports the direct presentation of cultural activity (a poetry reading, for example) and services which assist in the presentation of cultural activities. The program provides funds for the International Reading Series at Harbourfront, the Idler Pub Reading Series, the League of Canadian Poets, and other literary events. E-mail address: irene_r._bauer@metrodesk.metrotor.on.ca

ONTARIO ARTS COUNCIL/CONSEIL DES ARTS DE L'ONTARIO

Literature Office, 151 Bloor Street West, Suite 500, Toronto, Ontario M5S 1T6

Telephone: (416) 969-7437; Ontario only: 1-800-387-0058   Fax: (416) 961-7796

Literature Officer: Lorraine Filyer

The mandate of the OAC is to promote the study and enjoyment of, and the production of, works in the arts.

The OAC's Literature Office gives grants to literary book and periodical publishers. Literary associations may be granted support for various projects and workshops. Grants are also awarded to individual writers under the Works in Progress program. The OAC provides funding for the Writers' Reserve, a program of individual grants awarded on the recommendation of Ontario book and magazine publishers.

The Ontario Writers in the Schools program is another example of the OAC's support of writers and creative writing. One-time literary projects/performances can also receive OAC funding.

OAC programs are currently under review because of cutbacks; current data can be had from the Council.

ONTARIO MINISTRY OF CITIZENSHIP, CULTURE AND RECREATION/MINISTÈRE DES CITOYENS, DE LA CULTURE ET DE LA RECREATION

Arts Branch, 77 Bloor Street West, 3rd Floor, Toronto, Ontario M7A 2R9

REGIONAL MUNICIPALITY OF OTTAWA-CARLETON/MUNICIPALITÉ RÉGIONALE D'OTTAWA-CARLETON

Ottawa-Carleton Centre, Cartier Square, 111 Lisgar Street, Ottawa, Ontario K2P 2L7

SCARBOROUGH ARTS COUNCIL

1859 Kingston Road, Scarborough, Ontario MIN IT3

Telephone: (416) 698-7322   Fax: (416) 698-7972

Surface & Symbol editor: Vivian Snead

The Council seeks to promote and develop the literary, visual, and performing arts in Scarborough. It runs an annual poetry competition. It also publishes poetry in *Surface & Symbol*, its tabloid newsletter.

TORONTO ARTS COUNCIL

141 Bathurst Street, Toronto, Ontario M5V 2R2

Telephone: (416) 392-6800   Fax: (416) 392-6920

Grants Officer: Nalo Hopkinson

Writers must have lived in the City of Toronto for two years to apply for a grant. Unpublished writers can apply for up to $1,500; published writers for up to $4,500. Grants are for research or writing re: a work-in-progress. Only one grant per writer in any three-year period. Awards are made to poets, fiction writers, playwrights (but not for film scripts), and non-fiction writers.

Travel grants of up to $5,000 are also available. These can be for either domestic or international travel.

PRINCE EDWARD ISLAND

GOVERNMENT OF PRINCE EDWARD ISLAND

Community and Cultural Affairs/Affaires communautaires et culturelles, PO Box 2000, Charlottetown, Prince Edward Island CIA 7N8

PRINCE EDWARD ISLAND COUNCIL OF THE ARTS

PO Box 2234, Charlottetown, Prince Edward Island CIA 8B9

Telephone: (902) 368-4410   Fax: (902) 368-4418

The Council sponsors the annual Island Literary Awards with prizes for poetry, fiction, non-fiction, and children's literature. It also organizes a Festival of the Arts and helps support the National Milton Acorn Festival in Charlottetown every August.

QUEBEC

[none that wanted to be listed]

SASKATCHEWAN

CITY OF SASKATOON
Leisure Services Department, City Hall, 222 Third Avenue North, Saskatoon, Saskatchewan S7K 0J5

REGINA ARTS COMMISSION
Arts & Culture Section, Community Services, Parks and Recreation, City of Regina, PO Box 1790, Regina, Saskatchewan S4P 3C8

SASKATCHEWAN ARTS BOARD
3475 Albert Street, 3rd Floor, Regina, Saskatchewan S4S 6X6
Telephone: (306) 787-4056; Saskatchewan only: 1-800-667-7526   Fax: (306) 787-4199
Literary Officer: Gail Paul Armstrong
Information Officer: Nik L. Burton
The Board offers four types of grants to individual writers: A Grants, B Grants, C Grants, and Travel Grants. The A Grants are for senior writers and can be up to $20,000 for creative work, $10,000 for professional development, or $5,000 for research. B Grants are for professional writers and have maximums of $12,000 for creative work, $7,500 for professional development, or $3,500 for research. C Grants, for writers striving to establish themselves, provide maximum grants of $4,000, $4,000, or $1,500. The Travel Grants are worth $1,000. Application deadlines are March 1 and October 1.

The Arts Board's Literary Arts Program supports book and periodical publishers, the Literary Playscript Commissioning Program, and the Literary Script Reading Service, among other things. The Reading Service provides, at a subsidized rate, professional evaluation of manuscripts. The Board also cooperates with other agencies and organizations to promote writing, publishing, and reading in Saskatchewan.

SASKATCHEWAN MUNICIPAL GOVERNMENT
Arts, Cultural Industries & Multiculturalism Branch, 1855 Victoria Avenue, Suite 420, Regina, Saskatchewan S4P 3V7
Telephone: (306) 787-4753   Fax: (306) 787-8560
Arts Policy Consultant: Andras Tahn
The Arts Branch works to develop policy for the arts. It provides funding for the arts and cultural industries, including SaskFILM.

YUKON

YUKON ARTS COUNCIL
PO Box 5120, Whitehorse, Yukon Y1A 4S3
Telephone: (403) 668-6284   Fax: (403) 668-6803
Information Officer: Lilyan Grubach
The Council aims to develop opportunities for writers in the Yukon through

education, training, promotion, and both public and private sector programs. There is a Literary Touring Program for Yukon writers. The Council runs a Writer-in-Residence Program that is open to both Yukon and non-Yukon authors. There is also an Artist-in-the-School Program (Yukon authors only).

YUKON TOURISM
Arts Branch, PO Box 2703, Whitehorse, Yukon Y1A 2C6
Telephone: (403) 667-8589; Yukon only: 1-800-661-0408 Fax: (403) 667-4656
Director: Rick Lemaire
Arts Consultant: Laurel Parry
The Arts Brance offers funding assistance to arts organizations and individual artists. Grants to writers can be for literary creation, training, or travel. The deadlines are April 1 and October 1. The Branch also provides support for Special Projects (ie, festivals and seminars).

4.4 UNIVERSITY AND COLLEGE CREATIVE WRITING COURSES AND WORKSHOPS

One way to hone your poetry skills is to join a creative writing course or workshop at the college or university level.

Often these workshops are led by published authors who can also provide marketing information and advice.

Creative writing courses and workshops come in many varieties. There are night-school as well as day-school programs, summer programs, and weekend workshops. Some come with full university or college credits while others are non-credit. In fact, some schools— The University of Victoria, for example— offer day, night, and summer creative writing courses.

Survey forms were sent to all 52 universities in Canada and to 107 English-language community colleges. In each case our inquiry went to the Continuing Education office because night, summer, and weekend courses seemed better suited to people who are not full-time students.

Some secondary schools also offer creative writing courses or workshops which can be as useful as the university and college programs. We have not surveyed the public school systems but you might contact your board of education for this information.

Creative writing workshops tend to come and go, depending on student interest. Do not assume that your local college or university has nothing to offer if it is not listed here. This list only covers the 19 schools that responded to requests for data. Also note that this list covers only programs that were offered during 1995. New ones start all the time.

In addition to ongoing workshops and courses, some one-day seminars are offered. Seminars are not listed here because they are not set up far in advance. Check with your college or university for specific information on seminars.

ACADIA UNIVERSITY
Division of Continuing Education, Wolfville, Nova Scotia B0P 1X0
Telephone: (902) 542-2201, Ex. 1371 or Ext. 1111 or Ext.1502   Fax: (902) 542-3715 or 542-4727
Contact persons: Judy Noel-Walsh & Donna Smyth

Runs both day-school and summer-school classes. Three credit courses: English 2003 - Intro. to Creative Writing; English 3083 - Creative Writing I; English 3093 - Creative Writing II. Also has some non-credit offerings such as Fiction Writing and The Writer You Are. Hosts readings and talks by visiting authors.

ALGONQUIN COLLEGE of Applied Arts and Technology
1385 Woodroffe Avenue, Nepean, Ontario K2G 1V8
Telephone: (613) 727-4723, Ex. 6150 or Ex. 6156   Fax: (613) 733-6170
Contact person: Lucette Potvin

Offers two non-credit writing courses: ENL5201 & ENL5267.

AUGUSTANA UNIVERSITY COLLEGE
4901 46th Avenue, Camrose, Alberta T4V 2R3
Telephone: (403) 679-1100   Fax: (403) 679-1129
Contact person: Anne Le Dressay

Has one credit course: ENG 215 - Creative Writing.

CONCORDIA UNIVERSITY
Department of English, 1455 de Maisonneuve Blvd. West, Montréal, Québec H3G 1M8
Telephone (undergraduate): (514) 848-2342, (graduate studies): (514) 848-2344   Fax: (514) 848-4501
Contact person (undergraduate): Sharon Frank
Contact person (graduate studies): Susan Brown

Offers a B.A. in Creative Writing, an Honors B.A. in Creative Writing, and an M.A. in English with Creative Writing Option. Also has non-credit courses. Offers both day and night school courses. Talks and readings by 6 to 8 visiting writers per year. Large faculty helps keep creative writing workshops small. Also runs special workshops on topics such as the novella, cross-genre writing, and feminist "writing the body". Always has a writer-in-residence. The literary review *Matrix* is associated with the program.

CONFEDERATION COLLEGE of Applied Arts and Technology
PO Box 398, Thunder Bay, Ontario P7C 4W1
Telephone: (807) 475-6158, Toll-free in Ont., Man., & Sask.: 1-800-465-5493
Contact person: Linda Fodchuk

One non-credit offering: Creative Writing, Final Manuscript Workshop. This runs on Saturdays.

LAKELAND COLLEGE
Bag 5100, Vermilion, Alberta T0B 4M0
Telephone: 1-800-661-6490   Fax: (403) 853-2955

Offers a summer writing school during July with workshops on both poetry and fiction, among other topics.

MOUNT ALLISON UNIVERSITY
Department of English, Sackville, New Brunswick E0A 3C0
Telephone: (506) 364-2543 or 364-2549
Contact person: Deborah Wills

Offers only one credit, day class: Advanced Creative Writing (English 3850). Workshop format. Visiting writers provide readings and, whenever possible, talks. There is also a student run Creative Writing Group.

QUEEN'S UNIVERSITY
Department of English, Kingston, Ontario K7L 3N6
Telephone: (613) 545-2153   Fax: (613) 545-6872
Contact person: Carolyn Smart

Two half-credit offerings: WRIT 295 - Creative Writing Workshop and WRIT 296 - Advanced Creative Writing Workshop. Holds lectures, special seminars, and poetry readings (off-campus) by visiting writers.

SAINT MARY'S UNIVERSITY
Robie Street, Halifax, Nova Scotia B3H 3C3
Telephone: (902) 420-5715   Fax: (902) 420-5561
Contact person: Brian Bartlett

Offers credit courses that focus on the writing of poetry, fiction, plays, and non-fiction. A Minor in Creative Writing is available. Public readings are often featured. There are night school, as well as day school, offerings.

SENECA COLLEGE of Applied Arts and Technology
1750 Finch Avenue East, North York, Ontario M2L 2X5
Telephone: (416) 491-5050
Contact person: Lawrence G. Hopperton

Offers credit courses in Creative Writing (EAC 384), Freelance Writing (EAC 248), and Print Journalism (EAC 409). These are evening and/or weekend classes.

TRENT UNIVERSITY
Peterborough, Ontario, K9J 7B8
Telephone: (705) 748-1011
Contact person: Professor Orm Mitchell, Department of English.

Runs one night-school credit course: English 375 — Creative Writing Workshop. Portfolio required. Twelve-student limit. Has concentrated on fiction but plans a poetry workshop in future. Guest readers and workshop leaders. Publication: *Freefall and Stories*.

TRINITY WESTERN UNIVERSITY

7600 Glover Road, Langley, British Columbia V2Y IYI
Telephone: (604) 888-7511   Fax: (604) 888-7548
Contact person: Lynn Szabo

Two seminar-format credit courses (which can be taken on a non-credit basis). Small class size. Guest lecturers are included in the program. The focus is on poetry and short stories. They look at the techniques of imaginative writing and the development of a critical appreciation of the art. Day school only.

UNIVERSITÉ SAINTE-ANNE

Department of English, Pointe-de-l'Église, Nouvelle-Écosse B0W IM0
tel: (902) 769-2114   telecopie: (902) 769-2930
Contact person: Robert Finley

Offers a few writing courses in French and in English. Students have the opportunity to work in either or in both languages. Also offers courses in literary translation. Publishes the arts journal *Feux Chalins*.

UNIVERSITY COLLEGE OF THE FRASER VALLEY

32335 Fletcher Avenue, Mission, British Columbia V2V 4N3
Telephone: (604) 826-9544   Fax: (604) 826-0681
Contact persons: Anne Russell & Catherine McDonald

Courses take place at the Mission campus. Offers eight courses on creative writing and publishing. These include The Poetry Project, Songwriting, and Fiction for Fun & Profit. Classes tend to be held on weekends or during the evening.

UNIVERSITY OF NEW BRUNSWICK

English Department, PO Box 4400, Fredericton, New Brunswick E3B 5A3
Telephone: (506) 454-9153   Fax: (506) 453-3572
Contact person: Glenda Turner

Offers both day and night school classes, and both credit and non-credit courses. Program includes talks and readings by guest writers. Holds the annual Maritime Writers' Workshop in July. This offers workshop sessions plus lectures/discussions and public readings.

UNIVERSITY OF OTTAWA

Department of English, PO Box 450, Station A, Ottawa, Ontario KIN 6N5
Telephone: (613) 562-5764   Fax: (613) 562-5990
Contact person: Seymour Mayne

Credit courses only. These take place during the evenings. The program features talks and lectures by guest writers. Advanced seminars/workshops are also offered. The program is associated with the magazine *Bywords* as well as a regular poetry reading series.

UNIVERSITY OF VICTORIA

Department of Writing, PO Box 1700, Victoria, British Columbia V8W 2Y2
Telephone: (604) 721-7306
Contact person: Lana Richardson

Offers a bachelor program in creative writing. Runs creative writing classes in day, night, and summer programs. All courses are for credit. Has special programs/workshops in drama, fiction, non-fiction, and poetry. Also offers a co-operative education program. Contact Don Bailey, (604) 721-7627, for information on the Co-Op program. Hosts a poetry reading series. Features visiting writers and speakers. Also offers the Harvey Southam Diploma in Writing and Editing and a Certificate Program in Native Indian Creative Writing.

UNIVERSITY OF WATERLOO

Continuing Education, Waterloo, Ontario N2L 3G1
Telephone: (519) 888-4002 or 888-4567, Ex. 6034   Fax: (519) 746-4607
Contact person: Maureen Jones

Offers two non-credit courses on fiction writing. These are evening classes in a workshop format. Focus is on plot, characterization, conflict development, and narrative structure. E-mail address: conted@corr1.uwaterloo.ca

UNIVERSITY OF WINDSOR

Department of English, 401 Sunset Avenue, Windsor, Ontario N9A 3P4
Telephone: (519) 253-4232, Ex. 2289   Fax: (519) 973-7050
Contact person: Wyman H. Herendeen

Offers degree programs in English Literature/Creative Writing that can led to an Honours B.A. and an M.A. Also offers the Summer Writing Institute with non-credit workshops. Hosts various poetry readings, seminars, guest lectures, and colloquia. Publishes the *Windsor Review*, the *Wayzgoose Anthology*, and *Generation*. The program always has a writer-in-residence. There are special facilities for students working in hypertext. E-mail address: whh@uwindsor.ca

THE UNIVERSITY OF WINNIPEG

English Department, 515 Portage Avenue, Winnipeg, Manitoba R3B 2E9
Telephone: (204) 786-7811 or 786-9292   Fax: (204) 786-1824
Contact person: Uma Parameswaran

Offers two day school credit courses (17:3101:1 & 17:3112.1) in Creative Writing. Classes are kept small (15 students max.). The focus is on the act of writing and students are required to write, as their final projects, four short stories or four chapters of a novel or a collection of poems. Also has non-credit night school courses. Hosts guest lectures about three times per year as well as poetry readings three times per year. The university's Theatre Department offers courses in Playwriting. Published *Prairie Gold*.

The following 36 colleges and universities did not respond to inquiries. They are believed to offer creative writing courses.

Banff Centre School of Fine Arts
PO Box 1020
Banff, Alberta, T0L 0C0
Telephone: (403) 762-6100

Brandon University
270 18th Street
Brandon, Manitoba, R7A 6A9
Telephone: (204) 728-9520

Brock University
Merrittville Highway
St. Catharines, Ontario, L2S 3A1
Telephone: (905) 688-5550, Ex. 3469

Capilano College
2055 Purcell Way
North Vancouver, British Columbia,
V7J 3H5
Telephone: (604) 984-4957

Cariboo University College
PO Box 3010
Kamloops, British Columbia, V2C 5N3
Telephone: (604) 828-5223

Carleton University
Ottawa, Ontario, K1S 5B6
Telephone: (613) 788-2312

Champlain Regional College
Lennoxville, Québec, J1M 2A1
Telephone: (819) 564-3666

Cypress Hills Regional College
Beatty Campus
129 2nd Avenue N.E.
Swift Current, Saskatchewan, S9H 2C6
Telephone: (306) 773-1531

Douglas College
PO Box 2503
New Westminster, British Columbia,
V3L 5B2
Telephone: (604) 527-5289

East Kootenay Community College
PO Box 8500
Cranbrook, British Columbia, V1C 5L7
Telephone: (604) 489-2751

Grant MacEwan Community College
PO Box 1796
Edmonton, Alberta, T5J 2P2
Telephone: (403) 441-4863

Lakehead University
Thunder Bay, Ontario, P7B 5E1
Telephone: (807) 343-8375

Lambton College
PO Box 969
Sarnia, Ontario, N7T 7K4
Telephone: (519) 542-7751

Laurentian University
Ramsey Lake Road
Sudbury, Ontario, P3E 2C6
Telephone: (705) 675-1151, Ex. 4340

Lethbridge Community College
3000 College Drive South
Lethbridge, Alberta, T1K 1L6
Telephone: (403) 320-3200

Marianopolis College
3880 Côte des Neiges
Montréal, Québec, H3H 1W1
Telephone: (514) 931-8792

Memorial University of Newfoundland
St. John's, Newfoundland, A1B 3X9
Telephone: (709) 737-8277

Prairie West Regional College
PO Box 700
Biggar, Saskatchewan, S0M 0M0
Telephone: (306) 948-3363

Red Deer College
PO Box 5005
32 Street & 56 Avevue
Red Deer, Alberta, T4N 5H5
Telephone: (403) 342-3304

Red River Community College
2055 Notre Dame Avenue
Winnipeg, Manitoba, R3H 0J9
Telephone: (204) 632-2446

Selkirk College
PO Box 1200
Castlegar, British Columbia, V1N 3J1
Telephone: (604) 365-7292

Sir Sandford Fleming College
Sutherland Campus
Peterborough, Ontario, K9J 7B1
Telephone: (705) 749-5520

Université Laval
Québec, Québec, G1K 7P4
Telephone: (418) 656-2131

Université du Québec
C.P. 8888, succursale A
Montréal, Québec, H3C 3P8
Telephone: (514) 282-3000

Université de Sherbrooke
Études anglaises
Sherbrooke, Québec, J1M 2R1
Telephone: (819) 821-7277

University of British Columbia
Vancouver, British Columbia, V6T 1Z2
Telephone: (604) 228-2212

University of Calgary
2500 University Drive N.W.
Calgary, Alberta, T2N 1N4
Telephone: (403) 220-5470

University College of Cape Breton
PO Box 5300
Sydney, Nova Scotia, B1P 6L2
Telephone: (602) 539-5300

University of Guelph
Guelph, Onartio, N1G 2W1
Telephone: (519) 824-4120,
Ex. 3882 & Ex. 6315

The University of Lethbridge
4401 University Drive
Lethbridge, Alberta, T1K 3M4
Telephone: (403) 329-2378

University of Regina
Regina, Saskatchewan, S4S 0A2
Telephone: (306) 585-4140

University of Saskatchewan
Saskatoon, Saskatchewan, S7N 0W0
Telephone: (306) 966-5500 & 244-4343

The University of Western Ontario
London, Ontario, N6A 3K7
Telephone: (519) 679-2111, Ex. 5796

Wilfrid Laurier University
75 University Avenue
Waterloo, Ontario, N2L 3C5
Telephone: (519) 884-1970

York University
4700 Keele Street
North York, Ontario, M3J 1P3
Telephone: (416) 736-2100

4.5 PRACTICAL BOOKS FOR CANADIAN AUTHORS

The following is a short list of books (including one newsletter) that will prove useful to Canadian writers. All of these publications contain information on publishers and magazines that use poetry and/or fiction.

I can personally recommend the products of Dustbooks. I find them to be the most complete American reference books around. You will, it must be said, find quite a few mistakes in the listings published by Dustbooks. Still, they are what I use. (I should note that some of my fellow poets favour the titles put out by Writer's Digest Books.)

Most of these titles can be found at better literary bookshops. Public libraries may also have them. All are certainly worth reading. It pays to study your markets.

THE CANADIAN WRITERS' CONTEST CALENDAR
Susan Ioannou, Editor, Wordwrights Canada, PO Box 456, Station O, Toronto, Ontario M4A 2P1
Over 55 fiction, essay, and poetry competitions, arranged year-round in deadline order. 20 pages.

THE CANADIAN WRITER'S GUIDE
Fred Kerner & Gordon E. Symons, Editors, Fitzhenry & Whiteside Ltd., 91 Granton Drive, Richmond Hill, Ontario L4B 2N5

THE CANADIAN WRITER'S MARKET
Adrian Waller & Jem Bates, Editors, McClelland & Stewart Inc., 481 University Avenue, Toronto, Ontario M5G 2E9

DIRECTORY OF LITERARY MAGAZINES
Poets & Writers, Inc., 72 Spring Street, New York, NY 10012
Compiled by the Council of Literary Magazines and presses. 500 entries for poetry and fiction magazines. Detailed information on editors, editorial requirements, and payment policies. 270 pages.

DIRECTORY OF POETRY PUBLISHERS
Len Fulton, Editor, Dustbooks, PO Box 100, Paradise, CA 95967
Features twenty-one pieces of information on each magazine and book publisher. Over 2,000 listings. Covers editorial biases and names of contact people. 364 pages.

GUIDE TO LITERARY AGENTS
Kirsten C. Holm, Editor, Writer's Digest Books, 1507 Dana Avenue, Cincinnati, OH 45207-1005
Find everything you need to know about choosing an agent. More than 400 listings plus valuable information on the agent-author relationahip. 236 pages.

THE INTERNATIONAL DIRECTORY OF LITTLE MAGAZINES AND SMALL PRESSES

Len Fulton, Editor, Dustbooks, PO Box 100, Paradise, CA 95967

More that 6,000 publishers of poetry and fiction from thirty different countries. Extensive data on editorial likes and dislikes. Over 1,000 pages of detailed information on literary magazines and presses.

LITERARY AGENTS: A WRITER'S GUIDE

Adam Begley, Editor, Poets & Writers, 72 Spring Street, New York, NY 10012

Complete information on what literary agents do and usual fees. Covers query letters, submissions of manuscripts, and selecting an agent. Details exactly how the process works.

LITERARY ARTS DIRECTORY II

Gail D. Whitter, editor, The Federation of British Columbia Writers, PO Box 2206, Main Post Office, Vancouver, British Columbia V6B 3W2

The Canadian writer's desk-side resource book. Contains information on provincial and national writers' organizations, federal and provincial funding sources, and book and periodical publishers of poetry, fiction, and essays. Also includes several how-to articles on writing and publishing.

LITERARY MARKET DIRECTORY

Susan Ioannou, Editor, Wordwrights Canada, PO Box 456, Station O, Toronto, Ontario M4A 2P1

LITERARY MARKET PLACE

Karen Hallard, Editor, Reed Reference Publishing, 121 Chanlon Road, New Providence, NJ 07974

Recommended by most major American trade publishers. More than 1,200 listings. Information on magazines, publishers, agents, and book manufacturing companies. Also covers publicity outlets and editorial services. 2,000 pages.

LITERARY MARKETS THAT PAY

Susan Ioannou, Editor, Wordwrights Canada, PO Box 456, Station O, Toronto, Ontario M4A 2P1

NOVEL & SHORT STORY WRITER'S MARKET

Robin Gee, Editor, Writer's Digest Books, 1507 Dana Avenue, Cincinnati, OH 45207-1005

Get published with over 1,900 markets, contests, and other opportunities. Also offers information on conferences & writers' colonies. 624 pages.

POETRY LISTING

David Hart, Editor, Wood Wind Publications, 42 All Saints Road, Kings Heath, Birmingham, B14 7LL England

Lists books by individual poets, audiotapes, anthologies, and British literary magazines. Also covers resource books and handbooks. Publishes interviews with writers, publishers, and booksellers. 82 pages.

POET'S MARKET
Christine Martin, Editor, Writer's Digest Books, 1507 Dana Avenue, Cincinnati, OH 45207-1005

Over 1,700 listings with complete submission information. Enlightening articles and interviews by and with professional poets and editors. 552 pages.

SASKATCHEWAN LITERARY ARTS HANDBOOK
Saskatchewan Writers Guild, PO Box 3986, Regina, Saskatchewan S4P 3R9

Covers all aspects of the Canadian literary scene: writing, publishing, information technologies, film, video, and audiotapes. Also covers literary agents and self-promotion. Has a comprehensive list of awards and contests.

SMALL PRESSES & LITTLE MAGAZINES OF THE UK AND IRELAND
Peter Finch, Editor, Oriel Bookshop, The Friary, Cardiff, CF1 4AA Wales

Lists the vast majority of creative small presses and little magazines in the UK and Ireland. Data includes full name of press or magazine, editors' names, addresses, and a brief, one-line description of editorial content. Constantly updated.

WORDS FOR SALE
Eve Drobot & Hal Tennant, Editors, Periodical Writers Association of Canada, 54 Wolseley Street, Toronto, Ontario M5T 1A5

THE WRITER'S HANDBOOK
Barry Turner, Editor, Macmillan Publishers Ltd., 45 Islington Park Street, London, N1 1QB England

The essential reference book for all writers, whatever their market. Over 5,000 entries. Complete data on addresses, telephone & fax numbers, and key personnel. Also includes articles on poetry, talking books, translation, freelance earnings, and on the state of the English language.

WRITER'S MARKET
Mark Garvey, Editor, Writer's Digest Books, 1507 Dana Avenue, Cincinnati, OH 45207-1005

Over 4,000 magazines and book publishers that will condsider freelance submissions. Complete information: addresses, names of editors and contact people, and editorial requirements. 1,008 pages.

AUTHOR & EDITOR: A Working Guide
The Book and Periodical Council, (distributed by Prentice-Hall of Canada Ltd., 1870 Birchmount Road, Scarborough, Ontario M1P 2J7)

Written by experienced writers and editors. Focuses on the complex and sometimes delicate relationship between author and editor during the editing of a manuscript. Also outlines how the decision is made to publish a book, how book prices are determined, and how books are produced. Although it contains no market listings, I suggest that Author & Editor is well worth reading. It is a must for writers who are seeking book publication.

4.6 CRITICAL JOURNALS

The following seven journals are important sources of poetry information. Some, like *Studies in Canadian Literature*, are university publications. Others, like *Brick*, have no university affiliation. All publish book reviews, critical essays, and literary studies that relate directly to Canadian poetry.

Book reviews by influential critical journals can be most important to your life and work as a poet. Not only will reviews stimulate sales of your titles, they will provide valuable feedback on your poetry. You would be wise to ensure that your publisher sends review copies of your books and chapbooks to these addresses.

Aside from what they may do for you by reviewing your books, they are good to read simply because of their pure literary value. Your local university or public library should subscribe to some, if not all, of these periodicals. They are also readily available through leading literary bookshops. One can always learn more about poetry, and critical journals can be a fine place to start. After all, first-rate poetry goes hand in hand with first-rate criticism. One cannot exist without the other.

ARIEL
Victor J. Ramraj, Editor, The University of Calgary, Department of English, 2400 University Drive N. W., Calgary, Alberta T2N 1N4

BRICK
PO Box 537, Station Q, Toronto, Ontario M4T 2M5

CANADIAN LITERATURE
Eva-Marie Kröller, Editor, University of British Columbia, 2029 West Mall, Room 225, Vancouver, British Columbia V6T 1Z2

CANADIAN POETRY: Studies, Documents, Reviews
D.M.R. Bentley, Editor, University of Western Ontario, Department of English, London, Ontario N6A 3K7

ESSAYS ON CANADIAN WRITING
Jack David & Robert Lecker, Editors, 307 Coxwell Avenue, Toronto, Ontario M4L 3B5

JOURNAL OF CANADIAN POETRY
David Staines, Editor, 9 Ashburn Drive, Nepean, Ontario K2E 6N4

STUDIES IN CANADIAN LITERATURE
Kathleen Scherf, Editor, University of New Brunswick, PO Box 4400, Fredericton, New Brunswick E3B 5A3

FIVE: LITERARY AWARDS AND CONTESTS

Various awards are made annually to Canadian poets. These awards can be in recognition of sustained and outstanding achievement, or they can come from a specific contest.

The following list of 123 contests gives some examples of the types of awards and competitions that Canadian poets can win. The list is far from complete.

Most contests have specific and detailed rules. Many require an entrance fee. Some require the completion of an official entry form. Because these rules can be quite long and because fees can vary from year to year, complete information is NOT included here. The following list contains merely brief descriptions of some of the better known awards and contests, as well as the addresses to contact for more information. When requesting rules and entry forms, it is best to include an SASE. For foreign competitions, you should send an International Reply Coupon with your request.

THE above/ground press CHAPBOOK CONTEST
586 McLeod Street, #2, Ottawa, Ontario K1R 5R3
Telephone: (613) 231-7722
Open to poets not yet published in book form. Entry fee: yes. Official form: no. Blind judging: ? Deadline: June 30. Prize: chapbook publication plus small honorarium. All entrants receive the winning chapbook. Send 15 to 25 pages of work. E-mail address: az421@freenet.carleton.ca

THE ACORN-RUKEYSER CHAPBOOK CONTEST
Unfinished Monument Press, 237 Prospect Street South, Hamilton, Ontario L8M 2Z6
Telephone: (905) 312-1779   Fax: (905) 312-8285
An international contest open to all poets. Entry fee: yes. Official form: no. Blind judging: no. Deadline: October 31. Prize: chapbook publication of winning manuscript plus $100. All entrants receive the chapbook. Submit up to 30 poems. Poems must be in the People's Poetry tradition. E-mail address: ad507@freenet.hamilton.on.ca

AFTERTHOUGHTS POETRY AWARDS
Pacific Centre North, 701 Granville St., PO Box 54039, Vancouver, BC V7Y 1K6
Open to all poets. Entry fee: no. Official form: no. Blind judging: no. Deadline: April 30. Two categories: rhymed verse and free verse. Prize: engraved plaque.

THE AIR CANADA AWARD

Canadian Authors Association, 27 Doxsee Avenue North, Campbellford, Ontario
K0L 1L0

Telephone; (705) 653-0323   Fax: (705) 653-0593

Open to writers who are 30 years old or younger. Entry fee: no. Official form: no. Blind judging: no. Deadline: April 30. Prize: roundtrip tickets for two to an Air Canada destination.

ALCUIN SOCIETY CITATIONS AWARDS

The Alcuin Society, PO Box 3216, Vancouver, British Columbia V6B 3X8

Telephone: (604) 888-9049

Entry fee: yes. Official form: yes. Blind judging: no. Deadline: March 15. Four categories: general trade books, limited editions, text & reference, and juveniles. Annual prizes for excellence in book design.

DR. ALFRED BAILEY PRIZE

The Writers' Federation of New Brunswick, PO Box 37, Station A, Fredericton, New Brunswick E3B 4Y2

Telephone: (506) 459-7228

Entry fee: ? Official form: ? Blind judging: ? Deadline: ? Prize: $400 for best manuscript.

THE ALTA LIND COOK AWARD

University of Toronto, Victoria College, Office of the Registrar, 73 Queen's Park Crescent, Toronto, Ontario M5S 1K7

THE AMETHYST REVIEW WRITING CONTEST

23 Riverside Avenue, Truro, Nova Scotia B2N 4G2

Telephone: (902) 895-1345

Entry fee: yes. Official form: no. Blind judging: yes. Deadline: January 31. Two categories: poetry and fiction. Prize: $50 plus publication in *The Amethyst Review*. All entrants receive a subscription to the review. The contest has a different theme each year.

THE ANNUAL LOVE POEM AWARD

The Muse Journal, 226 Lisgar Street, Toronto, Ontario M6J 3G7

Telephone: (416) 539-9517   Fax: (416) 539-0047

Open to all poets. Entry fee: yes. Official form: no. Blind judging: no. Deadline: October 30. Prizes: $300, $200, $100.

ARCHIBALD LAMPMAN AWARD FOR POETRY

Ottawa Independent Writers, 265 Elderberry Terrace, Orléans, Ontario K1E 1Z2

Telephone: (613) 841-0572

Open to poets who live in the National Capital Region. Entry fee: no. Official form: no. Blind judging: no. Deadline: February 29. Prize: $400. Award is for a book or chapbook published during the pervious two years.

ATLANTIC WRITING COMPETITION

Writers' Federation of Nova Scotia, 1809 Barrington Street, Suite 901, Halifax, Nova Scotia B3J 3K8

Telephone: (902) 423-8116

Open to writers who live in Atlantic Canada. Entry fee: yes. Official form: yes. Blind judging: yes. Deadline: August 25. Prizes (poetry category) $100, $75, $50. Various categories— three prizes per category. For unpublished manuscripts.

BETTER POEMS AND GARDENS POETRY CONTEST

Dandelion Magazine, The Alexandra Centre, 922 9th Avenue S.E., Calgary, Alberta T2G 0S4

Telephone: (403) 265-0524

Entry fee: yes. Official form: no. Blind judging: yes. Deadline: March 31. Poems must be about gardens and gardening. All entrants receive a subscription to the magazine.

The bpNichol Chap-Book Award

Therafields Foundation, 316 Dupont Street, Toronto, Ontario M5R 1V9

Annual prize for the best poetry chapbook.

THE BRIDPORT PRIZE

Bridport Arts Centre, 9 Pier Terrace, West Bay, Bridport, Dorset, DT6 4ER England

Entry fee: yes. Official form: yes. Blind judging: yes. Deadline: June 30. Prizes (in British pounds) 2,500, 1,000, 500.

THE BRONWEN WALLACE MEMORIAL AWARD

The Writers' Development Trust, 24 Ryerson Avenue, Suite 201, Toronto, Ontario M5T 2P3

Telephone: (416) 504-8222   Fax: (416) 504-4490

Open to writers who are under 35 years old and have yet to publish a book. Entry fee: ? Official form: no. Blind judging: ? Deadline: January. Prize: $1,000. The award is for poetry in even numbered years and for short fiction in odd numbered years. Work must be unpublished.

THE BURNABY WRITERS' SOCIETY WRITING COMPETITION

6584 Deer Lake Avenue, Burnaby, British Columbia V5G 2J3

Telephone: (604) 435-6500

Open to B.C. writers only. Entry fee: ? Official form: ? Blind judging: ? Deadline: May 31. Cash prizes. Categories vary year to year, but poetry is always one of them.

BURNISHED PEBBLES COMPETITION

White Mountain Publications, Box 5180, R.R. 2, New Liskeard, Ontario P0L 1P0

Open to all poets. Entry fee: yes. Official form: no. Blind judging: yes. Deadline: March 31. Small cash prizes and publication in the poetry calendar. For poems of eight lines or less: haiku, senryu, sijo, cinquain, limerick, couplet, tercet.

CANADA-AUSTRALIA LITERARY PRIZE

The Canada Council, PO Box 1047, Ottawa, Ontario K1P 5V8

An English-language prize awarded in alternate years to an Australian or Canadian writer.

CANADA-BELGIUM LITERARY PRIZE

The Canada Council, PO Box 1047, Ottawa, Ontario K1P 5V8

A French-language prize awarded in alternate years to a Belgian or Canadian writer.

CANADA-ITALY LITERARY PRIZE

The Canada Council, PO Box 1047, Ottawa, Ontario K1P 5V8

English-language and French-language works are, in alternate years, translated into Italian. Italian works are translated into English or French.

CANADA-SWITZERLAND LITERARY PRIZE

The Canada Council, PO Box 1047, Ottawa, Ontario K1P 5V8

A French-language prize awarded in alternate years to a Swiss or Canadian writer.

CANADIAN AUTHORS ASSOCIATION LITERARY AWARDS

27 Doxsee Avenue North, Campbellford, Ontario K0L 1L0
Telephone: (705) 653-0323   Fax: (705) 653-0593

Open to Canadian writers. Entry fee: no. Official form: yes. Blind judging: no. Deadline: December 15. Prize: $5,000. Several awards for published books; poetry always one of the categories.

CANADIAN AUTHORS ASSOCIATION STUDENTS' CREATIVE WRITING CONTEST

Box 32219, 250 Harding Blvd. West, Richmond Hill, Ontario L4C 9R0

Open to Canadian students (high school, college, or university) living at home or abroad. Entry fee: yes. Official form: yes. Blind judging: yes. Deadline: March 22. Prizes: $500 each for the best poem, story, and essay.

CANADIAN WRITER'S JOURNAL POETRY COMPETITION

PO Box 6618, Depot 1, Victoria, British Columbia V8P 5N7
Telephone: (604) 477-8807

Open to all poets. Entry fee: yes. Official form: no. Blind judging: yes. Deadline: June 30. First, second, and third cash prizes. Four categories: free verse, traditional verse, haiku, and sijo.

CAPRICORN INTERNATIONAL POETRY AND SHORT STORY COMPETITION

17 West Lea Road, Weston, Bath, BA1 3RL England

Open to all writers. Entry fee: yes. Official form: no. Blind judging: yes. Deadline: November 30.

CHARTERHOUSE INTERNATIONAL POETRY COMPETITION

Charterhouse Poetry Festival, Brooke Hall, Charterhouse, Godalming, Surrey, GU7 2DX England

Two categories: Open (any age) and Under 19. Poems must be 50 lines or less.

THE CHELSEA AWARDS
PO Box 1040, York Beach, ME 03910
Open to all writers. Entry fee: yes. Official form: no. Blind judging: yes. Deadlines: Fiction - June 15; Poetry - December 15. Prizes: $500 plus publication. (General submissions to the magazine: PO Box 773, New York, NY, 10276-0773, USA)

CITY OF CARDIFF INTERNATIONAL POETRY COMPETITION
PO Box 438, Cardiff, CFI 6YA Wales
Open to all poets. Entry fee: yes. Official form: yes. Blind judging: yes. Deadline: August 18. Prizes: (in British pounds) 1,000, 750, 500, 250 (three prizes), and 200 (four prizes).

CITY OF REGINA WRITING AWARD
Saskatchewan Writers Guild, PO Box 3986, Regina, Saskatchewan S4P 3R9
Telephone: (306) 757-6310 Fax: (306) 565-8554
Open to Regina writers only. Entry fee: ? Official form: ? Blind judging: ? Deadline: ? Prize: $4,000.

CITY OF TORONTO BOOK AWARD
City of Toronto, City Clerk's Department, City Hall, Toronto, Ontario M5H 2N2
Telephone: (416) 392-0468
Open to Toronto writers only. Entry fee: no. Official form: no. Blind judging: no. Deadline: January 30. Prizes: $1,000 in each category. Focus is on fiction, non-fiction, and children's books. Only very seldom makes an award for a poetry title.

CLAREMONT REVIEW POETRY CONTEST
4980 Wesley Road, Victoria, British Columbia V8Y 1Y9
Telephone: (604) 658-5221 Fax: (604) 658-5387
Open to poets aged 13 to 19. Entry fee: yes. Official form: no. Blind judging: yes. Deadline: November 1. All entrants receive a subscription to the review.

COMMONWEALTH POETRY PRIZE
Commonwealth Institute, Kensington High Street, London, W8 6NQ England
Several poetry prizes. Open to all published commonwealth poets.

COMPACT FICTION/SHORT POEM COMPETITION
Pottersfield Portfolio, 5280 Green Street, PO Box 27094, Halifax, Nova Scotia B3H 4M8
Telephone: (902) 443-9178
Entry fee: yes. Official form: no. Blind judging: ? Deadline: ? Poems must be 20 lines or less; stories must be 1,500 words or less.

CutBank LITERARY AWARDS
The University of Montana, Department of English, Missoula, MT 59812
Open to all writers. Entry fee: yes. Official form: no. Blind judging: yes. Deadline: January 10. Prizes: $200, $100, $50. Two categories: poetry and fiction. All entrants receive a subscription to the magazine.

CV2 ANNUAL WRITING CONTEST
PO Box 3062, Winnipeg, Manitoba R3C 4E5
Telephone: (204) 949-1365
Entry fee: yes. Official form: no. Blind judging: yes. Deadline: March 31. Two categories: poetry and short fiction. All entrants receive a subscription to the quarterly.

DARK ROASTED ARABICA
Canadian Poetry Association, London Chapter, PO Box 340, London, Ontario N6A 4W1
Telephone: (519) 433-8994 & 439-3562
Open to all writers. Entry fee: yes. Official form: no. Blind judging: no. Deadline: May 1. Prize: publication of the story in chapbook form. For stories of up to 3,000 words. E-mail address: cpa@zap.wwdc.com

THE E.J. PRATT MEDAL AND PRIZE IN POETRY
University of Toronto, Admissions and Awards, 315 Bloor Street West, Toronto, Ontario M5S 1A3
Limited to students at the University of Toronto. Entry fee: no. Official form: no. Blind judging: yes. Prize: a gold medal and $100.

THE ELIZABETH MATCHETT STOVER MEMORIAL AWARD
Southwest Review, Southern Methodist University, 307 Fondren Library West, Box 374, Dallas, TX 75275-0374
Telephone: (214) 768-1036   Fax: (214) 768-1408
Open to all poets. Entry fee: no. Official form: no. Blind judging: no. Deadline: none. Prize: $150 for the best poem published in *Southwest Review* during the preceding year.

FESTIVAL WRITING COMPETITION
The Federation of British Columbia Writers, 905 West Pender Street, 4th Floor, Vancouver, British Columbia V6C 1L6
Telephone: (604) 683-2057   Fax: (604) 683-8269
Open to B.C. writers who have no more than three publishing credits. Entry fee: yes. Official form: no. Blind judging: yes. Deadline: March 15. Prizes: six of $100 each.

THE FIDDLEHEAD ANNUAL CONTEST
Campus House, University of New Brunswick, PO Box 4400, Fredericton, New Brunswick E3B 5A3
Telephone: (506) 453-3501   Fax: (506) 453-4599
Open to all writers. Entry fee: yes. Official form: no. Blind judging: yes. Deadline: December 15. Two categories: poetry and fiction. All entrants receive a subscription to the quarterly. There is a different theme each year; please send SASE for rules.

THE FOLEY POETRY AWARD
America, 106 West 56th Street, New York, NY 10019
Telephone: (212) 581-4640
Open to all poets. Entry fee: no. Official form: no. Blind judging: ? Deadline: submit

poems between January 1 and April 25. Submit only one poem per year. Envelope must have "The Foley Poetry Award" clearly indicated. Prize: $500 plus publication.

49th PARALLEL POETRY CONTEST
1007 Queen Street, Bellingham, WA 98226
Open to all poets. Entry fee: yes. Official form: no. Blind judging: yes. Deadline: submit poems between September 15 and December 1. Prizes: $150, $100, $50.

GEORGETOWN REVIEW POETRY CONTEST
400 East College Street, Box 227, Georgetown, KY 40324
Open to all poets. Entry fee: yes. Official form: ? Blind judging: ? Deadline: August 1. Prize: $150 plus publication. Runners-up receive publication in the review.

THE GERALD LAMPERT MEMORIAL AWARD
The League of Canadian Poets, 54 Wolseley Street, Suite 204, Toronto, Ontario M5T 1A5
Telephone: (416) 504-1657   Fax: (416) 703-0059
Open to Canadian poets only. Awarded annually for the best first book of poems. Prize: $1000. E-mail address: league@io.org

GOVERNOR GENERAL'S LITERARY AWARDS
The Canada Council, PO Box 1047, Ottawa, Ontario K1P 5V8
Various annual literary prizes including awards for the best English-language and French-language poetry books. Cash prizes.

THE GREENSBORO REVIEW LITERARY AWARDS
University of North Carolina, Department of English, Greensboro, NC 27412-5001
Telephone: (910) 334-5459   Fax: (910) 334-3281
Open to all writers. Entry fee: no. Official form: no. Blind judging: no. Deadline: September 15. Prize: $250 plus publication in the review. Two categories: poetry and fiction.

HAMILTON BOOK AWARDS
Hamilton & Region Arts Council, 116 King Street West, Hamilton, Ontario L8P 4V3
Telephone: (905) 529-9485   Fax: (905) 529-0238
Open only to writers living in or from the area of Hamilton-Wentworth, Grimsby, and Burlington. Entry fee: no. Official form: no. Blind judging: no. Deadline: June 15. Cash prizes for poetry, children's books, and fiction/non-fiction. Books must have been published during the preceding year. E-mail address: harac@freenet.hamilton.on.ca

HAMILTON SHORT PIECE AWARDS
Hamilton & Region Arts Council, 116 King Street West, Hamilton, Ontario L8P 4V3
Telephone: (905) 529-9485   Fax: (905) 529-0238
Open only to writers living in or from Hamilton-Wentworth, Grimsby, and Burlington. Entry fee: no. Official form: no. Blind judging: no. Deadline: June 15.

Cash prizes for poetry, fiction, and non-fiction. Entries must have been published in a periodical during the preceding year. E-mail address: harac@freenet.hamilton.on.ca

HASTINGS NATIONAL POETRY COMPETITION
and

CHILDREN'S 1066 POETRY COMPETITION
First Time, Burdett Cottage, 4 Burdett Place, George Street, Old Town, Hastings, East Sussex, TN34 3ED England

Open to all poets 18 years old and over. Entry fee: yes. Official form: yes. Blind judging: yes. Deadline: October 15. Prizes: (in British pounds) 100, 50, 25 plus publication in *First Time*. Also runs the Hastings Poetry Festival and winners invited to read there.

THE HAWTHORNE SOCIETY POETRY CONTEST
1051 Roslyn Road, Victoria, British Columbia V8S 4R4

Open to all Canadian poets. Entry fee: yes. Official form: no. Blind judging: yes. Deadline: April 1. First prize: $500 plus chapbook publication. Other prizes: publication of runners-up in an annual anthology. Contest is for manuscripts of 12 to 20 poems.

HEAVEN BONE PRESS INTERNATIONAL CHAPBOOK COMPETITION
PO Box 486, Chester, NY 10918
Telephone: (914) 469-9018

Open to all poets. Entry fee: yes. Official form: no. Blind judging: no. Deadline: July 15. Prize: chapbook publication. All entrants receive the winning chapbook.

THE HENRY FUERSTENBERG MEMORIAL AWARD
Jewish Book Awards Committee, Koffler Centre of the Arts, 4588 Bathurst Street, North York, Ontario M2R 1W6
Telephone: (416) 636-1880, Ex. 299   Fax: (416) 636-5813

Open to books by Canadian poets, published in Canada, on subjects of Jewish interest. Entry fee: no. Official form: no. Blind judging: no. Deadline: February 1. Cash prize. Note: the Jewish Book Awards Committee also offers cash prizes for books of fiction, biblical/rabbinic scholarship, history, children's literature, Holocaust literature, and translation. Please write for complete information.

THE HERB BARRETT HAIKU AWARD
Hamilton Haiku Press, 237 Peospect Street South, Hamilton, Ontario L8M 2Z6
Telephone: (905) 312-1779   Fax: (905) 312-8285

An international competition open to all poets. Entry fee: yes. Official form: no. Blind judging: yes. Deadline: November 30. Prize: publication by the Hamilton Haiku Press. All entrants receive the resulting publication. This competition is run by the Canadian Poetry Association, Hamilton Chapter. E-mail address: ad507@freenet.hamilton.on.ca

HOPE WRITERS' GUILD ANNUAL POETRY CONTEST
PO Box 1683, Hope, British Columbia V0X 1L0
Open to all poets. Entry fee: yes. Official form: no. Blind judging: yes. Deadline: July 31. Prizes: $100, $50, $25.

ICARUS COMPETITION
PO Box 2181, Kill Devil Hills, NC 27948
Entry fee: yes. Official form: no. Blind judging: yes. Deadline: September 30. Please write for information on special themes.

INTERACTIONS OPEN POETRY COMPETITION
PO Box 250, St. Helier, Jersey, JE4 8TZ Great Britian
Open to all poets. Entry fee: yes. Official form: yes. Blind judging: yes. Deadline: September 30. Prizes: (in British pounds) 100 and 50 plus anthology publication for both winners and the runners-up.

JANE JORDAN POETRY CONTEST
Tree Reading Series, 586 McLeod Street, #2, Ottawa, Ontario K1R 5R3
Telephone: (613) 231-7722
Open only to poets living in the National Capital Region. Entry fee: yes. Official form: no. Blind judging: yes. Deadline: February 28. Prizes: $200, $100, $50 plus publication in *Bywords*. E-mail address: az421@freenet.carleton.ca

JEWISH BOOK AWARDS
Jewish Book Awards Committee, Koffler Centre of the Arts, 4588 Bathurst Street, North York, Ontario M2R 1W6
Telephone: (416) 636-1880, Ex. 299   Fax: (416) 636-5813
Open to books by Canadian authors, published in Canada, on subjects of Jewish interest. Deadline: February 1. Offers eight different prizes ($1,000 to $250) for works of poetry, fiction, children's literature, history, Yiddish writing, translations, Holocaust literature, and biblical/rabbinic scholarship.

THE JIM OVERTON POETRY PRIZE
R.R. 3, Box 5, Site 2, Hampton, New Brunswick E0G 1Z0
Telephone: (506) 642-5229
Open to all poets. Entry fee: yes. Official form: no. Blind judging: yes. Deadline: October 31. Prize: cash plus a plaque.

THE KALAMALKA NEW WRITERS COMPETITION
7000 College Way, Vernon, British Columbia V1B 2N5
Telephone: (604) 545-7291   Fax: (604) 545-3277
Open to Canadian poets who have yet to be published in book form. Entry fee: yes. Official form: yes. Blind judging: yes. Deadline: ? Prize: book publication by Kalamalka Press. All entrants receive the previous winner's book.

THE KENNETH PATCHEN COMPETITION
Pig Iron Press, PO Box 237, Youngstown, OH 44501
Telephone: (216) 747-6932
Open to all writers. Entry fee: yes. Official form: no. Blind judging: yes. Deadline:

December 31. Prize. $100 plus book publication. Competition is for poetry in odd numbered years and for fiction in even numbered years.

KENT & SUSSEX POETRY SOCIETY OPEN POETRY COMPETITION
7 Southfield Road, Tunbridge Wells, Kent, TN4 9UH England

Open to all poets. Entry fee: yes. Official form: no. Blind judging: yes. Deadline: January 31. Prizes: (in British pounds) 300, 100, 50, 20 (five 20 pound prizes). The eight prize winning-poems as well as the runners-up will be published in an anthology.

LAST POEMS POETRY CONTEST
sub-TERRAIN Magazine, 175 East Broadway, Suite 204-A, Vancouver, British Columbia V5T 1W2
Telephone: (604) 876-8710   Fax: (604) 879-2667

Open to all North American poets. Entry fee: yes. Official form: no. Blind judging: no. Deadline: January 31. Prize: $200 plus publication in sub-TERRAIN. All entrants receive a subscription to the magazine. Note: there are two more contests— The International 3-Day Novel-Writing Contest and The Penny Dreadful Short Story Contest. Please send SASE for complete details on all three contests.

LITERARY WRITES
The Federation of British Columbia Writers, 905 West Pender Street, 4th Floor, Vancouver, British Columbia V6C 1L6
Telephone: (604) 683-2057   Fax: (604) 683-8269

Open only to Canadian writers. Entry fee: yes. Official form: no. Blind judging: yes. Deadline: send submissions between June 1 and September 8. Prizes: $500, $350, $75. Three categories: poetry, fiction, and non-fiction.

THE LYCIDAS AWARD
Hellas, 304 South Tyson Avenue, Glenside, PA 19038
Telephone: (215) 884-1086   Fax: (215) 884-3304

Open to all poets. Entry fee: yes. Official form: no. Blind judging: no. Deadline: December 31. Prize: $100 plus publication of the winning manuscript in chapbook form by Aldine Press.

MAINICHI AWARDS
Kazuo Sato, editor, Mainichi Daily News, 'Haiku in English', 1-1-1 Hitotsubashi, Chiyoda-ku, Tokyo, 100 Japan

Open to all English-language haiku poets. Prizes for the best haiku published in the Mainichi Daily News. Ten prizes are awarded for 17-syllable haiku and ten prizes are awarded for free-form haiku. Considers entries year-round.

THE MALAHAT REVIEW LONG POEM CONTEST
University of Victoria, PO Box 1700, Victoria, British Columbia V8W 2Y2

Entry fee: yes. Official form: no. Blind judging: yes. Three prizes for long poems or cycles of poems— flexible minimum length is 5 pages; flexible maximum length is

20 pages. A subscription to *The Malahat Review* goes to all entrants. Winning poems are published in the review.

MANITOBA LITERARY AWARDS
Manitoba Writers' Guild Inc., 100 Arthur Street, Suite 206, Winnipeg, Manitoba R3B 1H3
Telephone: (204) 942-6134 Fax: (204) 942-5754
Several awards are offered: the McNally Robinson Award for the Manitoba Book of the Year; the John Hirsch Award for the Most Promising Manitoba Writer, le prix littéraire La Liberté, and others. Complete details from the Manitoba Writers' Guild.

McGILL STREET MAGAZINE POETRY CONTEST
193 Bellwoods Avenue, Toronto, Ontario M6J 2P8
Telephone: (416) 538-0559
Entry fee: yes. Official form: no. Blind judging: yes. Deadline: February 15.

MILTON ACORN MEMORIAL PEOPLE'S POETRY AWARD
People's Poetry, PO Box 51531, 2060 Queen Street East, Toronto, Ontario M4E 3V7
Open to Canadian poets writing in the People's Poetry tradition. Entry fee: no. Official form: no. Blind judging: no. Deadline: books are judged during August. Books can be submitted any time. Prize: cash plus the People's Poetry Medal. Winner is invited to read at the National Milton Acorn Festival in Charlottetown. This award is offered annually for a book or chapbook of poems that sustains the tradition, embodied by Milton Acorn's work, of a people's literature in Canada.

MILTON ACORN POETRY AWARD
Prince Edward Island Council of the Arts, PO Box 2234, Charlottetown, Prince Edward Island C1A 8B9
Telephone: (902) 368-4410 Fax: (902) 368-4418
Limited to Prince Edward Island poets. Entry fee: yes. Official form: no. Blind judging: yes. Deadline: February 15. First prize: trip for two to Montreal or Ottawa. Other prizes: $200 and $100. The Council also offers four other awards: the Carl Sentner Short Story Award, the Feature Article Award, the Lucy Maud Montgomery P.E.I. Children's Literature Award, and the Cavendish Tourist Association Creative Writing Award for Young People.

{m}Öthêr Tøñgué Press POETRY CHAPBOOK CONTEST
290 Fulford-Ganges Road, Salt Spring Island, British Columbia V8K 2K6
Fax: (604) 537-4725
Open to all poets. Entry fee: yes. Official form: no. Blind judging: yes. Deadline: November 30. Prizes: $300 plus chapbook publication. Contest is for manuscripts of between 10 to 15 poems.

NATIONAL CAPITAL WRITING CONTEST
Canadian Authors Association, 23 Kenwoods Circle, Kingston, Ontario K7K 6Y1
Limited to poets of the National Capital Region. Entry fee: yes (except for CAA members). Official form: no. Blind judging: yes. Deadline: November 30. Prizes:

$100 cash, $50 gift certificate, $25 gift certificate in each category. Three categories: free verse, formal verse, and haiku.

NATIONAL POETRY COMPETITION
The Poetry Society, 22 Betterton Street, London, WC2H 9BU England

Open to all poets. Entry fee: yes. Official form: yes. Blind judging: yes. Deadline: October 30. Prizes: (in British pounds) 4,000, 1,000, 500 plus membership in the Poetry Society.

THE NATIONAL POETRY CONTEST
The League of Canadian Poets, 54 Wolseley Street, Suite 204, Toronto, Ontario M5T IA5
Telephone: (416) 504-1657   Fax: (416) 703-0059

Canadian poets only. Entry fee: yes. Official form: no. Blind judging: yes. Deadline: January 31. Prizes: $1,000, $750, and $500 plus anthology publication for the winners and 47 runners-up. Maximum length: 75 lines per poem. E-mail address: league@io.org

NEW MILLENNIUM WRITINGS CONTEST
PO Box 2463, Knoxville, TN 37901

Entry fee: yes. Official form: no. Blind judging: ? Deadline: December 1. Three categories: poetry, fiction, and essays.

NEW MUSE MANUSCRIPT AWARD
PO Box 596, Station A, Fredericton, New Brunswick E3B 5A6
Telephone: (506) 454-5127   Fax: same

Open to all poets who have yet to be published in book form. Entry fee: yes. Official form: no. Blind judging: yes. Deadline: January 31. Prize: book publication of winning manuscript by Broken Jaw Press. All entrants receive the winning book. E-mail address: jblades@nbnet.nb.ca

NIMROD LITERARY PRIZE COMPETITION
Pablo Neruda Prize for Poetry, Arts and Humanities Council of Tulsa, 2210 South Main Street, Tulsa, OK 74114
Telephone: (918) 584-3333   Fax: (918) 582-2787

An international contest open to all poets. First and second place prizes offered annually. Poetry word limit: 1,800 words. This can be one long poem or several short pieces.

THE NORMA EPSTEIN AWARD FOR CREATIVE WRITING
University of Toronto, University College, Office of the Registrar, Toronto, Ontario M5S IA1

Open to students who are registered at any Canadian university.

THE OBSERVER ARVON INTERNATIONAL POETRY COMPETITION
Kilnhurst, Kilnhurst Road, Todmorden, Lancashire, OL14 6AX England

Open to all poets. Entry fee: yes. Official form: yes. Blind judging: yes. Deadline:

November 30. First prize: 5,000 pounds. Other prizes: 5 prizes of 500 pounds each and 10 prizes of 250 pounds each.

OPEN UNIVERSITY POETS OPEN POETRY COMPETITION
The Observatory, Cyncoed Gardens, Cardiff, CF2 6BH Wales
Open to all poets. Entry fee: yes. Official form: yes. Blind judging: yes. Deadline: June 30. Prizes: (in British pounds) one of 200, two of 150, and three of 100 plus publication in an anthology.

PAINTBRUSH AWARD IN POETRY
Painted Hills Review, 2950 Portage Bay West, Suite 411, Davis, CA 95616-2862
Entry fee: yes. Three cash prizes. Poems should be less than 100 lines.

THE PAT LOWTHER MEMORIAL AWARD
The League of Canadian Poets, 54 Wolseley Street, Suite 204, Toronto, Ontario M5T 1A5
Telephone: (416) 504-1657   Fax: (416) 703-0059
Open to Canadian women only. Awarded annually for the best book of poems by a woman. E-mail address: league@io.org

PEOPLE'S POEM CONTEST
and

PEOPLE'S POLITICAL POEM CONTEST
People's Poetry Letter, PO Box 51531, 2060 Queen Street East, Toronto, Ontario M4E 3V7
Entry fee: yes. Official form: no. Blind judging: no. Deadline: mid-October for the People's Poem Contest and mid-April for the People's Political Poem Contest. Prize: cash and book prizes plus publication in *People's Poetry Letter.* All entrants receive a subscription to *People's Poetry Letter.* Funds go to support the Milton Acorn Memorial People's Poetry Award.

PETERLOO POETS OPEN POETRY COMPETITION
2 Kelly Gardens, Calstock, Cornwall, PL18 9SA U.K.
Open to all poets. Entry fee: yes. Official form: yes. Blind judging: yes. Deadline: March 1. Prizes: (in British pounds) 3,000 plus publication in *The Independent,* 1,000, 500, 300, 200, 100.

PETRA KENNEY MEMORIAL POETRY PRIZE
Writers' Forum Magazine, 9/10, Roberts Close, Moxley, Wednesbury, West Midlinds, WS10 8SS England
Open to all poets. Entry fee: yes. Official form: yes. Blind judging: yes. Deadline: December 22. Prizes: (in British pounds) 500, 250, 150 plus magazine publication. For traditional poems on the theme of Spring.

POEM OF THE YEAR CONTEST
Arc, PO Box 7368, Ottawa, Ontario K1L 8E4
Entry fee: yes. Official form: no. Blind judging: yes. Deadline: June 30. Prizes: $300, $200, $100 plus publication in *Arc.* All entrants receive a subscription to the magazine.

POETRY LIFE OPEN POETRY COMPETITION

14 Pennington Oval, Lymington, Hampshire, SO41 8BQ England

Open to all poets. Entry fee: yes. Official form: no. Blind judging: yes. Deadline: July 10. Prizes: (in British pounds) 500, 100, and two of 50 plus publication in *Poetry Life*.

POETRY OF PLACE

Canadian Poetry Association, London Chapter, PO Box 340, London, Ontario
N6A 4W1
Telephone: (519) 433-8994 & 439-3562

Open to all poets. Entry fee: yes. Official form: no. Blind judging: no. Deadline: May 1. Prize: publication of up to 20 poems in chapbook form. E-mail address: cpa@zap.wwdc.com

POETRY POSTCARD QUARTERLY COMPETITION

PO Box 1435, London, W1A 9LB England

Open to all poets. Entry fee: yes. Official form: no. Blind judging: no. Deadline: December 22. Three prizes (1,000 pounds in total divided between the winners) plus publication.

POETRY SOCIETY OF AMERICA AWARDS

15 Gramercy Park, New York, NY 10003
Telephone: (212) 254-9628

Several annual awards which include the Frost Medal, the Shelley Memorial Award, the William Carlos Williams Award, the Norma Farber First Book Award, and the Alice Fay Di Castagnola Award. Please send SASE (U.S. postage) for complete details.

PRAIRIE FIRE POETRY CONTEST

100 Arthur Street, Suite 423, Winnipeg, Manitoba R3B 1H3
Telephone: (204) 943-9066   Fax: (204) 942-1555

Open to all poets. Entry fee: yes. Official form: no. Blind judging: yes. Deadline: September 30. Prizes: $300, $200, $100 plus publication in the quarterly. All entrants receive a one-year subscription. Note: *Prairie Fire* also runs three other contests: the Long Short Story Contest, the Short Fiction Contest, and the Micro Fiction Contest. Please send SASE for contest data.

THE RAINMAKER AWARDS IN POETRY

Zone 3, Austin Peay State University, PO Box 4565, Clarksville, TN 37044
Telephone: (615) 648-7031 & 648-7891

First, second, and third place prizes awarded. All entries will be considered for publication in *Zone 3*.

RHYME REVIVAL COMPETITION

Orbis, 199 The Long Shoot, Nuneaton, Warks, CV11 6JQ England

Offered annually by *Orbis* magazine. Poems may be submitted in two categories: Open Class (no longer than 50 lines) and Formal Class (poetry in any recognized rhymed form).

ROOM OF ONE'S OWN ANNUAL CONTEST
PO Box 46160, Station D, Vancouver, British Columbia V6J 5G5
Entry fee: yes. Official form: no. Blind judging: yes. Deadline: June 30. Three categories: poetry, fiction, and creative non-fiction. All entrants receive a subscription to the quarterly.

ROYAL SOCIETY OF LITERATURE AWARD
The Royal Society of Literature, 1 Hyde Park Gardens, London, W2 2LT England
Presented for a published literary work of distinction.

THE RUTH LILLY PRIZE
Poetry, 60 West Walton Street, Chicago, IL 60610
Telephone: (312) 255-3703
Given yearly to a poet whose published work merits special recognition. Note: several other prizes are offered by Poetry such as the Bess Hokin Prize, the Levinson Prize, the Oscar Blumenthal Prize, the Eunice Tietjens Memorial Prize, the Frederick Bock Prize, the George Kent Prize, and the Union League Prize. Details from the magazine; please send your SASE (U.S.) postage.

THE SANDBURG-LIVESAY ANTHOLOGY CONTEST
Unfinished Monument Press, 237 Prospect Street South, Hamilton, Ontario L8M 2Z6
Telephone: (905) 312-1779   Fax: (905) 312-8285
An international contest open to all poets. Entry fee: yes. Official form: no. Blind judging: no. Deadline: October 31. First prize: publication plus $100 (U.S.). Other prizes: anthology publication. All entrants receive the anthology. Poems must be in the People's Poetry tradition. E-mail address: ad507@freenet.hamilton.on.ca

THE SARA HENDERSON HAY PRIZE
The Pittsburgh Quarterly, 36 Haberman Avenue, Pittsburgh, PA 15211-2144
Telephone: (412) 431-8885
Open to all poets. Entry fee: yes. Official form: no. Blind judging: no. Deadline: July 1. Prize: $200 plus publication in the quarterly. All entrants receive a one-year subscription.

SASKATCHEWAN BOOK AWARDS
Saskatchewan Writers Guild, PO Box 3986, Regina, Saskatchewan S4P 3R9
Telephone: (306) 757-6310   Fax: (306) 565-8554
Saskatchewan writers only. Entry fee: ? Official form: ? Blind judging: no Deadline: ?

SCARBOROUGH ARTS COUNCIL POETRY CONTEST
1859 Kingston Road, Scarborough, Ontario M1N 1T3
Telephone: (416) 698-7322
Limited to Canadian citizens currently living in Canada. Entry fee: yes. Official form: no. Blind judging: yes. Deadline: June 15. Prize: $100 (for adults) plus prizes of $50, $30, and $20 for poets aged 13 to 18. Note: poets in the Youth category pay no entry fee. All winning poems are published in Surface and Symbol, the journal of the arts council.

THE SHAUNT BASMAJIAN CHAPBOOK AWARD

Canadian Poetry Association, PO Box 22571, St. George Postal Outlet, Toronto, Ontario M5S 1V0

An international competition open to all poets. Entry fee: yes. Official form: no. Blind judging: yes. Deadline: ? Prize: publication of the winning manuscript in chapbook form.

SHORT GRAIN WRITING CONTEST

PO Box 1154, Regina, Saskatchewan S4P 3B4

Telephone: (306) 244-2828 Fax: (306) 565-8554

Open to all writers. Entry fee: yes. Official from: no. Blind judging: yes. Deadline: January 31. Prizes: $500, $300, $200 in each category. Three categories: prose poem, postcard story, and dramatic monologue. All entrants receive a subscription to *Grain*. All winners will be published in the quarterly.

THE SKOOB/INDEX COMPETITION

Skoob Books Publishing Ltd., 25 Lowman Road, Holloway, London, N7 6DD England

Prizes for individual poems. No restrictions as to length, style, or subject.

SLIPSTREAM ANNUAL POETRY CHAPBOOK CONTEST

PO Box 2071, New Market Station, Niagara Falls, NY 14301

Telephone (716) 282-2616 (after 5 pm)

Entry fee: yes. Official form: no. Blind judging: no. Deadline: December 1. Prize: chapbook publication of winning manuscript. All entrants receive a copy of the winning chapbook as well as a subscription to *Slipstream*. Send up to 40 pages of poetry.

SPRING POETRY CHAPBOOK CONTEST

White Eagle Coffee Stroe Press, PO Box 383, Fox River Grove, IL 60021-0383

Telephone: (847) 639-9200

Open to all poets. Entry fee: yes. Official form: no. Blind judging; yes. Deadline: March 30. Prize: chapbook publication of the winning manuscript. All entrants receive the winning chapbook. Send 20 to 24 pages of poetry.

STAPLE OPEN POETRY COMPETITION

Tor Cottage, 81 Canvendish Road, Matlock, DE4 3HD England

Open to all poets. Entry fee: yes. Official form: yes. Blind judging: no. Deadline: March 1. Prize: publication as a perfect-bound chapbook. Manuscripts should be between 32 and 45 pages of poetry.

STARVING ROMANTICS' POETRY COMPETITION

93 Charnwood Place, Thornhill, Ontario L3T 5H2

Entry fee: yes. Official form: no. Blind judging: yes. Deadline: July 31. For Romantic poetry only.

STEPHAN G. STEPHANSSON AWARD FOR POETRY
The Writers Guild of Alberta, Percy Page Centre, 3rd Floor, 11759 Groat Road, Edmonton, Alberta T5M 3K6
Telephone: (403) 422-8174   Fax: (403) 422-2663
Open to Alberta poets only. Entry fee: no. Official form: no. Blind judging: no. Deadline: December 31. Prize: $500 and a leather-bound copy of the winning book. Note: the Guild also offers awards for children's literature, novels, non-fiction, short stories, and drama. Please send your SASE for competition information.

THE STEPHEN LEACOCK POETRY AND LIMERICK AWARDS
The Orillia International Poetry Festival, PO Box 2307, Orillia, Ontario L3V 6S2
Open to all poets. Entry fee: yes. Official form: no. Blind judging: ? Deadline: November 30.

STUDENT WRITING AWARDS
Books in Canada, 130 Spadina Avenue, Suite 603, Toronto, Ontario M5V 2L4
Telephone: (416) 703-9880   Fax: (416) 703-9883
Open to full-time undergraduate students at Canadian colleges and universities. Entry fee: no. Official form: no. Blind judging: yes. Deadline: July 14. Prizes: $1,000, $500, $250 plus publication in *Books in Canada*. Two categories: poetry and short fiction.

SWG ANNUAL LITERARY AWARDS
Saskatchewan Writers Guild, PO Box 3986, Regina, Saskatchewan S4P 3R9
Telephone: (306) 757-6310   Fax: (306) 565-8554
Saskatchewan writers only. Entry fee: ? Official form: ? Blind judging: ? Deadline: ? Cash prizes are awarded in four categories: poetry, fiction, non-fiction, and children's literature.

TABLA POETRY MAGAZINE POETRY COMPETITION
7 Parliament Hill, London, NW3 2SY England
Open to all poets. Entry fee: yes. Official form: yes. Blind judging: yes. Deadline: September 1. Prize: 50 pounds plus publication in the magazine.

TEARS IN THE FENCE PAMPHLET COMPETITION
38 Hod View, Stourpaine, Blandford Forum, Dorset, DT11 8TN England
Open to all poets. Entry fee: yes. Official form: yes. Blind judging: yes. Deadline: December 31. First prize: chapbook publication of the winning manuscript. Other prizes: anthology publication of the runners-up. Submit up to 24 pages of poetry.

TILDEN CANADIAN LITERARY AWARDS
CBC Radio Performance, PO Box 500, Station A, Toronto, Ontario M5W 1E6
Open only to residents of Canada. Blind judging: yes. Deadline: January 9. Three categories: poetry, short story, and the personal essay.

TOP 40
Hamilton Wentworth Creative Arts Inc., 401 Main Street West, Hamilton, Ontario L8P 1K5
Telephone: (905) 525-6644   Fax: (905) 525-8292
Open only to poets from the greater Hamilton area and Burlington. Entry fee: yes.

Official form: yes. Blind judging: yes. Deadline: September 30. Prizes: $150, $75, $50 and anthology publication. 37 runners-up also receive anthology publication.

TRILLIUM AWARD
Ontario Ministry of Culture and Communications, Arts Branch, 77 Bloor Street West, Toronto, Ontario M7A 2R9

English-language and French-language books are considered if their authors have lived in Ontario for at least three years. The winning book must contribute to a better understanding of Ontario and its culture.

WHISKEY ISLAND PRIZE
Cleveland State University, English Department, Cleveland, OH 44115
Telephone: (216) 687-2056

Open to all poets. Entry fee: yes. Official form: no. Blind judging: ? Deadline: none. Cash prizes for both poetry (submit up to 10 poems) and fiction (up to 6,500 words).

WHITE MOUNTAIN PUBLICATIONS POETRY COMPETITION
PO Box 5180, New Liskeard, Ontario P0J 1P0

Open to all poets. Entry fee: yes. Official form: no. Blind judging: yes. Deadline: April 30. Cash prizes and publication.

WRITER'S BLOCK CONTEST
Box 32, 9944 33rd Avenue, Edmonton, Alberta T6N 1E8
Telephone: (403) 486-5856   Fax: (403) 444-7504

Open to all poets. Entry fee: yes. Official form: no. Blind judging: no. Two deadlines each year: March 1 and September 1. Cash and book prizes.

THE WRITERS' FEDERATION OF NEW BRUNSWICK LITERARY COMPETITION
PO Box 37, Station A, Fredericton, New Brunswick E3B 4Y2

Open only to New Brunswick poets. Two categories: single poems (up to 5 pages) and manuscript collections of poems. Cash prizes.

INDEX